After Germany's defeat in 1945, West German chemical firms made the transition from traditional coal-based chemistry to modern petrochemical technology, thus ensuring their long-term competitiveness. This book investigates the causes, course, and consequences of that major change in West German chemical technology. In seeking to explain the actual process of that transition and its broader cultural implications, the author examines the factors that led key chemical firms to pursue petrochemical production, the basis on which the chemical industrialists chose among the competing technologies, the process of technology transfer (primarily from the United States and Great Britain to Germany, but also the reverse), and the trends in German research, production, investment, and marketing after the war.

Using approaches drawn from the history of technology, business history, and political and economic history, and taking advantage of material from a broad range of public and private archives, this study argues that it is impossible to explain technological developments in the chemical industry from the end of the war until 1961 without exploring a number of other areas, including corresponding changes in the West German and worldwide political economies during the same period, as well as German traditions regarding technological change. Neither the move to petroleum-based feedstocks nor the pace of the transition was inevitable; rather, both depended on choices made by politicians and industrialists within the context of the political economy of the 1950s, as well as the context of prior German experience.

This study addresses a wide variety of issues: the problems of continuity and change in German history; the origins and impact of the decision to divide Germany; the origins, unfolding, and effects of the *Wirtschaftswunder,* or economic miracle; European integration; the changing role of the West German Federal Republic in the international political order; and the bases of the international competitiveness of West German industry.

Opting for Oil

Opting for Oil

The political economy of technological change in the
West German chemical industry, 1945–1961

RAYMOND G. STOKES
Department of Science and Technology Studies
Rensselaer Polytechnic Institute

CAMBRIDGE
UNIVERSITY PRESS

338.4766
S87o

Published by the Press Syndicate of the University of Cambridge
The Pitt Building, Trumpington Street, Cambridge CB2 1RP
40 West 20th Street, New York, NY 10011-4211, USA
10 Stamford Road, Oakleigh, Melbourne 3166, Australia

First published 1994

Printed in the United States of America

Library of Congress Cataloging-in-Publication Data
Stokes, Raymond G.
    Opting for oil : the political economy of technological change in
the West German chemical industry, 1945–1961 / by Raymond G. Stokes.
        p.   cm.
    ISBN 0-521-45124-8
    1. Chemical industry – Germany (West) 2. Chemical industry –
Germany (West) – Technological innovations.   I. Title.
    HD9656.G38S77   1994
    338.4'766'00943 – dc20   93-3922
                                                                     CIP

A catalog record for this book is available from the British Library.

ISBN 0-521-45124-8 hardback

To Anne Marie, Jonathan,
and Nikolas

Contents

Preface

I began work on this project shortly after sending off the final manuscript of
*Divide and Prosper: The Heirs of I. G. Farben under Allied Authority, 1945–
1951* (Berkeley: University of California Press, 1988) in November 1987. Because it was related to the first project, it seemed at the start a relatively
straightforward task. As it turned out, things were not that simple, for concentrating on the political economy of technological change involved questions
completely different from those animating my first study. It also involved using
new and different documentary materials, some of which became available only
as I was writing (or rewriting) this book. As I wrestled with these problems, I
benefited from a number of conversations with Alan Beyerchen, whose ideas
and work have influenced my own considerably. Working in Rensselaer's Department of Science and Technology Studies has also affected the final results of
my research – my colleagues will no doubt recognize their influences.

I would like to thank various organizations for financial support for this undertaking. I received generous support to complete much of the research for this
book from the Berlin Program for Advanced German and European Studies at
the Freie Universität, Berlin, between May 1988 and August 1989. The Social
Science Research Council administers the program, which is funded by the Stif-

tung Volkswagenwerk and the German Marshall Fund of the United States. Writing and additional research were facilitated by a grant during 1991 from the National Science Foundation Program in the History and Philosophy of Science and Technology (grant number DIR-90-23462). Rensselaer Polytechnic Institute also provided me with two Beer Trust minigrants, research assistants, and two leaves of absence to take up the fellowship and the grant.

Various individuals were extremely helpful in allowing me access to the documents on which this study is based; they also afforded me a hospitable atmosphere in which to work. They include Lothar Meinzer and Ruth Fromm at the BASF archives; Michael Pohlenz, Herr Pogarell, and Michael Frings at the Bayer archives; W. Metternich and M. Wex from the Hoechst archives; Gert Wlasich from Schering A. G.; and Herren Lenz and Baumgarten and Frau Wagner from the Bundesarchiv in Koblenz. I am also grateful to Kurt Hansen, H. J. Hubert, Heinz Nedelmann, and Bernhard Timm for granting me interviews. Drs. Hubert and Nedelmann also provided copies of documents from their personal collections that contributed substantially to the study.

Access to material from three additional archives came, unfortunately, too late for full inclusion in this book. I would nevertheless like to express my appreciation for their efforts on my behalf to Frau Ahlefeld of the Buna-Werksarchive, Schkopau, to Frau Schatz and Frau Haberland of the Leuna archives, Merseburg, and to Dr. G. Franz of the Chemische Werke Hüls.

I would like to thank the following people personally for their help during various stages of the project, primarily in reading and commenting on the drafts of funding proposals, outlines, or drafts of chapters: Volker Berghahn, Alan Beyerchen, Hans-Joachim Braun, P. Thomas Carroll, Burghard Ciesla, John Gillingham, Shirley Gorenstein, Peter Hayes, Carl-Ludwig Holtfrerich, Rainer Karlsch, Matt Levinger, Monika Medick-Krakau, Jeff Newcomer, Ken Resnik, Harm Schröter, Anne-Marie Stokes, Elisabeth Vaupel, Claudia Wörmann, and anonymous readers for Cambridge University Press, the National Science Foundation, and *Technology and Culture*. Natasha Ozo and Xuemei Xie provided research assistance. I am grateful also to Linda Jorgensen, who managed the file for and made the corrections to various drafts of the manuscript. Special thanks go to Peter Morris, who read and commented on various early versions of chapters. He also reviewed the penultimate draft of the manuscript with me during a marathon session at the York Railway Museum on a warm summer day in 1992. I particularly appreciate his close attention to the technical aspects of the developments described in the book, which prevented some errors. Those that remain are my responsibility.

I have enjoyed working with representatives of Cambridge University Press in producing this book. Special thanks to Frank Smith and Camilla T. K. Palmer.

Portions of Chapter 4 appear in my article "Technology Transfer and the Emergence of the West German Petrochemicals Industry, 1945–1951," in Jeffrey Diefendorf, Axel Frohn, and Hermann-Josef Rupieper, eds., *American Policy and the Reconstruction of West Germany, 1945–1955* (Cambridge University Press, 1993). My thanks to Cambridge University Press for permission to use this material.

And last, but not least, as usual, my family and friends helped me enormously as I pursued this project. Thanks to all of them, but particularly Anne Marie, whose companionship has sustained me and whose criticism of my writing has improved it substantially, and to Jonathan and Nikolas, who for their entire lives have cheerfully accepted their father's frequent distraction as he wrote this book.

Introduction

When World War II ended in 1945, the damage to German cities and industry had been so severe that most observers, whether Allies or Germans, realized that the country's economy was on the verge of collapse. Nonetheless, already in the 1950s commentators had begun to notice the West German *Wirtschaftswunder,* its "economic miracle," which led to rapid growth into the 1960s; the West German economic performance since then has evoked both admiration and envy. Macroeconomic explanations for the miracle abound,[1] as well as for the continuing West German ability to compete in world markets. Yet decisions at lower levels – by politicians, bureaucrats, businessmen, consumers, and others – clearly had significant impacts on that macroeconomic performance, and we still know very little about the processes of economic and technological change that occurred at the level of the various industries, with the possible exceptions of coal and steel.[2]

---

[1] Much of the literature on the economic miracle is cited by Rolf Dumke, "Reassessing the *Wirtschaftswunder:* Reconstruction and Postwar Growth in West Germany in an International Context," *Oxford Bulletin of Economics and Statistics* 52(1990):451–91.

[2] Studies of heavy industry include the following: Werner Abelshauser, *Der Ruhrkohlenbergbau seit 1945. Wiederaufbau, Krise, Anpassung* (Munich: Beck, 1984); Volker Berghahn, *The*

The West German chemical industry deserves attention in this regard. Like other industries, it was severely affected by the war, but rebounded quickly from those effects. It performed especially well in export markets, which were essential bases for the economic miracle. Unlike the heavy industries, the chemical industry was research-intensive, like many others that helped account for the impressive West German economic performance in the postwar period.

Why was the West German chemical industry able to recover from the effects of the war and perform so well in world markets in the postwar period? Part of the explanation is institutional, because in the aftermath of the war the Allies divided the most important German chemical firm, Interessengemeinschaft Farbenindustrie Aktiengesellschaft (variously referred to as I.G. Farbenindustrie A.G., I.G. Farben, or the I.G.), into component parts that were much more rational and competitive.[3] But one of the most important factors in the success of West German chemical firms in the postwar period was a major technological change: their gradual transition from traditional, coal-based chemistry to modern petrochemical technology.

This book investigates the causes, course, and consequences of that major change in West German chemical technology, covering the period from the German defeat in 1945 through 1961, the year in which petroleum replaced coal as the industry's primary starting material, or feedstock. My major concern is to examine why and how the transition from coal chemistry to petroleum chemistry occurred in West Germany as well as the political, economic, and cultural impacts of that technological change. This book thus examines the factors that led key chemical firms to opt for petrochemical production, the basis on which the chemical industrialists chose among the competing technologies, the process of technology transfer (primarily from the United States and Great Britain to Germany, but also the reverse), and the trends in German research, production, investment, and marketing after the war. In addition, I argue that it is impossible to explain the technological developments in the chemical industry between 1945 and 1961 without exploring a number of other areas, including corresponding changes in the West German and worldwide political economies during the same period, as well as German traditions regarding technological change. Neither the changeover to petroleum-based feedstocks nor the pace of the transition was inevitable; rather, both depended on choices made by politicians and industrialists within the context of the political economy of the 1950s, as well as the context of prior German experience.

Few technological developments have had greater impact on the daily lives of people in this century than those in the chemical industry. Large-scale production of chemicals and new applications for plastics, coatings, adhesives, syn-

---

Americanisation of West German Industry, 1945–1973 (Cambridge University Press, 1986); John Gillingham, *Coal, Steel, and the Rebirth of Europe, 1918–1955: The Germans and French from Ruhr Conflict to Economic Community* (Cambridge University Press, 1991); Mark Roseman, *Recasting the Ruhr, 1945–1958* (New York: Berg, 1992).

[3] See Raymond G. Stokes, *Divide and Prosper: The Heirs of I. G. Farben under Allied Authority, 1945–1951* (Berkeley: University of California Press, 1988).

thetic fibers, and a host of other products have literally transformed our material world. Proponents of the industry argue that all this has improved our standard of living by extending the range of products available and making them less expensive; critics point to the environmental costs of the industry's development and to the alleged cheapening of mass tastes. But neither side would deny that chemistry has fundamentally altered the way we have lived during the course of this century.

The startling expansion in the range and quantities of chemical products owed much to a change in the industry's preferred feedstock, from coal to petroleum. The first moves in that direction came in the early 1920s in the United States, when Carbide and Carbon Chemicals Company, a subsidiary of what later became Union Carbide Corporation, began production of ethylene glycol from ethylene. Expanded output of gasoline to meet the needs of the growing number of automobiles on U.S. roads led to an increase in the availability of olefins, which were by-products of the refining process and served as feedstocks for chemical manufacturing. Research by both chemical and oil companies led to new products and processes to utilize the increased output, and wartime demand for various materials such as explosives, synthetic rubber, and other substitute materials stimulated the petroleum-chemical industry still further. Postwar demand showed no signs of slackening. Between 1940 and 1950, the industry's output quadrupled. By 1955, more than 25 percent of all organic chemicals in the United States were produced using petroleum feedstocks, and they were being called "petrochemicals." On the eve of the oil crisis of 1973–4, the petrochemical share of the worldwide production of organic chemicals had grown to about 90 percent. What is more, by replacing coal with petroleum as its premier feedstock, the industry was able to produce goods in far greater quantities than would have been possible using only the traditional sources of coal-based feedstocks.

The German chemical industry, which led the world in output and technological sophistication through the 1920s, at first did not share in the new developments. Bound by tradition and (in the 1930s) by government policy to use their abundant supplies of domestic coal, German manufacturers, led by the giant combine I.G. Farbenindustrie A.G., fell far behind their U.S. counterparts in petrochemical technology. The German industry's relative technological backwardness ranked alongside the wartime destruction, the disruption of traditional production relationships (because of the division of Germany), and the breakup of I.G. Farben as key problems facing the industry during the immediate postwar years.

Still, West German industrialists representing the successors to I.G. Farben moved quickly during the 1950s and 1960s to replace coal-based feedstocks with petroleum-based feedstocks. By 1961, more than 50 percent of all organic chemicals in the Federal Republic of Germany were produced from petroleum, up from just 15 percent in 1950; in 1964, the proportion rose to 69 percent. As a result of that transition, West German firms regained a competitive position in international markets; by the 1970s, the I.G. Farben successors Badische Anilin-und Soda-Fabrik (BASF), Bayer, and Hoechst all ranked among the world's top five chemical producers. Its embrace of petrochemicals thus enabled the organic chemical industry to contribute substantially to West Germany's economic miracle and to the country's continuing economic success.

What would prompt the West Germans – or anyone else – to change from coal-based to petroleum-based feedstocks? Most commentators find the reason too obvious for lengthy comment. A. L. Waddams, for instance, in the third edition to his handbook on the petrochemical industry, put it simply: "the reason for the development of chemicals from a petroleum source as an alternative to, or at the expense of, other sources, is an economic one."[4] In his history of the rise of the petrochemical industry, Peter Spitz makes a similar point, stressing that all companies in all countries that wanted to remain competitive were forced to follow suit once U.S. pioneers in the industry began the transition:

It didn't matter that coal, alcohol, crude oil, or natural gas could all be transformed into many of the same organic chemicals. The important thing was that this could be done most inexpensively from feedstocks derived from petroleum or from . . . natural gas. . . . When these materials became abundantly available, coal and alcohol chemistry was no longer economically viable for the production of commodity organic chemicals . . . [T]he future of organic chemicals was going to be related to petroleum, not coal, as soon as companies such as Union Carbide, Standard Oil (New Jersey), Shell, and Dow turned their attention to the production of petrochemicals.[5]

These and many other commentators on the industry's development have found the process of that technological change less interesting than the virtues of the new technology. For them, the move from coal- or alcohol-based chemistry to petrochemistry appears to have been preordained, given the overwhelming cost advantages of petrochemical production. There were some international variations in the adoption of the new technology, as well as differences between companies, but they had to do primarily with how quickly a country's industry or a particular company could accept and act upon the inevitability of the change.

In the long run, petrochemical production was indeed less expensive, in most cases, than coal-based chemical production. However, stressing this long-term conversion to the exclusion of shorter-term developments can obscure several significant factors, as a closer look at the West German case will make clear. For one thing, such an interpretation implies that the transition from coal-based to petroleum-based chemistry was inevitable and, furthermore, that the future development of the industry must already have been obvious in the late 1940s and early 1950s to any reasonably informed observer. But in fact, from the perspective of those years, the fate of coal chemistry was far from evident; even in the latter half of the 1950s it continued to dominate worldwide production methods and to provide apparently viable alternatives to petrochemicals. Even in the United States, where the petrochemical industry was most advanced, about three-fourths of all organic chemicals were produced using coal or alcohol feedstocks in the mid-1950s. Petrochemicals had made inroads primarily in what be-

[4] A. L. Waddams, *Chemicals from Petroleum: An Introductory Survey,* 3rd ed. (New York: Wiley, 1973), p. 295.

[5] Peter Spitz, *Petrochemicals: The Rise of an Industry* (New York: Wiley, 1988), p. xiii.

came known as "commodity chemicals" (such as ethylene and propylene) and were especially important for the rapidly expanding plastics industry, but production in other areas, such as dyes, pharmaceuticals, solvents, and detergent intermediates, continued to be dominated by coal-based feedstocks, especially in Europe. Most European benzene, for instance, continued to be produced from coal through the mid-1960s.[6]

What is more, through the early 1960s there were alternatives to petrochemical production. Acetylene-based chemistry, for instance, was developed first and most extensively by BASF's Walter Reppe; it relied on carbide produced from coal, and it seemed particularly promising in the late 1940s and during the 1950s. Chemistry based on acetylene began its relative decline only in the 1960s, when U.S. chemical firms developed methods for producing acetylene from petroleum and found a number of alternative routes to manufacturing some of its products. In addition, another older German chemical process, the Fischer-Tropsch process, could use either coal or natural gas to produce chemical feedstocks. That process was modified during the late 1940s and 1950s and also seemed a promising alternative to petrochemicals.[7] In West Germany, Fischer-Tropsch plants continued to produce "petrochemicals" from coal into the early 1960s.

The persistence of Fischer-Tropsch plants, despite the inroads made by petrochemicals, brings up a second shortcoming of the interpretation that would stress the inevitable triumph of petrochemical technology. By focusing only on the success of petrochemicals, it neglects technological developments in the coal-chemical industry, in effect implying that it came to a standstill. In West Germany, however, innovations in coal-based processes continued throughout the 1950s and into the 1960s. Reppe chemistry remained vital to BASF's research effort into the 1960s, for instance. One of the Fischer-Tropsch facilities, in part owing to its research-and-development effort, was able to move into lucrative niche markets, producing those chemical raw materials and intermediates from coal that could not yet be produced from oil.

One key reason for the persistence of the coal-based chemical industry in the face of the apparently overwhelming superiority of petroleum-based processes was that coal chemistry was part of a distinguished industrial tradition in Germany. Producing petrochemicals would require that German chemists and industrialists begin to think in ways completely different than they had before. There were differences, for example, in terms of the optimal scale for an industrial plant, with petrochemical plants generally being much larger than coal-chemical facilities. In addition, the security of the feedstock supply became a much more difficult issue, because petrochemicals required reliance on overseas sources of oil, rather than on domestic coal. The Suez Crisis of 1956, occurring just as major West German firms were moving into petrochemical production on a large scale, brought home the potential dangers of such a course. Design traditions also had to change, because the new technology required that German

[6] Waddams, *Chemicals from Petroleum*, pp. 4–6.
[7] Melvin J. Astle, *The Chemistry of Petrochemicals* (New York: Reinhold, 1956), p. 5.

designers – who were trained primarily as chemists – abandon their traditional regard for "elegance," that is, for processes in which the theory was well understood and the highest possible yields were obtained. Instead, they had to learn to concentrate on the most direct path to the final product (which often was poorly understood theoretically and yielded far less product), relying on recycling of part of the reactant to increase yields.[8] It took time to alter habits that had led to such success from the 1860s through the 1940s, especially when the new alternative did not yet appear suitable for all types of organic chemical manufacturing.

An additional shortcoming of the emphasis on economic determinism is that it simply assumes, rather than describing or explaining, the process of technology transfer. The focus here is, instead, on the existence of alternatives, which makes the details of the technology transfer more vital, because the range of choices is seen to have been so much wider. Again, concentration on the West German experience is instructive because it illustrates the complexities of the transfer process. Not surprisingly, key West German firms sought out British and American oil and chemical firms to supply them with petrochemical feedstocks and technology. For instance, in 1955, BASF, in cooperation with Shell, established the first plant in Germany dedicated entirely to petroleum feedstocks, and Bayer and British Petroleum (BP) opened their plant at Dormagen in 1958. Both firms sought out American engineering companies to help them begin petrochemical production.

What is surprising is the extent to which the transfer process operated in the other direction, that is, the degree to which German firms – which were behind their American counterparts in petrochemical technology – had something to offer foreign (especially American) companies. American petrochemical producers showed considerable interest in Reppe's acetylene chemistry, the products of which often proved impossible to reproduce when starting from the less expensive petrochemical products. Representatives of U.S. chemical companies, hoping to use natural gas rather than coal to produce acetylene, were therefore extremely interested in Reppe chemistry. In addition, U.S. firms, which had extensively automated the production of chemicals in their large-scale factories, used centralized laboratories for product analysis and hence were interested in the complementary plant-stream analyzers pioneered by the Germans to allow on-the-spot analysis of product.[9]

---

[8] Waddams, *Chemicals from Petroleum*, pp. 12–13. Waddams claims that, in general, those working for established chemical companies found it difficult to make the conceptual switch necessary for the new technology. Petroleum producers, in contrast, were relatively unencumbered by that traditional regard for "elegance." Peter Morris makes a similar point with regard to the choice of feedstocks for synthetic rubber at I. G. Farben in the late 1920s and 1930s: "The Development of Acetylene Chemistry and Synthetic Rubber by I. G. Farbenindustrie Aktiengesellschaft, 1926–1945" (dissertation, Oxford University, 1982), pp. 197–8.

[9] M. H. Bigelow (Plaskon Division of Libbey-Owens-Ford Glass Co.), a technical investigator who studied Germany's wartime technological advances in the aftermath of the conflict, conveyed the American excitement in "Reppe's Acetylene Chemistry," *Chemical and Engineering News* 25(1947):1038–42. Some firms later acted on the matter. Monsanto was one; material on their negotiations with BASF is in BASF Unternehmensarchiv, Ludwigshafen (hereafter, BASF),

The ability of West German firms to offer technology that would appeal to their U.S. counterparts even during the 1950s brings up another important point. On account of this, West German companies possessed substantial bargaining power vis-à-vis foreign corporations, and the evidence indicates that they used it to wait for the best available deal. Bayer managers, for instance, were able to keep BP waiting in the wings on a proposed joint petrochemical deal while they negotiated with Esso. When, in 1954, after a number of years, the Esso deal fell through, BP was still waiting and quickly came to terms with Bayer on a joint venture. Shell's representatives sought out cooperation with BASF in the petrochemical field as early as 1948, but BASF managers chose to wait until 1952 to engage in the detailed negotiations that led to the creation of a joint venture in 1955.

This exploration of the competing technologies, the possible alternative paths of development, and the complex process of technology transfer draws evidence from a wide range of sources and speaks directly to a number of issues raised in several different but complementary bodies of literature. This book focuses, for example, on technological change, and in the process addresses a number of questions central to the history of technology. How decisions are reached on competing technologies, the role of the state in technological change, the process of technology transfer, the acknowledgment of real alternatives in the face of apparent technological determinism – all of these aspects of the "cultural ambience" of technological development are themes both in the contextual history of technology and in this book.[10] Various aspects of this study are also linked to themes and approaches dominant in business history, particularly in the work of Alfred D. Chandler, Jr.[11] Five of the book's chapters center on the

B4/1395 and F9/248. On acetylene chemistry's potential to produce goods that petrochemical technology at first could not, see Walter Reppe, "Die Bedeutung der Acetylenchemie für die Industrie der Kunststoffe im Vergleich mit anderen Grundstoffindustrien," *Chemische Industrie* 3(1951):602; BASF Patentabteilung, "Bericht über den Besuch der Herren Wilson und Menke der Monsanto Chemical Co. vom 15., 16. und 19 März 1951," March 29, 1951, 6, BASF, B4/1395. On plant-stream analysis, see B. Sturm, "Betriebskontrolltechnik in den USA und in Deutschland. Eine vergleichende Betrachtung über den Stand der Automatisierung," *Chemische Industrie* 7(1955):19.

[10] On competing technologies, see W. Brian Arthur, "Positive Feedbacks in the Economy," *Scientific American* (February 1990):92–9; and Arthur, "Competing Technologies, Increasing Returns, and Lock-in by Historical Events," *The Economic Journal* 99(1989):116–31. For a historical example of competing technologies, see Ian Inkster, *Science and Technology in History* (New Brunswick, NJ: Rutgers University Press, 1991), esp. p. 20. On nonlinear science more generally, see Alan Beyerchen, "Nonlinear Science and the Unfolding of a New Intellectual Vision," in Richard Bjornson and Marilyn Waldman, eds., "Rethinking Patterns of Knowledge," *Papers in Comparative Studies* 6(1988–9):25–50. The concept of competing technologies is related to, but is analytically distinct from, that of failed innovations. On the latter, see Hans-Joachim Braun's "Introduction" to a special issue of *Social Studies of Science* 22(1992):213–30. The term "cultural ambience" comes from John Staudenmaier, *Technology's Storytellers: Reweaving the Human Fabric* (Cambridge, MA: Society for the History of Technology and MIT Press, 1985), esp. pp. 121–61.

[11] See, for instance, Alfred D. Chandler, Jr., *The Visible Hand* (Cambridge, MA: Belknap Press, 1977); and Chander, *Scale and Scope: The Dynamics of Managerial Capitalism* (Cambridge, MA: Belknap Press, 1990).

individual firm as the locus of inquiry and employ a case-study approach, which allows in-depth study of the decision-making process regarding technological change and technology transfer, while highlighting the similarities and differences in the experiences of individual firms.

Finally, because all too often historians of technology and business historians deal with particular technologies or firms, with little or no regard for the context in which technological changes and business decisions take place, this book relies heavily on certain issues and approaches defined in the rapidly growing literature on the history of post-1945 Germany.[12] Among the central themes that scholars in this area have identified are the following: the problems of continuity and change in German history; the origins and impact of the decision to divide Germany; the origins, unfolding, and effects of the *Wirtschaftswunder,* or economic miracle; European integration; and the changing role of the Federal Republic in the international political order.

Besides drawing from the historiography of postwar Germany, this study attempts to make a significant contribution to it. There have been few intensive investigations of the development of a single industry in West Germany since 1945, and this is one of the first to stress the role of technology in postwar German history.[13] It makes use of previously unavailable archival sources to test and refine some of the existing broad hypotheses regarding German political and economic history. The story of the changes in the chemical industry between 1945 and 1961 is particularly appropriate for this task. As mentioned earlier, the persistence of coal-chemical technology was in some respects a concrete manifestation of the persistence of ideas from pre-1945 German history that stressed economic self-sufficiency. In addition, the steadily deteriorating position of coal-based technology vis-à-vis petroleum-based technology mirrored heavy industry's steadily eroding position of power in West Germany during the 1950s and 1960s. Furthermore, coal chemistry, with its secure domestic supplies of raw materials, shared a state of tension with petrochemical technology, whose

[12] Among the large and growing literature on this subject, see, for instance, John Gimbel, *The American Occupation of Germany* (Stanford University Press, 1968); Gimbel, *The Origins of the Marshall Plan* (Stanford University Press, 1976); Werner Abelshauser, *Die Wirtschaftsgeschichte der Bundesrepublik Deutschland* (Frankfurt: Suhrkamp, 1983); Alan Milward, *The Reconstruction of Western Europe, 1945–1951* (London: Methuen, 1984); Berghahn, *The Americanisation of West German Industry;* Ludolf Herbst, *Option für den Westen. Vom Marshallplan bis zum deutsch-französischen Vertrag* (Munich: DTV, 1989); Christoph Buchheim, *Die Wiedereingliederung Westdeutschlands in die Weltwirtschaft 1945–1958* (Munich: Oldenbourg, 1990); Gillingham, *Coal, Steel, and the Rebirth of Europe;* Hartmut Kaelble, ed., *Der Boom 1948–1973. Gesellschaftliche und wirtschaftliche Folgen in der Bundesrepublik Deutschland und in Europa* (Opladen: Westdeutscher Verlag, 1992).

[13] Among the industry studies to this point are the following: Abelshauser, *Der Ruhrkohlenbergbau seit 1945;* Berghahn, *The Americanisation of West German Industry;* Gillingham, *Coal, Steel, and the Rebirth of Europe;* and Roseman, *Recasting the Ruhr, 1945–1958.* One of the few full-length studies centering on technology is by John Gimbel, *Science, Technology, and Reparations: Exploitation and Plunder in Postwar Germany* (Stanford University Press, 1990). A review of recent literature on the subject is available: Raymond G. Stokes, "Technology and the West German *Wirtschaftswunder,*" *Technology and Culture* 32(1991):1–22.

adoption would mandate a Germany committed to export, to an integrated world economy, and to reliance on Anglo-American oil firms for supplies of feed-stocks. Both the old, coal-based and the new, petroleum-based technologies were vital to the origins and unfolding of the *Wirtschaftswunder*.[14] At the same time, the ultimate ascendancy of petrochemicals is part of the reason the Federal Republic of Germany has performed so well in the international economic arena – and the political arena – since 1945.

This study combines approaches drawn from the history of technology, business history, and political and economic history. It therefore deals with a variety of issues, including German technological traditions, the traditions within individual firms, and their impact on the decisions made after 1945 in both Germanies; technology transfer in its political context; the roles of economic determinants or constraints in technological choice; and the role of the state in shaping technological development. These themes are covered in four parts, which are divided chronologically. Part I (Chapters 1 and 2) establishes the background. Chapter 1 outlines the connections between politics and technological excellence in Germany between 1860 and 1945, focusing on the organic chemical industry, and identifies some of the key elements of the German technological tradition. Chapter 2 covers the period 1945–9, when the Allies at first tried to hold Germany at a standstill politically and technologically, and then slowly moved away from such policies. Part II (Chapters 3 and 4) deals with the political economy of technological change between 1949 and 1955, when the Korean War, the negotiations on rearmament, and the reorganization of European coal and steel production gave West Germany a much stronger bargaining position not only in foreign policy but also in negotiations with foreign firms to transfer technology. At the end of that period, the Federal Republic had regained virtually full political sovereignty, and the first large-scale petrochemical facility began production.

Part III (Chapters 5–9) compares and contrasts the varied paths to petrochemical production taken by major German firms: the experiences of the major West German successors to I.G. Farben, two of which entered into partnerships with major oil producers, while a third developed petrochemical technology and feedstock production on its own; the experience of the former I.G. Farben subsidiary Hüls, which borrowed extensively from American firms for rubber production while relying heavily on the West German state for guidance in technological change; and the experiences of non-I.G. coal-chemical producers in West Germany. Part IV (Chapters 10 and 11) covers the parallels between the consolidation of the new technological regime between 1957 and 1961 and the consolidation of the new political regime, especially noticeable because of what seemed to be the increasingly obvious permanence of the division of Germany. It also surveys the importance of those changes and explores the study's main themes and conclusions.

[14] Stokes, "Technology and the West German *Wirtschaftswunder*."

Part I
Background

1
Politics and technological excellence

Organic chemicals, 1860–1945

On 18 January 1871, rulers and representatives from the various German principalities assembled in the Hall of Mirrors at Versailles to proclaim King Wilhelm I of Prussia emperor of the Germans. German unification marked the conclusion of decades of debate on that nation's proper constitution. It also brought to a close a remarkable series of diplomatic and military triumphs for the Prussian state. Led by the Iron Chancellor, Otto von Bismarck, the Prussians had gone to war successfully against the Danes in 1864; against the Austrians, their main rivals for power within the German area, in 1866; and against the French, the main opponents of German unification on the Continent, in 1870. Intensive diplomatic preparation had preceded each of those wars, and shrewd diplomacy had followed each victory, paving the way for achievement of the ultimate objective: a united Germany dominated by Prussia.

During the same decade that Bismarck was planning and conducting that series of wars, a new and vibrant industry was taking shape in the German area; it became one of the power bases of the newly established German state. From 1871 until 1914, the new German organic chemical industry helped propel a tremendous burst of economic growth in the country. Especially successful in developing new technologies based on their domestic supplies of raw materials,

technologies designed to capture foreign markets, the organic chemical manufacturers bolstered the political power of the German state, not only in the years
prior to the outbreak of the Great War (World War I) but also as Germany recovered from defeat in the 1920s and 1930s.

This chapter explores the interactions among technological excellence, economic power, and the political system as reflected in the case of the German
organic chemical industry from about 1860 to 1945. One objective of this exploration is to introduce the actors (the firms and the individuals from government and industry) who play key roles in subsequent chapters; another is to place
the developments of the post–World War II period in historical context. But the
chapter goes beyond a synopsis of the developments between 1860 and 1945,
especially because that would add little to the excellent body of literature already
available on this topic.[1] By and large, there is consensus (both in the specialized
literature and in the more general interpretations of German history) that chemical technology often was an *instrument* of German power and politics, especially during the National Socialist period from 1933 to 1945.[2] I shall argue that
the mystique of organic chemical technology and its products became part of the
fiber of German political life by 1914 at the latest: It became an element in the
hopes, dreams, and desires of the German people and of those who sought to
influence them. The accomplishments of Germany's organic chemical industry
symbolized for many the country's ability to overcome resource limitations
through ingenious technological ability.

Establishing technological excellence: 1860–1914

At the beginning of the nineteenth century, "Germany" was a distant prospect
that existed only in the imagination of a few, with unification a long way off.
What is more, industrialization in the patchwork of German principalities –
there were more than three hundred of them before Napoleon rationalized the
map, leaving more than thirty – lagged far behind that in Great Britain, Belgium, and France. But the area had some significant advantages that became
increasingly obvious during the first half of the century. Its geographic position
in the center of Europe, for one thing, despite its drawbacks in regard to military

---

[1] Readers interested in detailed interpretations of aspects of the political economy of chemistry in
those years should consult the following sources: John J. Beer, *The Emergence of the German Dye
Industry* (Urbana: University of Illinois Press, 1959; reprinted New York: Arno Press, 1981); L. F.
Haber, *The Poisonous Cloud: Chemical Warfare in the First World War* (Oxford: Clarendon Press,
1986); Helmuth Tammen, *Die I.G. Farbenindustrie Aktiengesellschaft (1925–1933). Ein
Chemiekonzern in der Weimarer Republik* (Berlin: Verlag H. Tammen, 1978); Peter Hayes, *Industry and Ideology: I.G. Farben in the Nazi Era* (Cambridge University Press, 1987); Peter Morris, "The Development of Acetylene Chemistry and Synthetic Rubber by I.G. Farbenindustrie
Aktiengesellschaft, 1926–1945" (dissertation Oxford University, 1982). The newest, most comprehensive treatment of the entire history of the I.G. is by Gottfried Plumpe, *Die I.G. Farbenindustrie A.G.* (Berlin: Duncker & Humblot, 1990).
[2] See, for example, in addition to the sources cited in note 1, William Carr, *Arms, Autarky, and
Aggression: A Study in German Foreign Policy, 1933–1939* (New York: Norton, 1972).

strategy, meant that the German states had great potential for the development of foreign trade. Geography contributed to the area's promise in other ways as well. Coal was one of the few natural resources available in what was to become Germany, but its quality was high, and it was plentiful. Water was also available in abundance – for industrial production, for cooling and cleaning, and for low-cost transportation of raw materials and finished goods. That was especially true in the northern and western parts of the German area, where the Rhine River and its tributaries constituted a magnificent natural system of water transport that was supplemented by newly constructed canals and rail systems. A large and growing population that was well educated by the standards of the day added to the limited but geographically fortunate advantages of the German area as it stood poised to industrialize.

German entrepreneurs had begun the process of industrialization in earnest by the mid-1830s.[3] By the time the country was unified, that process was far advanced; in fact, industrialization was an important precondition for the success of the Prussian armies. But the "industrialization process" in Germany was something far different from what had taken place anywhere else. Growth and development were "relatively rapid, very uneven, and quite unique"; advances in industrial productivity far outpaced those in agriculture; heavy industry (coal, iron, and steel) rather than light industry (textiles) led the way.[4] The German path to industrialization differed markedly from that followed by the British, who had been the first to industrialize.

One of the "peculiarities of German history"[5] was therefore the early and sustained influence of heavy industry on the country's history. Coal and steel came to epitomize German military and economic power, as well as the close working relationships between industries and the state. If asked to name a prominent industrialist from German history, many would choose a member of the Krupp family. The family's World War I product, "Big Bertha," a gigantic piece of artillery, symbolized the frightening triumph of German steel and armaments technology. After World War II, during the trials at Nuremberg, members of the famous Krupp family were accused of complicity in the crimes of the National Socialist regime. In the late 1940s, knowledgeable observers recognized that German coal was the key to European reconstruction. Fear of a resurgent German heavy industry played a large role in convincing French Foreign Minister Robert Schuman to take up Jean Monnet's suggestion to establish the European Coal and Steel Community in May 1950.[6]

[3] Martin Kitchen, *The Political Economy of Germany, 1815–1914* (London: Croom Helm, 1978), p. 22.

[4] Kitchen, *Political Economy*, p. 61. The idea that German developments were somehow "quite unique" has been the subject of a debate extending well beyond the economic sphere. See, for example, David Blackbourn and Geoff Eley, *The Peculiarities of German History* (Oxford University Press, 1984).

[5] This phrase comes from Blackbourn and Eley, *The Peculiarities of German History*.

[6] Heavy industry in Germany has been one of the most studied, not only because of its economic importance but also because of its political importance into the postwar period. A sampling of studies: Gerald Feldman, *Iron and Steel in the German Inflation, 1916–1923* (Princeton University

But even at the height of the heavy industries' glory in the late nineteenth century, the German economy had begun to depend heavily on certain newer industries, as the German military would soon come to do. The newcomers were the chemical and electrical industries, both central to the so-called Second Industrial Revolution. Both were more capital-intensive than many earlier industries; they utilized more skilled workers, and they pioneered in infusing science into technology through industrial research and development. They also came to play important roles in domestic and foreign markets.[7] From its beginnings, the organic chemical industry in Germany was based on coal, both for energy and for raw materials.

These new industries were not at all unique to Germany. As John Beer has pointed out, Britain and France pioneered in the new organic chemical technology of the late nineteenth century.[8] Thomas Hughes has examined the parallel (and, to a large extent, interwoven) paths in electrical technology taken by the United States, Britain, and Germany through 1930.[9] David Noble identified the practitioners of chemical and electrical engineering as chief among those who made the United States a great power in the late nineteenth and early twentieth centuries.[10]

What was peculiar to Germany was the preponderance of its chemical industry, both at home and in international markets. In Noble's scenario, developed for the United States, both of these key new industries of the Second Industrial Revolution were important in shaping production processes, patterns of industrial relations, and, ultimately, society itself. But Noble concentrated almost exclusively on the electrical industry before 1914; he was hard pressed to find examples of important leadership in the chemical industry among American organic chemical companies before the outbreak of the war. The reason is that the Germans controlled the most important sectors of the trade, including about 88 percent of the value of the world's dyestuff sales in 1913.[11] As John Beer noted,

never before or since in the history of dye manufacture has a small group of industrialists come closer to monopolizing the world's color market than did the directors of the two German syndicates during the decade 1904–14. Given a few more years of peace, the

Press, 1977); Berndt Weisbrodt, *Schwerindustrie in der Weimarer Republik. Interessenpolitik zwischen Stabilisierung und Krise* (Wuppertal: Hammer-Verlag, 1978); Reinhard Neebe, *Grossindustrie, Staat und NSDAP 1930–1933* (Göttingen: Vandenhoeck & Ruprecht, 1981); Henry A. Turner, Jr., *German Big Business and the Rise of Hitler* (Oxford University Press, 1985); John Gillingham, *Industry and Politics in the Third Reich: Ruhr Coal, Hitler and Europe* (New York: Columbia University Press, 1985); Gillingham, *Coal, Steel, and the Rebirth of Europe, 1945–1955: The Germans and French from Ruhr Conflict to Economic Community* (Cambridge University Press, 1991); Volker Berghahn, *The Americanisation of West German Industry, 1945–1973* (Cambridge University Press, 1986).

[7] On the Second Industrial Revolution, see David Landes, *The Unbound Prometheus: Technological Change and Industrial Development in Western Europe from 1750 to the Present* (Cambridge University Press, 1969), pp. 231–358, esp. pp. 235, 249–90.

[8] John Beer, *Emergence*, e.g., p. 9.

[9] Thomas Parke Hughes, *Networks of Power* (Baltimore: Johns Hopkins University Press, 1983).

[10] David Noble, *America by Design: Science, Technology, and the Rise of Corporate Capitalism* (Oxford University Press, 1977).

[11] Plumpe, *Die I.G. Farbenindustrie*, pp. 50–7. By volume, the figure was over 90 percent.

chances are they would have gained control of the remaining 12 per cent of the business which was not yet in their hands.[12]

That 88 percent of worldwide production of dyes was indeed a formidable achievement, for organic chemicals composed the leading sector of the chemical industry. How did German firms come to dominate and practically monopolize world markets? The answer lies in the 1860s, when the most important firms were founded and key traditions were formed.

Chemical production involves fundamental transformations of matter (as opposed to merely reshaping it) and has been important almost since the beginning of human existence. Technological advances and large-scale production coincided with the beginnings of the Industrial Revolution in Britain, France, and Belgium in the late eighteenth and early nineteenth centuries. Inorganic chemical production grew first and most intensively, mainly to supply the soap-making and glass-making industries with salt and alkalis. Demand for chlorine bleach for the booming textile industry also stimulated growth and technological change in the chemical industry.[13] Expansion of inorganic chemical production thus formed part of the synergy that developed between and among various industries during the Industrial Revolution: Increased output in one industry led to increased demand for the products of others, and the possibility of exploiting the waste products of a given industry stimulated technological change in others.

Waste products from the manufacture of illuminating gas played a pivotal role in the development of the organic chemical industry, which began in the 1850s. One by-product of the production of illuminating gas was a foul-smelling, sticky coal tar, which was initially discarded. But chemical researchers found the substance interesting for experiments. Michael Faraday, for instance, isolated benzene in 1825. Three years later, Friedrich Wöhler discovered the isomerism of organic chemical compounds. A. W. Hofmann, a German researcher who had studied in Giessen under Justus Liebig and began lecturing in 1845 at the Royal College of Chemistry in London, had his students analyze and fractionalize coal tar during the late 1840s and 1850s. It was in London that researchers devised the first major commercial uses for coal tar in the form of synthetic dyes in the late 1850s. French chemists and entrepreneurs quickly followed in British footsteps.[14]

Although they had pioneered in the manufacture of coal-tar dyes, the British and French producers did not succeed in maintaining their position. Instead, world leadership in this still-new industrial sector had passed to their counterparts in Switzerland and the German area by the 1870s. By and large, German and Swiss companies maintained their leading positions in subsequent decades.

[12] Beer, *Emergence*, p. 134.

[13] A concise overview of these developments is available: The Open University, *The New Chemical Industry* (Milton Keynes: Open University Press, 1973), esp. pp. 25–55.

[14] Landes, *Unbound Prometheus*, pp. 274ff.; Beer, *Emergence*, passim, esp. pp. 5–30; for the most recent work on Hofmann and the relationship between his science and contemporary technology, see Anthony Travis, "Science's Powerful Companion: A. W. Hofmann's investigation of aniline red and its derivatives," *British Journal of the History of Science* 25(1992):27–44.

The return of some prominent German chemists to the German area from Britain symbolized the transfer of leadership in the new industry. Hofmann himself, frustrated by the British industry's unwillingness to invest in a solid program of training chemists and carefully planning research, responded to an attractive offer from the Prussian government and returned to Germany in 1865 as professor of chemistry at the University of Berlin. He was not alone. Heinrich Caro, who eventually became director of research at the Badische Anilin- und Soda-Fabrik (BASF) in Ludwigshafen, left England for Heidelberg in 1866. Carl Alexander Martius returned from Britain to the German area in the late 1860s and subsequently, together with Paul Mendelssohn-Bartholdy, founded the Berlin-based Gesellschaft für Anilinfabrikation, which later became Agfa.[15] These and other prominent figures led their companies to dominate the world's production of and trade in organic chemicals on the eve of World War I.

What accounts for the German success? Unquestionably, superior training of chemists for research and production work in the new industry was a factor, and the British and French fell short in that crucial task. Already in the late eighteenth century, German chemists had begun thinking of themselves as a scientific community, "that is, to regard one another as important peers, as primary arbiters of truth and merit."[16] Later, in the middle of the nineteenth century, German chemists would build on that foundation of an emerging scientific community, forcing reforms in the educational standards for chemists. Superior training in chemistry began early in the German area: In 1843, in his laboratory in Giessen, Justus Liebig pioneered in the early introduction of students to systematic, hands-on research in organic chemistry, especially in coal tars. Liebig also appreciated early on the relationship between science and industry, relying on industrialists to provide equipment and samples and to pose problems, and he was quite willing to enter into agreements with industry to commercialize his discoveries. Liebig established a pattern that was to be of enormous significance for the subsequent development of the industry in Germany. As John Beer pointed out, "the Germans, unlike the French and British, succeeded in removing the intellectual and social barriers between fundamental and applied science," especially in chemistry.[17]

Clearly, however, training excellent chemists was not in itself sufficient for a successful industry, as the short-term habitation of Hofmann and others in England demonstrated. Numerous other factors were also important. Arriving later on the scene than had the British and French pioneers in applied organic chemistry, German entrepreneurs were able to avoid some of the earlier mistakes of those pioneers; at the same time, they did not arrive so late that the cost of en-

---

[15] Beer, *Emergence*, pp. 42–3.

[16] Karl Hufbauer, *The Formation of the German Chemical Community (1720–1795)* (Berkeley: University of California Press, 1982), p. 1.

[17] Beer, *Emergence*, pp. 9ff., 18–20, 34–5, 57ff.; quotation, p. 61. See also Alan Beyerchen, "On the Stimulation of Excellence in Wilhelmine Science," in Jack R. Dukes and Joachim Remak, eds., *Another Germany: A Reconsideration of the Imperial Era* (Boulder: Westview Press, 1988), pp. 143–5.

tering into the competition, whether in terms of capital or inadequacy of scientific knowledge, was prohibitive.[18] Most of the German firms that would dominate the organic chemical industry were founded in the 1860s and 1870s (including Bayer, the predecessor of Hoechst, and Kalle & Co., all founded in 1863; BASF, in 1865; and Farbenfabriken ter Meer, in 1877),[19] in other words, not long after the founding of the earliest British and French firms. Surprisingly, in that rapidly changing industry, the slight German lag proved an advantage.

The slight but significant delay of German firms in entering organic chemical production also dovetailed well with one of the key political developments of the late nineteenth century: German unification. When it was accomplished in 1871, these firms stood ready to take advantage of the enlarged trading area that the new Reich entailed. Unification brought about a number of other advantages as well. The new, powerful German state was able to press for terms of trade advantageous to its industry, of particular importance in organic chemical production, which relied heavily on foreign trade. In addition, the Reich Patent Law of 1876, which took effect on 1 June 1877 and which "was framed with the help of the dye companies . . . , proved itself the world's most efficient legal instrument for the protection of chemical inventions."[20] Unlike French patent law, which protected a particular product and thus discouraged process innovation in the chemical industry, the German law protected only a production process. By coming up with a more efficient way to produce a popular dye, a firm could undercut a rival, even though that rival had been the first to develop the dye.

Other organizational changes, both within the industry and within German society as a whole, contributed to the success of the German organic chemical industry in the late nineteenth and early twentieth centuries. One key development was the rise of the industrial research laboratory within the German chemical industry, an innovation that was crucial to success in this science-intensive industry.[21]

---

[18] Wolfram Fischer makes a similar point for German industry in general in "The Role of Science and Technology in the Economic Development of Modern Germany," in William Beranek, Jr., and Gustav Ranis, eds., *Science, Technology, and Economic Development: A Historical and Comparative Study* (New York: Praeger, 1978), pp. 71–113, esp. p. 79.

[19] See Jürgen Kocka and Hannes Siegrist, "Die hundert grössten deutschen Unternehmen im späten 19. und frühen 20. Jahrhundert. Expansion, Diversification und Integration im internationalen Vergleich," in Norbert Horn and Jürgen Kocka, eds., *Recht und Entwicklung der Grossunternehmen im 19. und 20. Jahrhundert* (Göttingen: Vandenhoeck & Ruprecht, 1979), pp. 103–4, 11.

[20] Beer, *Emergence*, pp. 49ff., 67–8, 105–6; quotation, p. 56. For more on the patent law, see Paul M. Hohenberg, *Chemicals in Western Europe, 1850–1914: An Economic Study of Technical Change* (Chicago: Rand McNally, 1967), pp. 71ff.; Henk van den Belt and Arie Rip, "The Nelson-Winter-Dosi Model and Synthetic Dye Chemistry," in Wiebe Bijker, Thomas Hughes, and Trevor Pinch, eds., *The Social Construction of Technological Systems* (Cambridge, MA: MIT Press, 1987), pp. 135–58.

[21] Beer, *Emergence*, pp. 70–93; Georg Meyer-Thurow, "The Industrialization of Invention: A Case Study from the German Chemical Industry," *Isis* 73(1982):363–81; for the most recent work on industrial laboratories in the German chemical industry (and an article that revises fundamentally the findings of Beer and Thurow), see Ernst Homburg, "The Emergence of Research

BASF pioneered the concept. Gradually, between 1868 and 1877, the firm's chief, Friedrich Engelhorn, brought Heinrich Caro, who had recently returned from England to nearby Heidelberg, into an increasingly close relationship with his firm, culminating in Caro's appointment as research director. Once Caro began direction of BASF's main laboratory, he presided over its rapid expansion from just two to five and then to six full-time chemists by the beginning of the 1880s. By 1887, there were eighteen laboratories at BASF, ranging from factory to research laboratories. Hoechst also had a full-fledged research organization in place by 1880, though Bayer A.G. followed more slowly. To that point, the relationships between chemical companies and their laboratories had evolved gradually and without much strategic planning on the part of management. But a major change in the perception of the laboratory and its role in the company took place in the early 1880s. Management began to conceive of formal research within the firm as a tool, an aspect of corporate strategy. The founding of the Hoechst central laboratory in 1883 for pharmaceutical research was the first instance of this new conceptualization, and other companies quickly followed suit.[22]

Once the laboratories were in place, they were clearly significant. One set of figures clearly indicates the importance of the products of research laboratories for such firms: In the 1890s, 70–90 percent of company income came from sales of dyestuffs; by 1914, the figure had dropped to 60–70 percent, which was still substantial, but clearly on the downturn.[23] New products, which could be developed only through intensive research, were needed to ensure continued competitiveness in the face of such developments.

German firms also moved early to create effective sales organizations throughout the world. Sales representatives carefully cultivated new customers, and the services they offered – products that met the specific needs of particular customers, attention to quality, and so on – encouraged considerable loyalty. Linkages between the sales organization and other parts of the companies were also extremely important. Technical services to customers were a common feature. In addition, cooperation between sales offices and industrial laboratories helped to increase sales of chemical products throughout the world and provided a stimulus for invention. Moreover, in some cases the chemists spent time working with their customers to better learn their needs.[24]

Changes in educational and research arrangements in Germany, furthermore, provided competition for the somewhat complacent universities and thus ensured continuing success for the organic chemical industry, as well as for other sectors of the German economy. In October 1899, Kaiser Wilhelm II gave German polytechnics (Technische Hochschulen, THs) the right to confer advanced research degrees. Government and industry also skirted the fiefdoms of the uni-

Laboratories in the Dyestuffs Industry, 1870–1900," *British Journal of the History of Science* 25(1992):91–111.

[22] Homburg, "The Emergence of Research Laboratories."   [23] Beer, *Emergence*, p. 97.

[24] Beer, *Emergence*, pp. 91–3; L. F. Haber, *The Chemical Industry, 1900–1930: International Growth and Technological Change* (Oxford: Clarendon Press, 1971), pp. 123–4.

versities in founding research institutes in applied sciences, such as the Physikalisch-Technische Reichsanstalt (PTR), which served as the German bureau of standards, in addition to carrying out some research. Later, the universities responded to those threats to their scientific leadership and to rising enrollments by helping establish the Kaiser Wilhelm Society, which was announced in October 1910 and founded in January 1911. The Kaiser Wilhelm Society eventually set up laboratories, funded privately, for the most part, but under state auspices, which pursued research at the cutting edge of science, often in new hybrid fields such as physical chemistry.[25]

In sum, the competition in the German scientific community and that in its industry were intertwined. Individual institutions such as universities or industrial laboratories did not account for that competitiveness on their own; rather, the relationships between institutions led to the success of the German enterprise. As Alan Beyerchen pointed out,

crucial to their [German] scientific competitiveness was the institutionalization of a synergistic system for the generation and dissemination of knowledge that functioned in a sophisticated, modern manner. The distinctions between pure science, applied science and technology were blurred by constant interaction and mutual invigoration. This complex dynamic arrangement, rather than any one institution or even set of institutions, was the key to the success and excellence of Wilhelmian science.[26]

By 1914, many of the patterns of technological tradition and institutional relationships that would characterize German organic chemical production through at least 1945 (and in some cases, to the present) were becoming evident.[27] Elsewhere, I have argued that West German industry drew "upon a set of German technological traditions that emerged in the late 19th and early 20th centuries, major characteristics of which include[d] a drive for technical excellence tempered by gradual implementation of new technologies."[28] At first glance, German organic chemical technology, at the forefront of technological change through at least 1914, would seem to have violated that emerging tradition. After all, the infusion of science into industrial production was clearly "modern," as was the sales organization. Eventually, the combination of the better part of the industry into a giant trust, I.G. Farbenindustrie A.G., gave it a modern management structure as well.[29]

---

[25] Beyerchen, "Stimulation of Excellence," esp. pp. 150–5, 156ff.

[26] Beyerchen, "Stimulation of Excellence," p. 161.

[27] For an overview of the German chemical industry on the eve of the Great War, see Haber, *The Chemical Industry, 1900–1930*, pp. 108–34.

[28] Raymond G. Stokes, "Technology and the West German *Wirtschaftswunder*," *Technology and Culture* 32(1991):1–22.

[29] Alfred D. Chandler, Jr., dates the emergence of modern management in the German chemical industry even earlier: "By World War I the German dye companies had become the world's first truly managerial industrial enterprises." *Scale and Scope: The Dynamics of Industrial Capitalism* (Cambridge, MA: Belknap Press of Harvard University Press, 1990), pp. 474–81, 563–9; quotation, p. 481.

But to say that industry was truly modern would be somewhat misleading. In fact, organic chemical manufacturing in Germany involved grafting some new techniques of production, research, and management onto older traditions of work and technology. When the industry first emerged in the German area in the 1860s, for instance, it introduced a traditional guild system into its factories. Only gradually did firms change in the 1870s to a system involving technically trained foremen.[30] Even after that time, craft traditions continued to be strong in the industry. In his study of labor unrest during the German inflation of the 1920s, for instance, Craig Patton pointed out "that while labor protest at the major German chemical firms in 1914–1924 displayed some of the traits attributed to mass production industries, it often resembled that typical of artisanal industries."[31] What is more, the production technologies for dyes and pharmaceuticals, although they yielded state-of-the-art products that were the results of painstaking research and development, continued to demonstrate traditional characteristics. Workers produced the goods in small quantities in batch processes; the extremely high markup for the value added in the manufacturing process accounted for the success of the industry. Even in high-pressure chemistry, into which German firms had begun to move on the eve of World War I, there was no assembly line or even "mass production" in the sense we use those terms today.[32] Thus, although it was in many ways a modern industry, organic chemical manufacturing featured a surprising variety of traditional characteristics.

Another key instance of such an emerging pattern of technological traditions was the increasing awareness of the close connections among scientific and technical advances, economic success, and the power of the nation-state, an awareness that is also striking in its modernity. Werner Siemens, one of the pioneers of the electrical industry in Germany, had clearly articulated that perception in the early 1880s, when industrialists and government officials had debated the creation of an institute for precision mechanics, which eventually became the PTR:

Research in the natural sciences will always remain the firm foundation of technical advance, and the industry of a country will never be able to acquire and hold an international leading position if it is not simultaneously at the forefront of natural scientific advance.[33]

The rewards from that strategy of infusing science into industry quickly became obvious in the organic chemical industry. In 1895, for instance, the 1.1 per-

[30] Beer, *Emergence*, pp. 74ff.

[31] Craig Dean Patton, "Labor Protest and the German Inflation, 1914–1923: The Case of the Chemical Industry" (dissertation, University of California, Berkeley, 1985), p. 528. For an overview of labor relations in the German chemical industry compared with other countries, see Haber, *The Chemical Industry, 1900–1930*, pp. 376–403.

[32] For this final point, see Christopher S. Allen, "Political Consequences of Change: The Chemical Industry," in Peter Katzenstein, ed., *Industry and Politics in West Germany: Toward the Third Republic* (Ithaca: Cornell University Press, 1989), pp. 163–4. More generally, see Charles Sabel and Jonathan Zeitlin, "Historical Alternatives to Mass Production: Politics, Markets and Technology in Nineteenth-Century Industrialization," *Past and Present* 108(1985):133–76.

[33] Translated and quoted by Beyerchen, "Stimulation of Excellence," p. 146.

cent of the total German labor force that worked in chemical manufacturing produced 9.8 percent of the total value of the country's exports.[34] Because Germany depended heavily on exports for its economic well-being, that was indeed significant.

Ties between the chemical industry and the German state were at that early date nowhere near as close as they were to become. Decisions on the levels of chemical production and the funding of applied research remained in private hands. The state had a significant role in the success of the industry, but functioned primarily in the context of traditional nineteenth-century economic liberalism: Its role was to provide the legal, infrastructural, and foreign-trade framework within which industrialists could conduct their business most effectively. World War I fundamentally changed people's perceptions of the connection between industrial performance and state power by making it much more obvious and concrete. The chemical industry began to take a leading role in undergirding the power of the German state, not simply by figuring largely in the balance of trade (a relatively abstract concept), but also by providing some crucial instruments of state power, such as synthetic nitrates and poison gas. It thus freed Germany from dependence on foreign supplies of nitrates for fertilizers and ammunition and provided one of the most important weapons of World War I. Representatives of the state, recognizing the importance of the relationship between the performance of the chemical industry and the state's military and political power, began to take a much more active role in its management.[35]

The impact of war: 1914–18

When hostilities broke out in August 1914, BASF scientists were already working toward implementing on an industrial scale their new and promising process for fixing nitrogen from the air. The company's management was attracted to nitrogen-fixation technology for a number of reasons, the most important being the cyclical nature of the organic chemical industry: New products tended to pay off handsomely for a few years, followed by rapid deterioration in earnings. Dye sales already indicated that trend; thus, there was a need to develop new areas.[36]

Nitrate production seemed particularly interesting because the potential markets were very large indeed: Densely populated European countries needed to farm intensively, which would necessitate heavy use of nitrogenous fertilizers/ the military demand for nitric acid to produce nitroglycerin, dynamite, and trinitrotoluene (TNT) was also significant. Germany, like most other countries, depended heavily on overseas supplies, drawn mainly from deposits of sodium nitrate in Chile, which had replaced the traditional source, guano, in the second

[34] Beyerchen, "Stimulation of Excellence," p. 150.

[35] Haber makes this point as well, noting that it applied to all major chemical-producing countries: *The Chemical Industry, 1900–1930,* pp. 218–246. See also Jeffrey Johnson, *The Kaiser's Chemists* (Chapel Hill: University of North Carolina Press, 1990), passim, esp. chapter 9.

[36] On dye sales, see Beer, *Emergence,* p. 97. On product cycles and their effects on corporate strategy by the I.G. and its predecessors, see Hayes, *Industry and Ideology,* esp. pp. 2–5. On the development of synthetic nitrates, see, in addition to the sources listed in notes 37 and 38, Plumpe, *Die I.G. Farbenindustrie,* pp. 203–43.

half of the nineteenth century. One alternative was sulfate of ammonia, recovered from gasworks and coke ovens, but their production fluctuated considerably according to the needs of gas customers and the steel industry, and they could never be counted on to meet the demand for ammonia.

Two other alternatives appeared promising early in the twentieth century: the arc process and the cyanamide process. The former, however, used massive quantities of electricity, and the process could be economical only in areas that had abundant, low-cost hydroelectric power. The cyanamide process, which involved heating finely ground calcium carbide in the presence of nitrogen to form calcium cyanamide, also used considerable amounts of electricity, and the end product met with resistance from German farmers. Thus, even though alternative sources of nitrates existed, they were all more or less unsatisfactory. If BASF, using a chemically simple but technically challenging process based on the research of Fritz Haber (1868–1934), could produce nitrates at reasonable cost, it would be assured of a large market.[37]

Moving into this new production area would require investigating a new technological frontier in chemical manufacturing: high-pressure chemistry. The confluence of technological developments in different industries was crucial: High-pressure chemistry depended on the ability of steel producers to provide metals capable of withstanding unprecedented temperatures and pressures. By 1909, when Haber demonstrated, on laboratory scale, that yields of ammonia produced from hydrogen and nitrogen under pressure, and in the presence of a catalyst, appeared to be industrially viable, the steel industry was indeed up to the task. Carl Bosch (1874–1940), a high-ranking BASF engineer and the man who began to bring the process up to industrial scale, expressed his full confidence: "I believe it can work. I know the technical capability of the steel industry precisely."[38]

For a time, however, Bosch's confidence seemed misplaced. Converters of the size needed for the project had never been made before; they required a single casting of high-quality steel. Bosch turned to the Krupp steelworks to produce the converters, but he soon discovered that the steel weakened and the vessels burst after very short running times. It turned out that heated hydrogen used in the process was reacting with the carbon in the steel pipes, decarbonizing and weakening them. Bosch's solution reflected his ingenuity. He directed that the pipes be made of two layers. The inner pipe, fashioned of softer, low-carbon steel, did not react with the hydrogen. To give it strength, it was encased in a high-strength steel pipe, which had holes bored in it to allow hydrogen molecules to escape. Supplying sufficiently pure gases proved another technical problem, but Bosch and his co-workers were able to solve

---

[37] Haber, *The Chemical Industry, 1900–1930,* pp. 85–102; Harry A. Curtis, "A History of Nitrogen Fixation Processes," in Harry A. Curtis, ed., *Fixed Nitrogen* (New York: Chemical Catalog Company, 1932), pp. 77–89; Morris, "Development of Acetylene Chemistry," pp. 84–7.

[38] Thomas Parke Hughes, "Technological Momentum in History: Hydrogenation in Germany, 1898–1933," *Past and Present* 44(August 1969):106–8; Walter Witschakowski, *Hochdrucktechnik* (Ludwigshafen: BASF, 1974), pp. 10–15, quotation, p. 10; Haber, *The Chemical Industry, 1900–1930,* pp. 90–7.

that as well. By 1913, a small reactor was in production at Oppau, not far from the original BASF plant in Ludwigshafen.[39]

Development of the new process would have continued on that gradual path had it not been for the war. The British blockade of Germany made it abundantly clear just how dependent the country was on overseas supplies of nitrates, despite the availability of the alternative processes. The war effort's insatiable demand for ammunition, and the need for fertilizers for additional agricultural production, drew down stockpiles quickly. In 1915, industrialists significantly expanded their capacity for calcium carbide production with the erection of two new plants at Piesteritz and Königshütte, and they increased production capacity at Knapsack, near Cologne, and Trostberg, in Bavaria.[40] But even as the cyanamide producers geared up carbide production in anticipation of war orders, it was clear that they would not be able to meet the pressing needs of the war effort. Equally important, the amount of electricity needed for the process taxed the German war economy still further. With government financial encouragement, BASF responded to nitrate shortages by rapidly expanding its synthetic ammonia output by means of the superior Haber-Bosch process. Had the chemical industry and its technology not come to the rescue, there is no question that Germany would have collapsed long before November 1918, perhaps as early as mid-1915.[41]

The significance of the story of the wartime development of nitrogen-fixation technology is threefold. First, the war clearly accelerated the pace of change in Haber-Bosch technology. Second, the success of BASF's process occurred at the expense of other nitrogen-fixation processes, particularly the cyanamide process, although the overwhelming success of the Haber-Bosch process was not clear early in the war. That was why calcium carbide capacity was increased considerably in 1915. That expansion in carbide capacity had indirect but important consequences. After the war, "Germany was effectively self-sufficient in carbide."[42] In fact, the industry suffered from overcapacity and had to search for new markets. That was one important motivation behind the search for new uses for acetylene as a chemical feedstock, which, as we shall see, was a crucial scientific and technological development during the Third Reich.[43]

Third, the state became more involved in guiding the directions of technological change in the chemical industry. Some have suggested that the wartime experience was an aberration in the traditional patterns of state–chemical-industry relationships in Germany.[44] I would argue that the closer relations between the state and industry during the Great War simply made more explicit

[39] Witschakowski, *Hochdrucktechnik*, pp. 10–11; Haber, *The Chemical Industry, 1900–1930*, pp. 94–6.

[40] Morris, "Development of Acetylene Chemistry," pp. 86–7.

[41] Alan Beyerchen made this point to me in conversation in 1980. For a similar line of argument, see Johnson, *The Kaiser's Chemists*, p. 187.

[42] Morris, "Development of Acetylene Chemistry," pp. 86–7.   [43] Ibid.

[44] Peter F. Hayes, by stressing the economic liberalism of the German chemical industry until the Nazi period, implies this in "Carl Bosch and Carl Krauch: Chemistry and the Political Economy of Germany, 1925–1945," *Journal of Economic History* 47(1987):353–63.

and concrete the earlier perceptions of the connection between industrial and technological prowess and political power. Although the government-financed nitrogen-fixation plants were privatized during the great inflation of the 1920s – on terms very favorable to private industry[45] – that wartime experience set the tone for the later close identification of interest between I.G. Farben and the Third Reich. Finally, the development of this new technology underscored the chemical industry's ability to overcome at least some of Germany's resource limitations, something that synthetic-dye technology had already made clear. An awareness of that ability helped shape perceptions of the policy options during the Weimar period.

The Great War also introduced a new and direct use of chemicals on the battlefield: poison gas. L. F. Haber, the son of Fritz Haber, the chemist who had demonstrated the viability of nitrogen fixation in the laboratory and had led the German poison-gas effort, has detailed the history of chemical warfare during World War I in *The Poisonous Cloud*.[46] He contends that the widespread fear of gas warfare and the exaggerated stories about it were far out of proportion to the actual effects of the gas, especially because defensive technologies kept pace with offensive developments, and because of the mitigating effects of weather and other variables during gas attacks. Although it is difficult to make even rough estimates of the casualties from the poison gas, "set against the millions killed and wounded on the Western Front, the casualties of chemical warfare were insignificant."[47] Still, Haber sees the long-term consequences of gas warfare as far more significant than the tactical use of gas itself: Gas warfare affected military thinking about direct applications of science and technology to the conduct of war. Because of that experience, after 1918 (or, in any case, well before 1939), the indispensability of science and technology to the war effort was simply taken as a given.[48] Just as was the case with nitrogen-fixation technology, poison-gas development profoundly affected the political and strategic climate in Germany during the Weimar Republic and the Third Reich.

The war clearly altered the trajectory of technological development in the chemical industry and brought crucial changes in state–industry relations. The war had a direct impact, too, on the international role and domestic organization of the German chemical industry.[49] The British blockade not only prevented much-needed raw materials from reaching Germany but also blocked shipment from Germany of organic chemical intermediates and finished products. The utter dependence of many foreign companies on German producers became quickly and painfully evident, and especially after German firms began to provide the military with poison gas, the British, French, and American governments, among others, encouraged expansion of their domestic production of organic chemicals. After the war, therefore, German firms would face unparalleled competition in their former markets.

---

[45] Hayes, *Industry and Ideology*, pp. 12–13.   [46] Haber, *Poisonous Cloud*.

[47] Haber, *Poisonous Cloud*, pp. 239–58; quotation, p. 245.   [48] Haber, *Poisonous Cloud*, p. 315.

[49] For a more detailed look at the effects of World War I on the chemical industry, see Plumpe, *Die I.G. Farbenindustrie*, pp. 96–114.

Mindful of that fact, and in the interest of conducting the war effort more effectively, the six major German organic chemical companies coordinated their resources, beginning in 1916, under the auspices of Interessengemeinschaft der deutschen Teerfarbenfabriken (''community of interest of German coal-tar dye factories''). Two other producers joined in the following year, and Interessengemeinschaft also acquired a number of other factories. The companies agreed to pool profits and redistribute them based on fixed percentages. They also coordinated their acquisitions, the raising of capital, and their exchanges of knowhow.[50] Although each company retained some measure of independence by reserving the right to withdraw from the cartel and to set its own production programs, the formation of the Interessengemeinschaft was an important step along the path to concentration of organic chemical production in Germany into a single company, a step that would be taken during the Weimar Republic.

The tumultuous twenties: 1918–29

The last months of the Great War and the five years following the armistice constituted perhaps the most traumatic period in German history to that point. The kaiser was forced to abdicate in November 1918. At about the same time, revolutionary activity swept through the collapsing country, and a German republic was proclaimed. The provisional government, composed of socialists and others who had been kept out by the ruling elites in the imperial period, faced enormous difficulties on all sides: Communists insisted that the revolution be carried through to its logical conclusion, that is, to the complete overthrow of capitalism and the remaking of German society; rightists plotted the new republic's overthrow from the beginning of its existence, with a variety of aims, ranging from re-establishing the monarchy to creating a new, fascist state; less extreme political groups, big business, and the military supported the new government only when it was clearly in their best interests, certainly not out of any conviction. Faced with pressure from the extremists, representatives of the new regime made deals with the latter groups, thus guaranteeing that German society would not be made over. Economic instability paralleled political upheaval. Already, between 1914 and 1918, the German mark had lost about half its value against the dollar in international markets because of deficit financing. After the war, inflation began a dizzying upward spiral, with the mark's value dropping from 8.28 to the dollar in December 1918 to 317.14 to the dollar by June 1922.[51]

Foreign political problems were both causes and consequences of the domestic political and economic instability. The new German government expected to sign a peace based on President Woodrow Wilson's Fourteen Points – a ''peace with no victors'' – but its representatives were in for a rude awakening. At the end of the peace process in June 1919, representatives of the new German

---

[50] Hayes, *Industry and Ideology*, pp. 11–13.
[51] Carl-Ludwig Holtfrerich, *The German Inflation, 1914–1923: Causes and Effects in International Perspective* (Berlin: Walter de Gruyter, 1986); mark–dollar rates from Appendix 1 of Feldman, *Iron and Steel in the German Inflation, 1916–1923*, p. 472.

government signed the punitive Treaty of Versailles under duress. Among other things, the treaty mandated massive cutbacks in German armed forces, severely curtailed the country's ability to determine its foreign-trade policy, transferred territory to Germany's victorious or neutral neighbors, and demanded large but unspecified reparations from the defeated nation. Historians have debated at length whether or not Germany deserved such treatment.[52] All agree, however, that the Treaty of Versailles undermined the authority of the new republican government; at the same time, those who had prosecuted the war, because they were no longer in the government, were effectively exonerated of responsibility for the German defeat. Politicians who promised nonfulfillment of the treaty and who opposed the government enjoyed substantial popular support.

Such was the situation in mid-1922, when things spiraled out of control. In late June 1922, right-wing extremists assassinated the foreign minister, Walther Rathenau, who had advocated fulfillment of the treaty. By 11 January 1923, French troops had occupied the Rhineland. The German government responded by funding a financially ruinous policy of passive resistance: It paid workers in the occupied areas not to work, but at the same time it failed to increase its revenues through taxes or other measures. Hyperinflation began, with the mark losing value at a breathtaking rate: Its official value fell from 4.2 to the dollar in 1914 to 4.2 *trillion* to the dollar by the fall of 1923. Political chaos accompanied the economic chaos. Governments came and went with astonishing rapidity, while Adolf Hitler and his Nazis attempted an abortive coup in Bavaria. Only in late 1923 and early 1924 did the situation stabilize: Hans Luther and Hjalmar Schacht engineered the stabilization of the mark (at 4.2 to the dollar once again); an American loan and mediation on the reparations issue (the Dawes Plan) helped the German government consolidate its financial situation; and Gustav Stresemann began his five-year tenure as foreign minister, stressing reconciliation with the French and fulfillment of the Treaty of Versailles.[53]

This digression on the political economy of Weimar Germany is necessary for a full understanding of what became of the country's chemical industry in the interwar years; at the same time, the changes in the organization of the industry and in chemical technology had certain effects on the Weimar political economy. The formation of I.G. Farbenindustrie A.G. and the development of new technologies for synthesizing petroleum from coal, and then rubber from coal, resulted from this interplay of industry–state relations.

The major German chemical producers emerged from the turmoil of war, revolution, and inflation in decent shape. Because no fighting had taken place on German soil, and because the air war had been a negligible factor in World War I, the chemical plants were intact, and had even grown to meet wartime de-

[52] The literature on this subject is enormous. For a brief introduction to some of the most important contributions, see the extracts in Holger H. Herwig, ed., *The Outbreak of World War I*, 5th ed. (Lexington, MA: D. C. Heath, 1991).

[53] The best overview of the economic and political causes and effects of inflation (in their international context) is by Holtfrerich, *German Inflation*.

mands. More important, domestic inflation had little effect on the ability of chemical firms to sell abroad; in fact, the international competitiveness of German firms may actually have increased because of the inflation.[54] In addition, they, like other surviving businesses, produced goods that people wanted, which meant that it was possible to avoid some of the worst effects of inflation through nonmonetary transactions. Inflation also had some positive effects: The companies could pay off their loans painlessly with inflated currency, and they were able to buy government-financed synthetic-nitrogen plants built during the war in the same way.

But the chemical firms had their share of problems. Wartime expansion had led to overcapacity for the domestic market. The war had also disrupted their sales networks abroad, and because other countries had been cut off from their German sources of organic chemicals, they had begun to create their own organic chemical industries. Synthetic-nitrogen production was reasonably profitable in the short term, although, again, wartime expansion had led to some oversupply. Still, top-level managers could see that within a relatively short time, the product cycle for synthetic nitrogen would run its course, just as it had for dyes. Its manufacture would therefore steadily become less profitable. The firms would have to enter new production areas, and research-and-development costs would of necessity be exorbitant.

Key German chemical producers had already gained experience coordinating some of their operations through the Interessengemeinschaft during the war. When Carl Duisberg of Bayer and Carl Bosch of BASF began to press for still closer cooperation to combat some of the problems just outlined and to reestablish German leadership in organic chemical production, high-ranking managers of other firms were receptive. By late 1925, they went so far as to fuse into a single corporation. Bayer, Agfa, Farbwerke Hoechst, Cassella Farbwerke, Kalle & Co., Chemische Fabriken vorm. Weiler ter Meer, and Chemische Fabrik Griesheim Elektron sold all of their shares to BASF, which renamed itself Interessengemeinschaft Farbenindustrie Aktiengesellschaft (I.G. Farbenindustrie A.G., I.G. Farben, or the I.G.). The new corporation established headquarters in Frankfurt. A giant trust, I.G. Farben immediately became the largest industrial corporation in Europe and the largest chemical firm in the world. It dominated the most lucrative and technologically sophisticated sectors of organic chemical production and the nonferrous-metals industry in Germany, and by capitalizing on prewar Germany's worldwide reputation in the field and on extensive foreign sales experience, I.G. Farben soon captured large markets abroad as well.[55]

Carl Bosch, who became chairman of the managing board of the I.G., saw the firm's premier project as that of putting into industrial production an efficient process to synthesize liquid fuels from coal. In the mid-1920s, synthetic fuel seemed a particularly viable source of profit to succeed synthetic nitrogen and

---

[54] Holtfrerich, *German Inflation*, esp. pp. 279–300.
[55] For additional material on the formation and structure of I.G. Farben, see Plumpe, *Die I.G. Farbenindustrie*, pp. 131–63.

dyes: Forecasters were predicting that supplies of natural petroleum would be declining rapidly, while at the same time automobile production and thus the demand for fuel were on the rise. The curve for the extremely profitable synthetic-fuel product cycle would begin to rise just as synthetic-nitrogen profits would be leveling off. Moreover, because synthetic-fuel processes would be based on coal, Germany would be in a particularly advantageous position with its assured supplies of raw materials for synthetic fuels. BASF (later I.G. Farben) used its experience in high-pressure chemistry to good effect, and by 1927 the Farben plant at Leuna was producing fuel at a rate of 90,000 metric tons annually. Unfortunately for Farben's management, however, the start-up of production at Leuna was followed closely by a collapse in world prices of many commodities, including petroleum, a downturn that anticipated the Great Depression that began in 1929.[56] As the Depression worsened, top personnel at the I.G. were placed in the uncomfortable position of having to decide whether to continue research, development, and production of synthetic petroleum or to cut their very considerable losses. As we shall see, they decided to continue their efforts, but they had to turn to the German government for help.

Most nations did not have secure supplies of rubber, another crucial commodity in an industrialized society, and that provided potentially lucrative opportunities for German chemical firms in the mid-1920s. At the beginning of the century, natural rubber came from the Amazon basin, and when supplies from that source proved inadequate, plantations were started in the Far East, with one of the key producing areas being British Malaya. When prices for natural rubber plummeted in the early 1920s, the British government stepped in to limit exports from Malaya, thus increasing prices substantially. Higher prices and the desire to avoid British manipulation of the market prompted researchers in the Soviet Union, Germany, and the United States to explore the possibilities of synthetic-rubber production.[57]

Bayer scientists had already come up with a process for producing a synthetic "methyl rubber," and in 1912 they added it to natural rubber to make automobile tires of semiartificial rubber. Owing to the British blockade during the war, the German government substituted methyl rubber for natural rubber in many applications, but its poor performance and high prices forced Bayer to abandon production after the war. The events of the early 1920s prompted renewed interest in artificial rubber. When I.G. Farben was formed in 1925, its management placed a high priority on developing satisfactory and relatively inexpensive substitutes for natural rubber. I.G. scientists made significant progress through 1930, coming up with two very promising artificial rubbers, Buna S and Buna N, both of which had desirable wear characteristics compared with natural rubber. Just as in the case of synthetic-fuel development, however, the I.G.'s timing could not have been worse. A sharp drop in natural-rubber prices combined with the Depression to force practical suspension of artificial-rubber research at the

[56] Hughes, "Technological Momentum."
[57] Peter Morris, "Transatlantic Transfers in Synthetic Rubber Technology, 1930–1960" (unpublished manuscript in author's possession), pp. 3–6.

I.G. in fall of 1930. Again, though, as in the case of synthetic petroleum, government intervention would later resuscitate the I.G.'s synthetic-rubber program.[58]

More than the mere unfortunate happenstance of investing heavily in new substitute technologies just as natural-commodity prices fell connected I.G. Farben's experiences with synthetic petroleum and synthetic rubber. Both products were at the cutting edge of technological development, thus conforming to traditions in the organic chemical industry. Both, furthermore, drew heavily on the chemical firms' technological experience in high-pressure chemistry, hydrogen production, and, in the case of rubber, polymerization. Both represented potential successors, at the beginning of their product cycles, to synthetic dyes and nitrogen.

There were other similarities as well. Both technologies conformed closely to the previous patterns of relationships between industrial and technological development on the one hand and the German political economy on the other. I.G. Farben executives meant eventually to sell their wares on world markets and to compete effectively with natural petroleum and rubber. To that extent, production of synthetic petroleum and rubber would fit in with the liberal traditions of free trade in the German chemical industry that Peter Hayes has described.[59] But stressing exclusively the foreign-sales policies of I.G. management does not take into consideration the manufacturing process as a whole; it neglects the source of raw materials and the actual manufacture of the finished product. Production of the substitute materials was based ultimately on secure supplies of the most important raw material, domestic coal, which German factories transformed into a saleable product. For the domestic market, moreover, synthetic petroleum and rubber were meant to liberate Germany from dependence on foreign supplies. In other words, if one considers not only the foreign-trade policy of I.G. Farben but also its domestic-market strategies, raw-materials procurement policies, and manufacturing practices, it is clear that the new technologies were also designed to ensure the largest possible measure of self-sufficiency, or autarky, for Germany in these crucial areas. They therefore conformed closely to the traditional patterns of relationships between the German organic chemical industry and the political economy established by the dyestuffs and synthetic-nitrogen technologies. National Socialists and other right-wing groups drew upon this aspect of the new technology for inspiration during the Weimar period: I.G. Farben's ability to overcome Germany's natural-resource limitations in so many vital areas made it possible for the Nazis and others to dream of German self-sufficiency, which for the Nazis was both a preliminary to and an objective of an aggressive war of expansion.

Heavy investment in synthetic fuel and synthetic rubber meant continuing, indeed increasing, the I.G.'s reliance on coal. In the process of enabling

---

[58] Morris, "Transatlantic Transfers," pp. 6, 8–11.

[59] See Hayes, "Carl Bosch and Carl Krauch," for the argument of continuity in the liberal tradition in the German chemical industry. Gottfried Plumpe also stresses dependence on foreign trade as one major factor distinguishing I.G. Farben from other major firms under Weimar and the Third Reich; see *Die I.G. Farbenindustrie*, pp. 498–506, 560–91.

Germany to become more independent of foreign raw materials, did the firm itself become more dependent on the industrialists in heavy industry, who controlled most of Germany's coal? In fact, that was not the case: The I.G. pursued a strategy of maximum energy and raw-materials independence within Germany, even purchasing coal mines during the 1920s and 1930s.[60]

Finally, there was a fairly close connection between the emergence of these two new technologies and the formation of the I.G. The recognition that it would be necessary to combine forces to explore new and very expensive technological possibilities in order to find profitable new organic chemical products was part of a broader awareness of the advantages of fusion. Only a company of the scale of I.G. Farben could bring the necessary resources to bear to develop the new technologies. Only a company the size of I.G. Farben could find ways of continuing to pursue the new technologies as it weathered the economic and political storms that wracked Germany beginning in 1929.

Depression and descent into war: 1929–45

The periodization for this last section of this chapter is somewhat unorthodox. Let me explain briefly. The Nazi seizure of power, beginning on 30 January 1933, certainly entailed a new and horrible era in the organization of the German polity. But the date that Hitler assumed the chancellorship should not obscure the continuities from the late Weimar Republic through the Nazi period. The world economic collapse that followed the Wall Street crash of August 1929 helped bring about the end of democracy in the Weimar Republic; the death of Gustav Stresemann, who had done much to help stabilize the fragile republic, in October of the same year did not help matters. Beginning in the summer of 1930, the emergency clause (Article 48) of the Weimar constitution was invoked; thereafter, although the Reichstag, the German parliament, continued to have some political weight, chancellors ruled by decree with the assent of the president, the former field marshal Paul von Hindenburg. The beginning of Hitler's chancellorship in January 1933, because it was not based on a majority in the Reichstag, and because it, too, depended on rule by decree, shared important elements with the immediate Weimar past.

In terms of the relationship between I.G. Farben and the state, 1929–30 was a more important breaking point with the immediate past than was 1933. The collapse of world prices for petroleum, in particular, prompted I.G. executives to join with other German oil producers in seeking support from the state to protect their investment in substitute technologies. The Weimar state responded with tariff protection measures: In April 1930, the duty on imported gasoline rose from the equivalent of 8.6 cents per U.S. gallon to 14.3 cents; a year later, the government raised the duty per gallon still further to 24.4 cents.[61] During the National Socialist period, those duties were increased, and in 1933 the govern-

---

[60] See Plumpe, *Die I.G. Farbenindustrie*, pp. 165–8.

[61] U.S. Strategic Bombing Survey (European War), USSBS Report 113, *The German Oil Industry, Ministerial Report 78* (January 1947), p. 19, seen in U.S. National Archives, Washington, DC, Record Group 243.

ment and the I.G. signed a contract, the *Benzinvertrag,* through which the government agreed to purchase a significant part of the output by synthetic-gasoline plants in return for expansion of production.[62] Closer industry–state relations to deal with the economic crises of the late Weimar period recapitulated similar patterns implemented to deal with the crisis of World War I and established the basis for still closer cooperation in the National Socialist period (which might be thought of as being, by virtue of deliberate government policy, in a permanent state of crisis). This is not to say that there was no difference between the late Weimar period and the National Socialist period in this or any other respect, because, after all, the German political economy and society looked far different in 1936 than they had in 1930, and far different in 1944 than in 1936; it is merely to point out that chemical-industry–state relations evolved gradually between 1929–30 and 1945 as the interests of the two groups of actors became intertwined more and more closely.

What were the major elements of that evolution? The first had to do with subtle changes in the meaning of "autarky," or economic self-sufficiency. As indicated earlier, trends in the German organic chemical industry through the late 1920s favored self-sufficiency in raw-materials supply and manufacturing and extensive foreign trade in finished materials. The collapse in world trade that was the most serious cause and consequence of the Great Depression forced I.G. Farben executives to abandon, to some extent, their former economic liberalism, to seek tariff protection – and a predominantly domestic market – for one of their key products: synthetic fuel. National Socialists, instead of viewing the abandonment of economic liberalism as a regrettable last resort, saw autarkic policies as a positive step, extricating Germany from reliance on foreign markets and serving as a precondition for their preparations for war.

Because world markets continued to be sluggish through the first half of the 1930s, and because Nazi policies of autarky benefited the chemical industry so much, I.G. Farben's management increasingly found common interests with Germany's new rulers. Synthetic fuel, synthetic rubber, nonferrous-metals production, plastics – all of these were production technologies in which the I.G. excelled; all of them were necessary to make Germany less reliant on overseas suppliers, and all of them were vital to the conduct of war. It is thus no accident that the first National Socialist Four Year Plan, an investment program to prepare Germany for the war that began in 1936, devoted the lion's share of its effort and resources to such technologies. Because the company's production palette so clearly matched the interests of the Nazi state in preparing for war, I.G. Farben benefited considerably from Four Year Plan investments, although Peter Hayes has demonstrated that the company's share in such investments was not as high as had been thought.[63]

---

[62] Hayes, *Industry and Ideology,* pp. 115–20. Hayes makes the important point that the contract "astutely balanced the interests of the contracting parties" (p. 118), rather than benefiting the I.G. at the expense of the government (or vice versa).

[63] Hayes, *Industry and Ideology,* pp. 175–85, esp. pp. 183–4. Hayes suggests that I.G.'s share in the plan's investments varied over time, but that they probably were on the order of a fifth to a

The Four Year Plan represented an important stage in the evolution of industry–government relations for another reason as well: Personnel seconded from I.G. Farben participated in formation of the government's investment policy. Carl Krauch, a high-ranking I.G. Farben official who became head of research and development in the Plan Office and in 1938 became commissioner-general for the problems of the chemical industry, was the most prominent of these, but there were several others. The I.G. moved from a posture of rejecting overt government interference in the industry in the 1920s to appealing to the government for protection and purchase guarantees in the late Weimar and early Nazi periods. Finally, key I.G. executives began to participate actively in government decision-making, although the extent to which they privileged their firm's interests over the interests of others while serving in that capacity has been questioned effectively.[64]

Peter Hayes has argued that the participation of personnel from the I.G. in government did not differ from that of personnel from other major chemical firms in other countries, especially during the war itself: High-ranking DuPont officials did service as "dollar-a-year men" in the U.S. government, for example, and representatives of ICI were active in British government circles.[65] Still, the I.G.–National Socialist relationship was different from the chemical-firm–state relationships in other highly industrialized countries, for at least two reasons. First, the I.G. dominated the German economy in a way that chemical firms in other countries did not. Second, the National Socialists, because of the combination of German resource limitations and their own aggressive designs, needed the I.G. to an extent unparalleled in other countries. Given the state of the world economy when the National Socialists came to power, such attention was certainly welcome in many quarters at the I.G. Thus, although it may well be that "relatively traditional commercial and technological considerations . . . underlay the combine's conduct" throughout most of the Nazi period,[66] the firm and its political masters grew together over the course of that period.

I.G. Farben's research policies also closely followed that evolution toward closer identification with prevailing National Socialist goals and practice. The organic chemical industry had traditionally invested heavily in research and development, with considerable emphasis on research that would have no immediate applications. The Depression, besides forcing the I.G. to seek government help for its production technologies, forced it to cut its research budget drastically. As a result of the transformation of the German economy to a war footing by 1936, and then because of the pressures of the war itself, I.G. Farben continued to emphasize applied research.[67] Research and development (R&D) in the

     fourth of the total, a far cry from the two-thirds to three-fourths proportions usually cited by, for
     instance, Joseph Borkin and Dietmar Petzina. See sources cited by Hayes, p. 182, n. 37.
[64] Hayes, *Industry and Ideology*, pp. 156–8, 175–8; Morris, "Development of Acetylene Chemistry," pp. 61–2.
[65] Hayes, *Industry and Ideology*, pp. 118, 158, 327ff.   [66] Hayes, *Industry and Ideology*, p. 161.
[67] Raymond G. Stokes, *Divide and Prosper: The Heirs of I.G. Farben under Allied Authority, 1945–1951* (Berkeley: University of California Press, 1988), pp. 25–7.

National Socialist period produced some very impressive products and results, but the experience of I.G. Farben fit in with the general tendency during the period to favor applied research over basic research.[68]

Thus, two key areas of development for the I.G. during the period were synthetic fuel and synthetic rubber, two areas in which the company (or its constituent companies) had done more-fundamental research in the 1920s and earlier. The most important new field for I.G. Farben's R&D in the Nazi era was acetylene chemistry, particularly the branch of acetylene chemistry associated with Walter Reppe, a researcher at I.G.'s plant at Ludwigshafen. After the war, allied investigators, chemists, and chemical industrialists identified Reppe chemistry (along with synthetic-fuel and synthetic-rubber technologies) as one of the few fields in which the Allies could learn something from the Germans. One chemist went so far as to say that the central thrust of Reppe chemistry "undoubtedly represents one of the finest pieces of organic research carried out in recent years."[69]

Acetylene was a compound that was well known and often used around the world by the 1920s: as a welding gas; for lighting; and in the production of inorganic chemicals, such as nitrogen fertilizers.[70] For those applications, as well as for its much more limited use in the production of organic chemicals, there were some disadvantages: Manufacturing acetylene, which featured a triple bond between its constituent carbon atoms, required tremendous amounts of energy and was quite expensive; more important, the compound could readily form explosive mixtures. Using it under pressure was considered especially unsafe.[71]

Despite such cost and safety concerns, acetylene-based organic chemistry occupied an important niche in the industry beginning during World War I. Its application in the production of acetone was another excellent example of a technology meant to overcome Germany's resource limitations. Acetone was vital to the manufacture of smokeless powder, which composed about 50 percent of the

[68] See Stokes, *Divide and Prosper;* see also Mark Walker, *German National Socialism and the Quest for Nuclear Power, 1939–1949* (Cambridge University Press, 1989); John Gimbel, *Science, Technology, and Reparations: Exploitation and Plunder in Postwar Germany* (Stanford University Press, 1990). This is not meant to imply that no fundamental research was done in the Nazi period. Fundamental work on polymers and acetylene chemistry was carried out, for instance. I thank Peter Morris for his comments on an earlier draft of this chapter, and especially for his comments on the following section.

[69] Morris, "Development of Acetylene Chemistry," pp. 111–17; Peter Morris, "Strategy and System: Reppe and the Development of Organic Chemicals in I.G. Farben," presented at a meeting of the Society for the History of Technology, Madison, WI, 3 November 1991; M. H. Bigelow, "Reppe's Acetylene Chemistry," *Chemical and Engineering News* 25(14 April 1947):1038–42; quotation from Ernst Bergmann, *The Chemistry of Acetylene and Related Compounds* (New York: Interscience, 1948), p. 42; Peter Spitz, *Petrochemicals: The Birth of an Industry* (New York: Wiley, 1988), pp. 51, 55–6. For an English-language treatment based on Reppe's own recollections and notes in the aftermath of the war, see John W. Copenhaver and Maurice H. Bigelow, *Acetylene and Carbon Monoxide Chemistry* (New York: Reinhold, 1949).

[70] See the discussion of cyanamide earlier in this chapter.

[71] Morris, "Development of Acetylene Chemistry," pp. 84–249; Alfred von Nagel, *Aethylen–Acetylen* (Ludwigshafen: BASF, 1971), pp. 38ff.

weight of gun cotton, and was therefore of obvious military significance. Before the war and in its initial stages, most of the acetone supply came as a by-product of wood distillation in the United States and the Austrian Empire. As those sources were taxed by wartime demand and supply lines were disrupted by the hostilities, the Allies, and especially Britain, turned to fermentation of grain for additional supplies. The Germans chose an alternate route, using carbide produced from domestic coal and lime to make acetylene, from which acetaldehyde and then acetic acid could be produced, ending up finally with acetone.[72]

Acetone certainly was not the only product of those early efforts at acetylene-based organic chemistry. Indeed, during the 1920s and 1930s, Hoechst was already developing a whole "acetylene family tree" (*Acetylen-Stammbaum*), which eventually

featured a large number of aliphatic compounds which are obtainable from acetylene through relatively simple transformations. To this large number belong above all chlorinated hydrocarbons, acetaldehye, acetone, acetic acid, vinyl acetate and vinyl chloride.[73]

The Hoechst family tree constituted a complicated path to a limited number of fairly straightforward organic chemicals, a situation that did not satisfy a young researcher at BASF, Walter Reppe (1892–1969). Reppe, who rarely was photographed without a cigar and never tired of promoting himself (Figure 1.1), began working intensively on acetylene chemistry in 1928. He saw great possibilities in utilizing acetylene to produce plastics. To do that, however, would require rendering acetylene more reactive by manipulating catalysts and employing higher pressures. Reppe therefore selected as one of his main research areas the feared problem of handling acetylene under pressure, a task he undertook at great personal risk.[74]

By 1934, Reppe and his co-workers, then operating in the new Intermediates and Plastics Laboratory in Ludwigshafen, succeeded in finding ways of handling acetylene under pressure and in finding new ways to produce polymers. They came up with a whole family of "vinylation" (*Vinylierung*) reactions, which paid off in production of polyvinyl ethers for the glue, paint, rubber, and cable industries, polyvinyl isobutyl ether for plastics and chewing gum, and polyvinylpyrrolidone for use as a blood-plasma substitute. Those were important accomplishments, but vinylation had one important drawback: The triple carbon bond in acetylene became a double bond, which was accompanied by a considerable loss of energy.[75]

Reppe and his staff achieved their key breakthrough in 1937 when they discovered a way to maintain the triple bond of acetylene when it reacted with formaldehyde to produce 1,4-butynediol, which allowed a two-stage route,

[72] Haber, *The Chemical Industry, 1900–1930*, pp. 211–14; Morris, "Development of Acetylene Chemistry," pp. 84–93.

[73] von Nagel, *Aethylen–Acetylen*, p. 39; for a diagram of "traditional acetylene chemistry," see Morris, "Development of Acetylene Chemistry," p. 91.

[74] von Nagel, *Aethylen–Acetylen*, pp. 38–41; Morris, "Strategy and System."

[75] von Nagel, *Aethylen–Acetylen*, pp. 42–3.

Figure 1.1. Walter Reppe, head of the main research laboratory, BASF, Ludwigshafen. (Courtesy BASF Unternehmensarchiv, Ludwigshafen.)

rather than a four-stage route, to butadiene, a key building block of Buna synthetic rubber.[76] As a reward for that accomplishment, Reppe was appointed director of the Central Research Laboratory at Ludwigshafen, where he spent the remainder of the National Socialist period working out the implications of his important discovery for production of other organic chemicals. Although "it is well to recall that the Reppe products accounted for [just] 2 ½ percent of all acetylene-based chemicals in 1943,"[77] Reppe's processes yielded important new plastics (and new routes to old ones) during the war and held great promise for the postwar period.

Less than two years after Reppe assumed the directorship of the Ludwigshafen main laboratory, the war began, in September 1939. Thereafter, patriotism – or, put somewhat differently, the desire to avoid the appearance of undermining the war effort – placed more pressure than ever on I.G. Farben executives to conform with National Socialist wishes. But I.G. managers probably were also tempted by the wealth and power such conformity would entail. The two tendencies combined to bring about an even greater coincidence of interests between the chemical firm and Germany's ruling party; there was a growing

---

[76] von Nagel, *Aethylen–Acetylen,* p. 43; Morris, "Development of Acetylene Chemistry," pp. 123–33, esp. pp. 123–4.
[77] Morris, "Development of Acetylene Chemistry," p. 133.

tendency for I.G. Farben personnel to howl with the Nazi wolves. The I.G.'s participation in the occupation, exploitation, and plunder of Germany's neighbors was one example of this tendency. The firm's implementation of many of the regime's racial policies was another; the I.G., like most other German firms, did not hesitate to use forced labor and slave labor in its factories to try to fulfill the demands of the Nazi war machine.[78]

It was, however, at Auschwitz that German history – and the history of the German organic chemical industry – reached its nadir. Under pressure from the Nazi regime, but having also assured themselves of the viability of the investment using traditional methods of business decision-making, I.G.'s leaders decided in February 1941 to establish a plant – primarily for producing synthetic rubber, methanol, and oil – near what was to be a factory for murdering the victims of Nazi racial policies. There is no evidence that the abundance of slave labor in the area was a factor in the I.G. decision, because in fact the firm planned to lure German workers to the site, nor did the implementation of the Final Solution start at Auschwitz until after the plant was under construction. But it is certain that top officials of the chemical combine knew about the killing, and there is no evidence that they considered any course other than going along with the butchery.[79]

For many Germans, including the leaders of I.G. Farben, the situation at Auschwitz involved and illustrated an appalling moral lapse. Farben's unpardonable moral failing at Auschwitz corresponded to a decline in its technological capabilities as well, although it is impossible to establish a causal relationship in this regard.[80] The plant was intended to implement the firm's latest technologies, but to construct it, the company had used the most primitive, barbaric methods. What is more, the descent into barbarism was as ineffective as it was outrageous: The plant never produced any rubber for the German war effort.

Conclusions

In this first chapter, the aim has been to give an overview of the history of the German organic chemical industry through 1945, not only to provide necessary background information for what is to follow but also to demonstrate the intimate connections between business and technological decision-making and the German political economy between 1860 and 1945. Clearly, throughout German history, the organic chemical industry and its products were necessary for the country to gain and maintain its world-power status: Its virtual monopoly of for-

---

[78] Hayes, *Industry and Ideology*, pp. 266–376.

[79] Morris, "Development of Acetylene Chemistry," pp. 321–6, 330–45; Hayes, *Industry and Ideology*, pp. 347–68. See also Joseph White, "The Politics of Labor Utilization: I.G. Farben, the SS, and Auschwitz" (M.A. thesis, Georgia State University, 1989).

[80] Nicholas Wade, reporting on research by Robert Berger, as published in the *New England Journal of Medicine*, suggests that there is a relationship between moral deficiency and bad science. Describing the discrediting of Nazi hypothermia experiments, he notes that "any experiment grossly deficient in ethics is likely to be defective in other ways as well." See "The Errors of Nazi Science," *New York Times* (27 May 1990). Perhaps the same is true with regard to technology.

eign trade in organic chemicals before 1914 contributed substantially to Germany's overall economic competitiveness; during World War I, the industry's contributions in the form of synthetic nitrogen and poison gas staved off certain German defeat for four years; during the Nazi period and World War II, I.G. Farben's foreign-trade earnings aided the cause of German rearmament substantially, and its synthesis technologies provided the basis for a war of aggression that was initially frighteningly successful.

The close connections between excellence in organic chemical technology and political and economic power in Germany helped orient the industry toward a self-serving mixture of economic liberalism (in the area of foreign trade) and autarky, or self-sufficiency (in raw-materials supply and manufacture). Over time, and especially after 1930, more generalized autarkic policies overcame even the modest liberal strain in that tradition. That changing pattern of relationships between industry and the state helped shape the technological course of the major organic chemical producer, I.G. Farben. Because of ingrained technological traditions, Germany's abundant supplies of coal, and autarkic policies (of necessity during World War I and in the Weimar period, and partly by choice in the Nazi period), I.G. officials chose to develop technologies that would produce substitute products to ease German reliance on overseas supplies, technologies that were based on German coal.

That pattern of reliance on coal continued even as U.S. chemical firms began to move in the 1920s (and even more rapidly during the war) into new, larger-scale technologies that were based on petroleum feedstocks. Petrochemical production allowed unparalleled scales of manufacturing for certain new (and some old) products – mostly synthetic polymers – at a fraction of the cost of using other starting materials. After the war, it appeared that the Germany that would renounce autarky and begin to compete once again in world markets using the most efficient feedstocks probably would have to become a petrochemical producer, at least for part of its production palette.

But in 1945, such considerations were still academic. The fate of Germany itself remained unclear. Its economy and infrastructure were devastated. The central German government had collapsed, its functions taken over by the four Allies (the Soviet Union, the United States, France, and Great Britain), each of which had responsibility for a zone of occupation. And the Allies came with an explicit policy of radically reforming the German organic chemical industry, beginning by breaking up the giant combine I.G. Farben.

2
Western German chemicals in flux, 1945–1951

As Allied troops swarmed into Germany in the spring of 1945, the Nazi government and economy collapsed. By April, the once mighty German organic chemical industry, along with virtually all other industries, sat idle, the victim of Allied bombing attacks, transportation outages, and disruptions in supplies of energy and raw materials. Its resuscitation did not appear imminent: All four of the Allies agreed that they should denazify, decartelize, and deconcentrate the German economy, and one of their top targets was I.G. Farbenindustrie A.G. In addition, the Allies sent teams of scientists and engineers to the defeated nation to scour university and industrial laboratories for scientific and technical information.[1] They also set strict controls for future German research. The combined effects of the initial Allied policies therefore undermined the technological basis of Germany's economic and political power. By 1948, however, in view of

[1] The most comprehensive treatment of the American side of that effort is John Gimbel's *Science, Technology, and Reparations: Exploitation and Plunder in Postwar Germany* (Stanford University Press, 1990); the activities of the other Allies remain little researched. For one exception dealing with an aspect of the French effort, see Marie-France Ludmann-Obier, "Un aspect de la chasse aux cerveaux: les transferts de techniciens allemands en France: 1945–1949," *Relations internationales* 46 (1986): 195–208.

the fluctuating international political situation and the costs of those initial draconian policies, western Allied policy had begun to change. Key figures in German industry were faced with a variety of technological choices, and they had to formulate their plans for the future under the constraints of that changing policy.

Politics and technology at the "zero hour," 1945–8

The chemical industry had provided the German war machine with such key goods as synthetic gasoline, synthetic rubber, and other substitute materials, and therefore control over that industry was an important objective of the Allied occupation officials. Restraints on technological development were central to the control effort, with limitations on production and control over research initiatives as key policy elements. Even the Allied breakup of I.G. Farben affected the industry technologically, by ending the traditional production and research relationships among individual factories.[2] Forced transfers of technology from Germany to Allied countries comprised a critical element in the control program, and that appropriation occurred on a massive scale; still, such transfers proved a rather blunt instrument for accomplishing the initial Allied objectives.

Although most severe in the Soviet zone of occupation,[3] physical removal of industrial plant and equipment also occurred in the western zones and was one aspect of the wider technology transfer from Germany to its former enemies. Chemical plants represented a key policy objective. As the occupation began, well over half of the industry's facilities were slated for removal; even the revised level-of-industry plan issued in August 1947 for the combined American and British zones stated that "between 40 and 50% of the total chemical capacity . . . will . . . be removed as reparations or destroyed."[4]

---

[2] Joint Chiefs of Staff directive JCS 1067 states U.S. policy in those areas. The April 1945 version (made public in October of the same year) is in U.S. Department of State, *Germany 1947–1949: The Story in Documents* (Washington, DC: U.S. Government Printing Office, 1950), pp. 22–33.

[3] Dismantling in the Soviet zone reached a scale unknown in the other zones; e.g., Sachsen-Anhalt, an industrial province, lost about 40% of its total industrial substance; Leuna, the largest I.G. Farben plant, lost half of its capacity that remained after the bombing. See "Demontage in der Ostzone," *Angewandte Chemie* B20(1948):148–9. An internal document prepared by the Decartelization and Deconcentration Division of the U.S. High Commission in Germany (apparently at the end of 1953) indicated that 40% of the production capacity of the former I.G. Farben plants was lost through dismantling through 1948. Reconstruction and upgrading of those plants began in that same year, however, with the result that "it is considered that at present the total production capacity of all the former Farben plants in the Soviet zone exceeds substantially that of any one of the individual big three successor companies carved out of the former Western zonal Farben estate." Decartelization and Deconcentration Division, "Notes on the Soviet Zonal Assets of the I.G. Farbenindustrie A.G. and Analysis of the Effects of a Possible Restoration on the Allied Deconcentration Program," n.d. (ca. end of 1953), NA, RG 466, HICOG, Office of General Counsel, Decartelization and Deconcentration Division, Cartel Subject Files, 1947–1955, Box 22: Future of Soviet Zone Assets. For more on the Soviet zone and East Germany, see Chapter 10.

[4] "Revised Plan for Level of Industry in the Combined U.S.-U.K. Zones of Germany: Joint Statement by State and War Departments," 29 August 1947, in U.S. Department of State, *Germany 1947–1949*, pp. 361–2.

Still, that figure overstated the extent of dismantling in the west: More than three-fourths of the total capacity slated for removal represented war-related explosives plants, and the actual dismantling never reached even those revised targets. A more reasonable estimate compiled in late 1949 by the Bremen Committee for Economic Research, at the behest of the German Office for Peace Questions, pegged the average loss of postwar capacity by the chemical industry at 6 percent.[5] That figure had distinct advantages over many other estimates: It eliminated from consideration purely war-related plants, while at the same time including measures of the effects of wartime destruction and of reconstruction in the immediate aftermath of the war. It thus reflected the scale of dismantling of physical plant as a form of technology transfer, although the broad range of firms and countries involved and the differing methods of valuing the seized assets continue to impede a more precise assessment.[6]

That something on the order of 94 percent of the 1936 western German chemical capacity was available in November 1949, however, tells us remarkably little about the quality of the intact capacity. In fact, it varied tremendously. Bombing had destroyed or damaged only 5 percent of Hoechst's main production facilities; they were little affected by reparations or dismantling, as was the case with most factories in the U.S. zone. Hoechst's physical plant was, however, relatively old and worn out. BASF's main factories at Ludwigshafen and Oppau represented the other end of the spectrum, with relatively modern plant that was both more heavily bombed and more affected by dismantling.[7] Other major chemical factories lay between the extremes.

Variations in Allied dismantling policy and practice determined the differing experiences of chemical factories. American occupiers, finding little equipment

[5] Bremer Ausschuss für Wirtschaftsforschung, "Gesamtumfang der Demontagen" (end of November 1949), Bl. 22, Bundesarchiv, Koblenz (hereafter, BAK), Z35/317. "Postwar capacity" is all intact capacity in 1945 plus machinery repaired or rehabilitated as of 1947–8 (about an additional 10% of 1945 capacity). Postwar western German chemical and chemical-technical capacity was approximately that of the equivalent area in 1936. "Demontagen in Westdeutschland," *Chemie-Ingenieur-Technik* 23(1951):593–4, provides a critical review of the report.

[6] Critiquing estimates of dismantling and reparations, Werner Abelshauser states bluntly that "an exact reckoning of the actual extent of reparations and their capacity-reducing effect on the fixed assets of West German industry is not possible." See "Neuanfang oder Wiederaufbau? Zu den wirtschaftlichen und sozialen Ausgangsbedingungen der westlichen Industrie nach dem Zweiten Weltkrieg," *Technikgeschichte* 53(1986):264–6; quotation, p. 265. For a more recent attempt to estimate the value of both physical and "intellectual" reparations, see Christoph Buchheim, *Die Wiedereingliederung Westdeutschlands in die Weltwirtschaft 1945–1958* (Munich: Oldenbourg, 1990), pp. 89ff. To illustrate the complexity of formulating such figures, in 1950, BASF reported differences of about DM 25 million between Allied and German estimates of the current value of assets seized from its factories. BASF, "Meldung an Landesregierung Rheinland-Pfalz, Wirtschaftsministerium Ref. IX," 7 December 1950, 1, BASF Unternehmensarchiv, Ludwigshafen (hereafter, BASF), B4/659.

[7] Production Control Agency, SHAEF, "Industrial Investigation Report 16: I.G. Farbenindustrie A.G., Werk Hoechst," 1945, p. 2, in Hauptstaatsarchiv Hessen, Wiesbaden, 649, OMGH Bipartite Liaison Division ED, 17/164-1/12; Herbert Moulton, "Subject: The Höchst Plant of I.G. Farbenindustrie A.G.," 30 July 1945, Hoechst Firmenarchiv, Frankfurt-Hoechst; BASF, "BASF schreibt Geschichte," *Chemische Industrie* 4(1952):A580.

worth carting away, and charged with seeing that the German economy did not become a major burden for the U.S. taxpayer, chose other means of realizing their policy objectives: Information, not hardware, was the preferred means of transfer. The Russians found much equipment that seemed worth removing, and the French and British removals ranked intermediate between those by the two superpowers.

Given such variability, how is one to sum up the experience of western German chemical firms with regard to dismantling? For one thing, for the factories involved, losing some plant represented an unpleasant experience, but it also had positive points: It provided some impetus for technological improvement. On the other hand, one must not ascribe too much weight to this point. Few factories lost more than a fraction of their capacity. Most used prewar and wartime equipment to reenter domestic and export markets.[8]

Despite dismantling, then, the overwhelming majority of capacity remained intact in western Germany, and as the Allied policies changed, all (including the latest) equipment fell from the dismantling lists. Even the worst-affected emerged with something to be happy about. BASF, for instance, reported in the early 1950s that

measured against the original dismantling program, . . . it has to be seen . . . as a success that the proportion of the factory that fell victim to dismantling was not much larger. It was particularly fortunate that it was possible to retain the facilities for large-scale synthesis on the basis of acetylene, which were especially endangered. This furnished promising preconditions for further development, especially in the plastics area.[9]

The picture was even less gloomy than BASF indicated: Already in mid-1948, despite dismantling, chemical plants in the French zone, led by BASF, were producing at 91 percent of their 1936 level. Factories in the combined American and British zones (the bizone) lagged behind, but still produced at more than half their 1936 rates despite their earlier bombing damages, reparations, transportation outages, and fuel and raw-materials shortages. Inadequacies in transportation, fuel, and raw materials – *not* insufficient production capacity – were the most important bottlenecks in the reconstruction of the industry.[10] Of course, virtually all of the chemical production capacity remaining after the war in what became West Germany was based on coal-chemical technology; it and the new capacity built after 1945 generally retained that coal basis well into the 1950s.

Physical removal of machinery represented a relatively minor form of technology transfer; much more substantial was the Allied effort to seize *geistige*

[8] Raymond G. Stokes, "Technology and the West German *Wirtschaftswunder*," *Technology and Culture*, 32(1991):1–22.

[9] BASF, *Bericht über die Neugründung 1952–1953*, pp. 28–9. A brief summary of the end of the dismantling effort is in "Demontagen in Westdeutschland," pp. 593–4.

[10] Werner Abelshauser, *Wirtschaftsgeschichte der Bundesrepublik Deutschland 1945–1980* (Frankfurt: Suhrkamp, 1983), p. 38, for zonal figures; Raymond G. Stokes, *Divide and Prosper: The Heirs of I.G. Farben under Allied Authority, 1945–1951* (Berkeley: University of California Press, 1988), pp. 95–6, for BASF performance; pp. 109–51, for factors impeding recovery of the chemical industry immediately after the war.

Reparationen, or intellectual reparations, from the defeated country. Allied teams gathered information on the wartime scientific and technological developments in Germany by investigating plants and interrogating personnel, all for the purpose of meeting the military and industrial needs of the former Allies, already splitting into East and West blocs. Information transfer also occurred when German scientists and technicians were recruited to emigrate to the various Allied countries, although that form of technology transfer apparently was relatively unimportant for the chemical industry.[11]

Chemical and Engineering News (CEN) reported in late 1946 on the scale and objectives of one important American group of "more than 200 civilian technicians [who] have been sent to Germany to seek out scientific and technical information of value to United States industry." Sponsored by private firms, those men became nominal employees of the U.S. Department of Commerce and wore the uniforms of army officers, with shoulder patches identifying them as "Scientific Consultants."[12]

Chemical technology constituted a primary target. Of the 200-plus technicians described by *CEN,* some seventy were in the chemicals unit. In addition, several other units, including those looking for fuels and lubricants, metals and minerals, pharmaceuticals and medical technology, rubber, and textiles, engaged in investigations of interest to the chemical industry. Of course, the group sponsored by the Department of Commerce was only one of many sent (not only by the Americans, but also by the other Allies) to investigate the state of German technology. Were its interests representative of the investigative effort as a whole? Numerous publications describing the state of German technology in specialized areas, which were among the most important products of that group and other investigatory groups, provide additional evidence of the extent of interest in chemical technology, especially in the developments at I.G. Farben during the war. Reports by the investigators concentrated heavily on synthetic fuels, synthetic rubber, and acetylene chemistry.[13]

---

[11] Allied organizations conducting the "exploitation" effort (as internal documents termed it) included the British Intelligence Objectives Subcommittee (BIOS), the Field Information Agency, Technical (FIAT), and a number of others.
    The best overview of those efforts is by Gimbel, *Science, Technology, and Reparations.* An earlier and still useful work on American use of German scientists is by Clarence Lasby, *Project Paperclip: German Scientists and the Cold War* (New York: Athenaeum, 1971), esp. pp. 18–26, 129–30, 163–4. On technical investigations, see, e.g., Leslie E. Simon, *German Research in World War II* (New York: Wiley, 1947); Arnold Krammer, "Technology Transfer as War Booty: The U.S. Technical Oil Mission to Europe, 1945," *Technology and Culture* 22(1981):68–103; and Peter Spitz, *Petrochemicals: The Rise of an Industry* (New York: Wiley, 1988), who deals specifically with chemical-industry investigations, pp. 2–17, 48–52, 113–14, 303–4, 346.

[12] "Civilian Scientists Sent to Germany," *Chemical and Engineering News* 24(1946):2637–8; quotation, p. 2637.

[13] Ibid., pp. 2637–8. I base my remarks on the subjects the Allies investigated on an evaluation of the "Alphabetical Subject Index of CIOS, BIOS, FIAT, and JIOA Final Reports," n.d., a copy of which is in the Public Record Office, London (Kew) (hereafter, PRO), FO1005/1602. Gimbel describes some of the missions to study processes (such as Reppe chemistry and synthetic rubber)

What those investigations brought to Allied firms is unclear. Peter Spitz, a participant in and student of the history of the petrochemical industry, contends that Vladimir Haensel's experience in Germany as a member of a technical team was helpful to his work in the United States on catalytic processes for hydrocarbon conversions, and Spitz himself used some of the reports as aids in designing chemical plants.[14] Still, Spitz and others often encountered the pitfalls inherent in relying exclusively on such written reports. Almost invariably they had to turn to German chemists and German firms for the know-how to utilize the new information.[15] That accounts in part for the sometimes contradictory actions and statements by the representatives of the U.S. firms: They often would write to the Office of Technical Services and the Department of Commerce to comment on the positive impact of the written technical reports, but later would deny the use or value of such information.[16]

The evidence regarding the effects on German companies is also mixed. On the one hand, given the estimates of the value of the patents that the Allies seized from German industry, those seizures, exacerbated by the technological investigatory effort, would appear to have doomed Germany's competitive prospects. In February 1947, for instance, a German patent attorney claimed that "American experts estimate the worth of confiscated German patents abroad to be several million dollars."[17] The Munich-based economic think tank Ifo-Institut pegged the losses of patents and trademarks by the German chemical industry alone at $10 billion, including 200,000 foreign patents, 24,000 internationally registered trademarks, and about 200,000 foreign-registered trade names.[18]

On the other hand, as mentioned earlier, printed technical information is useful only insofar as know-how is also available. Eventually, German patentholders sold or bartered their know-how to minimize the effects of patent seizures. What is more, the rapid advances being made in the chemical industry meant that in a relatively short time, newly developed and patentable products would account for significant and increasing portions of chemical firms' revenues. In 1963, for example, Gilbert Burck wrote in *Fortune* that "today probably more than half the [European chemical] industry's revenues come from products

developed and employed at I.G. Farben facilities: *Science, Technology, and Reparations*, e.g., pp. 9–15, 30–1, 88.

[14] Spitz, *Petrochemicals*, pp. 176, 329–31. Gimbel discusses this problem in *Science, Technology, and Reparations*, pp. 95–101, 224.

[15] For instance, BASF L.-K. Abteilung, "Aktennotiz: *Betr.* Besuch der Herren von der Mitsubishi Chemical Industries Limited," 27 July 1953, BASF, F9/79; Spitz, *Petrochemicals*, pp. 329–31. That experience is not surprising in light of recent research; see Keith Pavitt, "Technology Transfer among the Industrially Advanced Countries: An Overview," in N. Rosenberg and C. Frischtak, eds., *International Technology Transfer: Concepts, Measures, and Comparisons* (New York: Praeger, 1985), pp. 3–23.

[16] Gimbel, *Science, Technology, and Reparations*, pp. 96–101, 224, gives examples of these apparently contradictory comments.

[17] Werner Colrausz, "Vorschläge für das Patentgesetz," *Angewandte Chemie* 19B(1947):50.

[18] Ifo-Institut, Bearb., *Chemie einschl. Kunststoffe* (Munich: Ifo-Institut, 1952), N5.

that did not exist twenty-five years ago." For Bayer A.G., in particular, Burck went on, "nearly 60 percent of . . . world sales . . . now come from products that did not exist fifteen years ago."[19] The same was true for other major West German chemical producers.

All in all, the dismantling and information-gathering efforts illuminate some crucial aspects of occupation policy in the immediate postwar period. For one thing, their consequences differed significantly by zone; such zonal variation in the full range of policies and practices was typical of the early occupation period.[20] Only later did the U.S. aim of allowing Germany a modicum of economic health gain the upper hand in western German occupation policy. More important, "policy," in the American zone in particular (though in the other zones as well), remained an elusive concept; in fact, occupation practices mirrored the vagueness and ambiguity in Allied policies. If the primary policy objective – to curb future German war potential – seemed clear enough, the means to accomplish it was not. Was elimination of the defeated country's war-related facilities the best way to prevent future German aggression? Was undermining German industry's competitiveness through transfer of equipment and information to Allied firms the best means to that end? By answering, "all of the above," the Americans and their Allies meant to signal their determination to root out any potential for German aggression. But it was far from clear how undermining competitiveness would accomplish the objective of curbing the German war potential. Unless the policy were carried out ruthlessly and to its logical conclusion, which was never likely to be the case, German disaffection was a likely outcome. What is more, an intact industrial capacity had the potential to enable that disaffection to become dangerous. In any case, one effect of concentrating so heavily on the transfer of information from German industry to Allied industry was to undermine the credibility of the Allies, especially the Americans, regarding their claim of being interested primarily and unselfishly in future peace.

There were even more basic problems in occupation policy. What, for instance, constituted war-related industry, as opposed to peacetime industry? Explosives manufacturing seemed a clear candidate for removal, as being purely war-related. Even in that extreme case, though, ambiguities were rife: Explosives were needed for clearing away the debris of war, for mining, and for building roads – all peacetime pursuits. Of course, explosives were available from foreign suppliers, but that would require foreign exchange, and the Americans were the only ones who could supply that. They were generally unwilling to do so when German sources were available. In other words, curbing war potential often conflicted with other fundamental objectives, such as keeping the occupation as short and as inexpensive as possible. The same sort of conflicts emerged in the exploitation efforts, because curbing war potential and constraining future German industrial competition – objectives them-

[19] Gilbert Burck, "Chemicals: The Reluctant Competitors," *Fortune* 68(1963):148, 152.
[20] For a similar point, see John Gimbel, *The Origins of the Marshall Plan* (Stanford University Press, 1976), pp. 143–6.

selves not fully compatible with one another – contradicted the desire to limit the costs and length of the occupation.

Dismantling and exploitation soon fell victim to other considerations, however. The more perceptive occupation officials quickly recognized that their main problem was not how to contain the German economy, but rather how to keep it from collapsing, and within a fairly short time that reality became clear to key policymakers.[21] The spiraling costs of occupation soon took their toll. British officials, in particular, began to doubt that they could afford the spoils of victory. Added to that was growing tension between the East and West blocs, which contributed gradually to a belief that western Germany might serve as an indispensable ally and as an engine for western European economic growth. One important result of those developments was the official end of technical investigations in the combined British and American zones in June 1947.[22] Dismantling stopped, and production prohibitions were slowly lifted between April 1949 and April 1951.[23] That period from the end of the technical-investigation effort to the lifting of production prohibitions was critical: At the same time that political choices were being made (choices that themselves placed constraints on technological development), there emerged several viable technological alternatives for the future of the chemical industry.

Technological alternatives and evolving political constraints, 1948–51

With the enactment of currency reform in the three western zones of occupation in June 1948, Germany was divided into two, rather than four, successor states. All that remained was to formally establish the successor states that would replace the Reich. The total control by the Soviets in the "eastern zone" and the equally evident hegemony of the Americans in the western zones would fundamentally shape the political economies of the new Germanies. Economic liberalization (removal of price controls and cessation of rationing for many commodities), which came quickly on the heels of the currency reform, was another step along that path in the West. By September 1949, the Federal Republic of Germany (West Germany) had come into existence, a parliamentary democracy with a capitalist economic system that would participate in the U.S.-dominated world economic and political order. In October, the German

[21] An indication of the policy change was U.S. Secretary of State James F. Byrnes's Stuttgart speech in September 1946; see Beate Ruhm von Oppen, *Documents on Germany under Occupation, 1945–1955* (Oxford University Press, 1955), pp. 152–60. A concrete expression of the change was the founding of the combined British and American zone of occupation, or the bizone, on 1 January 1947. For the text of the agreement of 2 December 1946 creating the bizone, see von Oppen, pp. 195–9.

[22] OMGUS, Public Relations Office, "Press Release," 27 March 1947 (Abschrift), BASF, B4/ 1543. General Lucius Clay opposed aspects of the program from at least October 1946; he believed it represented concealed reparations and benefited the United States more than other countries. See Clay (personal) for Daniel Noce, 22 January 1947, in Jean Edward Smith, ed., *The Papers of General Lucius Clay* (Bloomington: Indiana University Press, 1974), vol. I, pp. 305–6. A file on discontinuing the Allied investigations is in PRO, FO371/65032.

[23] Stokes, *Divide and Prosper*, pp. 170–3; "Demontagen in Westdeutschland," pp. 593–4.

Democratic Republic (East Germany) was founded, a "peasants' and workers' state" on the Soviet model that featured thinly veiled party dictatorship and a centrally planned, full-employment economy.

The United States had invested considerable effort in the emergence of the Federal Republic and had helped shape its political economy, and U.S. officials both wanted and needed to see the newly formed West German state succeed. The perceived Soviet threat was a primary force behind that desire, together with the perception that a thriving German economy would provide the impetus for reconstruction and recovery throughout Europe. But the outbreak of the Korean War in June 1950 gave a more concrete reason for a strong West Germany: Many U.S. troops had to be withdrawn, and only the Germans could take up the slack in defending Europe against the Russians. It would take several years, until 1954–5, to work out the details of German rearmament, but it was already in the cards in the early 1950s.[24]

From its inception, therefore, and increasingly over time, West Germany was needed for its economic leadership in Europe, and later for the defense of Europe. Thus, although it can hardly be argued that the Federal Republic in its early years had independence (or even full sovereignty, because officially West Germany was under the authority of the Allied High Commission until 1955, and the Allies retained some rights on German soil until 12 September 1990), the Cold War served to increase the nascent regime's leverage and freedom of movement. Of course, participation in the postwar economic order of the Western bloc also constrained West German choices: Autarky, in the sense of freedom from reliance on imports and exports, was, for instance, no longer a viable option, because West German firms had to become "competitive" in world markets. But such constraints did not determine specific choices; in that, the West Germans had considerable freedom of movement.

For the chemical industry, precisely what it would take to become competitive was far from clear. There is evidence that German industrialists were well aware of the promise of petrochemical technology even before World War II, and certainly immediately afterward. Peter Spitz, for instance, reported that Carl Krauch of I.G. Farben confided to his son in the 1930s that it was the elder Krauch's dream "to marry German high-pressure technology and catalytic know-how with the hydrocarbon resources of a large oil company, thus creating the conditions for producing almost unlimited amounts of light hydrocarbon fuels and chemical feedstocks." In December 1946, a group of BASF researchers listened closely as one of their number reported on "Recent American Work on Petro-chemistry." They made preparations to work intensively on the same subject. Other major German chemical firms began significant R&D efforts in the same direction.[25]

---

[24] Michael Geyer, *Deutsch Rüstungspolitik 1860–1980* (Frankfurt: Suhrkamp, 1984), pp. 185–204; Volker Berghahn, *The Americanisation of West German Industry* (Cambridge University Press, 1986), pp. 260–82.

[25] Spitz, *Petrochemicals,* p. 514; Dr. Reitz, "Neuere amerikanische Arbeiten über Erdölchemie," 11 December 1946, BASF, F9/66; an overview of some of the accomplishments of German firms

But it would be a mistake to view the German effort solely from the perspective of what was to come, because it was far from evident in the late 1940s and early 1950s that petrochemicals would eventually (by the 1980s) account for virtually all organic chemical production. Through the mid-1950s, at least, coal chemistry dominated the worldwide chemical industry, even in the United States, where the petrochemical industry was most advanced.[26] Petrochemicals had made inroads in certain key areas, especially in plastics and "commodity chemicals," but large segments of organic chemical production were still using coal-based processes.

Alternatives to petrochemicals also existed, at least through the 1960s. Acetylene-based chemistry, as developed by BASF's Walter Reppe, relied primarily on carbide produced from coal.[27] Acetylene from carbide offered a route to production of vinyl chloride, acrylics, vinyl acetate, and a number of other products, and chemistry based on acetylene began its relative decline only in the 1960s, when U.S. chemical firms developed methods for producing acetylene from natural gas and petroleum; a number of alternative routes to manufacturing some of its products were also devised. Another older German chemical process, Fischer-Tropsch synthesis, could use either coal or natural gas as primary feedstock to convert carbon monoxide and hydrogen to hydrocarbons. Depending on the catalyst used, the hydrocarbon mixture would be some mixture of gasoline, diesel fuel, alcohols, ketones, and so on. The process, as modified during the late 1940s and 1950s, seemed a promising alternative to petrochemicals, certainly in West Germany and even in the United States. As Melvin J. Astle, author of a textbook on petrochemicals, wrote in 1956, "at the present time the process is thought by some to be competitive with petroleum for the production of fuels and, in addition, to be an excellent source of chemicals."[28]

Before proceeding further with discussions of technological alternatives and the evolving political constraints between 1948 and 1951, a brief digression and a clarification are in order. In purely chemical terms, it is generally possible to come up with the desired product whether one uses coal, alcohol, natural gas, or petroleum as the starting material. What might vary would be the series of reactions leading to that product, the scale and arrangement of the reaction equipment employed, and the cost of using a particular starting material. To the extent that any two or more of these feedstocks can produce the same thing in their own ways, but at comparable costs, they represent technological alternatives, or, in the words of the economist W. Brian Arthur, "competing technologies."[29] My contention throughout this book is that during the 1950s,

---

and the potential of petroleum-based chemistry is in "Die Welt-Erdölwirtschaft," *Chemische Industrie* 1(1949):23.

[26] G. H. Lehmann, "Entwicklung der Erdölchemie als Bilanz Zweier Weltkriege," *Chemische Industrie* 4(1952):195.

[27] For more on Reppe chemistry, see Chapter 1.

[28] Melvin J. Astle, *The Chemistry of Petrochemicals* (New York, Reinhold, 1956), p. 5.

[29] W. Brian Arthur, "Increasing returns, competing technologies, and lock-in by historical events," *Economics Journal* 99(1989):116–31.

various coal-based technologies and petrochemical technology represented competing technologies.

Having said that, it is crucial to keep in mind that the situation appeared somewhat different to German engineers, scientists, and industrialists in the late 1940s and early 1950s. Most of them foresaw a future in which there would be some sort of equilibrium, some sort of peaceful co-existence among the various technologies.[30] Petroleum, they thought, would supplant coal as the primary feedstock in a number of areas, but the newer starting material would be much more important in producing a whole range of new products (demand for which was growing apace) than in supplanting old ones. Coal chemistry, and especially Reppe acetylene chemistry, would continue, however, to hold a prominent and vital place in organic chemical production, because it could produce a range of products that were thought to be inaccessible for petroleum-based technology.[31] In addition, prominent journal articles echoed the widespread belief that, especially in the German area, coal would continue to be "the foundation of chemistry" for some time to come, simply because it was readily available and involved little foreign exchange. One commentator noted that although theoretically it had become possible to make many organic chemicals from coal, alcohol, or petroleum, "for every country the choice must be made basically according to practical criteria, e.g. available sources of raw materials and various economic and technical – including financial – aspects of the situation."[32] Three things, then, would limit the competition between coal and petroleum technologies: massive demand for new products; frequent absence of direct competition between the two in manufacturing certain products; and Germany's substantial coal supplies and its limited supplies of both oil and foreign exchange.

There was one exception, in which two different technologies did meet head-on in the period from 1948 to 1951: a brief skirmish between interests supporting Fischer-Tropsch synthesis and those favoring petrochemical production. The story of the confrontation is significant, because the outcome was a harbinger of the later wholesale confrontation between coal chemistry and petrochemistry, which eventually resulted in much of the coal-chemical industry being phased out. It also forced supporters of the Fischer-Tropsch process to change tactics in their attempt to stave off a complete victory for petrochemicals, a story that will be the subject of a later chapter.

[30] This is the contention of a pair of articles that appeared together in a special section of a prominent West German trade periodical in 1950. See the articles in the section on "Kohle-, Acetylen- und Erdölchemie," *Chemische Industrie* 2(1950):207–14. Heinz Nedelmann, the head of the Coal-Chemical Trade Association, was even more explicit in 1955: He contended "daß eine scharfe Abgrenzung zwischen Kohlechemie und Petrochemie nicht existiert, daß also Kohle und Erdöl auf dem Gebiet der Chemie zusammengehören." See "Technik und Wirtschaft der Kohlechemie," *Erdöl und Chemie* 8(June 1955):387.

[31] Interview of Dr. Hubert, Schering A.G., Bergkamen, 3 April 1989.

[32] First quotation, Dr. Wilhelm von Haken, "Inventur der wichtigsten Chemierohstoffe," *Chemische Industrie* 7(1955):777; second quotation, "Die wirtschaftliche Entwicklung der Erdölchemie," *Chemische Industrie* 2(1950):213.

The Fischer-Tropsch process

The history of Fischer-Tropsch synthesis, first developed to industrial scale in Germany in the 1930s, provides an excellent example of the political malleability of technology. Intended initially to produce primarily synthetic liquid fuels, the process clearly fit in with the goal of German self-sufficiency that was pursued during the National Socialist period. As a result of state support, Fischer-Tropsch production grew impressively. Its eventual significance, however, lagged considerably behind that of Bergius coal hydrogenation, as developed by I.G. Farben.[33] In part, the reasons were technical: Gasoline produced via the Fischer-Tropsch process was inferior to that produced via the Bergius-I.G. process, a consideration of prime importance in the National Socialist war economy.[34] However, there were also political reasons: I.G. Farben's backing of the Bergius process played a role in its ascendance during the Nazi period.[35]

Six plants in what would later become West Germany used the Fischer-Tropsch production process: installations at Bergkamen (Chemische Werke Essener Steinkohle), Moers (Chemische Werke Rheinpreussen), Oberhausen-Holten (Ruhrchemie A.G.), Dortmund (Dortmunder Paraffinwerke), Wanne-Eickel (Krupp Treibstoffwerke), and Castrop-Rauxel (Gewerkschaft Victor). Developed by researchers at the Kaiser Wilhelm Institute for Coal Research in Mülheim in the late 1920s, the Fischer-Tropsch process involved chemical combination of carbon monoxide and hydrogen obtained from coke by means of the water–gas reaction, all at relatively low pressures and temperatures and in the presence of a catalyst (generally based on cobalt and iron).[36]

Fischer-Tropsch plants shared the fate of those producing synthetic fuel by other means. In mid-1944, General Carl A. Spaatz of the U.S. Army Air Force

---

[33] Hydrogenation was a result of the pioneering research of Friedrich Bergius in the years before World War I and the research, production experience, and financial might of the I.G. Farbenindustrie A.G. It involved the combination of coal (or other carbonaceous materials) with free hydrogen under high temperatures and pressures, producing a high-quality light hydrocarbon readily usable as a motor fuel. Four hydrogenation plants were located in what became West Germany, although the more significant ones were located in central and eastern Germany. For a discussion of the development and technology of hydrogenation, see Anthony N. Stranges, "Friedrich Bergius and the Rise of the German Synthetic Fuel Industry," *Isis* 75(1984):643–67. The synthetic-oil industry as a whole is discussed at length by Wolfgang Birkenfeld, *Der synthetische Treibstoff 1933–1945* (Göttingen: Musterschmidt, 1964); for a more general discussion of the oil industry as a whole in Nazi Germany, see Arnold Krammer, "Fueling the Third Reich," *Technology and Culture* 19(July 1978):394–422. For a concise description of the differences between hydrogenation and Fischer-Tropsch technology and the relative positions in the Nazi regime of producers favoring each process, see Raymond G. Stokes, "The Oil Industry in Nazi Germany, 1933–1945," *Business History Review* 59(Summer 1985):254–77.

[34] Birkenfeld, *Der synthetische Treibstoff*, passim; Stokes, "Oil Industry," pp. 265ff.

[35] Stokes, "Oil Industry," pp. 254–77.

[36] Astle, *The Chemistry of Petrochemicals*, pp. 5–9. The water–gas reaction involves heating coke using a blast of air. After incandescence is reached, steam is introduced, producing carbon monoxide and hydrogen. The optimum gas mixture features a carbon monoxide : hydrogen ratio of 1 : 2; therefore, some of the carbon monoxide is converted to carbon dioxide, which is removed from the gas stream by absorption in water.

directed that "the primary strategic aim of U.S. Strategic Air Forces is now to deny oil to enemy air forces."[37] Allied bombing raids damaged the plants again and again, resulting in severely curtailed production in the synthetic-oil industry by late 1944 and early 1945. Cumulatively, the bombing contributed significantly to the downfall of the German economy. Fischer-Tropsch facilities at Moers, Oberhausen-Holten, and Dortmund, for instance, emerged from the war so severely damaged that they could never resume production. As for the remaining synthetic-fuel plants (both Fischer-Tropsch and hydrogenation), Allied investigators estimated that it would be at least a year (until June 1946) before any could return to production, owing to bombing damage and heavy usage, with insufficient maintenance, during the war.[38]

The synthetic-fuel industry had been closely linked to the production of other goods directly related to Germany's ability to wage war. That meant, according to the provisions of the Allied Control Council's plan for reparations and restrictions on the postwar German economy, issued on 28 March 1946, that synthetic-fuel production would never again be permitted in Germany. To that end, the Allies planned to dismantle all synthetic-fuel plants and give them away as reparations to Germany's former enemies.[39] Hydrogenation and Fischer-Tropsch plants were also important targets of the Allied investigation teams, which reported their findings – including considerable quantities of commercially important technical information – to their companies at home.[40]

At the same time the Allies were punishing the industry, all of them made provision in the short term to use the synthetic-fuel capacity of Germany to meet the needs of the occupation forces,[41] and they soon found that their problems in conducting the occupation, along with the increasing tensions between East and West, necessitated implementation of that provision, even though it involved a war-related industry. By 1947, two Fischer-Tropsch plants were again in production to aid in providing raw materials for soaps and detergents.

[37] U.S. Strategic Bombing Survey (USSBS), Final Report 109, *Oil Division Final Report,* 2nd ed. (January 1947), p. 1.

[38] See Stokes, "Oil Industry," pp. 272–6, for a summary of bombing losses; on Allied estimates, see D. M. S. Langworthy to members of the Army-Navy Petroleum Board, 24 May 1945, in National Archives (Washington, DC), Record Group 165, Records of the War Department General and Special Staffs, CAD 463(6-1-43), sec. 2.

[39] The text of the "Plan for Reparations and Level of Postwar German Economy" is printed in full in B. U. Ratchford and W. D. Ross, *Berlin Reparations Assignment* (Chapel Hill: University of North Carolina Press, 1947), pp. 225–30. It was specifically meant to carry out the provisions of the Potsdam protocols of 1 August 1945. For the text of the protocols, see 1477–98 of U.S. Department of State, *Foreign Relations of the United States* (hereafter, *FRUS*), *The Conference of Berlin (Potsdam Conference), 1945,* vol. II (Washington, DC: U.S. Government Printing Office, 1960), esp. pp. 1483–7.

[40] See Gimbel, *Science, Technology, and Reparations,* esp. pp. 85, 101, 224, n. 26. For an overview of the organization and activities of the technical oil mission, see Krammer, "Technology Transfer as War Booty," pp. 68–103.

[41] The amendments made to the directive to the commander in chief of the U.S. occupation forces in Germany were JCS 1067/8 and 1067/9, 10 and 11 May 1945, respectively, in NA, Washington, Record Group 218 (U.S. Joint Chiefs of Staff), CCS 383.21 Germany (2-22-44), sec. 8.

The Bizonal Refinery Plan, negotiated in 1947 and 1948 and implemented in 1949, called for resumption of production in some of the hydrogenation plants in West Germany.[42]

At the same time, official policy lagged significantly behind practice: Reparations and dismantling orders remained in force through late 1949, and many production prohibitions remained on the books until 1951. Obviously, key German interest groups, including the industrialists who owned the plants, the workers in those plants, and the politicians seeking increased responsibility and power over German affairs, had a stake in promoting liberalization of the Allied occupation policies, and they were active in helping to change those policies. The primary responsibility for that lobbying effort lay with the Coal Chemical Trade Association (Fachverband Kohlechemie, FVK). Beginning in early 1947, the business manager of the FVK was Heinz Nedelmann.

Nedelmann's career paralleled to a remarkable degree the history of energy in Germany from the turn of the century to the mid-1960s. Born in Mülheim in the heart of the Ruhr coal region in 1901, Nedelmann grew up immersed in the milieu of the Ruhr coal industry in its heyday, lived through its crises in World War I, and experienced firsthand the vicissitudes of the industry during the 1920s.[43] He received his doctorate in chemical engineering shortly after the beginning of the Great Depression and soon began working in one of the most technologically sophisticated areas of the coal industry: production of synthetic fuels. By the early 1940s he was plant manager (*Werksleiter*) of the Union-Kraftstoff hydrogenation plant at Wesseling, near Cologne. As was typical of men in such positions of responsibility, Nedelmann became a member of the National Socialist party. He later claimed that his membership had been "nominal." In June 1945, American and British occupation authorities judged his association to have been less innocent: Nedelmann spent the period from mid-1945 to 1947 doing farmwork in the countryside, barred because of his membership in the Nazi party from working in the industry for which he had been trained.[44]

As the fortunes of German industry improved with changes in Allied policies in 1946–7, Nedelmann was able to return to work in the energy field as the first business manager of the FVK.[45] He remained in that position until 1958, when he joined Deutsche BP A.G. in Hamburg, the German subsidiary of British Petroleum. His switch from the coal industry to the oil industry closely paralleled the major structural change in the West German energy economy from coal to petroleum as the preferred energy source.[46]

[42] Heinz Nedelmann, "Technik und Wirtschaft der Kohlechemie," *Erdöl und Kohle* 8(1955):386; Joint Chairmen, Bipartite Control Office, "Approval of the Oil Refining Plan for Bizonia," 9 April 1948, NA, Suitland, MD, Record Group 260 (OMGUS HQ), Box 1/176-3.

[43] For more on the Ruhr coal industry, see John Gillingham, *Industry and Politics in the Third Reich: Ruhr Coal, Hitler and Europe* (New York: Columbia University Press, 1985); Werner Abelshauser, *Der Ruhrkohlenbergbau seit 1945: Wiederaufbau, Krise, Anpassung* (München: Beck, 1984).

[44] Interview with Dr.-Ing. Heinz Nedelmann, 9 July 1984, Essen, West Germany.   [45] Ibid.

[46] On the transition from coal to oil, see Manfred Horn, *Die Energiepolitik der Bundesregierung von 1958 bis 1972)* (Berlin: Duncker & Humblot, 1977), passim.

As FVK business manager, Nedelmann represented a number of constituen-
cies, including firms in five distinct production areas: coal-mine cokeries, coal-
tar distilleries, benzol installations, hydrogenation plants, and Fischer-Tropsch
facilities. The interests of the firms in those five areas varied considerably. Cokeries, coal-tar distilleries, and benzol facilities, for instance, had not suffered
much damage during the war and were not targets of Allied restrictions. There
also were differences in interests between the generally larger hydrogenation
plants, with their links to international oil companies, and the smaller Fischer-
Tropsch works, generally owned by domestic coal interests. Much of the FVK's
initial work revolved around obtaining permission to resume production in the
Fischer-Tropsch plants in the British zone of occupation. In the course of that
campaign, conflicting interests within the West German coal-chemical industry
became evident: Because of the new regime in Germany, Fischer-Tropsch plants
would have to reorient production away from fuel and toward production of
chemical feedstocks, bringing those plants into direct conflict with petroleum
interests. A closer examination of the tactics and results of that campaign will
therefore be instructive.

Two Fischer-Tropsch facilities in the Ruhr district, the Krupp facility at
Wanne-Eickel and Gewerkschaft Victor at Castrop-Rauxel, had received permission from the British military government to resume production in 1946. Manufacture of motor fuels was discouraged. Instead, the occupation authorities
instructed factory directors to produce other hydrocarbon fractions, insofar as
was possible, and in particular to concentrate on intermediate materials to alleviate shortages of soaps and detergents in the West zones. Other Fischer-
Tropsch plants had not yet been allowed to resume production. As noted earlier,
the threat of being dismantled and carted away remained in force for all of the
plants throughout the occupation period.

In the spring of 1948, Heinz Nedelmann developed arguments for retention of
the Fischer-Tropsch plants that would be used throughout later negotiations with
the Allies. The most serious Allied objection to those facilities was that they
represented German war potential, especially because they made possible the
production of gasoline from domestic coal. Nedelmann countered that the
Fischer-Tropsch process was not well suited for production of gasoline and that
"even during the war, when everyone tried to produce as much synthetic fuel as
possible, the Fischer-Tropsch plants were not in the position to produce much
more than 50 percent of their total production in the form of gasoline-like products." Instead, he claimed, the process was suited for the production of "*basic
chemical products* for a *pure peacetime economy*," including fatty acids, paraffin, soap, detergent intermediates, softeners and solvents for the plastics and
paint industries, and so on.[47] In effect, then, Nedelmann argued that the very
deficiencies in performance of the Fischer-Tropsch plants during the Third Reich
were grounds for allowing them to continue production in the postwar period.

---

[47] Memorandum (no author noted, but clearly Nedelmann), "Fischer-Tropsch-Industrie," 7 April
1948, Bayerwerksarchiv, Leverkusen (hereafter, BWA), 186/K1.15.

Table 2.1. *Products of the Fischer-Tropsch plant of Krupp Kohlechemie, Essen, 1939–49.*

Product	Boiling point (°C)	Percentage by year								
		1939	1940	1941	1942	1943	1944	1947	1948	1949
Power gas	to 40	9.3	5.3	8.2	10.5	11.9	9.0	11.0	12.7	14.6
Gasoline	40–100	82.4	50.7	44.9	46.0	42.7	43.8	43.2	40.3	32.4
Aliphatics (0,I,II)	100–230								18.8	26.7
Diesel	180–230	8.3	32.1	19.3	16.4	16.1	16.0			
Kogasin I & II	180–320		5.4	14.9	15.6	17.6	17.7	34.2	17.4	14.8
Crude paraffin	320–450		2.9	8.8	7.7	8.1	9.1	8.6	7.8	8.7
Other paraffin fractions	>450		3.7	3.9	4.1	3.6	4.4	3.0	3.0	2.8

Source: Deutsche Revisions- und Treuhand A.G., "Bericht D 1415 A . . . über die bei der Krupp Kohlechemie Gmb, Essen durchgeführte Subventionsprüfung," n.d. (1951), Anhang, Bl. 3, Bundesarchiv, Koblenz, B102/1479, Heft 1.

Before considering other aspects of Nedelmann's argument, it will be useful to examine briefly the accuracy of his claims about the optimum production mix in Fischer-Tropsch plants. Table 2.1 contains information on the changing mix of production at Krupp's Wanne-Eickel plant from 1939 to 1949. Initially, in 1939, its output of gasoline accounted for more than 80 percent of the plant's production, but that figure quickly dropped to about 50 percent in 1940 and hovered around 43–46 percent for the remainder of the war. These figures tend to support Nedelmann's claim. On the other hand, during the war, diesel fuel generally accounted for about 15–20 percent of its total output. In other words, the plant's total production of motor fuels was 60 percent or more of its output throughout the war, and Nedelmann's claims were therefore somewhat misleading. After the war, however, the mix of outputs at the Krupp plant did change significantly, although that was due less to any decline in production of gasoline than to elimination of diesel-oil output, at least until 1949. Instead of diesel fuel, plants began producing more of other fractions that could be used as starting materials for chemical production.

Nedelmann went on, however, to replicate some of the arguments he had developed earlier for retention of hydrogenation facilities.[48] He held, for instance, that resumption of production in the Fischer-Tropsch plants would alleviate the foreign-exchange crisis: The process would produce goods made from German coal that would yield up to twice the revenue that could be expected from direct export of the same amounts of coal or coke. He also argued that the owners of the plants had already spent RM 27 million on repairs to their facilities and that they should not be punished for having done so. Finally, he claimed that

[48] Heinz Nedelmann, memorandum, "Betr.: Hydrierwerke," 27 January 1948, BWA, 186/K1.13.

dismantling would yield only "about 30 percent of the present value of the plants" to the countries receiving them.[49]

The agreements reached between the hydrogenation plants and certain Allied oil companies later in 1948,[50] however, caused Nedelmann and the FVK to change tactics. Most important, they decided to move away from the strategy of broad agitation to save all synthetic plants toward a more focused strategy. They turned their attention to an effort to obtain permission for the Essener Steinkohle plant at Bergkamen to resume production. The largest of the Fischer-Tropsch facilities in the West zones of occupation, Essener Steinkohle was owned by major Ruhr coal interests and had been sufficiently repaired that it could function if it could gain a waiver from the Allied policy.

Another key component of Nedelmann's new tack was to argue that oil interests in the Allied countries were responsible for the delays in receiving the necessary permits to operate. He made the accusation first in a letter to Dr. Karl Schnurre, a former German diplomat, in which he asked for help in establishing contacts with the British Foreign Office. He pointed out that Bergkamen was ready to resume production, but that the Bipartite Control Group (British and American military-government officials) had refused permission because official policy forbade production. Nedelmann, however, had "the impression . . . that it was primarily reasons of competition [rather than to curtail German war potential] that [brought] the English to this opinion." Nedelmann went on to specify the source of the British attitude. He compared the treatment accorded the hydrogenation facilities with that received by the Fischer-Tropsch plants and contended that the hydrogenation works had received permission to operate simply "because it is in the interests of the English and American petroleum industry (Standard Oil, [Socony]-Vacuum, Shell)." He went on to ask Schnurre to help him make contacts in influential circles in Britain so as to bring pressure to bear on the military government in Germany.[51]

Following a conversation with President W. A. Menne of the western German Chemical Industry Trade Association on 6 December 1948, Nedelmann could be even more specific in his allegations. Menne reported an encounter a few days earlier with Mr. Zwegintzov, who had been the head of the chemical-industry section of the Control Council for Germany (British Element) immediately after the war, and who in late 1946 had returned to work for Shell in London. Zwegintzov informed Menne of Shell's plans for the German market. Besides signing contracts with the hydrogenation plant at Wesseling, which would produce gasoline and diesel oil, for the most part, Shell hoped to expand its refinery in Hamburg-Harburg to begin producing petrochemicals, which would be processed further in chemical plants. The products would include solvents, raw and intermediate materials for the production of soaps and detergents, basic materials for the production of plastics, and pesticides. Shell would not concern itself

---

[49] Ibid.   [50] Ibid.

[51] Nedelmann to Dr. Karl Schnurre, 11 October 1948, BWA, 186/K1.14.

with the final processing of these materials, "but rather wants to allow German firms to do further processing of the products."[52]

Menne asked Zwegintzov a few questions about the Fischer-Tropsch plants and their prospects. Zwegintzov responded simply that they were "entirely un-economic" and that it was unlikely that British policy toward them would change. In light of Shell's plans to move into the petrochemical industry in Germany (which would involve manufacturing products in direct competition with those of the Fischer-Tropsch plants), Zwegintzov's response had suggested only one conclusion to Menne: "It thus seems to be clear that the primary opposition to the allowance of permission for reconstruction and for production in the still inactive Fischer-Tropsch plants comes from the side of Shell."[53] Although Menne directed Nedelmann not to circulate any written account of his conversation with Zwegintzov, he indicated that he would have nothing against oral transmission of it to appropriate interested parties.[54] In fact, Nedelmann wrote a memorandum on the subject on 7 December 1948 and circulated it (albeit with the heading "strictly confidential") to Dr. Krueger, from Harpener Bergbau A.G., Dr. Tramm, from Ruhrchemie A.G., and Herr Stork, from the Chemical Industry Trade Association. Through "an indiscretion," Nedelmann's memorandum eventually landed in the hands of a reporter for *Die Welt*, a major national newspaper, and an article on the subject appeared on 16 April 1949. None of those who possessed the 7 December memorandum admitted to the leak, but Nedelmann himself may well have been responsible.[55]

---

[52] Nedelmann, Aktennotiz, "Betr.: Fischer-Tropsch-Werke," 7 December 1948, BWA, 186/K1.15. The distribution list for the memorandum included Dr. Krueger, from Harpener Bergbau, Dr. Tramm, from Ruhrchemie, and Herr Stork, from the Wirtschaftsverband der chemischen Industrie, even though an appended note from Nedelmann indicated that Menne requested that it not be circulated; however, Menne had nothing against orally transmitting the information to interested parties "in vorsichtiger Form."

[53] Ibid.   [54] Ibid.

[55] The memo in question was Nedelmann, Aktennotiz, "Betr.: Fischer-Tropsch-Werke," 7 December 1948, BWA, 186/K1.15; for discussions on containing the damage of the "indiscretion," see Nedelmann, "Aktennotiz über die Besprechung mit Herrn Präsident Menne am 16.5.1949," 17 May 1949, in BWA, 186/K1.18; the article in question was "Erdöl – der künftige chemische Rohstoff," *Die Welt* (16 April 1949), seen in BWA, 186/K1.18. *Die Welt* was not the only newspaper to publish articles in that vein. The rumor was dealt with implicitly in the article "Nahostöl für Westdeutschland," *Industriekurier* (4 March 1949), in BWA, 186/K1.13, which draws attention to the type of crude being imported from the Middle East, to the credence thus lent to rumors that Shell planned production of petrochemicals in Harburg, and to the fact that such production would compete directly with the products of Fischer-Tropsch plants. The obvious conclusion is left to the reader's imagination. Another such piece is " 'Unwirtschaftliche' Fischer-Tropsch-Synthese?" in *Westecho* no. 187(19/20 June 1949), seen in BASF Unternehmensarchiv, Ludwigshafen, B4/1825.

I base my speculation about Nedelmann's possible role on the frequency (in correspondence) with which he made known his "feeling" that Shell was behind the problems faced by the Fischer-Tropsch plants, and also his additional "indiscretion" in his correspondence with Hermann Abs (notes 58–60).

The piece published by *Die Welt,* which featured entire paragraphs lifted without alteration from Nedelmann's document, was a curious composition. The text consisted of two parallel stories, one about the Allies' policy on synthetic-fuel facilities and the dismantling of Fischer-Tropsch plants, the other about Shell's new refining center in Hamburg-Harburg. Little attempt was made to tie the two together in the article itself, and in fact the author switched from one subject to the other without transition more than once. Still, the series of headlines made its message clear: "Consequences of the Fischer-Tropsch Prohibition. Petroleum – the future chemical raw material. Refinery center Harburg – Six Fischer-Tropsch facilities to be dismantled."[56]

Shell responded politely but firmly to the article in *Die Welt* on 4 May through its German subsidiary. Mr. Hofland of the Deutsche Shell A.G. managing board wrote Menne that the conversation had been misconstrued: "Unfortunately these two aspects of the conversation – Shell's interests in the area of petrochemicals and the Fischer-Tropsch process – have been connected in the press so that the stories read as if Shell had an interest in suppressing the Fischer-Tropsch process, and we therefore place value on making it clear that this is not the case." Hofland asked, in addition, for Menne's assistance in correcting the misinformation in the press.[57]

Shell tried to exert additional pressure on Nedelmann through the offices of one of the most influential men in western Germany, Hermann J. Abs. Abs, like Nedelmann, had been born in 1901, and he had risen quickly through the ranks of the Deutsche Bank A.G. during the Nazi period, becoming a member of the bank's managing board in 1938. By virtue of that office, he had also been a member of the supervisory boards of several major companies. Removed from his positions and placed by the Allies in the automatic-arrest category immediately after the war, Abs soon became an adviser to the British military government and began returning to his former business posts by the spring of 1946. One of those was on the supervisory board of Deutsche Shell A.G.

Abs was on the mailing list of the FVK, and as a powerful individual in the German political economy, he was someone to whom Nedelmann could turn for advice. On 12 May 1949, Nedelmann wrote Abs in conjunction with the projected publication of a newsletter that would bring to the attention of "influential personalities" in the Allied countries the plight of the Fischer-Tropsch plants. Asking for suggestions regarding potential foreign recipients of the newsletter (the draft of which was dated 9 May), Nedelmann also took the opportunity to inform Abs privately of the probable source of the misery for Germany's "coal-enrichment" (*Kohleveredlung*) processes, hydrogenation, and Fischer-Tropsch synthesis. He noted that "we have the distinct feeling that the prohibition of Fischer-Tropsch synthesis can be traced back to the influence of foreign oil concerns, especially

---

[56] "Erdöl – der künftige chemische Rohstoff," *Die Welt* (16 April 1949).
[57] Deutsche Shell A.G. Vorstand (Hofland) to W. A. Menne, 4 May 1949 (*Abschrift*), BWA, 186/K1.18.

Shell."[58] Abs wrote two separate letters in response, the first somewhat mysterious, the second decidedly blunt. Abs briefly informed Nedelmann on 17 May that he had received the material on the prohibition of the Fischer-Tropsch plants. He went on to note dryly that something had been sent to him by mistake along with the draft newsletter. The enclosure was an astonishing one: It was a "strictly confidential" memorandum of 17 May 1949 recording a conversation between Nedelmann and Menne, and it outlined the genesis of the "indiscretion" that had led to the story in *Die Welt* and the denial of responsibility by all parties. More important, it noted that Menne wanted to use that opportunity to approach Herr Hofland from Shell: "At this opportunity the attempt must be made by us to get Shell to do something for the Fischer-Tropsch works."[59]

In his capacity as a member of the Shell supervisory board, Abs made his own position much more clear to Nedelmann in a terse note on 25 May 1949. Nedelmann should keep his opinions to himself: "I have to take issue with the news in your letter that you have the distinct feeling that [the] reason for the prohibition of Fischer-Tropsch synthesis is to be found in the influence of foreign oil concerns, specifically that of Shell. At least as far as Shell goes, your presumption is not correct. Therefore I would like to ask you to be more careful in the expression of speculations and intuitions."[60]

Nedelmann and the FVK were already retreating from their accusations against Shell. In another "strictly confidential" note of 11 May 1949, Menne wrote Nedelmann and other prominent members of the FVK that he planned to respond to Hofland's letter of 4 May as quickly as possible "and to inform the gentlemen that their belief that this article [in *Die Welt*] has something to do with me is completely off the track."[61] The campaign against Shell stopped abruptly, and Nedelmann changed the tactics of the FVK once again. Before exploring that change in tactics, however, we should pause briefly to consider the motivations for and the effects of that brief conflict between Shell and the FVK, as well as its broader significance.

Clearly, Nedelmann's attempt to take on Shell, and, by implication, the hydrogenation plants as well, was ill-advised. What prompted his actions? One key motivation was to pin the blame for the plight of the Fischer-Tropsch plants on the Allies, and especially on the unfair influence exerted by private industries in the Allied countries. The story of the Anglo-American oil companies' fear of German competition and their consequent attempts to influence occupation policy fit the bill nicely, providing an intuitively plausible explanation for why the Allies refused to grant Fischer-Tropsch plants permission to produce. The

[58] Nedelmann to Abs, 12 May 1949, BWA, 186/1.18.
[59] Abs to Nedelmann, 17 May 1949, and Anlage, BWA, 186/K1.18.
[60] Abs to Nedelmann, 25 May 1949, BWA, 186/K1.18. Biographical information on Abs comes from the book by GDR historian Eberhard Czichon, *Der Bankier und die Macht: Hermann Josef Abs in der deutschen Politik* (Cologne: Pahl-Rugenstein, 1970).
[61] W. A. Menne to Nedelmann (and others in the Fachverband Kohlechemie and in the A.G. Chemische Industrie), 11 May 1949, BWA, 186/K1.18.

intense interest of Allied investigators in the Fischer-Tropsch process following the war may have lent further credence to that explanation.[62]

Closer attention to Nedelmann's explanation, however, reveals that his scenario was extremely unlikely, if only because the potential threat that the Fischer-Tropsch plants posed to the interests of the Anglo-American oil companies was very small. None of the synthesis facilities could produce feedstocks at anywhere near the rates achieved by modern petrochemical facilities. Also, the product range for the Fischer-Tropsch plants was much narrower than that for petrochemical facilities. At the same time, petrochemical production constituted only a small part of the output of oil companies, which were, of course, primarily in the business of refining and marketing fuels.

If, then, fear of competition was a factor in the conflict between Shell and other oil companies, on the one hand, and the Fischer-Tropsch producers, on the other, it was more likely that the Fischer-Tropsch interests feared the oil producers, rather than the reverse. Such fear seems the most likely motivation for the campaign against Shell, even though that campaign was doomed from the start: It was impossible to attack the oil companies as the villains behind unfair Allied policies without at the same time taking on German firms and individuals as well. Given the Germans' need to present a united front in trying to change Allied policy, that strategy had obvious drawbacks.

The failure of the attack on Shell led Menne, Nedelmann, and the FVK to change their tactics. Instead of confronting Shell, they sought cooperation. In discussing the letter that Shell wrote to Menne to gain his support in "correcting" the impression promulgated by the news media, Menne told Nedelmann that although the story in the paper was completely misleading and off track, "here is an opportunity to get to talk with Shell." The idea was "namely perhaps to come to an agreement that brings the interests of the Fischer-Tropsch factories as well as those of Shell into harmony."[63]

Thus, the effect of the rumors about Shell – in all probability started and certainly propagated by Nedelmann – was to increase the possibility of combined action by Fischer-Tropsch interests and Shell to influence Allied policy. Given, though, that the outcome could have been otherwise, that is, that Shell's managers could have been irretrievably estranged from the FVK as a result of Nedelmann's actions, perhaps it is more accurate to say that Nedelmann and Menne, through luck and political jockeying, limited the potential damage from the Shell–Fischer-Tropsch dispute so that it did not interfere significantly with German attempts to change Allied policy.

Nedelmann next abandoned the tactic of focusing on the interests of a single plant and instead began again to build a still broader German consensus to push for changes in Allied policy. He announced at a meeting on 29 April 1949 that the German Coal-Mining Directorate (Deutsche Kohlenbergbauleitung), the Chemical Industry Trade Association (AG Chemische Industrie), and the trade unions would begin a common action "which was supposed to enlighten the

[62] Gimbel, *Science, Technology, and Reparations*, pp. 85, 101, 224, n. 26.
[63] Menne to Nedelmann, 11 May 1949, BWA, 186/K1.18.

German public about the consequences'' if Allied policy were not changed.[64] Cooperation between the coal and chemical industries was to be expected, but it was also fairly easy to convince representatives of West German trade unions to support the FVK in its campaign to avoid dismantling of the synthesis works. The destruction of the works would, after all, involve dismissing an estimated 4,000 German workers.

To counteract that threat, August Schmidt, head of the German Miners' Union, sent an appeal in June 1949 to his U.S. counterpart, John L. Lewis of the United Mine Workers, asking Lewis to use his influence to prevent the destruction of the synthesis plants. The German workers, claimed Schmidt, did not want to be absolved from responsibilities incurred as a result of the war, nor from reparations. They were entirely willing to ''recognize our duty as to what we have to make up for, but shall be prevented from doing so if the destruction continues.''[65] The tactics of the unions extended to more than just rhetoric, however. German workers blocked attempts to begin dismantling work at Bergkamen, and their protest had to be broken up by Belgian troops.[66]

The activities of German trade unions in support of the cause of retaining and restarting the synthetic-fuel plants unquestionably had some effect on the course of Allied policy development. For one thing, the letter from Schmidt to Lewis and the resistance shown by the miners at Bergkamen demonstrated that German workers were, at least on that issue, in full agreement with German industrialists and politicians. For another, the fact that the resistance at Bergkamen forced the Allies to send in troops gave the action notoriety and probably caused labor opinion throughout the world to become more sympathetic to the German cause. Still, Nedelmann's actions in other areas probably were more significant in influencing policy changes.

For instance, Nedelmann also convinced the major political parties to support the industry in its effort. On 4 November 1949, at the behest of George Radin, an American lawyer who had been hired by the FVK to present its case to the Allied High Commission in Germany, Nedelmann, Radin, and representatives of the major synthetic-fuel plants met with representatives of the Free Democratic Party (FDP) and Christian Democratic Union (CDU) in the chambers of the vice-president of the Bundestag. Nedelmann proposed, and the representatives of the FDP accepted, that he meet with members of the Bundestag to go over the issues regarding dismantling, which they did on 10 November.[67]

[64] Nedelmann, ''Aktennotiz über die Besprechung am 29.4.49 im Sitzungssaal des Landesverbandes Nordrhein, des Chemieverbandes in Düsseldorf,'' 9 May 1949, BWA, 186/K1.21. Those present were Min.-Dir. Dr. Schlafejew, Dir. Eger, Dr. Witte, Dr. Gummert, Oberbergrat Hess, Dr. Kluitmann, and Dr. Nedelmann.

[65] Quoted by Dorothy Thompson, ''On the Record: Ruhr Miners Call on Lewis to Block Destruction of Coal-Conversion Plants,'' *Washington Star* (16 June 1949), a copy of which is in BWA, 186/K1.19.1.

[66] Thompson, ''On the Record.''

[67] Nedelmann, ''Aktennotiz über die Besprechung am 4.11.1949 im Zimmer des Herrn Vize-Präsidenten des Bundestages Dr. Schäfer, Betr.: Demontage der kohlechemischen Werke,'' 4 November 1949, BWA, 186/K1.19.2.

It was through such measures that a consensus among leading German politicians, trade unionists, and industrialists was formed. It reached to the highest levels in the new West German regime, including Economics Minister Ludwig Erhard and Chancellor Konrad Adenauer. German unity on the issues of dismantling and production prohibitions and American pressure on the British were the preconditions for obtaining a change in policy. The proximate cause of the change was that the Allies needed German support in attempting to solve the problem of the disposition of the Ruhr district. In return for West German support for an international authority for the Ruhr,[68] the Allied High Commission agreed to suspend dismantling in the chemical and steel industries and agreed to other economic concessions in the Petersberg agreement of 22 November 1949.[69]

It would be another year and a half, until 3 April 1951, before the West German government and the High Commission would agree to lift all production prohibitions on synthetic-oil plants (along with shipbuilding and synthetic rubber),[70] but the key victories in the battle to retain and restart synthetic-fuel facilities in West Germany had been won by the end of 1949. Heinz Nedelmann and the FVK had succeeded in forging a consensus among all major economic and political groups in West Germany in favor of retaining German synthetic-fuel plants, and that consensus had been supplemented by actions taken to influence Allied policymakers abroad, a strategy particularly successful in influencing the United States. That preparation allowed the Germans to take advantage of a changing political constellation in the late 1940s and early 1950s to gain changes in Allied policy.

Nedelmann and the FVK thereupon turned their attention to an effort to gain tax breaks and import protection for the coal-chemical industry from the West German federal government.[71] Aspects of that successful campaign will be discussed in more detail later. It is important to note here that the unsuccessful confrontation with Shell in the spring of 1949 marked a major turning point for those championing the interests of the Fischer-Tropsch plants. Unsuccessful under the National Socialist regime, as compared with their counterparts that produced synthetic fuels via high-pressure hydrogenation, the Fischer-Tropsch producers tried, through the FVK, to reassert their interests under the new postwar regime, only to run into powerful opposition once again: During the Nazi period, hydrogenation, owned or licensed by the powerful I.G. Farben concern, had offered greater outputs of apparently more useful products than had Fischer-Tropsch; during the occupation period, petrochemicals, backed by the even more

[68] See, for instance, Acting U.S. POLAD to Germany (Riddleberger) to U.S. Secretary of State (from McCloy), 14 September 1949, in *FRUS*, 1949, vol. III, pp. 598–9; "Draft Directive to the High Commissioners on Dismantling," in SecState to President and Acting SecState, 11 November 1949, in *FRUS*, 1949, vol. III, pp. 635–6.

[69] Text is in the U.S. High Commissioner (McCloy) to SecState, 22 November 1949, in *FRUS*, 1949, vol. III, pp. 343–6.

[70] Fachverband Kohlechemie, "Rundschreiben 4/51," 6 April 1951, p. 2, BWA, 186/K1.8.

[71] There is some material on the tax incentives for the industry, in particular for the hydrogenation plants, in Horn, *Die Energiepolitik*, p. 243. See also Chapter 3.

powerful Anglo-American oil interests, could offer greater outputs of apparently less expensive and more useful products than could Fischer-Tropsch. Following the failure of their campaign to take on a major oil company, Fischer-Tropsch producers agitated for tariff protection and embarked on a niche strategy to produce chemical feedstocks that would not compete directly with petrochemical plants. The "end-game strategy" of the Fischer-Tropsch plants will be the subject of a later chapter.

The change in strategy for Fischer-Tropsch producers coincided with a shift in the ground rules for all chemical producers that occurred primarily as a result of the Cold War and its intensification during the period 1950–5. Foreign policy had a major impact on the framework within which business was conducted, and that impact extended even to the technological options available to chemical producers. The changing political economy of chemical technology in the early 1950s is the subject of the following two chapters, which form Part II.

Part II
Bargaining from strength: the political economy of technological change, 1949–1955

3

A new agenda, 1949–1955: Cold War, changing energy patterns, and the development of West German chemical technology

Writing in 1950 in West German chemical trade journal *Chemische Industrie,* Alfons Metzner, a frequent contributor of articles on the political economy of chemical technology, claimed that the Cold War had "convulsed [*erschüt-tert*]" the chemical industry: "The chemical industry is taking on a key position in the interplay of political forces and is therefore being brought into line [*aus-gerichtet*] with purely political considerations."[1] As a key supplier to all other industries, including defense-related ones, the chemical industry did indeed play a central political role during the Cold War. But if one views the Cold War not simply as an attempt by both East and West to assert military ascendance over the other, but as a broader confrontation that was meant to demonstrate the superiority of one political-economic system over another, the chemical industry is seen to have been even more central: As an engine for economic growth, and especially as it contributed to an enhanced standard of living, the chemical industry could be instrumental in helping one of the sides to prevail in that struggle.

---

[1] Alfons Metzner, "Entwicklungstendenzen der Weltchemiewirtschaft," *Chemische Industrie* 2(1950):597.

In the first half of the 1950s, then, just as had been the case in their previous experience, German chemists and chemical industrialists developed technologies in the sway of broader political and economic currents, with many of those currents originating outside German borders. This is not to say that the Cold War and issues associated with it determined what happened in the industry in any detail, but rather that they defined the limits of the technological and production options available to it.

The first section of this chapter examines aspects of the intensification of the Cold War in the first half of the 1950s, looking in particular at the first Berlin crisis, the official division of Germany into two successor states, the Korean War, and Germany rearmament. All of those developments, as well as the Schuman Plan to integrate continental Europe's heavy industry, had direct bearings on the future of the German chemical industry and its technology. The next two sections in this chapter focus on important issues related to the final breakup of I.G. Farben and the changing Allied policies regarding research and production. Both the final disposition of the I.G. and the changing Allied policies can be understood only in the context of the Korean War and West German rearmament. The chapter's fourth section deals with a related development in the first six years of the 1950s: the changing world energy order, particularly the importance of the Suez Crisis and the domestic considerations entailed in that changing order.

Two key "global" issues are not examined in this chapter: The re-internationalization of chemical technology after the war is important enough to warrant a chapter of its own. The impact of changes in the industry on the environment, though equally international and at least as important from a present-day perspective, was not something to which contemporaries gave much thought. Consideration of this issue is taken up in Chapter 11.

The intensification of the Cold War

As noted in Chapter 2, the founding of the West German state in 1949 was in part a function of the growing tension between East and West. No one can say exactly when the division of the country occurred and who was at fault. Many of the actions taken by the two sides were precipitated not simply by political developments, but also by economic considerations. Western Allied officials, in particular, acted on the basis of perceived economic deterioration in their zones. Thus, the British and American occupiers combined their zones economically into the bizone on 1 January 1947, despite Soviet protests that they were violating the Potsdam agreement, which called for treating Germany as a single economic unit. The currency reform of June 1948, which applied not only to the bizone but also to the French zone and the Western zones of Berlin, provoked a much more significant response from the Soviets. They were forced to create a new currency in their zone as well, thus institutionalizing the financial division of the country. The currency reform in the West also brought about the first Berlin crisis, as the Soviets closed off access by road and rail to the former capital.

Finally, formal creation of the West German Federal Republic between May and September 1949 was followed closely by the creation of the German Democratic Republic on 7 October 1949.

One major consequence of the growing realization of the German area's centrality for European political and economic stabilization and reconstruction was increased German control over their own affairs. As Western Allied dependence on the new West Germany grew, the country's leaders could push more insistently for full sovereignty. Shortly after the founding of the Federal Republic, for instance, the Allied–German Petersberg agreement of November 1949 traded short-lived concessions on control of Ruhr coal and steel resources for independent West German participation in the Organization for European Economic Cooperation (OEEC) and for removal of key chemical and steel factories from the Allied dismantling lists. During the following six years, diplomats from the Federal Republic chipped away effectively at most remaining restrictions.

Intensification of the East–West conflict in the Korean War, which began in June 1950, forced the United States to withdraw troops from Europe and send them to Asia. Who would provide the forces believed to be necessary to contain the Soviet threat in Europe? Only one country had sufficient manpower: West Germany. Chancellor Konrad Adenauer used the issue of German rearmament to gain concessions on a number of other issues. Rearmament was no simple issue, of course, especially so soon after the end of World War II. As he secretly began rearmament negotiations with the Allies in the summer of 1950, Adenauer faced strong antiwar sentiment at home and considerable fear of renewed German military might, particularly in France. During the course of long and difficult political maneuvering, made considerably easier by the apparent increase in the Soviet threat, Adenauer was able, by 1955, to create a new German army, the Bundeswehr, which would be fully integrated into the North Atlantic Treaty Organization (NATO) and would use only conventional weapons.[2] It was no accident that German rearmament coincided closely with the final diplomatic agreements to return virtually full sovereignty to the Federal Republic through the German Treaty of 1954 and the official end of the occupation in 1955.[3]

Major changes in the organizational framework of the chemical industry constituted a central objective in, and consequence of, the push toward sovereignty. Adenauer and his economics minister, Ludwig Erhard, often intervened personally to promote those changes, because they recognized that an internationally competitive chemical industry would increase the diplomatic leverage of the Federal Republic. As had been the case between 1871 and 1945, politicians realized that a vital chemical industry would be an indispensable prerequisite for a sound and strong state, even if the international conditions under which that state would operate would be fundamentally changed. The industry's vitality

---

[2] Michael Geyer, *Deutsche Rüstungspolitik 1860–1980* (Frankfurt: Suhrkamp, 1984), pp. 185–204; Volker Berghahn, *The Americanisation of West German Industry* (Cambridge University Press, 1986), pp. 260–82. See also Anne Marie Stokes, "German Writers and the Intermediate-Range Nuclear Forces Debate" (Ph.D. dissertation, Ohio State University, 1991), chapter 1.

[3] The Allies had some rights on German soil through the autumn of 1990.

depended, first and foremost, on a satisfactory resolution to key problems associated with the breakup of I.G. Farben.

Breaking up I.G. Farben

As World War II ended, all four of the victorious Allies agreed that I.G. Farben must be broken up. That firm, along with a few others, such as Vereinigte Stahl-werke, represented, in their view, an excessive concentration of economic power. A glance at the proportion of total German production of key products controlled by I.G. Farben through 1945 confirms that impression: The giant firm produced all of Germany's synthetic rubber and methanol, 90 percent of its organic intermediates and plastics, 84 percent of its explosives, and three-fourths of its nitrogen and solvents. But the corporation did not monopolize German chemical manufacturing; it produced much smaller proportions of other products, such as pharmaceuticals (about 50 percent) and synthetic gasoline (about 33 percent, although I.G. licensees controlled much of the remainder of synthetic-gasoline output). Nevertheless, it is clear that I.G. Farben controlled key sectors of the chemicals market, in particular those high-pressure organic processes at the technological cutting edge of the industry.[4] I.G. Farben's economic might, moreover, translated into political power, a power perceived to be more dangerous because of the fact that the firm could supply any German government with the synthetic materials that could help overcome domestic raw-materials limitations. It was believed that breaking up the I.G., combined with restrictions on research and production, would prevent Germany from ever making war again.

Although one can well understand the rationale for the breakup of I.G. Farben, even passing consideration of the problems associated with it reveals its astonishing complexity. I.G. Farben's holdings included not only production, sales, and research facilities within the German borders of 1937 (i.e., before the annexation of Austria) but also banks, patents, mortgage companies, and insurance companies in Germany, in addition to overseas holdings, as well as factories and other assets in Poland and other eastern European countries. Which successors would inherit which patents? Which successor firms (and in what proportions) would have to answer the enormous claims against the old company – by creditors, government tax collectors, and those who were owed pensions, not to mention the survivors of slave labor and forced labor and the heirs of those who did not survive? Who would be responsible for trying to win back foreign holdings (patents, production facilities, and sales offices) for the suc-

[4] On the story of the breakup of the firm, see Raymond G. Stokes, *Divide and Prosper: The Heirs of I.G. Farben under Allied Authority, 1945–1951* (Berkeley: University of California Press, 1988), esp. pp. 11–14. Rather than merely recapitulating the arguments of *Divide and Prosper*, this section explores, in particular, areas related to the roles of state actors in the breakup, as well as matters that extend beyond the chronological scope of my earlier study and matters of special interest for the history of the West German petrochemical industry. Figures on the proportions of particular production areas controlled by the I.G. are drawn from Karl Falk, "What Has Happened to Germany's Divided Chemical Industry," *Chemical Engineering* 56(May 1949):146–7.

cessor firms? By October 1949, of course, the "foreign holdings" of West Germans also included properties in East Germany.

The central issue, however, was to determine the optimum sizes and numbers of the successor firms. This seems a purely technical matter that might be resolved easily by a committee of engineers, bankers, and businessmen conversant with the firm and its assets. But as Hans-Dieter Kreikamp has shown, technical arguments were at their root ambiguous: One might conceive of any number of possible combinations of factories that might constitute viable independent units.[5] Decisions on whether there should be a large number of small successors or a small number of large ones, or something in between, and on which factories would be combined to form a given successor, were therefore fundamentally political and economic issues. Their outcome would depend heavily on assumptions about postwar Germany's most desirable socioeconomic order, the perceived importance of competitiveness in the U.S.-dominated postwar international system, and a number of other, less important issues.

Such basic disagreements hampered the Allied powers from the beginning of the occupation, despite attempts to coordinate policy.[6] As the occupation continued, harmonizing the disparate Allied concerns proved impossible, especially when heightened Cold War tensions brought formal four-power cooperation in the breakup to a halt in the spring of 1948. Still, the net effect of the fundamental differences in policy and practice among the victorious powers was that, de facto, from the beginning of the occupation I.G. Farbenindustrie A.G. ceased to function as a single corporation. Although the final outcome of the breakup was not predictable in 1945, zonal policies helped prejudice its general contours. Practically speaking, the major Western successors of I.G. Farben were going to be the three large works units of the old firm, the central factories of which lay in different zones: the Upper Rhine group, with headquarters in Ludwigshafen in the French zone, and comprising key factories of the old BASF; the Middle Rhine group, with headquarters in Frankfurt-Hoechst in the U.S. zone, and comprising the factories of the old Meister Lucius & Brüning, later Farbwerke Hoechst A.G.; and the Lower Rhine group, with headquarters in Leverkusen in the British zone, and comprising the factories of the old Bayer corporation.

Reconstitution of BASF, Hoechst, and Bayer as independent companies provided the core of the solution to the problem of breaking up the I.G. Two major trends had shaped that solution by the late 1940s. First, as a result of changes in occupation policy, owing to the intensification of the Cold War, the Western Allies allowed the Germans a steadily increasing voice in the negotiations on the breakup. Second (and this is one of the more peculiar developments of the occupation), each of the Western Allies became increasingly protective of the interests of the former I.G. group in its zone.

[5] Hans-Dieter Kreikamp, "Die Entflechtung der I.G. Farbenindustrie A.G. und die Gründung der Nachfolgegesellschaften," *Vierteljahrshefte für Zeitgeschichte* 25(1977):221, 247; Stokes, *Divide and Prosper*, pp. 173–9.
[6] Stokes, *Divide and Prosper*, passim; on diversity in the U.S. camp, see pp. 41–8, 153–4, 177–8; on the breakup (*Entflechtung*) of the firm itself, see pp. 118–22, 173–9.

German participation in the I.G. breakup began in earnest in the summer of 1948, following the breakdown in four-power cooperation, the currency reform, and the beginning of the Berlin crisis. In August, American and British occupation officials created the Bizonal I.G. Farben Control Office (BIFCO) to control and decartelize the firm, but they also created a parallel German organization responsible for devising the final plans for breaking up the firm: the I.G. Farben Dispersal Panel (FARDIP). The complexities of their task kept the members of FARDIP busy for some time, but on 29 June 1950 they delivered their recommendations to the Western Allies. They called for the creation of twenty-two independent units to succeed the I.G., but the most important feature in their suggestions was the idea of *Kerngesellschaften,* or "nuclear firms." These would, of course, be BASF, Hoechst, and Bayer, which would be approximately equal in size and would be by far the largest firms in the West German chemical industry.[7]

The occupiers, for their part, began official moves to break up the firm in the summer of 1950. On 17 August they enacted Allied High Commission (AHC) Law 35, which provided the legal basis for the stock transfers that would complete the process. Implementation of Law 35, however, required still more German participation. Konrad Adenauer and Ludwig Erhard took active personal roles, but they also turned over part of the task to two key figures in the Economics Ministry: Felix Prentzel and Heinrich von Rospatt. Prentzel and von Rospatt marshaled support from government, industry, and labor groups to present a united German front in negotiations with the Allies. Their arguments stressed, throughout, the concept of *Kerngesellschaften* and the importance of the international competitiveness of the successor firms.[8]

The ascendance of those ideas was assured when, in October 1950, a committee of three Allied experts endorsed them in a final report, which the AHC accepted in full on 23 November and forwarded to the West German government for comment.[9] American chemist Erwin H. Amick, British chemical industrialist George Brearley, and French chemist Leon C. Denivelle agreed with the Germans that BASF, Bayer, and Hoechst should be approximately equal in size and that each should be composed of sufficient numbers of factories to be competitive in world markets. They disagreed with the Germans on a number of other points; some of those key areas of disagreement will be discussed later. Still, extensive agreement on the makeup of the major successors allowed them to be "re-founded" fairly quickly: Farbwerke Hoechst A.G. on 7 December 1951, Farbenfabrik Bayer A.G. on 19 December 1951, and BASF A.G. on 30

---

[7] Stokes, *Divide and Prosper,* pp. 174ff.   [8] Ibid., pp. 175ff.

[9] "Report of the Tripartite Investigation Team Appointed to Consider Dispersal Problems Relating to I.G. Farbenindustrie A.G.," August 1950 (signed October 1950 by the principal authors, Amick, Brearley, and Denivelle), Public Record Office, London (Kew) (hereafter, PRO), FO371/ 85684. On Allied approval and request for comment, see Allied High Commission for Germany, Allied General Secretariat (AGSEC) to Ministerialdirigent Dr. Dittmann, Office of the Chancellor of the FRG, "Subj.: I.G. Farben Dispersal Plan," 23 November 1950 [AGSEC(50)2018], PRO, FO371/85685.

January 1952, even though negotiations on the capital to be allocated to each successor would continue until the end of March 1953. The three successors differed from one another in terms of management, production, and research traditions, the extent of bombing damage, and the condition and modernity of physical plant, but they were all well situated to turn to capital markets to modernize in the 1950s. In the meantime, they produced at high volume for the practically insatiable domestic market, and they began exporting using equipment and technologies left over from the war.[10]

In addition to the increasing German participation in the process, a related trend helped shape the outcome of the negotiations on the breakup of I.G. Farben: the growing concern of each of the occupiers for the I.G. works group in its own zone. That became evident only gradually, mainly in the course of resolving the outstanding details of the breakup during the period from 1949 to 1955. Those details involved deciding the fates of several factories, including the Dormagen factory of the Leverkusen-based Lower Rhine group and the Agfa factories in Leverkusen and Munich, the Auguste Victoria mine, the acetylene works at Knapsack, and the synthetic-rubber and polymer factory of Hüls in Marl-Recklinghausen. It will thus be worth following more closely the Allied–German negotiations on those matters.

Leverkusen: Dormagen and Agfa

In considering the factories associated with the Leverkusen-based Bayer group, the Allied experts Amick, Brearley, and Denivelle recommended that Dormagen, which produced primarily synthetic fibers and was a long-time component of the Bayer (Lower Rhine) group, be separated from Bayer. Because they did not think the factory could survive independently, they suggested that Dormagen join other former I.G. factories at Rottweil and Bobingen to form a single company. The "Synthetic Fiber Company" would produce viscose rayon, cuprammonium filament and fiber, cellulose acetate, and Perlon fiber and silk. In addition, the experts recommended that Agfa, with works in Leverkusen and in Munich, be set up as an independent corporation producing a complete range of photographic products and equipment.[11] At a special meeting on 12 April 1951, the AHC decided that Dormagen would be established as a separate company, but changed its mind about Agfa:

AGFA should be established as a company subsidiary to Leverkusen. Chief considerations in reaching this decision were fears of political repercussions which would result from announcement at this time [of] separation of AGFA from Leverkusen, and particularly French anxiety reference Schuman Plan negotiations; fact that AGFA separated from Leverkusen would still be able to find capital more easily than competitors and thus in any event be likely to establish dominant position; extent of opposition to AGFA

---

[10] Stokes, *Divide and Prosper*, pp. 176–89; Stokes, "Technology and the West German *Wirtschaftswunder*," *Technology and Culture* 32(1991):1–22.

[11] "Report of the Tripartite Investigation Team," p. 35, PRO, FO371/85684; Kreikamp, "Die Entflechtung," pp. 234–5, 248–9.

separation expressed by German management, Federal Republic and Trade Unions; and finally, whereas Dormagen was located 15 kilos [kilometers] from parent concern, AGFA workshops located on Leverkusen site.[12]

Several implications of this summary should be emphasized. First, the fundamental importance of political factors, rather than purely technological or financial considerations, was clear. Second, concerted German efforts organized by Prentzel and von Rospatt had paid off. Finally, the importance of the Schuman Plan deserves emphasis. The French were anxious that the control mechanisms for European coal and steel production be clarified. For that, they would need the support of the Federal Republic, and they were unwilling to allow the Schuman Plan negotiations to be hindered by the final negotiations on the I.G. breakup. As we shall see, the Schuman Plan played a role in the negotiations on the Auguste Victoria coal mine as well.

The decision of the high commissioners on Dormagen was not to last, however, and that on Agfa was to be modified. One major factor in overturning the original order was British support for the Bayer position that both Agfa-Leverkusen and Dormagen be retained by the group. The British I.G. Farben control officer, E. L. Douglas Fowles, heavily and publicly favored retention of both from at least the summer of 1950.[13] What is more, about two weeks before the meeting of the high commissioners on 12 April, C. C. Oxborrow, the British head of the Industrial Control and Decartelisation Branch, wrote on the subject to G. W. Macready, the British economic adviser:

I have been thinking that it might be worth while to suggest to the [British] High Commissioner [Ivone Kirkpatrick] that he should make an eleventh hour attempt to settle this matter out of court with Mr. McCloy. [handwritten addition to this by Oxborrow: "I mean, of course, a settlement in our favour!"]

He thought that British acceptance of an American-backed coal/steel plan would make the American high commissioner much more likely to accept Britain's position.[14] It is not clear, but it may well have been such an argument that al-

---

[12] AGSEC from Slater, "Summary Report of Council Meeting held in Bonn-Petersberg, 12 April 1951," in U.S. National Archives, Washington National Records Center, Suitland, MD, Record Group (hereafter, NA, RG) 466, Records of the U.S. High Commission for Germany, Papers of High Commissioner John McCloy (hereafter, McCloy Papers), Classified General Records, Box 27, document D(51)480a.

[13] R. J. B. Williams (Ind. Control and Decart. Br., Frankfurt) to R. S. Swann (FO Ger. Comm. Rel. and Ind. Dept.), "Subject: I.G. Farben," 21 August 1950, PRO, FO371/85681. Fowles believed that American occupiers were the primary impediment to agreement on those questions: the members of the U.S. element "are fighting a rear-guard action and the Agfa and Dormagen problems represent the last 'bridgehead'. If Leverkusen is permitted to retain Dormagen and Agfa, it will be construed as a major U.S. defeat. The appointment, as U.S. I.G. Control Officer, of the chief prosecutor [sic] in the I.G. Farben Trial at Nuremberg – an emigrant German Jew who has anglicised his German name [Randolph Newman] – has not proved conducive to a change in the U.S. attitude to such matters." Draft brief for high commissioner submitted by Fowles per letter of Fowles to C. C. Oxborrow, 20 February 1951, PRO, FO1036/180.

[14] On British support for the German position: G. W. Macready (economic adviser) to British high commissioner, 5 April 1951, PRO, FO1036/179; quotation from memorandum to economic adviser from C. C. Oxborrow, "Subject: Agfa/Dormagen," 6 April 1951, PRO, FO1036/179.

lowed the compromise of 12 April separating Dormagen from Leverkusen, but giving Agfa-Leverkusen to Leverkusen.

Immediately after the high commissioners' meeting, Macready began to undermine their decision. He wrote to Kirkpatrick on 13 April to argue that another solution would have to be found if it proved impossible to create the synthetic-fiber company suggested by the Amick-Brearley-Denivelle report: "These three plants all make artificial fibres, and the British experts consider (in spite of what the U.S. expert told Mr. McCloy yesterday) that Dormagen could not hope to survive by itself. . . . [I]t would be unlikely to last eighteen months."[15] When the Germans protested the AHC action on Dormagen, internal British government correspondence noted that the British, too, opposed the decision.[16]

Given German and British unhappiness at the disposition of Dormagen and active British opposition to the High Commission's decision, it was bound to be reversed. On 11 January 1952, the AHC accepted the British argument: "As it subsequently [to the 12 April decision] proved financially impracticable to combine these three plants [Dormagen, Rottweil, and Bobingen] into one new company, decision was taken on 11 January and Fed Govt [*sic*] was informed that Dormagen plant would be assigned to new successor company, Farbenfabriken Bayer, which is to receive Leverkusen assets."[17]

Throughout that episode, the German management of the Bayer group was interested in maintaining its four main factories at Leverkusen (including the Agfa facility there), Elberfeld, Uerdingen, and Dormagen as a single, technically integrated unit.[18] Bayer's managers were able, by early 1952, to achieve that objective. But once again it is important to note that technical arguments were not in themselves persuasive in deciding the issue; instead, the political support of British occupation officials was crucial. British and German personnel did not see eye-to-eye on all issues regarding the breakup of the large firm, but from the beginning of the occupation they generally worked together to reestablish a viable successor company to the I.G. in the British zone, in part, at least, because of the tremendous cost of the occupation to the British economy.

BASF: Auguste Victoria

The British were not the only occupying power looking out for the interests of the works group in their zone. French occupation officials did so as well, although, from the beginning, their motivation differed from that of the British. As Douglas Fowles, the British I.G. control officer, characterized French policy: "*The French Element,* having in their zone only one really important under-

[15] G. W. Macready to high commissioner, 13 April 1951, PRO, FO1036/181.
[16] E. L. Douglas Fowles to G. W. Macready, "Subject: German Reactions to Allied Decision Concerning Dormagen," 5 May 1951, PRO FO1036/181.
[17] Telegram, AGSEC from Slater, "Summary report of Council meeting held 17 January with Kirkpatrick (UK), McCloy (US) and Poncet (Fr)," 17 January 1952, NA, RG 466, McCloy Papers, Classified General Records, Box 35, D(52)147a.
[18] On the integration of the Bayer-group factories, see Stokes, *Divide and Prosper,* pp. 72–3.

taking [BASF Ludwigshafen, together with the nearby Oppau plant], settled in that plant with a large contingent of technical and other officials and did their best to turn it and certain other plants in their zone into units of [the] French economy."[19] When he wrote that in early 1951, Fowles's views may have been somewhat exaggerated, but his statement gives a fairly accurate characterization of French policies through early 1948. Policies changed during 1948, however, for a variety of reasons, including growing tension in the Cold War, the need of the French to secure American and British political (and, in the case of the Americans, financial) support in their efforts at reconstruction, and increasing evidence that the practice of stressing production, without sufficient preventive maintenance, had reached its technical limits.[20] New occupation policies were meant to achieve some of the original ends through more subtle means: Occupation officials, for instance, facilitated the conclusion of technical and sales contracts between BASF and French firms in 1948 and 1949.[21] In addition, French Foreign Ministry officials were able to wrest financial concessions from the Germans as the last steps toward sovereignty were taken. In September 1953, for example, the Federal Republic agreed to pay the French government $11,840,000 because "between 8 May 1945 and 18 October 1948, France furnished Germany economic assistance" of approximately that amount.[22]

Clearly, the French continued to make use of their ascendance in their zone of Germany to wring concessions out of the country and its industry. At the same time, it is important to note that the French and the Germans began to reach an accommodation in that regard by mid-1948: German politicians and businessmen were willing to accept French views on a number of issues in return for French support on a number of others. French control officials, for instance, allowed (in fact encouraged) Karl Wurster to return to his former post as director of the Ludwigshafen-Oppau group within weeks after his acquittal at Nuremberg in mid-1948, thus ensuring continuity in the leadership of the works group from the 1930s into the 1940s and 1950s.[23] At about the same time, French military-government officials looked the other way when two representatives of the Royal Dutch Shell group (Mr. Mitchell from the Shell group in London and Herr Boeder from Deutsche Shell in Hamburg) showed up at Ludwigshafen to meet with Bernhard Timm, Wurster's assistant. Shell was interested in supplying BASF with petrochemical feedstocks.[24] Although the deal did not work out right

[19] Draft brief for high commissioner submitted by Fowles per letter of Fowles to C. C. Oxborrow, 20 February 1951, PRO, FO1036/180.
[20] Stokes, *Divide and Prosper,* pp. 86–108.   [21] Ibid., p. 97.
[22] Min. des Affaires Etrangéres, "Accord entre le gouvernement de la Republique française et le gouvernement de la Republique fédérale d'Allemagne sur le règlement de la créance du gouvernement français au titre de l'assistance économique fournie à l'Allemagne après la guerre," 2 September 1953, French Foreign Ministry Archives, Paris, Affaires Allemandes et Autrichiennes, Imprimés, AFA C4, Notes et Etudes Documentaires No. 1776. (Signed in London by R. Massigli and H. Abs on 27 February 1953; passed the Bundestag 190 to 147, with 17 abstentions, on 3 July 1953.)
[23] Stokes, *Divide and Prosper,* p. 155.
[24] Interview with Bernhard Timm, BASF Ludwigshafen, 10 August 1988.

away, that 1948 meeting laid the groundwork for later negotiations between the two firms, which eventually would result in the founding of Germany's first factory dedicated exclusively to petrochemical production.[25]

By early 1951, according to British I.G. controller Douglas Fowles, the French were willing to cut deals with the British, the Americans, or the Germans on a number of items related to the breakup of the I.G., because they had "obtained both Allied and German agreement to the only really important issue in which they are interested – the Ludwigshafen/Oppau fusion."[26] Fowles's insights, once again, were somewhat overstated. As noted earlier, the desire not to imperil negotiations on the Schuman Plan to create the European Coal and Steel Community continued to affect the French stance (and those of others) on the I.G. breakup. Attaining "the Ludwigshafen/Oppau fusion," Fowles implied, would mark the close of the issue for the French. In fact, attaining that fusion did not end French involvement; French officials continued to be vitally interested in the new company's prospects after its formal re-founding. The French inclination to safeguard the interests of the BASF group and the role of the Schuman Plan in the I.G. breakup were best illustrated in the negotiations surrounding the disposition of the Auguste Victoria coal mine. Debate on the issue also demonstrated some of the technical complexities of the breakup.

Gewerkschaft Auguste Victoria, the company that ran the coal mine, was one of many firms that were totally owned by I.G. Farben, and the task of assigning such subsidiaries to successor companies was complicated. The mine was adjacent to the main factory of the Chemische Werke Hüls, another I.G. subsidiary (discussed later in this chapter). The two shared rail links, water-transportation facilities, power-generation stations, workers' housing, and "welfare projects." Thus the Allies assigned Auguste Victoria to Hüls.[27] Another reason for that decision may have been concerns about Hüls's viability: In their recommendations on the breakup of the I.G., the Allied experts made it clear that they wanted to strengthen Hüls so as to keep it from being swallowed up by one of the large successors. They were also concerned about Hüls's ability to compete effectively over the long term.[28]

As the final disposition of the I.G. approached in 1952 and 1953, personnel from BASF, the West German government, and the French occupation authority became increasingly insistent that Auguste Victoria be turned over to BASF instead of Hüls. Their arguments were based on technical considerations. As Dr.

[25] These negotiations and their outcome are explored in detail in Chapter 5.

[26] Draft brief on I.G. Farben prepared by Douglas Fowles, submitted under cover of letter from control officer for I.G. (Fowles) to C. C. Oxborrow (office of the economic adviser), 20 February 1951, PRO, FO1036/180.

[27] H. Trevelyan to high commissioner, "Deconcentration of I.G. Farbenindustrie, A.G.," 21 November 1952, Appendix A, p. 1, PRO, FO1036/183.

[28] "Report of the Tripartite Investigation Team," pp. 24–5, PRO, FO371/85684. The experts were very concerned with Hüls's position if Allied prohibitions on production of synthetic rubber remained in force, because the new firm would have to enter new and often untried fields of polymer chemistry. Production controls were lifted in late 1951, improving the firm's chances of survival, but the experts were concerned about the fate of the new firm even in that case.

Westrick, state secretary in the West German Economics Ministry, presented it to Allied antitrust personnel in November 1952, "one of [BASF] Ludwigshaven's [sic] main production lines is nitrogen . . . [T]he production of nitrogen demanded a particular grade of coke and an absolutely uniform quality of that grade."[29] Auguste Victoria produced coke of the type and grade needed by BASF, and "the Victoria output of coke would cover about 70% of the BASF's requirements."[30]

British occupation officials were not particularly impressed with Westrick's arguments. Given the complicated intermingling of crucial infrastructure between Auguste Victoria and Hüls, an adviser to the high commissioner wrote, would it not "be simpler to provide BASF with a contract for the coke output"? The alternative would be to cover Hüls's transportation, power, and housing needs with more complicated long-term contracts. The British had no wish to "get tangled up in internal German arguments" and thus did not press their objections.[31] The French, on the other hand, supported the BASF/Auguste Victoria arrangement,[32] just as the British had supported Bayer in the Dormagen matter.

Still, the management of Hüls also needed to be convinced, and they were at first reluctant to even consider an arrangement by which the mine and its attendant support systems would be owned by BASF. Paul Baumann, the head of Hüls, in a memorandum to the federal Ministry of Economics in August 1952, stressed that in the strongest terms: "To sum up, a majority participation of BASF in the AV [Auguste Victoria] pit means of necessity control of CWH [Chemische Werke Hüls] by its largest competitor." Losing Auguste Victoria would deprive the smaller firm of a valuable source of hydrocarbons and electricity that it could use itself or sell to obtain needed feedstocks.[33]

By late November, however, those objections were "overcome by the gentle art of persuasion."[34] Quite probably, BASF's management reminded Baumann of the larger firm's agreement in May 1952 to license key patents to Hüls,[35] because whatever Baumann might say about the consequences of losing Auguste

[29] Minutes from C. C. Oxborrow to Mr. Trevelyan, "Outstanding items in the Farben Reorganisation," 7 November 1952 (seen by Trevelyan on 12 November), PRO, FO1036/183. Westrick was the top bureaucrat in the Economics Ministry (just under Ludwig Erhard, the minister) for most of the 1950s.

[30] H. Trevelyan to high commissioner, "Deconcentration of I.G. Farbenindustrie, A.G.," 21 November 1952, Appendix A, p. 1, PRO, FO1036/183.

[31] Ibid.

[32] C. C. Oxborrow to R. S. Swann, Foreign Office, "Subject: Law 35 – Reorganisation of I.G. Farbenindustrie," 25 November 1952, PRO, FO1036/183.

[33] Paul Baumann, "Stellungnahme der Chemischen Werke Hüls (CWH) zu einer 51 %igen Zuteilung der Zeche Auguste Victoria (AV) an die Badische Anilin- & Soda-Fabrik (BASF)," 27 August 1952, Bundesarchiv Koblenz (hereafter, BAK), Records of the Federal Ministry of Economics, B102, File 442, vol. 1 (hereafter, B102/442, Heft 1).

[34] H. Trevelyan to high commissioner, "Deconcentration of I.G. Farbenindustrie, A.G.," 21 November 1952, Appendix A, p. 1, PRO, FO1036/183.

[35] Paul Baumann to H. von Rospatt, 6 May 1952, BAK, B102/411. BASF held the majority of the patents that Hüls needed to operate its facilities.

Victoria, gaining licenses to the BASF and other I.G. patents was crucial to the firm's future.[36] In November, Baumann reported to British military-government officials that BASF's Karl Wurster had personally assured him that "all demands of Chemische Werke Hüls will be fulfilled when Zeche [mine] Auguste Victoria is transferred to BASF 100 percent. I suggest to approve the general demand of a 100% transfer of Auguste Victoria to BASF."[37]

Everything appeared to be lined up for BASF to get its wishes, when a major complication arose at an AHC meeting on 25 November 1952. The Economics Committee of the Allied High Commission for Germany (HICOG) warned the AHC that giving Auguste Victoria to BASF "would prejudice future action by the Schuman High Authority to prevent similar concentrations of economic power in the future." The French, of course, could not afford to appear to be undermining the spirit of the Schuman Plan and therefore altered their tactics. Instead of Auguste Victoria going to BASF, they suggested, the Federal Republic should have the choice of either setting up the mine as an independent company or giving it to Hüls. A British participant saw through the French ploy immediately: "The idea behind complete independence is, of course, to leave the door open for BASF to make an application to the High Authority for the acquisition of the mine at a later date; and for the same reasons the Federal Government may prefer it." Still, he noted that "in view of the injection of the Schuman Plan we felt we could not oppose the French proposal on Auguste Victoria."[38]

Just as we have seen before, the negotiations surrounding the Schuman Plan exerted a powerful effect on those concerning the breakup of I.G. Farben. Neither the French nor the British – nor even the Americans – were willing to accept any decision on the breakup that might somehow derail the initial work of the European Coal and Steel Community (ECSC). The Germans, though also anxious to keep the ECSC on track, were unwilling to allow Allied anticipation of the ECSC's decisions to dissuade them from pursuing their objectives on the last details of the I.G. breakup. At a meeting between the high commissioners and the chancellor of the Federal Republic on 10 December 1952, Ivone Kirkpatrick asked Adenauer to consider suggesting a compromise on Auguste Victoria and other matters. Adenauer replied through the state secretary of the Foreign Ministry (Hallstein) in a letter of 9 February: "On the basis of renewed careful investigation and extensive conversations with experts, the federal

---

[36] This is evident from a number of documents in the Federal German Archives, e.g., Fritz ter Meer, "Chemische Werke Hüls GmbH, Stellungnahme zur Patententflechtung" (Abschrift), 23 February 1952, BAK, B102/411; Baumann to von Rospatt, 5 May 1952, BAK, B102/411; Baumann to Bundeswirtschaftsministerium (Federal Ministry of Economics) (BWM), Unterabteilung IV B, "Patententflechtung I.G. Farbenindustrie A.G. in Auflösung, Durchführungsverordnung zum Gesetz 35, BAK, B102/441, Heft 2; Baumann, "Produktionsprogramm der Chemischen Werke Hüls," 13 June 1952, BAK, B102/442, Heft 1.

[37] Memorandum (probably by C. C. Oxborrow), "Telephone call from Mr. Watson 13.10 hours," n.d. (middle to late November 1952), PRO, FO1036/183.

[38] C. C. Oxborrow to R. S. Swann, "Subject: Law 35 – Reorganisation of I.G. Farbenindustrie," 25 November 1952, PRO, FO1036/183.

government has now come to the conviction that it is impossible for it to find a compromise.'' For Auguste Victoria in particular, the German federal government was unwilling to delay the decision to give it to BASF, ''since it is important with regard to the Schuman Plan to establish clear relationships in this matter in the framework of the break-up of the I.G.'' The Germans thus used the Schuman Plan to bolster their own argument. They rejected explicitly the reasoning used by the Allies: ''The federal government considers this [giving Auguste Victoria to BASF] now as before urgently necessary, even if your experts do not concur with the opinion that the requirements of the Schuman Plan could be of significance in this matter.''[39]

The German government was in a good bargaining position as the Allies tried to move quickly to resolve most of the outstanding difficulties regarding the breakup of the I.G. J. A. Douglas of the British Foreign Office reported in March 1953, about a month after Hallstein's letter, that the Germans had achieved their goals on the disposition of Auguste Victoria, as well as other key I.G. properties:

In return for the Federal Govt's [sic] acceptance of the Allied drafts on share distribution, appointment of trustees, tax and pensions liabilities, the Federal Govt's [sic] proposals for dealing with:–
    Auguste Victoria mine;
    [and several other matters]
have been accepted.[40]

Hoechst: getting Knapsack

Bayer negotiated with the support of the British to get Dormagen and Agfa. BASF, supported by the French, received Auguste Victoria. With support from all three Allied experts, Hoechst was also able to achieve one of its main goals in the breakup, that is, control of the Knapsack acetylene production facility. For Hoechst, however, that achievement probably was much more significant than the victories of the other two members of the ''Big Three'': Controlling Knapsack, the supply base for Hoechst's acetylene-chemistry family tree, or *Stammbaum*,[41] was vital to the firm's survival in the immediate aftermath of the I.G. breakup. The difficulties of the Hoechst group were recognized from the beginning of the occupation.

In a report prepared in July 1945 for the Production Control Branch of the U.S. occupying forces in Germany, Lt. Col. Herbert G. Moulton presented an overview of the past performance and future potential of the main plant of the I.G. Farben Hoechst group, located at Frankfurt-Hoechst. The factory, he

---

[39] Walter Hallstein to Samuel Reber (acting U.S. high commissioner), 9 February 1953, NA, RG 466, HICOG Office of the General Counsel, Decartelization and Deconcentration Division, Cartel Subject Files, 1947–1955, Farben, I.G., Box 20: FEDREP, Views of the Federal Republic.

[40] J. A. Douglas (Foreign Office, German General Department), ''Minute,'' 13 March 1953, PRO, FO371/105762.

[41] See Chapter 1.

pointed out, "manufactured heavy basic chemicals – sulphuric, nitric and hydrochloric acids and chlorine; also fertilizers, refrigerants, solvents, detergents, dye-stuffs and pharmaceuticals," in other words, a full range of modern chemical products. Altogether, its production amounted to "about 10% of the total business of I.G.F., or 22% of the general chemical business of the company (excluding aluminum, magnesium and synthetic oils)." Although Hoechst clearly was a major factory within the I.G. Farben complex, Moulton's report went on to note that the state of its technology was unremarkable and to emphasize its dependence on firms outside the American zone of occupation for crucial supplies of feedstocks and energy:

The plant is an ordinary, average chemical factory, with much obsolescent, old equipment and some new modern equipment, following usual, common, more or less standard production practices. The site is far from sources of raw material, power and fuel supply, and has no advantages except inland waterway transportation.

Practically all raw material, fuel, power and operating supplies are dependent on sources in the British, French and Russian Zones. The operations of all departments of the plant in the last analysis depend primarily, directly or indirectly, on coal, coke, coke-oven by-products and coke-oven gas from the RUHR (British Zone).

What was true for the Hoechst plant in general applied also to the factory's production in the most modern areas of organic chemistry, solvents, and plastics. That, Moulton pointed out, was "based on calcium carbide and acetaldehyde (from the British Zone, but with possible substitution from plants in the American Zone which in turn require RUHR coal)."[42]

Moulton's overview of the state and potential of the laboratories at Hoechst was more positive. Indeed, he contended, "THE PRINCIPAL ASSETS OF THE [HOECHST] PLANT ARE BRAINS AND SKILL RATHER THAN BRICKS AND MORTAR." Hoechst's Catalytic Research Laboratory was one area with potential for the future. Even though much of the research in the laboratory had been of narrow focus (involving, for instance, incremental improvements in the catalysts used at the Hoechst main plant), researchers had also done work to maximize olefin production, rather than paraffin production, with a view toward organic chemical synthesis. In addition, "much work was done on a scientific level in connection with to [sic] substitution of carbon monoxide for calcium carbide as a starting point for various lines of solvent production." Moulton, however, doubted the wisdom of continued research into catalysis at Hoechst, because those forays into alternative technologies still involved coal-based chemicals as the fundamental building blocks for organic synthesis. He noted that "further research on catalysis might by chance or design fit in with some future scheme of German self-sufficiency through the manufacture of synthetics."[43]

[42] Herbert G. Moulton, memorandum, "The Höchst [sic] Plant of I.G. Farbenindustrie A.G.," 30 July 1945, pp. 1, 40 (final quotation, p. 40; all others, p. 1), Firmenarchiv Hoechst, Frankfurt-Hoechst.

[43] Moulton, "The Höchst Plant," pp. 37–43, 48; quotations, pp. 48, 40, 42.

Regardless of the wisdom of Moulton's suggestion, it was clear to everyone associated with the chemical industry in Germany in the immediate postwar period that domestic coal would be the primary source of raw materials for some time to come. It was equally clear that acetylene chemistry, based on German coal, would be the dominant mode for producing sophisticated organic chemicals. Hoechst thus desperately needed a source of supply for carbide and acetaldehyde, and it was for that reason that its top managers began to fight to gain control of its former supplier, the A.G. für Stickstoffdünger, at Knapsack, near Cologne.

In the first months of the occupation, the future relationship between Hoechst and Knapsack was problematic: The Allied division of Germany into four practically airtight zones of occupation left little chance for interzonal trade. That changed somewhat at the beginning of 1947, when the Americans and the British decided to merge their zones economically into the bizone. The main plant of the Hoechst group was able to purchase needed supplies from Knapsack. Still, that solution was not completely satisfactory. Hoechst's solvents and plastics sections counted for about one-fifth of the firm's total revenue by the end of the occupation period, and the company needed 30–35 percent of Knapsack's total production of carbide to manufacture its solvents and plastics.[44] Purchasing carbide on the open market would put the firm at a cost disadvantage, but if it were almost totally dependent on Knapsack (a company that was legally completely separate) for its raw materials, it could not be absolutely sure of its source of supply.

The founding of the Federal Republic coincided with a general loosening of Allied policy that favored accommodation rather than confrontation with West German companies. By 1950, all parties negotiating the breakup of I.G. Farben – including the Western Allies, the West German federal government, state governments, and industry – agreed that Hoechst and Knapsack should be bound together in some way.[45] The new Allied stance was embodied in the 1950 report of the three Allied experts. They recommended full fusion of the main Hoechst plant with the A.G. für Stickstoffdünger in Knapsack, as well as other independent factories at Offenbach, Griesheim, and Marburg. The experts spelled out their reasons in the report's conclusion:

The most difficult problem, and the one that consumed the major portion of time, was to find a workable procedure for creating a Main [Hoechst] Group of sufficient strength as to insure its continued existence and progress side by side with the two strong organizations of Farbenfabriken Bayer and BASF. It was concluded that to achieve this, certain factories . . . should be linked. It is not the intention that these factories should be joined to Hoechst as several were formerly [that is, as largely independent operating units], but

---

[44] Der Hessische Minister für Arbeit, Landwirtschaft und Wirtschaft, "Die Dekonzentrierung der IG-Farbenindustrie A.G. unter Berücksichtigung der wirtschaftlichen und sozialen Belange des Landes Hessen," 28 October 1950 (Abschrift), p. 5, in Hauptstaatsarchiv Hessen, Wiesbaden, 507/1667.

[45] Much of the following is drawn from Hans-Dieter Kreikamp, "Die Entflechtung," pp. 220–51, esp. pp. 238–9. I expand on Kreikamp's observations later using relevant documentary materials.

rather that a new organization be set up for which the best possible managerial personnel be selected from the individual units involved and from the outside, if necessary. . . . The success or otherwise of the Main Group and consequently of the deconcentration plan as a whole is greatly dependent upon a satisfactory solution of this organizational problem.[46]

Even before the experts submitted their report in August 1950, George Brearley, the British chemical industrialist who served on the committee, underscored the centrality of Hoechst's strength to attaining the Allied goal of effective and long-lasting deconcentration, in a conversation with a representative of the British Foreign Office:

Mr. Brearley [believes] that the Frankfurt plans should be combined in one complex under strong direction which is entirely lacking at present. It is his belief that any deconcentration or leaving of the other two complexes alone without a combination of the Frankfurt plants would create the very opportunity of the construction of I.G. Farben under another name so soon as the allied control disappears. On the other hand, if a strong complex in the Frankfurt area could act as a counterpoise to the other two complexes then the eventual chances of cartelisation are much diminished.[47]

Hoechst's control of Knapsack was thus vital to the firm's long-term health and to a permanent restructuring of the German chemical industry.

The conclusions of the Allied experts met with the approval of a significant portion of the German side in the discussion, although not all agreed with the idea of full fusion of the two firms. It went without saying that Hoechst's managers were in favor of fusion, and they were supported by W. A. Menne, representing the Chemical Industry Trade Association, and by the Hessian state government (where the main Hoechst plant was located).[48] However, the federal Ministry of Economics and the state government of North Rhine–Westphalia, where Knapsack was located, saw the issue as more complicated. For the Economics Ministry, the main concern was not only to ensure Hoechst's supply but also to ensure supplies of carbide to other chemical producers who depended on Knapsack and who purchased the remaining 55–60 percent of its carbide production. Ministry officials therefore suggested some sort of legal connection with, but official independence from, Hoechst that would leave open the question of Knapsack's continued role as supplier of carbide to a broad segment of the chemical industry. They also suggested that Knapsack be fused with the

---

[46] "Report of the Tripartite Investigation Team Appointed to Consider Dispersal Problems relating to I.G. Farbenindustrie A.G.," August 1950, pp. 7, 33; quotation, p. 33; from Archives of the French Occupation Forces, Colmar (seen in Paris), C96, Archives Tripartite, Groupe de contrôle de l'IG Farben, Caisse 221, Dossier: Rapport des experts alliés.

[47] C. F. McFarlane, "Memo: Subject: Meeting with Mr. Brearley on 6 June," 7 June 1950, Public Record Office, Kew, PRO, FO371/85678.

[48] See, for instance, W. A. Menne (president, Arbeitsgemeinschaft Chemische Industrie) to federal minister of economics, "Betr.: Aufteilung der I.G.-Farbenindustrie" (Abschrift), from *Dokumente aus Hoechst-Archiven* 50, Teil 2: "Der Hoechst-Konzern entsteht" (Frankfurt-Hoechst: Hoechst A.G., 1978), pp. 124–5; Hessische Minister, "Die Dekonzentrierung der IG-Farbenindustrie A.G."

oxygen group of the old I.G., including Griesheim Autogen, Nordwestdeutsche Sauerstoffwerke Düsseldorf, and Südwestdeutsche Sauerstoffwerke Stuttgart, plants that were related technically and commercially to Knapsack's production palette.[49] Officials of the state government of North Rhine–Westphalia also insisted on legal independence for Knapsack, although their motives probably were less noble; they wished to retain "the possibility of influencing a business located in the state [of North Rhine–Westphalia]."[50]

The Allies, by 1951 eager to complete the work of starting up the successor firms, soon compromised with the German government's position. Despite protests from the Hessian Ministry of Economics that continued into May 1951, at least,[51] the A.G. für Stickstoffdünger and the I.G. oxygen group were combined into a new firm, Knapsack-Griesheim A.G., on the same day that Farbwerke Hoechst A.G. was founded: 7 December 1951. Knapsack-Griesheim was a totally owned subsidiary of Hoechst, but it retained its own separate legal existence.[52] Eight years later, on 15 December 1959, Knapsack-Griesheim A.G. fused with Hoechst by turning over its property to its parent firm. It continued to operate its factories under the old name, but "under the commission of" ("im Auftrag") the main firm; the former subsidiary also signed a profit-and-loss contract with Hoechst.[53]

Hüls

Hüls was mentioned briefly in the discussion of Auguste Victoria, and the firm and its technical development are dealt with in much more detail in Chapter 8. Here, the point is to sketch the impact of the Allied breakup of I.G. Farben – in the context of the Cold War – on the firm and its technological prospects.

Chemische Werke Hüls GmbH was founded pursuant to National Socialist autarky policies in May 1938 to produce synthetic Buna rubber from coal-based feedstocks. Located on a site owned by I.G. Farben at Marl on the Lippe River adjacent to the Auguste Victoria mine, the new factory also was not far from two hydrogenation plants: Gelsenberg Benzin A.G. in Gelsenkirchen and Hydrierwerk Scholven A.G. in Scholven. The factory's efficient operation depended heavily on being near those facilities: The river provided cooling water and transport; the proximity of the mine meant that rail links already existed, and the coal could be used to generate electricity; nearby hydrogenation plants could provide waste hydrocarbon gases, which could then be cracked (i.e., broken

---

49 "Erste Stellunghahme des Bundesministeriums für Wirtschaft zu den Ausführungen in dem Bericht des Tripartite Untersuchungsausschusses (ABD-Gutachten) ohne den bereits behandelten Komplex Leverkusen," 23 January 1951, pp. 1–2, in *Dokumente* 50, Teil 2, pp. 135–6.

50 Dr. Sträter to Konrad Adenauer (Persönlich) (Abschrift von Abschrift), 5 January 1951, in *Dokumente* 50, Teil 2, pp. 131–2; quotation from Kreikamp, "Die Entflechtung," p. 239.

51 Der Hessische Ministerpräsident (Zinn) to Herr Bundeswirtschaftsminister Prof. Dr. Erhard, "Betr.: Zusammenschluss von Knapsack mit der Maingau-Gruppe und die Zukunft der Behring-Werke," 18 May 1951, in *Dokumente* 50, Teil 2, pp. 154–9.

52 Farbwerke Hoechst A.G., *Geschäftsbericht 1952*, pp. 11–18.

53 Farbwerke Hoechst A.G., *Geschäftsbericht 1959*, p. 19.

down so that the number of carbon atoms in each hydrocarbon molecule became smaller) using the arc process to make acetylene, the starting material for the Hüls plant's four-stage process for producing synthetic rubber. Hydrogen was a by-product of that process for making acetylene, and the factory sent some of it to the hydrogenation plants.[54]

The technical interdependence (*Verbundwirtschaft*) between the synthetic-rubber factory and the hydrogenation plants was reflected in property relationships: I.G. Farben owned 74 percent of Chemische Werke Hüls's share capital, and the Prussian state's Bergwerksgesellschaft Hibernia (Hibernia Mining Company) owned 26 percent; the I.G. and the Prussian state also co-owned the Scholven hydrogenation plant. Gelsenberg Benzin, the largest of the West German hydrogenation plants, was originally part of the coal-mining property of the Vereinigte Stahlwerke, a major coal and steel conglomerate, and licensed its technology from the I.G.[55]

At the end of World War II, Hüls, as a partly owned subsidiary of I.G. Farben, was subject to the same controls as its parent firm. Practically from the beginning of the occupation it was clear that Hüls would be separated from the I.G.'s successors. That was important for several reasons, the foremost being that Hüls relied on I.G. patents for most of its processes. It was also important that the main research laboratory for synthetic rubber was located – and would remain – at Leverkusen. At first, however, production was largely unaffected. Because of the pressing needs of the German economy, British occupation authorities had allowed resumption of Buna production on 16 June 1945; by the end of 1945, the plant also had permission to manufacture a variety of other products, including solvents, cleaning materials, and technical gases.

To ensure that Hüls produced at the maximum level possible in the difficult early period of the occupation, the occupiers also retained managers who had run the factory from its beginnings. The most important was Paul Baumann. Former director of the Hüls production group within the I.G., Baumann was named works manager on 26 June 1945 and remained in that position through 1964. Other top factory managers from the I.G. period joined Baumann in forming the core of the Hüls leadership. By 1948, however, the apparent easing of the

---

[54] On the decision on the site for the Buna II (Hüls) plant, see Peter Morris, "The Development of Acetylene Chemistry and Synthetic Rubber by I.G. Farbenindustrie Aktiengesellschaft, 1926–1945" (dissertation, Oxford University, 1982), pp. 297–304; and Paul Kränzlein, *Chemie im Revier. Hüls* (Düsseldorf: Econ, 1980), pp. 32–4; for a detailed overview of technical interrelationships between Hüls and the hydrogenation plants, see Paul Baumann, "Verbundwirtschaft Chemische Werke Hüls-Ruhrbergbau," 14 June 1952, BAK, B102/442, Heft 1; on the four-stage process for producing synthetic rubber, see Morris, "The Development of Acetylene Chemistry," pp. 156–60, 199–203, and see the brief overview of acetylene chemistry in Chapter 1 of this book.

[55] Werner Abelshauser, *Der Ruhrkohlenbergbau seit 1945. Wiederaufbau, Krise, Anpassung* Munich: C. H. Beck, 1984), p. 55. On 17 June 1953, as part of the breakup of the Vereinigte Stahlwerke, Gelsenkirchener Bergwerks A.G. (GBAG), a holding company, was formed. Gelsenberg Benzin was one of its subsidiaries, along with three major coal-mining companies and Raab-Karcher GmbH, a coal-trading company.

European economic situation and the clear beginning of German reconstruction finally allowed the Allies to implement parts of the 1945 Potsdam agreements on prohibited and limited industries. For Hüls, on 30 June 1948, that meant a ban on production of synthetic rubber, the firm's main product.[56]

Although the factory was able to reorient its manufacturing program to make up for some of the losses that resulted from the shutdown of synthetic rubber – mainly by using acetylene for increased production of certain solvents in the middle- and high-boiling-point range, such as "butanol, butyl acetate, and the softening agent 'Vestinol','' and manufacturing more antifreeze and pure alcohol – it was necessary for Hüls to consider moving aggressively into new product lines, especially production of plastics. The latter area, given the growing demand and the firm's experience with polymerization, looked especially promising.[57] Despite such moves, as noted earlier, the Allied experts who recommended in the summer of 1950 that Hüls be formed as an independent successor concluded that its chances were somewhat shaky without the synthetic-rubber production line.[58] The impact of the Korean War on the European political economy changed everything: By April 1951, the Allies had lifted the prohibition of synthetic rubber and gradually loosened restrictions on synthetic-rubber production. Hüls resumed manufacture of its most important product on 29 November 1951.[59]

When the Allies and the Germans agreed in late 1951 and early 1952 to found the major successors of I.G. Farben, the precise status of Hüls was one of the issues left unresolved; the I.G.'s holdings in the factory were left in the hands of I.G. Farbenindustrie A.G. in Liquidation (I.G. Farben i.L.). That was because, even after the resolution, in April 1951, of the question whether or not the firm would be able to produce synthetic rubber, a number of other issues remained outstanding, including who would own the firm and in what proportions. The panel of German experts composing the I.G. Farben Dispersal Panel (FARDIP) outlined some of the outstanding questions in February 1951. FARDIP held that "the Hüls works, after separation from the I.G. concern, can be competitive and capable of survival as an independent company only under certain preconditions." The preconditions were as follows: (1) Hüls would gain property rights to its grounds from I.G. Farben and to a power plant that had been leased from STEAG (a power company owned by Ruhr coal interests[60]); (2) Ruhr coal companies would be willing to guarantee the firm's raw-materials supply; (3) all patent and trademark rights belonging to the I.G. that Hüls had used in its own

[56] Kränzlein, *Chemie im Revier,* pp. 45–67.   [57] Ibid., pp. 67–72.

[58] "Report of the Tripartite Investigation Team," pp. 24–5, PRO, FO371/85684. The experts were very concerned with Hüls's position if Allied prohibitions on production of synthetic rubber remained in force, because the new firm would have to enter new and often untried fields of polymer chemistry. Production controls were lifted in late 1951, improving the firm's chances of survival, but the experts were concerned about the fate of the new firm even in that case.

[59] Kränzlein, *Chemie im Revier,* pp. 89–92.

[60] John R. Gillingham, *Industry and Politics in the Third Reich: Ruhr Coal, Hitler, and Europe* (New York: Columbia University Press, 1985), p. 69.

production and sales program would be licensed to the firm; and (4) Hüls would become a joint-stock company (Aktiengesellschaft, or A.G.), instead of a limited-liability company (Gesellschaft mit beschrankter Haftung, or GmbH). Former I.G. shareholders would receive their proportion (i.e., 74 percent) of the new stock issued.[61]

The patent issue probably was the most important matter, because virtually the entire production program of Hüls depended on patents, processes, and experience that had been made available freely and without cost to the factory during the I.G. period.[62] Apparently the issue was also relatively easy to resolve: Baumann and the managers of the bigger successors simply met personally to discuss it. In early May 1952, for instance, Baumann reported that

we have already had the opportunity to conduct talks with the gentlemen of Badischen Anilin- & Soda-Fabrik, Ludwigshafen, which has been allocated the majority of the patents utilized in our factory. These talks resulted in an agreement between Badische Anilin- & Soda-Fabrik and the Chemische Werke Hüls which clears away all questions that came up during the "patent breakup" [*Patententflechtung*].[63]

BASF's attitude did not result from simple generosity. In return for those concessions and similar ones from Bayer (the other important holder of the patents in question), Baumann also went on record to assure BASF and Bayer that Hüls would stay out of some their most lucrative production areas. In June 1952 he wrote that

The Chemische Werke Hüls does not foresee becoming involved in the current production areas of the [original I.G.] works groups [*Stammwerke*], including production of synthetic nitrogen and its derivatives, of dyes and their intermediates, of pharmaceuticals and their intermediates, of photographic supplies, and in the area of recent Reppe chemistry, such as ethylinization chemistry.[64]

It was 16 December 1953 before the other questions were settled and the Chemische Werke Hüls A.G. was founded. A glance at Figure 3.1, which depicts the complicated ownership of the new joint-stock company, gives an indication of why it took so long: In order to meet the preconditions for the firm's competitiveness recommended by FARDIP, a number of other companies had to receive a stake in Hüls. Those included STEAG, Ruhrgas, and Gelsenberg Benzin, which combined their interests into another company, the Kohleverwertungs GmbH. Shares for the newcomers came primarily out of the old I.G. holdings. I.G. Farben i.L. sold about one-third of its share in Hüls GmbH (24 percent of the total capital of the factory) to them in order to break the logjam surrounding

---

[61] Kränzlein, *Chemie im Revier*, pp. 96–109; quotation, p. 99.
[62] This point is made forcefully by Fritz ter Meer, who contended *"dass Hüls trotz der nur 74 %igen Beteiligung der I.G. praktisch wie ein reines I.G.-Werk behandelt wurde,"* in "Chemische Werke Hüls GmbH, Stellungnahme zur Patententflechtung," 23 February 1953, BAK, B102/411; quotation, p. 2, his emphasis.
[63] Paul Baumann to H. von Rospatt, 6 May 1952, BAK, B102/411.
[64] Paul Baumann, "Produktionsprogramm der Chemischen Werke Hüls," 13 June 1952, BAK, B102/442, Heft 1; quotation, p. 4.

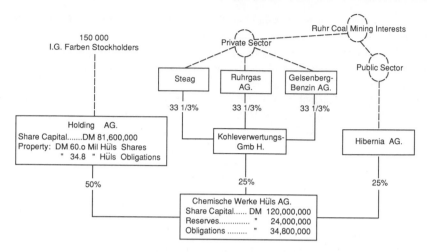

Figure 3.1. The Allied plan from 1953 for the breakup of Chemische Werke Hüls. (From S. E. Disney to W. A. Acton, "Subject: Reorganization of Hüls," 30 November 1953, U.S. National Archives, Washington National Records Center, Suitland, MD, Record Group 466, High Commissioner for Germany, Office of the General Counsel, Decartelization and Deconcentration Division, Cartel Subject Files, 1947–1955, Farben, I.G., Box 21.)

the negotiations; Hibernia sold one twenty-sixth of its share (1 percent of the total) to the newcomers for the same reason. Proceeds from the sale increased the value of I.G. Farben i.L. for former I.G. stockholders, and they also gained, through "Hüls Holding," 50 percent of the stock in the new company.[65]

Allied, and especially American, decartelization officials were wary of that arrangement. As U.S. Decartelization Division member S. E. Disney wrote on 30 November 1953, just before Hüls A.G. officially came into existence, "rumors have it that the Big Three (BASF, Bayer, and Hoechst) have requested the Federal Government to exert its influence in favor of a distribution of the present Farben participation in the Chemische Werke Hüls GmbH (74%) to the Big Three in equal proportions."[66] Because the Big Three did not directly control the old I.G. holdings in Hüls (I.G. Farben i.L. did), Disney's fears were not realized in any direct sense. Still, his suspicions were justified to some extent by subsequent events, as detailed in Chapter 8 and outlined only briefly here. In order to remain competitive in synthetic rubber, Hüls needed to develop new technologies, especially those for producing "cold rubber." They purchased catalyst and other technology from U.S. firms, but needed capital and know-how

[65] Kränzlein, *Chemie im Revier,* pp. 102–9; S. E. Disney to W. A. Acton, "Reorganization of Hüls," 30 November 1953, NA, RG 466, HICOG, Office of General Counsel, Decartelization and Deconcentration Division, Cartel Subject Files, 1947–1955, Farben, I.G., Box 21: Chemische Werke Hüls.

[66] S. E. Disney to W. A. Acton, "Reorganization of Hüls," 30 November 1953, NA, RG 466, HICOG, Office of General Counsel, Decartelization and Deconcentration Division, Cartel Subject Files, 1947–1955, Farben, I.G., Box 21: Chemische Werke Hüls.

from the Big Three in order to implement their plans. Thus, the limited-liability company founded on 1 June 1955 to pursue the cold-rubber project, Bunawerke Hüls GmbH, featured a 50 percent participation by Hüls A.G. and participations of $16\frac{2}{3}$ percent each by BASF, Bayer, and Hoechst.[67] Technical and personal connections between the old components of I.G. Farben proved resilient in the face of Allied attempts to break them.

With the founding of the Chemische Werke Hüls A.G. in December 1953, the basic organizational framework for the West German organic chemical industry in the postwar period was completed. The three major successors, BASF, Bayer, and Hoechst, dominated the industry in terms of sales, although other former I.G. companies, such as Hüls, were also important. Those firms also held commanding positions in West Germany in the development of chemical technology, and they were already in the process of enhancing their technological capability to reach world-class standards. Each of the decisions detailed here – the final dispositions of Dormagen and Agfa, of Auguste Victoria, of Knapsack, and of Hüls – would have an impact on technological development by each of the major successors. Those impacts will be examined further in the case studies in Part III. But there were also other matters that needed to be attended to, including, first, the re-establishment of close working relationships with the chemical industry outside of Europe and, second, reconstruction of their research establishments and removal of Allied production controls. The former is the subject of the next chapter, the latter the next section.

Controlling and rebuilding research and production in the chemical industry

Since its origins in the 1860s and 1870s, modern organic production has been a research-intensive industry; to gain a foothold in the dye trade, German firms pioneered in "the industrialization of invention" by founding the first modern industrial laboratories. That traditional emphasis on research and technological development as means to growth continued as the industry changed still further in the first half of the twentieth century. As profits on dye sales began to tail off by about the beginning of World War I, German firms invested heavily in research and development of new technologies, including, in turn, the processes for synthesizing nitrogen, petroleum, and rubber, the profits from which would finance research and development of the next product cycle for the industry.[68]

---

[67] Kränzlein, *Chemie im Revier,* pp. 122–6.
[68] Georg Meyer-Thurow, "The Industrialization of Invention: A Case Study from the German Chemical Industry," *Isis* 73(1982):363–81; Peter Hayes, *Industry and Ideology: I.G. Farben in the Nazi Era* (Cambridge University Press, 1987), pp. 2–5, 46–7; Alan Beyerchen, "On the Stimulation of Excellence in Wilhelmian Science," in Jack R. Dukes and Joachim Remak, eds., *Another Germany: A Reconsideration of the Imperial Era* (Boulder: Westview Press, 1988), pp. 150–1.

In the 1950s and 1960s, with practically insatiable consumer and industrial demand for chemicals, and faced with rapid technological change and production growth on all fronts, especially in the area of plastics, research became even more important.[69]

Germany's long-standing status and record of success in the chemical industry were thus in part functions of the commitment of individual firms to basic research, especially the firms discussed in this study. The products of those efforts were remarkable, ranging from the palette of dyes and a broad variety of pharmaceuticals in the late nineteenth and early twentieth centuries to high-pressure chemistry and new techniques for synthesis in the first decades of this century. During World War II, German chemistry was one of the few areas, besides rocket technology, to score major technological advances.[70] Still, it is not surprising that shortly after 1945, German chemical industrialists perceived their industry to be behind their American and British counterparts in technological developments, especially in exploiting the new possibilities of plastics and other products manufactured from petrochemical feedstocks.[71]

Isolation from international transfers of scientific and technical information during most of the National Socialist period accounted for some of that technological lag. But it also reflected a long-term problem that affected all German science and technology after 1945: For much of the twentieth century, for economic and political reasons, German scientists and engineers had placed more emphasis on applied research than on basic research. That relative neglect of basic research began in 1914, with the outbreak of World War I, and continued, with some brief periods of respite, through that war (1914–18), the ensuing inflation period (1914–24), the Great Depression (1929–33), the renewed preparations for war (1936–9), World War II (1939–45), and the occupation (1945–9).[72]

The initial occupation policies placed severe, if understandable, restrictions on German research. Motivated primarily by the belief that Germany's scientific and technological expertise had contributed substantially to its ability to make war, each of the Allies restricted the kinds of projects that German scientists and engineers could undertake. Furthermore, all four occupying powers agreed on

---

[69] See, for instance, Gilbert Burck, "Chemicals: The Reluctant Competitors," *Fortune* 68(1963): 148, 152.

[70] Thomas Stamm, *Zwischen Staat und Selbstverwaltung. Die deutsche Forschung im Wiederaufbau 1945–1965* (Cologne: Verlag Wissenschaft und Politik, 1981), p. 40. He singles out developments in Buna rubber and synthetic fuels.

[71] Dr. Reitz, "Neuere amerikanische Arbeiten über Erdölchemie," paper presented at the BASF Wissenschaftliche Aussprache, 4. Sitzung, on 11 December 1946, BASF Unternehmensarchiv, Ludwigshafen (hereafter, BASF), F9/66. For a similar sentiment, expressed even later, see Alfred von Nagel, "Einflüsse der deutschen Chemieproduktion auf den Weltmarkt," *Chemische Industrie* 4(1952):187.

[72] Alan Beyerchen, "Trends in the Twentieth-Century German Research Enterprise," in *The Academic Research Enterprise within the Industrialized Nations: Comparative Perspectives* (Washington, DC: National Academy Press, 1990), pp. 83–4.

29 April 1946 to Allied Control Council (ACC) Law 25 on control of German research.[73] The Allied restrictions on research affected the chemical industry directly by outlawing war-related research and limiting other types of research.

Despite ACC Law 25 and earlier restrictions, however, German chemical firms engaged in some research practically from the beginning of the occupation. One reason was the desperate situation of the European economy: It demanded new products, as well as modifications of old products, to prevent further economic and political deterioration (e.g., pesticides, photographic film and chemicals to aid the occupiers in controlling the population, medicines, chlorine, artificial sweeteners), and then for reconstruction (fertilizer, pesticides and herbicides, various plastics, and chemical products for other industries). Kurt Hansen (Figure 3.2), who later became chairman of the managing board of Bayer, for instance, was given the task in the early occupation period of finding a new means of diluting the strength of the Bayer pesticide E 605, because farmers could not use it full strength. The powder previously used to thin the agent was no longer available, and the material previously used to make it water-soluble was in short supply. As a result of his efforts, Bayer's Elberfeld plant began producing water-soluble E 605 in 1947.[74]

Allied restrictions in the area of production constituted an even more pressing reason for chemical firms to resume research as quickly as possible. Faced with the prospect of not being allowed to manufacture some of their most profitable product lines, firms scrambled to come up with new products that would not be subject to Allied restrictions. For instance, Hüls researchers, when faced with a ban on production of synthetic rubber, found that if they combined 30 parts butadiene with 70 parts styrene (the proportions would be reversed for synthetic rubber), they could produce a new material. Hüls's new "product 1073," nicknamed "upside-down Buna," was unsuitable for use in tires, and therefore its production would not conflict with Allied policy restrictions. However, the new material was extremely useful in a variety of applications important to the recovering German economy: It was used in the linoleum industry, it was used to make natural rubber more durable, and it was used as a waterproofing additive to paints.[75] Hüls also converted other parts of its factory to other uses as a result of Allied policy, "including seventy per cent of the aldol section, four of the butadiene ovens and five of the eight batteries in the co-polymerisation section." As a direct result of the prohibition of synthetic-rubber manufacture,

[73] Alan Beyerchen, "German Scientists and Research Institutions in Allied Occupation Policy," *History of Education Quarterly* 22(1982):289–99.

[74] Interview with Kurt Hansen, Bayerwerk, Leverkusen, 4 December 1984; Erik Verg, *Meilensteine* (Leverkusen: Bayer A.G., 1988), p. 307. Material on Hoechst's research efforts in the early occupation period is summarized in Stokes, *Divide and Prosper*, p. 62. BASF reported by 1953 that despite the difficult circumstances of the immediate postwar years, "schon wieder 2000 Anmeldungen beim Deutschen Patentamt eingereicht werden konnten," indicating an active research program. See BASF, *Bericht über die Neugründung 1952–1953* (Ludwigshafen: BASF, n.d.), p. 34.

[75] Kränzlein, *Chemie im Revier*, pp. 70–2.

Figure 3.2. Kurt Hansen, member of the managing board, Bayer A.G. (Courtesy Bayer Firmenarchiv, Leverkusen.)

the company "busily engaged in expanding its production of solvents and polymers."[76]

Whether conducted to find new products or processes that would meet pressing needs in the occupation period or to find substitute production areas, owing to Allied restrictions, those research efforts required the approval of and registration with military-government research-control officers, who made certain that they complied with Allied policies. As Allied policy toward Germany changed with the intensification of the Cold War, some loosening of restrictions was to be expected, and, indeed, in practice that did happen, if only because of the smaller number of occupation personnel to supervise German compliance with Allied policy. Still, western Germany's increasing voice in the control of its internal affairs during 1948 and 1949 did not translate immediately into a lifting of restrictions; in fact, the increasing German activity made some, most notably

[76] J. E. G. Harris (Chemical Industry Section, British HICOG) to A. H. Lincoln (Foreign Office, German Section), 29 September 1950, PRO, FO1013/1522.

the French, quite nervous. Thus, primarily for the purpose of preventing German aggression in the future, the Allies decided to maintain some control over scientific and technological research, as well as other key areas that might affect Germany's ability to wage war. However, the original severity of the policy was toned down to some extent, and the organization was altered in anticipation of the creation of the new West German state.

The three Western Allies moved in that direction with the establishment of a Military Security Board (MSB) on 17 January 1949. The military governors, who had approved that measure on 16 December 1948, created the MSB specifically ''to ensure the maintenance of disarmament and demilitarization in the interests of security.'' Headed by committees for oversight and administration, the MSB contained three functional divisions: Military, Industrial, and Scientific Research. Members of the divisions were responsible for inspection (to ensure compliance with Allied policy), as well as for making policy recommendations.[77]

The first task of the MSB Scientific Research Division was to come up with a replacement for ACC Law 25, and they submitted recommendations to the three military governors for approval on 9 July 1949. A closer look at the division's recommendations is worthwhile. Prohibition of war research continued to be one element of its control program, as did special attention to certain research areas. Those included ''chemical warfare; bacterial warfare; radar, guided missiles and similar subjects; nuclear physics.'' So far, there were no surprises, and very little had changed from earlier policy. But the recommendations went much further and demonstrated even more clearly the continuity with earlier policies. The division wished ''to establish and enforce a new notification and reporting procedure which although less onerous than the former procedure nevertheless will ensure maintenance of security requirements covering *all* German research.'' In explaining their recommendations, members of the division stressed that a broad program of monitoring all German research ''is the really important one,'' because ''the importance of our control lies not in the research leading to the known war-winning weapons, but rather in the watching of the whole of German research,'' in order to prevent Germany from building up its ''potential for the *next* war (not the *last* war).''[78]

The same spirit pervaded the more general AHC Law 24, authorizing ''control of certain articles, products, installations, and equipment,'' as agreed to by the military governors of the three Western occupation powers on 14 April 1949.[79] Specific policy measures on the chemical industry under AHC Law 24 came in the form of ''Regulation 8 under Law 24'' of 25 May 1950, which re-

[77] ''Directive on Organization of the Military Security Board (Note by the Secretariat),'' 17 January 1949, TRIB/P(48)17 (final), PRO, FO1074/106.
[78] Note by Tripartite Secretariat, ''Control of Scientific Research,'' 9 July 1949 [TRIB/P(49)53], NA, RG 466, McCloy Papers, Historical Analyses of the McCloy Administration, Box 1, D(49)96.
[79] F. Frowein, ''Produktionsverbote und -einschränkugen in der chemischen Industrie,'' *Chemische Industrie* 3(1951):116–18.

stricted the production and the installed capacity to produce chlorine, ammonia, styrene, butadiene, and Buna rubber, among other things.[80]

Naturally, the West Germans were not happy with that state of affairs, and given their increasing economic and political clout within Europe, in part as a result of the outbreak of the Korean War in June 1950, they were able to do something about it. The Chemicals Section of the German Ministry of Economics informed Economics Minister Ludwig Erhard in August that Hüls, BASF, and Bayer wished the AHC to remove production prohibitions on synthetic rubber, butadiene, and other materials.[81] By December, Chancellor Konrad Adenauer was pressing the Allies not only to remove such prohibitions but also to remove any limits on the production of chemicals. In and of itself that was not surprising, nor anything new: Using old arguments, for instance, he suggested that restrictions on chlorine and ammonia capacity should be lifted because they did not affect Allied security concerns. However, Adenauer's justifications for certain other requests completely disregarded security issues: He suggested that lifting restrictions on Bergius hydrogenation capacity would save foreign exchange; he claimed that white phosphorus, styrene, Buna, and butadiene were sorely needed in Germany, but were in short supply.[82] He was arguing that West Germany's economic well-being should be the primary criterion for determining Allied policy, not security concerns.

The Allies agreed, for the most part, with the German chancellor, largely as a direct result of the changing power relationships in Europe. In September 1950, the U.S., British, and French foreign ministers had agreed to review their restrictive policies "in the light of the developing relationship with the Federal Republic."[83] On 3 April 1951, the Western Allies removed prohibitions on a number of production areas, including synthetic fuel and rubber, and loosened restrictions over a number of others. Some restrictions remained in place, including those affecting the levels of synthetic-rubber production.

Clearly, however, the Allies' ability to control what the Germans were doing had already been severely eroded. MSB inspectors who visited BASF's Ludwigshafen plant on 6 June 1951, for example, found that "the B.A.S.F. has reinstalled three vessels for the polymerization of Buna, and had started to reinstall five others in the building where they were previously installed, without licence from the Military Security Board." Under AHC regulations, Buna production was prohibited, the inspectors' report continued (apparently they had not yet

---

[80] AHC, "Regulation No. 8 (chemical articles, products, installations, and equipment) under Law No. 24: Control of certain articles, products, installations, and equipment," 25 May 1950 [GEN/ P(50)20B], PRO, FO1074/14.

[81] Bundeswirtschaftsministerium (BWM), Abteilung IV, Vermerk für den Herrn Minister über den Herrn Staatssekretär, "Betrifft: Antragstellung auf Genehmigung zur Wiederaufnahme der nach Militärgesetz Nr. 24 verbotenen Produktion von synthetischem Kautschuk, Butadien u.ä. Stoffen," 29 August 1950 (marked "hat dem Minister vorgelegen"), BAK, B102/9238, Heft 2.

[82] Allied High Commission for Germany, Allied General Secretariat to chairman, MSB, "Subject: Revision of the Prohibited and Limited Industries Agreement," 30 December 1950 [AGSEC(50)2888], PRO, FO1013/1521.

[83] Ibid.

been informed of the decision to allow it again). But, they went on, BASF claimed "that it is intended to convert these vessels for other production not covered by Law No. 24 (butanetriol, polystyrol, etc.)." Because such conversion could be allowed only by MSB order, "you are requested to instruct the B.A.S.F. to suspend the work in hand as the Military Security Board has not approved these proposals for conversion, which the B.A.S.F. should submit in accordance with the terms of Directive No. 16."[84]

It was no accident that the loosening of restrictions and the more limited ability to enforce them coincided with the intensification of the Cold War, especially after the outbreak of war in Korea in 1950. By late 1952, Allied controls over German production had become less effective, and controls over research even less so. All restrictions were formally lifted in 1955.[85] What were the long-term effects of such controls? It is not clear to what extent Allied restrictions on German research and development functioned as a factor in technological choice for the chemical industry or any other industry in the postwar period. Certainly, however, anecdotal evidence makes it clear that some unintended consequences followed from the controls on research and production: They sometimes stimulated German industrial researchers to develop new products and new uses for old ones. Thus, the long-term economic and technological effects of such controls were mixed. In some ways, the restrictions hampered reconstruction; in others, they helped foster it.

The changing world energy order

Changes in the political economy of worldwide energy production and consumption also altered the context of technological choice for chemical industrialists in post-1945 Germany. Prewar Germany had used coal to supply approximately 90 percent of its energy needs, with petroleum accounting for only about 3 percent.[86] The feedstock structure of the pre-1945 German chemical industry had also been heavily oriented toward coal, although some small plants employed alcohol, natural gas, or even petroleum feedstocks.

In the aftermath of German defeat, that situation changed only gradually. The war itself had played some role in that: Bombing damage, lack of proper maintenance during the National Socialist period, and severe debilitation of the working population in the mines because of hunger and disease had contributed to inadequate coal production in the years immediately after 1945.[87]

[84] J. P. Guede (duty chief secretary, MSB) to land commissioner, Land Rhine Palatinate, "Irregularities under Regulation no. 8 to AHC Law No. 24 by the Badische Anilin- und Soda-Fabrik Ludwigshafen/Rhein," 21 June 1951 (translation), PRO, FO1074/14.

[85] Generally, on postwar German research, see Stamm, *Zwischen Staat und Selbstverwaltung;* Beyerchen, "Trends in the Twentieth-Century German Research Enterprise," pp. 84–7.

[86] Ferdinand Friedensburg, *Die Rohstoffe und Energiequellen im neuen Europa* (Oldenburg/Berlin: G. Stalling, 1943), p. 299.

[87] Abelshauser, *Der Ruhrkohlenbergbau seit 1945*, pp. 15–49. For a more recent assessment, in English, of German coal after the war, see Mark Roseman, *Recasting the Ruhr, 1945–1958: Manpower, Economic Recovery and Labour Relations* (New York: Berg, 1992). For a broader treat-

But even when the industry began to recover in the late 1940s, it was clear that German, British, and other European outputs of coal would not cover the energy needs of Europe. Imports could have been one alternative, from the United States or Poland. U.S. coal, however, was priced in dollars, which were in short supply in the late 1940s and early 1950s in Europe; shipping it would also be expensive. Polish coal was plentiful and cheap, but that would have involved western European dependence on a Communist country for a crucial raw material. In the context of the intensification of the Cold War, that was not a viable option. Instead, in the summer of 1947 the coal group of the Committee for European Economic Cooperation stated that "Europe's energy requirements must be met by 'the expansion of hydroelectric capacity and the increased use of petroleum products'."[88]

Although the increased production and energy utilization that followed the beginning of the Korean War underscored once again the limits of depending on coal and resulted in an energy crisis in 1950–1,[89] by the first years of the 1950s Europe's energy structure had changed very little. European countries used petroleum for 15 percent of their energy needs in 1951, up from just under 10 percent in 1938. A number of factors accounted for the slow transition. For one thing, at the end of April 1946, U.S. price controls on petroleum were lifted, resulting in a doubling of oil prices (from $1.32 to $2.68 per barrel by 1947). In addition, Europe's dollar shortage impeded purchase of oil, much of which was priced in dollars. There was also a shortage of refinery capacity in Europe. Finally, the Soviets always posed a threat to the Middle East, the major source of Europe's petroleum supplies.[90]

In large part because of the aid received through the European Recovery Program (the Marshall Plan), however, the basis had been laid during the period 1947–51 for more radical change: "an infrastructure of refineries and industrial boilers was emplaced that permitted increasing use of liquid fuel throughout the 1950s. At the same time, U.S. policies encouraged the development of Middle East concessions by its national companies."[91] The new infrastructure allowed expanded use of oil, and by 1955 petroleum accounted for more than 20 percent of Europe's energy consumption. By 1959, the figure had risen to 30 percent; by 1962, to 39 percent; and, by 1964, to 45 percent of total energy consumption.[92]

---

ment of German heavy industry in the context of postwar European politics, see John Gillingham, *Coal, Steel, and the Rebirth of Europe, 1945–1955* (Cambridge University Press, 1991).

[88] Ethan Kapstein, *The Insecure Alliance: Energy Crises and Western Politics since 1944* (Oxford University Press, 1990), pp. 51–2. For a general overview of American oil diplomacy in the postwar period that also covers the role of the Marshall Plan, see David Painter, *Oil and the American Century* (Baltimore: John Hopkins University Press, 1986). For a comparison of U.S. coal and oil policies in postwar Germany, See Raymond G. Stokes, "German Energy in the U.S. Postwar Economic Order, 1945–1951," *Journal of European Economic History* 17(1988):621–39.

[89] Werner Abelshauser, "Korea, die Ruhr und Erhards Marktwirtschaft. Die Energiekrise von 1950–51," *Rheinische Vierteljahrsblätter* 45(1981):287–316.

[90] Kapstein, *The Insecure Alliance,* pp. 60, 63–4.

[91] Ibid., p. 60.   [92] Ibid., pp. 105, 131.

Even in the mid-1950s the dangers inherent in that transition had become evident: 90 percent of Europe's energy supplies came from the Middle East, an extremely volatile region, and 70 percent of Middle Eastern oil shipped to Europe passed through the Suez Canal. Thus, when the Egyptian leader Gamal Abdal Nasser nationalized the canal in late July 1956, in order to gain funding for his Aswan Dam project, Europeans became nervous. In the fall of 1956, the British and the French, aided by the Israelis, decided to take the Suez Canal back by force. Taking advantage of the Soviet preoccupation with Hungary, which had been invaded in 24 October, Israeli troops, supported by French supply airlifts, moved into Egypt on 29 October. The United States did not support that action, which intensified in the following days. In response to the attack, Egypt scuttled ships in the canal on 2 and 3 November; on 4 November, explosions disrupted the flow of petroleum through the Iraq Petroleum Company's pipeline through Syria. Europe was faced with a massive oil shortage.[93]

Having provoked the Egyptians to the extreme action of closing the canal, the British and French decided to use force to reopen it. Their troops invaded the canal zone on 5 November, but faced with Soviet threats and pressure from the Americans, they called off the invasion the following day. The American action was especially important: President Dwight Eisenhower's refusal to activate emergency planning mechanisms that would make up for shortfalls in European oil with supplies from the Western Hemisphere, coupled with the rerouting of tankers around the tip of Africa, forced the Europeans to submit to American wishes. When they did, emergency supply operations began, with the United States and, to a greater extent, Venezuela supplying large quantities of petroleum to Europe. Shipowners also diverted more tankers to the Persian Gulf to try to offset the effects of the longer trip to Europe. As a result, "by the spring [1957] Europe was able to maintain pre-Suez consumption levels, if not exceed them." By May 1957, the canal and the pipeline had reopened.[94]

This brief overview of changes in the world energy economy during the period 1945–57 demonstrates the centrality of U.S. policy objectives in shaping European energy-consumption patterns.[95] This is not to say that the interests of American oil companies determined what happened in Europe. Rather, Europe's shift from coal to oil and, in particular, toward reliance on Middle East oil in the late 1940s and 1950s resulted from a complex interplay among U.S. government policy, American private interests, and global resource and economic constraints. From the outset, U.S. policy encouraged Europeans to integrate economically, a matter that became more pressing with the onset of the Cold War. The Cold War made West Germany's inclusion in the Western world order necessary and prompted a shift in occupation policy toward again encouraging industrial output, which required increased energy supplies. Given that West

---

[93] Ibid., pp. 103–15.　　[94] Ibid., pp. 115–24; quotation, p. 119.

[95] For more on this subject, see Painter, *Oil and the American Century*, and, more specifically, Painter, "Oil and the Marshall Plan," *Business History Review* 58(1984):359–83; on Germany, in particular, and on the connection between coal policy and oil policy, see Stokes, "German Energy in the U.S. Postwar Economic Order," pp. 621–39.

Germany and Britain did not produce enough coal and that supplies from the United States and Poland were, for different reasons, not feasible options, policymakers encouraged reliance on petroleum. U.S. firms already had a large presence in the oil industry, and their government supported them in expanding their holdings in the Middle East, which, because of the domestic-energy security concerns of the United States, would have to take the place of the Western Hemisphere as the primary supplier of petroleum products worldwide. That would ensure that Europe would have enough energy; at the same time, Germany, in particular, would have to become more reliant on foreign energy sources, controlled, at least in part, by U.S. firms.

Despite the complexity of this account of the interaction among government policy, private interest, and resource constraints, it still leads to an oversimplified version of events: It leaves out internal developments in the countries affected. For West Germany, in particular, internal political discussions and policy-making during that same period indicated that acceptance of new energy order was slow in coming. For a number of reasons, the West German government continued its restrictive policies on oil imports, pursuing policies designed to give preference to the use of domestic coal, rather than oil. Attempts by the chemical industry to gain tax and tariff concessions for the oil used in petrochemical processes provoked a discussion that illuminates the resistance to change in energy and raw-materials sources.

As noted earlier, the German chemical industry in the late 1940s relied overwhelmingly on coal as a feedstock. Two developments in the immediate postwar period prompted German chemical firms to move into the new area of petroleum chemistry. The first was the rising price of coal,[96] and the second was competition from abroad, especially from the United States.

As a result of Allied price controls and the Allies' desire to supply the European economy with relatively inexpensive coal, German coal prices remained at their prewar level of RM 10.50 per ton into 1948, despite rising labor costs and other costs at the mines. On the eve of the currency reform of June 1948, that figure rose to RM 25, and Ludwig Erhard found it necessary to raise the price again to DM 32.50 shortly after the currency reform on 1 August 1948. In other words, the nominal price of coal tripled within eight months, and given the currency reform, the real price increase was many times that. Even so, the coal industry continued to lose an average of DM 3.44 per ton of coal sold, a situation that was rectified only by further increases totaling more than 50 percent by 1955. When the authorities of the European Coal and Steel Community allowed Ruhr coal interests to set prices freely as of 1 April 1956, further steep increases were in order. Ruhr coal prices increased an average of 7–8 percent per year in the late 1950s and early 1960s. At the same time, the price of heavy

[96] Two representatives of Bayer (Holzrichter and Casper) made this point explicitly in their letter to the federal Ministry of Economics (to Dr. Lenz in the Chemicals Section), "Betr.: Entwicklung der Erdölchemie bei Farbenfabriken Bayer," 22 July 1955, BAK, B102/36054.

heating oil, one of coal's major competitors, declined sharply from DM 142 per ton in 1956 to DM 60 in 1960, at least in part because Erhard lifted the duty of DM 15 per ton on imported heating oil.[97]

Competition from their counterparts abroad was also a factor in the decision of German industrialists to enter new areas of chemical technology. U.S. chemical producers, who utilized petrochemical feedstocks extensively, were especially threatening to the Germans. One commentary in the spring of 1950 from the North Rhine–Westphalian Ministry of Economics, for instance, noted that the price of acetone in West Germany – produced from coal via acetylene – was twice as high as the price of that produced in the United States from oil via propylene. The report went on to point to "a large class" of solvents "which U.S. producers offer on the world market at prices so low that competition is not possible."[98]

Despite pressure from rising coal prices and devastating competition, however, chemical industrialists in West Germany did not move wholesale or wholeheartedly into petrochemical production in the early 1950s. Some specific reasons for that in particular firms will be explored in later chapters, but two developments of a more general nature were important: First, many chemical producers were content to pursue, at least in the short term, a policy of seeking government protection from foreign competition. In the short run they were successful, attaining tariff rates of more than 25 percent, and in some cases more than 35 percent for the products of acetylene, such as acetone. High tariff rates were justified explicitly on the basis of foreign competition, because in comparison with Germany's acetylene chemistry, "[foreign] ethylene chemistry enjoys a great advantage technically and economically since ethylene and other olefins result cheaply from petroleum refining according to a rather simple process."[99] Of course, even such high rates could not protect the market for German acetone production from American encroachment; even with a tariff of more than 35 percent, the American product was less expensive. But the rates did protect a number of other products of acetylene chemistry.

Second, it is clear that German coal-chemical producers hoped to expand further into the business of supplying feedstocks for the organic chemical industry. Once again, the tariffs provided an indication of that, and a later chapter will deal more fully with the arguments of the Fischer-Tropsch producers. But even the North Rhine–Westphalian report, which came down strongly in favor of moving into petroleum-chemical production, recognized that as well, although it

---

[97] Abelshauser, *Der Ruhrkohlenbergbau seit 1945*, pp. 65, 79, 80–7. Abelshauser sees a rapid "Wende am Energiemarkt" from coal to oil starting in 1958 (p. 87), which precipitated a crisis in the coal industry that lasted for the next ten years (pp. 87–117).

[98] Der Wirtschaftsminister des Landes Nordrhein-Westfalen III/5, "Zur Frage der Entwicklung einer deutschen Mineralölchemie," 31 March 1950, BAK, B102/513, Heft 2.

[99] Ibid.; "Auszug aus der Begründung zum Entwurf eines Zolltarifgesetzes, Kapitel 29, organische chemische Erzeugnisse," n.d. (ca. early 1950), BAK, B102/1462, Heft 1; quotation from "Auszug."

suggested that solvent manufacturers that produced on the basis of carbide at least consider carefully "whether it might be more advisable only to cultivate such production to which ethylene chemistry can present no competition."[100]

The tariff policy affecting the West German chemical industry thus resulted from a patchwork of competing and sometimes contradictory interests. Some firms wished to move forward with petrochemical production, whereas others did not. All, however, shared an aversion to rapid adoption of the new feedstock and its associated technologies. The same confusion of motivations and conflicting interests was obvious in tariff policies regarding petroleum, in particular for the chemical industry: The government and some segments of industry wished to promote technological change and competitiveness in world markets; at the same time, the government faced the social and economic might of the coal industry and, to a lesser extent, the coal-chemical industry, which insisted on preferences, subventions, and high tariffs as means of staving off the new energy source.[101]

Tariff rates on imported petroleum were high in West Germany in the first half of the 1950s, amounting to DM 129 per ton, which when added to the base price of about DM 100 per ton more than doubled it.[102] According to the Petroleum Tax Law (Mineralölsteuergesetz) of 22 March 1939, as amended on 19 January 1951, it was possible, with some exceptions, for the chemical industry to gain special dispensation from the Customs Office so that it could use petroleum tax-free "for chemical transformation into other materials than petroleum."[103] For those companies wishing to use petroleum as a feedstock, however, that policy presented difficulties. As their representatives pointed out in a meeting with the federal minister of finance on 14 January 1953, tax-free status was granted only if a company could prove that "the tax is unbearable." In other words, the law depended upon bureaucratic interpretation. The representatives requested a strengthening of the law by having it spell out clearly the petrochemical industry's "freedom from taxation." Without such a change in the law, they con-

---

[100] Der Wirtschaftsminister des Landes Nordrhein-Westfalen III/5, "Zur Frage der Entwicklung einer deutschen Mineralölchemie," 31 March 1950, BAK, B102/513, Heft 2.

[101] Abelshauser, Der Ruhrkohlenbergbau seit 1945, pp. 118–63. Subsidies to the hard-coal industry amounted to more than DM 15 billion during the years of crisis between 1958 and 1968, of which the Ruhr received about 70% (p. 150). On 14 June 1968, the Ruhr coal industry was consolidated into the Ruhrkohle A.G., a company that was meant to rationalize and systematically trim back the industry (pp. 150ff.). Subsidies continued to be a factor, however, amounting to a total of DM 9.6 billion from the taxpayer and the consumer of electricity (the so-called Kohlepfennig was introduced in 1975) (pp. 161–3).

[102] Tariff given in "Hinweise" (Vertraulich), attachment to letter from Verband der chemischen Industrie (Wurms) to the federal Ministry of Economics (Chemieref. Dr. Lenz, Mineralölref. Dr. Boecker), "Betr. Mineralölzollbefreiung für Entwicklungsarbeiten der Erdölchemie," 22 November 1956, BAK, B102/73343; base price (and tariff also) noted in BWM, IV B (Lenz) to Bundesministerium der Finanzen (Min. Dir. Himstedt), "Zollfreie Verwendung von Mineralöl in einer Versuchsanlage bei der Farbenfabriken Bayer AG, Leverkusen," 29 November 1955, BAK, B102/36054.

[103] Mineralöl-Handelsges. Hannig & Co., Das neue Mineralölsteuergesetz (February 1951), pp. 18–19, seen in BAK, B146/1923.

tended, "no investor would find himself in the position of placing at the industry's disposal investment amounts in the several hundred million DM range if the Federal Minister of Finance had the opportunity under the law to influence [cost] calculations through the petroleum tax."[104] The lobbying efforts of the petrochemical interests, supported by the federal Economics Ministry, were successful in 1953, when the tariff law was altered to allow tariff and tax freedom for oil used in new petrochemical production processes that would transform petroleum into nonpetroleum products. As a 1956 legal commentary on the changes in the law of 1953 put it, the finance minister had accepted the arguments of the industrialists in full:

The basis of the tax preference given through paragraph 1, number four, is the political-economic necessity of making possible a new development in the chemical industry which has been implemented elsewhere but in Germany is still new, a development in which petroleum serves as a raw material (so-called petrochemistry). This development is costly and appears only profitable if the raw materials can be utilized at world market prices. . . . The necessary investments require a firm basis for calculation, which the tax preference is supposed to create.[105]

Even the revised law, chemical producers soon found out, left something to be desired. Bayer A.G.'s Hermann Holzrichter, who was responsible for his company's development of petrochemical processes, for instance, co-authored a letter to Dr. Lenz in the Economics Ministry in July 1955 complaining that his application to the Finance Ministry for a tax exemption for petroleum used in a petrochemical pilot plant had been rejected. The pilot plant, a cooperative venture of Bayer, Lurgi Gesellschaft für Wärmetechnik, and Ruhrgas, used about one ton of petroleum per hour and was meant to test new technology that departed from practice abroad by processing petroleum so that, "in addition to unavoidable by-products, insofar as possible only chemical raw materials come into existence, in the first instance gaseous olefins." The process used sand "as a circulating heat-transfer agent" to crack petroleum at temperatures of 750–800°C, that is, 250–300°C higher than the catalytic cracking processes usually used in the oil-refining industry.

Because Bayer's new technology did not yet allow direct transformation of petroleum to nonpetroleum products, but instead required some interim storage of the cracked gases to determine their exact chemical compositions and levels of purity, the petroleum used in it did not qualify for exemption from tariffs. That delay in transformation was one of the technical problems that Bayer and its partners were working to solve. The firm then applied to the Finance Min-

---

[104] Min. Rat. z. Wv. Dr. Lenz, "Zoll und steuerliche Behandlung der Chemischen Industrie im Gesetz zur Neuregelung der Abgaben auf Mineralöl," 16 January 1953 (Abschrift für Entwurf), BAK, B102/9560, Heft 2.

[105] Commentary of von Schädel, *Mineralölsteuer und Mineralölzoll*, 2nd ed., 1956, as quoted in "Hinweise" (Vertraulich), attachment to letter from Verband der chemischen Industrie (Wurms) to the federal Ministry of Economics (Chemieref. Dr. Lenz, Mineralölref. Dr. Boecker), "Betr. Mineralölzollbefreiung für Entwicklungsarbeiten der Erdölchemie," 22 November 1956, BAK, B102/73343.

istry for relief from the tax on the grounds of fairness (*aus Billigkeitsgründen*), which was also permissible under the 1953 law, but it was turned down on 21 June 1955 on the grounds that "I cannot recognize sufficient reasons [for applying this clause]. The initial outlays for materials used in development belong to development costs; they must here as in other cases be borne by the firm." Holzrichter repeatedly complained in his letter that the process was new and that it was not technically possible to bring it up to industrial scale immediately, because the problem of delay in the use of the gases had been not yet solved, although solving that problem would relieve the firm of the tax burden. There was, therefore, a policy contradiction that had to be resolved.[106]

Holzrichter's letter set in motion a discussion that demonstrated the complex web of interests in West German industry and government. The federal Ministry of Economics supported Bayer's application fully, and its Chemicals Section, under Dr. Lenz, began discussions with officials in the Finance Ministry on removing the tax burden from development and experimental plants. On 26 October 1956, Lenz invited Holzrichter and other Bayer personnel to join him in direct discussions with Mr. Himstedt, the official from the Finance Ministry who had made the original ruling against Bayer. Lenz concentrated on trying to find some sort of bureaucratic formulation (however tortured) that would sway Himstedt. Insisting that he did not want to challenge the general rule that taxes on materials used in pilot plants were part of the unavoidable costs of research and development, Lenz nonetheless argued that Bayer's case was a special one. In most instances, oil used in experimental plants was subject to the same tariff as that imposed on the industrial-scale counterpart. The Bayer case, however, was one in which there would be no tariff whatsoever on feedstocks for industrial-scale plant, but petroleum used in the pilot plant would be taxed fully. Lenz clinched his argument by pointing out that under the current practice, if the cost estimates for the full-scale plant were based on the experience in operating the pilot plant, those cost estimates would be skewed:

In the case at hand, it is not something like a favoring of pilot plant operations in comparison to normal plant operations that is being applied for, but rather a placing of the pilot-plant operations on an equal footing in terms of cost. This alone should in my view make for sufficient grounds of fairness for the remission of the petroleum customs duty.[107]

When that argument failed to convince Himstedt, the Chemicals Section of the Economics Ministry tried a different tack, concentrating on technical and financial arguments. On 15 May 1956, one of its chemists joined Dr. Reitter from the Finance Ministry in a meeting at Leverkusen with Holzrichter and three

---

[106] F.F. Bayer (Holzrichter and Casper) to BWM (Dr. Lenz), "Betr.: Entwicklung der Erdölchemie bei Farbenfabriken Bayer A.G.," 22 July 1955, BAK, B102/36054.

[107] BWM, IV B (Lenz) to Bundesministerium der Finanzen (Min. Dgt. Himstedt), "Zollfreie Verwendung von Mineralöl in einer Versuchsanlage bei der Farbenfabriken Bayer AG, Leverkusen, Besprechung bei Herrn Min. Dgt. Himstedt am 26.10.1955," 29 November 1955, BAK, B102/36054.

other Bayer personnel. Reitter received a detailed briefing on the problems associated with the Ruhrgas-Lurgi-Bayer process for cracking Iraqi crude into petrochemical feedstocks. A large percentage – 44.3 percent – of the input could be converted directly into petrochemical feedstocks, including ethylene, propylene, butadiene, and butylene. About 11 percent of the input could be transformed into fractions with boiling points below 200°C which, it was hoped, would later be subjected to refining under pressure and Udex extraction[108] in order to gain aromatics. Although the report of the meeting did not say so directly, those were products for which the 1953 tax-exemption law had been intended.

The briefers went on to point out that some of the input, about 25 percent, was used up in the process in maintaining the reaction temperatures, and an additional 2 percent of the input was coke, which attached itself to the sand used in the process and was subsequently burned off. The tariff on those amounts should be paid back to the firm; an analogous compensation mechanism was already in place for catalytic cracking, where coke was burned off on the catalyst. Still, the yield of petrochemical feedstocks was not satisfactory, and the key problem lay in the unavoidable by-products of the process. About 21 percent of the input was transformed into by-product gases, "which because of their composition cannot at this time be processed further chemically in the firm's installation and therefore must be burned off." The firm sought relief, in particular, from taxes on that portion of the input of crude oil, because "if these gases . . . should be subject to full customs duties, the economic viability of the entire process and thus of the production of ethylene at a reasonable price [is] no longer a given, which would lead to a situation where the firm is no longer in the position to compete abroad."[109] Thus, the Bayer representatives tried in that meeting to overwhelm Reitter with technical details, and they combined those arguments with others stressing the need to support new technology and, more important, the need to enhance West Germany's competitive position.

Reitter visited Hoechst for a similar conference on 5 July 1956, but as late as November he had not yet decided what to do. On 6 November, Dr. von Buddenbrook of the Economics Ministry's Chemicals Section noted that the delay was because Reitter had gone on vacation and then had been engaged in intensive preparations for upcoming tariff talks in Brussels, but he went on to say that he had promised Holzrichter that he would arrange further discussions with the Finance Ministry as soon as possible, talks that would include representatives from Leverkusen and Hoechst, as well as Mr. Wurms of the Verband der Chemischen Industrie (VCI), the newly renamed chemical-industry trade

---

[108] On Udex extraction, see Basil Achilladelis, "History of UOP: From petroleum refining to petrochemicals," *Chemistry and Industry* (19 April 1975):337–44, esp. p. 343; see also Peter Spitz, *Petrochemicals: The Rise of an Industry* (New York: Wiley, 1988), pp. 185–7.

[109] BWM, IV B (Schneider), "Vermerk über Besprechung betr. Zollrückvergütung von Restmineralöl und Gas mit den Farbenfabriken Bayer A.G., Leverkusen, am 15. Mai 1956 in Leverkusen," 17 May 1956, BAK, B102/73343.

association.[110] The inclusion of Hoechst and of the VCI in further negotiations was significant because it represented an intensification of pressure on the Finance Ministry: The problem was no longer one of a solitary firm, but rather affected the entire chemical industry. What is more, the VCI took an active role in communicating its wishes to the Economics Ministry's Chemicals Section, where those wishes were represented virtually without alteration in subsequent actions to achieve Bayer's original goals.

The refusal of the Finance Ministry to change its decision prompted another change in tactics. On 16 November 1956, Wurms of the VCI asked for a meeting with Economics Ministry officials to discuss their options. Boecker, Lenz, and von Buddenbrook of the Chemicals Section joined Wurms for that meeting on 20 November. All agreed with Boecker's suggestion that they explore the possibility – "after exhausting all possibilities of negotiation with the Finance Ministry" – of a legislative solution rather than a bureaucratic solution to the problem. He suggested attaching an addendum to the twelfth "Law to Alter the Customs Tariff" that would extend to pilot plants the tax exemption given to full-scale petrochemical plants. Chemicals Section officials began to assist Wurms in drafting such an addendum.[111] They quickly came up with a formulation to be appended to the proposed law:

Petroleum products . . . and gaseous hydrocarbons . . . , which after manufacture abroad are imported or are manufactured from unrefined petroleum that has a duty placed on it here, and which are used for development of processes that have as their goal chemical transformation . . . are free [from duty].[112]

Wurms and VCI business manager Felix Ehrmann began contacting legislators to solicit support for the addendum and the votes to see it through the legislative process. At the end of November, they also tried to elicit the support of the petroleum-industry trade association, the Mineralölwirtschaftsverband (MWV).[113]

It took the MWV months to answer the VCI request, and its response indicated that the question of how to deal with pilot plants in the petrochemical industry had been taken quite seriously: The MWV letter of 14 February 1957 indicated that a number of meetings had taken place between the VCI and the MWV, that the MWV had consulted thoroughly with the Economics Ministry (in this case, the Petroleum Section) on the issue, and that eventually the MWV's official stand on the issue would be decided by a vote of its managing

[110] BWM, IV B 1 (Dr. von Buddenbrook), "Vermerk betr. Zollerlass aus Billigkeitsgründen für Mineraloel das in einer Versuchsanlage verwendet wird," 6 November 1956, BAK, B102/36054.

[111] BWM, IV B 1 (von Buddenbrook), "Vermerk: Betr. Mineralölzollbefreiung für Entwicklungsarbeiten in Versuchsanlagen der Erdöl-Chemie," 7 January 1957, BAK, B102/36054.

[112] VCI (Ehrmann) to Mineralölwirtschaftsverband (Dr. Moslener), "Betr. Abgabenfreiheit für Mineralöl für Entwicklungsanlagen der Erdölchemie," 30 November 1956 (Abschrift), BAK, B102/73343.

[113] VCI (Ehrmann) to Mineralölwirtschaftsverband (Dr. Moslener), "Betr. "Abgabenfreiheit für Mineralöl für Entwicklungsanlagen der Erdölchemie," 30 November 1956 (Abschrift), BAK, B102/73343.

board of directors. Dr. Weber of the MWV managing board wrote that this organization had no opposition in principle to the VCI suggestion for the addendum to the twelfth law. On the other hand, the MWV did not want "to burden" the current draft of the law with such an addition, because it bore no relationship to the primary questions dealt with in the proposed law. What is more, given the Finance Ministry's opposition to the proposed addendum, its representatives likely would testify against the proposal in committee hearings. Finally, a committee of experts from the MWV had noted a technical problem with the proposed addendum: It did not specify the means for guaranteeing that leftover petroleum and/or petroleum products arising from chemical processes would be subject to the correct tariff rates. The MWV planned to report that legal objection in their commentary on the VCI proposal to the Economics Ministry's Petroleum Section. On balance, then, it would not be possible for the MWV to support the request of the VCI.[114] It was clear from the tone and substance of the letter that the highest priority of the MWV was speedy passage of the law; the Finance Ministry's objections to the proposed VCI addendum threatened to delay passage and was the primary reason for the MWV's refusal to support their colleagues in the VCI.

Felix Ehrmann responded quickly to Weber's letter on 20 February 1957. He pointed out that experts from both the VCI and MWV had met on 23 January and had, he believed, dealt with the MWV's legal objection to the proposed addendum. For Ehrmann, the primary question was, Would the VCI proposal delay passage of the twelfth law? No, he argued. The discussions surrounding the passage of the 1953 law freeing petroleum used in petrochemical processes in general – although that had represented a fundamental change in petroleum tariff policy – had led to no substantial delay and had taken care of the general legal principle regarding petrochemical tariffs. Currently, the legislators had only to say whether or not the use of petroleum in pilot plants represented a special case to which that general principle applied. Regardless of the outcome, it would mean no delay. He went on to point out that the question was of "urgent" interest for a few key firms and would affect their research-and-development costs substantially. The alternative of proposing a special "initiative" separate from the twelfth law certainly would not pass during the current legislative session. In closing, Ehrmann accepted the MWV's lack of endorsement, but he believed, on the basis of discussions between the two organizations, that the MWV would not actively oppose the VCI's plans.[115]

The passage of the addendum on 27 July 1957 took care of a major cost consideration in research and development for the petrochemical industry, something that representatives of the major firms believed to be an important impediment to technological change and competitiveness for the West German organic chemicals industry. The agonizing negotiations surrounding the adden-

[114] Mineralölwirtschaftsverband (Weber) to VCI (Ehrmann), "Betr.: Abgabenfreiheit für Mineralöl für Entwicklungsanlagen der Erdölchemie," 14 February 1957, BAK, B102/73343.

[115] VCI (Ehrmann) to MWV (Weber), "Abgabenfreiheit für Mineralöl für Entwicklungsanlagen der Petro-Chemie," 20 February 1957, BAK, B102/73343.

dum, however, clearly demonstrated the extent to which technological changes and choices of feedstocks for the industry were held hostage to the existing legal framework of tariff policy (which, because it was based on a 1939 law, itself was an instance of continuity from the National Socialist period to the Federal Republic period) and to the persistent traditions in bureaucratic thinking, especially in the Finance Ministry.

Concluding remarks

During the first half of the 1950s, the impetus for change in the organizational structure and the technological infrastructure of the German chemical industry came primarily from abroad. Two momentous developments in power politics stand out above all others in shaping the direction of change. Germany's loss of World War II was the first of those, because the Germans, at least for a time, lost the ability to control events in their country. The onset and intensification of the Cold War between East and West composed the second such development, because it led to the division of Germany and the domination of the German successor states by the two superpowers. The two developments affected the chemical industry in different ways. The loss of the war, for instance, led directly to the breakup of I.G. Farbenindustrie A.G., whereas Cold War considerations helped bring about the large, internationally competitive units to replace it. Similarly, losing the war made it probable that Germany would permanently lose direct control over its coal resources and, at least in the short term, led to coal shortages throughout Europe; the intensifying Cold War helped push the Germans, and indeed all Europeans, toward heavy reliance on overseas sources of crude oil, primarily from the Middle East.

Those global trends in power politics, however, did not determine in any detail the organizational or technological construction of the West German chemical industry in the postwar period. Instead, the interactions among those global trends and a number of domestic considerations, over time, channeled the general tendencies into their specific forms. Shortages of coal supplies – at the same time that consensus reigned regarding the political and economic centrality of the coal industry – constituted one such domestic consideration. German traditions of government–business interactions constituted another, with firms' internal traditions of business organization and technological change forming yet a third.

German assumptions about the past and future political and economic significance of the coal industry, along with those political and intrafirm traditions, help explain why, despite coal shortages, chemical firms in West Germany only slowly began to use petroleum instead of coal-chemical feedstocks. Of course, there were other reasons as well, including shortages of capital and some feelings of uncertainty about the security of petroleum supply from the Middle East. Although long-held assumptions were beginning to change, even in the bureaucracy, most German industrialists, even in the forward-looking chemical industry, would not even consider using imported raw materials if perfectly good substitutes were available at home, as coal certainly was.

Thinking in terms of self-sufficiency, or autarky, in the supply of raw materials was only one example of the continuities from the pre-1945 period to the postwar period. Volker Berghahn has argued that, in addition, West German industrial elites in the postwar period continued to think in terms of cartelization and authoritarian approaches to industrial relations. Although the West German chemical industry was never fully "Americanised," as should become evident from a reading of the following chapters, Berghahn is persuasive in his contention that those old habits of thought, over time, began to give way in the face of the contrasting American traditions of open markets, oligopoly, and nonhierarchical, often cooperative approaches to industrial relations.[116]

That tension between the old traditions and new thinking emerged clearly in a document that reported a conversation between the American consul general in Düsseldorf and Ulrich Haberland, the head of Bayer A.G. The two were discussing Haberland's planned trip to the United States in September 1954. Although it is clear from other sources that most of Haberland's time would be spent dealing with American chemical industrialists as Bayer negotiated technology-sharing agreements and set up its postwar U.S. production and sales operations, that conversation focused on Haberland's complaints about Allied policy toward the chemical industry. Haberland was particularly upset about the "uneconomic" position of the successors to the I.G. in the fields of research and sales. Because "he had discussed this question with Allied officials in Germany without satisfaction . . . , he planned to call on high officials of the United States government in Washington. . . . He added that he would enlist the aid of the German ambassador to the United States in contacting the proper persons." After citing some examples to support his complaints, Haberland added the significant observation

that the important members of the German chemical industry will certainly re-establish close relationships as soon as the Allied governments are no longer able to exercise control over them. He said that this did not mean that they would necessarily regroup themselves into a single company but that they would cooperate to improve their collective position.[117]

Clearly, Haberland reflected the continuity in habits of thought among German industrialists from the period before 1945 to the postwar era that stressed

---

[116] Berghahn, *The Americanisation of West German Industry.*

[117] LaVerne Baldwin, American consul general Düsseldorf to Department of State, "Cartel Policy – Prospective visit to the United States of Dr. E. h. Ulrich Haberland of Farbenfabriken Bayer," NA, RG 469, European Cooperation Administration, Deputy Director for Operations, Office of European Operations, Office of the Director, Geographic Files, Box 103: Germany – Industry. A draft itinerary for the Haberland visit is in "Reise Prof. Dr. Haberland/Canada-USA-Mexico," 23 August 1954, in Bayer Werksarchiv, Leverkusen, Records of the Secretariat Dr. Haberland, 271/1.1.92; various documents in the same file also indicate that Haberland in fact made the trip approximately as planned.

cartels and cooperation. At the same time, because important stops during his trip would be aimed at facilitating international transfer of technology, at groping toward Bayer's emergence as a multinational corporation, and, through those measures, at improving Bayer's competitive position not only in the world but also in Germany, Haberland's visit also reflected an emerging attitude of understanding the new realities of the postwar political-economic order dominated by the United States.

Contact and cooperation with American and British firms provided one of the most important mechanisms for technological change in the chemical industry as it began to situate itself in the new international political economy. Describing and analyzing the process of technology transfer during the early 1950s is the objective of the next chapter. German industrialists used older, homegrown technologies to bargain for new ones that the Americans and the British had to offer.

4
Rejoining the international community: international cooperation and technology transfer, 1951–1955

The broad postwar changes that affected the place of the West German organic chemical industry in the political economy of the Western world, as described in Chapter 3, facilitated – and in part were facilitated by – the events to be described in this chapter: The return of German firms to respected and active membership in the international business community was, of course, a function of the re-achievement of sovereignty by the Federal Republic, but the economic performance engendered in part by rejoining the international community helped stabilize and increase the power of the West German state.

This chapter deals primarily with patterns of technology transfer[1] in the first

---

[1] There is no generally accepted definition of "technology transfer." See, for instance, O. Börnsen, H. Glismann, and E. -J. Horn, *Der Technologietransfer zwischen den USA und der Bundesrepublik* (Tübingen: J. C. B. Mohr/P. Siebeck, 1985), pp. 1–3. I use a commonsense definition of the concept here, i.e., adoption by a firm or firms in one country of production techniques developed by a firm or firms in another country. Useful overviews of international technology transfer include the following: Thomas Ilgen and T. J. Pempel, *Trading Technology: Europe and Japan in the Middle East* (New York: Praeger, 1987), pp. 1–25; essays in John R. McIntyre and Daniel S. Papp, eds., *The Political Economy of International Technology Transfer* (New York: Quorum, 1986); and Nathan Rosenberg and Claudio Frischtak, eds., *International Technology Transfer: Concepts, Methods, and Comparisons* (New York: Praeger, 1985), pp. 3–23.

half of the 1950s, although it explores some other forms of international cooperation as well. Because this material has the potential for such a wide range of ramifications, its treatment will be limited in several ways. The chapter concentrates, for instance, on relationships between German firms and their counterparts in the United States and, to a lesser degree, Great Britain, which were by far the most important foreign economic relations for the postwar chemical industry (and most other industries). This story involves, furthermore, only a small number of West German firms, mostly BASF and Bayer, with some attention to Hoechst A.G. and to Professor Karl Ziegler and his low-pressure process for producing polyethylene. Their experiences were not representative, but those firms were among the most active and most significant in positioning the West German chemical industry to recapture its former status in technology and markets worldwide. Finally, the chapter offers a case study of technological changes in the processes for manufacturing a single family of products, the polyethylenes, because of their overwhelming importance in the expansion and technological changes in the chemical industry worldwide during the 1950s and 1960s.

At the beginning of the 1950s, however, plans for changes in the industry were
Although in terms of technology the West German chemical industry lagged behind its American counterpart in many areas, especially in petrochemicals, negotiations over technology transfers and over international cooperation between firms were far from one-sided. West German firms had much to offer even the Americans, and they certainly had a great deal with which to bargain in their dealings with chemical industrialists in other countries. Their surprisingly strong bargaining position so soon after the war was based in part on personal relationships that had remained intact despite the conflict, as well as on some new, energetic personalities in the industry and a number of holdovers from the brilliant tradition of research and development at the I.G. Farbenindustrie A.G. The astonishing demand for chemical products around the world that characterized the decades following World War II was also a factor. Trading on the basis of their strong bargaining position, in turn, allowed them to "make haste slowly" in changing the technological and feedstock basis of the industry.

At the beginning of the 1950s, however, plans for changes in the industry were hampered by capital shortages, the still-visible aftereffects of the war, clear technological backwardness, the unresolved breakup of I.G. Farben, and legal restrictions (on research, on production, and, because of the tariff policy until 1953, on petrochemical manufacturing). The Americans implementing the Marshall Plan recognized the seriousness of the German situation in the context of the European devastation in general. One of the most important programs was the technical-assistance program, which was meant to further European integration, while at the same time helping the Europeans overcome their technological backwardness vis-à-vis the United States.

The technical-assistance program

Although technical assistance (TA) had its legal basis in a bilateral treaty on economic cooperation between the Federal Republic of Germany and the United

States of 15 December 1949, it had a distinct multilateral flavor in certain critical areas: Trips to the United States could be undertaken by single-country delegations from the industry, commerce, and agriculture sectors to study American techniques regarding statistical analysis, market research, trade-union structure, or generic industrial productivity; however, if the trips had anything to do with specific industries (such as chemicals, iron and steel, automobiles, and textiles), they had to be multinational missions coordinated by the Organization for European Economic Cooperation (OEEC). Officially, TA was an exchange program, allowing U.S. delegations to visit Europe as well. Still, the flow of information generally was in only one direction: from the United States to Europe. Europeans visiting the United States studied American technology, and Americans visiting Europe advised the Europeans on how to modernize their operations. The program also funded some intra-European exchanges and some services (such as an information service).[2] The year in which the program was started (1949), its connection to the Mutual Security Agency (MSA), and its emphasis on the OEEC all point to the multiple aims of the TA program. It was meant to promote Western European integration so as to foster economic growth and prevent future wars and, at the same time, to bolster the western part of the Continent economically so as better to contribute militarily to the new North Atlantic Treaty Organization.

Funding for TA was undertaken jointly by the MSA and the countries that participated in the program. Because of the shortage of dollars in Europe, the MSA paid for dollar expenses, and the participating European country (e.g., the Federal Republic) was required to deposit "counterpart funds" in the local currency (e.g., DM) against the dollar amount. That method of financing the dollar portion of expenditures allowed strapped European economies to save much-needed foreign exchange, while at the same time providing a source of capital for industrial expansion (over the expenditure of which American officials had some say). Participating countries also bore the local-currency costs of the program, although the counterpart funds themselves could be used for that purpose. Through the end of April 1952, TA had funded travel for 7,800 Europeans to the United States and 825 Americans to Europe, with an additional 6,000 Europeans and 600 Americans slated for fiscal year 1953.[3]

Funding was available for several missions related to the chemical industry, and the OEEC's Chemical Product Committee was the venue where representatives of the member states decided which areas to stress. In mid-April 1950, delegations from Austria, France, Italy, and Germany suggested four study projects to be pursued in the United States:

1. relations between research laboratories and the chemical industry
2. equipment in the chemical industry

---

[2] Ministry of Marshall Plan, "Vermerk Betr. Technical Assistance," 21 January 1953 (carbon copy), Bundesarchiv, Koblenz (hereafter, BAK), B146/1119; "MSA Policy and Programs for Productivity and Technical Assistance," 28 April 1952, pp. 2–3, United States National Archives, Washington National Records Center, Suitland, MD, Record Group (hereafter, NA, RG) 469, OEO Director's Office, Subject File, Box 21; Technical Assistance.

[3] "MSA Policy and Programs for Productivity and Technical Assistance," p. 3.

3. "study of chemical products derived from oil"

4. synthetic detergents and auxiliary products for textiles and leather

The delegate from Denmark suggested a fifth area of inquiry: problems of water and air pollution due to the chemical industry. The committee approved all five suggestions and submitted them "to the Council" of the OEEC for approval.[4] U.S. officials in Europe representing the Economic Cooperation Administration subsequently approved all five projects; they were given the designations OEEC-22 through OEEC-26.[5]

It is telling that the delegate from Denmark recommended the investigation of environmental problems. Industrialists and bureaucrats from the other, larger countries were, in 1950, more interested in economic growth than in environmental protection. The West Germans clearly focused their attention on the first four areas of inquiry, and one of their delegates, Otto Horn, representing the interests that would soon form Hoechst A.G., emphasized in a letter to Dr. Theurer of the Chemicals Section of the West German Ministry of Economics the critical importance of project three: petrochemicals. He began by stressing that the upcoming study trip should be under the auspices of the Chemicals Section, rather than the Petroleum Section, because the whole idea in petroleum cracking was to maximize fuel production and minimize "gaseous olefins," whereas chemical producers had the opposite objective. Continuing, he noted how critical it was for Germany to participate in the mission:

The modern development in the entire world, and of necessity also in Europe and in Germany, will move away partially from overbred [überzüchteten] acetylene chemistry in the next years and toward petroleum. The first signs of this are already obvious in England and Holland. If we want to participate in this development in the area of solvents and plastics, we must go down this path, especially since it is economically superior to the one pursued thus far. It therefore appears to us urgently necessary that we interest ourselves in this committee for petrochemicals.

Horn went on to outline the areas of interest for Germany and to offer his services for an upcoming Chemical Products Committee meeting: "Since we are interested in this development at Hoechst and since this is one of my working areas, I would be happy to participate in this meeting."[6] Horn's analysis, though incisive in retrospect, was not generally shared in 1950. His belief that acetylene chemistry was "overbred," for instance, was not a common opinion, and his statement that petrochemicals were inherently superior economically to coal-based chemicals would not have met with general approval. Some of the

[4] OEEC, Chemical Products Committee, "Report on the Work of the 12th Session (12.15. + 19.4.1950)," 27 April 1950 [CP(50)7] (Restricted, original French), BAK, B102/1468.

[5] "Technical Assistance Monthly Report, July 1951," NA, RG 469, ECA Productivity and Technical Assistance Division, Office of the Director, Technical Assistance Country Subject Files, Box 9: TA Reports.

[6] Otto Horn to Dr. Theurer (BWM, Chemicals Section), "Betr: Bericht C50/109 Annex 3 (Petrochemicals)," 6 June 1950, BAK, B102/1469, Heft 2.

more prevalent notions in West Germany regarding coal and petroleum chemistry are dealt with later in this chapter. Suffice it to say here that some key American decision-makers apparently considered the petrochemicals mission as important as he did; and for them, it was therefore threatening.

Dr. Theurer, in writing his report on the meeting at which the Chemical Products Committee decided on its five main areas of interest, had noticed that something was wrong:

The discussion about America's technical assistance is not yet finished. From the American side, considerable resistance to allowing trips and tours [of factories] as concerns all areas of chemistry showed itself. One tries for the present to restrict oneself to individual areas, whereby the area of plastics stands in the foreground.[7]

Theurer's instinct appears to have been correct. The Washington-based headquarters of the European Cooperation Administration (ECA) quickly turned down the synthetic-detergents project.[8] A report of June 1953 listed about two hundred separate industrial and agricultural projects under various headings. Only one was listed as not being implemented, "Petroleum Chemicals,"[9] and it does not appear that the mission ever took place. It is not clear just why that was so, but the American fear of renewed competition from the German chemical industry that Theurer had detected in mid-April 1950 may have been an important factor.

Whatever the fears of American industrialists, however, their own government's policies provided an alternative means to help the Europeans overcome their technological lag in petrochemicals. In early July 1953, the OEEC's Working Party 5 identified petrochemicals as a potential target for policies that would promote "selective expansion." The idea was to identify and assist industries that would be most likely to help the European countries close their dollar deficits with the United States – because of existing European dependence on the industry's products and the potential for existing European companies to produce in a particular sector of the industry. Working Party 5 requested that the Chemical Products Committee take up the task of preparing the case for petrochemicals.[10] The committee turned the work over to Working Party 7, which was slated to meet for the first time on 27 July 1953.

The West Germans were at first apprehensive concerning what was in store for them in that new OEEC working party. The staff of the Chemicals Section of the West German Ministry of Economics met to discuss strategy in mid-July. Dr. Prentzel, the head of the section, eventually decided not to send a represen-

---

[7] Dr. Theurer, "Bericht über die 12. Sitzung des Chemical Product Committees vom 12.4 bis 15.4.1950 [*sic*] in Paris," 18 April 1950, p. 4, BAK, B102/1468.

[8] OECE, Comité des produits chimiques, "Compte-Rendu des travaux de la 13ème Session (16.– 21.10.1950)," 23 October 1950 [CP(50)18] (Restricted), p. 3, BAK B102/1468.

[9] (Näher), "Vermerk für Herrn ORR Rochell, Betr. Technical Assistance," 24 June 1953, BAK, B146/1119.

[10] OEEC, "Working Party No. 5 of the Council: Questionnaire to the Chemical Products Committee," 7 July 1953 (Restricted), BAK, B146/1009.

tative from industry to the first meeting. Instead, Dr. Pohland, from the Chemicals Section, would represent the German side. Prentzel instructed him to take "a wait-and-see attitude." The reason was that "He would first ascertain whether or not the great European firms want to use the working group to push through their interests against those of the smaller chemical firms which are active in Germany in the area of petrochemistry [sic]."[11]

A member of the German delegation to the OEEC, von Wallenberg, warned that that might not be such a good idea; he suggested inviting Hans Freiensehner from BASF (whom Carl Wurster had volunteered for the job) as "a pronounced specialist" to complement Pohland's more general expertise.[12] Freiensehner would have been in good company. Shortly after the first meeting took place, von Wallenberg reported from Paris to Bonn that the British delegation included representatives from Imperial Chemical Industries (ICI), Shell Petrochemicals, and Petrochemicals Ltd.; the French delegation had one each from Rhone-Poulenc and Napthachemie; the Belgian delegation had two from the currently forming Société Chimique des Dérivés du Petrole; and the Italian delegation had one from Montecatini.[13] Contrary to the Germans' apprehension about being milked by their European competitors, perhaps German expertise would be necessary for the German delegation to hold its own.

By the fall of 1953, the West Germans had made up for lost time. Under the auspices of Prentzel, representatives of the Chemicals Section and Petroleum Section of the Economics Ministry and of the chemical and petroleum industries met to discuss "the future arrangement of national and international cooperation in this area." Nominations for participants in continued talks at the national level – which were to provide the basis for negotiations at the international level – included, from the chemical industry, Dr. Freiensehner from BASF, Dr. Thieβ from Hoechst, and Dr. Peukert from Hüls, and, from the petroleum industry, Mr. Lütkemeyer from Shell, Mr. Schneider from BP, and a third person to be named later. A blue-ribbon committee (*Spitzengremium*) that would represent the interests of the Federal Republic as a whole would include representatives from the bureaucracy, as well as Alexander Menne from Hoechst, Paul Baumann from Hüls, Dr. Boeder from Shell, and Dr. Wissel from Wesseling.[14] In practice, members of the national-level committees, as well as members of the blue-ribbon committee, could participate in Paris. For instance, Peukert, Freiensehner, and Lütkemeyer joined Pohland and Schneider from the Economics Ministry

[11] Bundesministerium für das Marshall-Plan, II/2c (Esche), memorandum "Betr.: Petro-Chemie," 20 July 1953, BAK, B146/1009.

[12] Deutsche Bundesvertretung beim Europäischen Wirtschaftsrat (von Wallenberg), "Betr. Chemieausschuss/Arbeitsgruppe Petrolchemie," 21 July 1953, BAK, B146/1009; BASF (Wurster/Timm) to Délégation Allemande auprès de l'OECE (Dr. Schulz), 6 July 1953 (Abschrift), BAK, B146/1009.

[13] Deutsche Bundesvertretung beim Europäischen Wirtschaftsrat (von Wallenberg), "Betr.: Chemieausschuss/Sitzung der Arbeitsgruppe Erdölchemie," 30 July 1953, BAK, B146/1009.

[14] Bundesministerium für das Marshall-Plan (Gerbaulet) to representation of Federal Republic at the OEEC, "Betr: Arbeitsgruppe 'Petrochemie' des Chemie-Ausschusses," 10 October 1953, BAK, B146/1009.

at the meetings during 26–29 October 1953.[15] All of the representatives from industry were members of the managing boards of their respective companies, an indication of the importance that companies attached to such discussions. Those talks also indicated the extent of government attention to and active intervention in technological changes in the postwar period. It appears that nothing substantive came out of those talks, but they provided a forum within which representatives of chemical firms and the oil industry could discuss common problems, whether from a national perspective or from a European vantage.

Still, however helpful government-sponsored trips to the United States or government-backed discussions of petrochemical technology may have been, they could not substitute for a visit by the employees of a given company to another company in America. The proposed OEEC trip, for instance, had it occurred, would have yielded little, if any, information that was not public (i.e., proprietary). For companies competing not just with the Americans, but also among themselves, that posed a problem. A similar difficulty arose in intra-German and intra-European discussions on new chemical technology: It was obviously of some use to the companies to conduct such discussions (otherwise they would not have sent such high-ranking members of their firms); still, such talks had to be conducted at a very general level to avoid giving away important information to industrial competitors. Thus, private trips by industry personnel, as early as 1948, proved an effective means of re-establishing prewar contacts between the Germans and the Americans and, more important, of assessing the opposition to see how far behind the German firms really were.

Private study visits to the United States, 1948–54

West German chemical industrialists saw that they had two prime tasks in the immediate postwar period: first, to recapture foreign markets; second, to catch up with the new standards of excellence in chemical technology. Sales and study visits were means to accomplish both. The earliest of those trips was an excursion in 1948 by high-ranking Bayer personnel (Ulrich Haberland, Otto Bayer, and Oskar Loehr) to the United States to visit DuPont, among other firms,[16] but that trip was not typical, and it was not until the early 1950s that most firms could afford such visits. Still, as soon as the legal position of the I.G. successors was secured, and insofar as foreign exchange was available, a steady stream of representatives from major firms re-established contacts with their counterparts abroad and eagerly toured foreign factories. The United States proved a favorite destination.[17]

---

[15] "Verzeichnis der von den Teilnehmerländer für die Sitzung 'Erdölchemie' vom 26.–29. Oktober 1953 entsandten Sachverständigen," n.d., BAK, B146/1009.

[16] Dr. Knauff, "Aktennotiz: Betr. DuPont de Nemours & Co.," 16 May 1952, Bayerwerksarchiv, Leverkusen (hereafter, BWA), Sekretariat Otto Bayer, Korrespondenz mit amerikanischen und englischen Behörden und mit ausländischen Firmen (hereafter, O. Bayer Korr.).

[17] W. A. Menne, head of the chemical-industry trade association and by 1952 a member of the Hoechst managing board, reported on two such visits to the United States in 1951: W. A. Menne,

In arranging their visits, German chemical industrialists possessed distinct advantages over those from other European countries, including extensive and close contacts from before the war and a long-standing reputation for high-quality chemical research and production. Two examples, one each from Bayer A.G. and BASF, will illustrate this.

Bayer began to move into petroleum-based chemical production after signing a contract with Ruhrbau in Mülheim at the end of 1952, and at the end of January 1953 it sent a five-man team to the United States. In addition to looking into specific technologies, the team had "the general task of looking around in petrochemistry and of ascertaining as far as possible the current state of cracking processes and of petrochemical-chemistry [sic]." Dr. H. Hanisch, who reported the results of the trip to the Bayer directors at a conference in April 1953, noted that the group had made important contacts with an American engineering firm, Hydrocarbon; personal connections dating from before the war were crucial to the Bayer-Hydrocarbon relationship:

Its [Hydrocarbon's] chairman of the board is Mr. Keith, who was with Kellogg [another American engineering firm] earlier and is known to many of the former members of the I.G. managing board. The Chairman for Europe is Dr. Ringer, who earlier led negotiations within the I.G. of I.G.'s Sparte I with the Standard Oil companies. The most prominent leader in the development section of Hydrocarbon, which has a quite impressive technology installation and laboratory in Trenton, is Dr. Pichler, one of the first and most well-known co-workers of Professor Franz Fischer from the KWI [Kaiser Wilhelm Institute] in Mülheim. Half of the Hydrocarbon, or rather Hydramin company here in Germany, which has its seat in Düsseldorf, belongs to Mr. Stinnes [who had helped arrange the visit].

It soon became clear to the Bayer team that Hydrocarbon was too small to give Bayer the kind of help it needed. Still, Hydrocarbon personnel helped arrange visits throughout the United States, including trips to the hotbeds of activity in large-scale petrochemical production in Texas, Oklahoma, and Louisiana.[18]

BASF, long a leader in high-pressure chemistry and in other sophisticated areas of chemical production, had better contacts in the United States than did Bayer. At the beginning of their visit to more than forty American firms in late 1953, two BASF engineers reported feeling especially concerned about how they would be received. Still, "we soon perceived that the 'Badische' [BASF] has a good name and has, even over there, friends who are happy to stand helpfully at our side." One key contact was Frank Howard, former vice-president of Standard Oil of New Jersey and a longtime associate of Ludwigshafen's leadership. Howard arranged visits to several firms, including Union Carbide & Carbon, Pittsburgh Consolidation Coal, Humble Oil in Houston, the Ethyl Corporation

---

"Der internationale Erfahrungsaustausch," *Chemische Industrie* 4(1952):1–2. See also the visits noted later, and see Stokes, *Divide and Prosper*, pp. 195–6, 204.

[18] Dr. H. Hanisch, "Eindrücke und Ergebnisse einer Amerikareise, Vortrag bei der Direktoren-Konferenz in Leverkusen am 14. April 1953," BWA, 700/1302.

in New York, and the American Viscose Company. He also facilitated visits by representatives of interested American firms to BASF.[19]

Given access by virtue of reputation and previous contacts, German firms scurried to send representatives to the United States in the first half of the 1950s. What were they interested in seeing? For one thing, as the Hanisch-led trip in 1953 for Bayer indicated, Germans were well aware that the burgeoning U.S. petrochemical industry represented a major challenge to future German competitiveness. Their on-site inspections of U.S. plants only strengthened that impression. In a presentation to top BASF officials in March 1954, two company engineers reported their sense of awe during a 1953 visit to a new Shell Chemical catalytic cracking plant in Houston: "Although we had, in the course of our other visits, already digested a few impressions of petrochemistry and had seen a few things from the highways as we drove by, I have to say this: as I now stood here before one of the most modern cat[alytic] crackers, I first had to take a deep breath."[20] Although they had worked for one of the most technologically advanced German firms, the two BASF engineers had witnessed something entirely new to them: Indeed, the *scale* of production in U.S. petrochemical factories constituted a qualitative change in chemical technology, especially in that it necessitated considerable automation.[21] German companies had just begun to make real progress in that area. Other aspects of petrochemical production differentiated it from coal-chemical technology, although many Germans persisted in believing that the new process did not differ substantially from those familiar to their own chemical technologists. In fact, American (and also British) petroleum and chemical firms had developed new methods – such as catalytic cracking, using, first, fixed-bed and then fluidized-bed process – to produce the feedstocks needed for petrochemical production. Subsequently, they also applied such processes to chemical production, as, for instance, in the use of fluidized-bed technology to synthesize acrylonitrile from propylene. Other areas of American petrochemical technology had also moved forward substantially during the war, even as German progress in such areas had ground to a halt; for example, "by the early 1950s, U.S. polymer technology [crucial for modern thermoplastic production] was well ahead of German research."[22]

[19] Frank Howard, *Buna Rubber, the Birth of an Industry* (New York: Van Nostrand, 1947); BASF LK-Abteilung, Dr. Günther Daumiller and Dr. Rudolf Keller, "Eindrücke einer Reise in den Vereinigten Staaten von Nordamerkika im Herbst 1953. Referat im Hauptlaboratorium am 1. März 1954 und Besuchsberichte," pp. 3–4, 67; quotation, p. 3, BASF Unternehmensarchiv, Ludwigshafen (hereafter, BASF), F9/39; BASF Patentabteilung (Kleber), "Aktennotiz: Betr. Besuch von Dr. Sidney Caldwell am 1.8.1951," August 1951, BASF, B4/1813.

[20] BASF LK-Abteilung, Dr. Günther Daumiller and Dr. Rudolf Keller, "Eindrücke einer Reise in den Vereinigten Staaten von Nordamerikika im Herbst 1953. Referat im Hauptlaboratorium am 1. März 1954 und Besuchsberichte," p. 17, BASF, F9/39.

[21] Menne, "Der internationale Erfahrungsaustausch," p. 1. More generally, see B. Sturm, "Betriebskontrolltechnik in den USA und in Deutschland. Eine vergleichende Betrachtung über den Stand der Automatisierung," *Chemische Industrie* 7(1955):17–19.

[22] On the basis of a study visit, H. Miessner, of F.F. Bayer, reported that American process technology (whether the processes themselves or the apparatus), with few exceptions, "were not

The need for German firms to catch up, already plain early in the occupation, became even more pressing when their representatives saw the progress that had been made in the United States. At the same time, German chemists, engineers, and managers did not despair. A report from December 1952 describing a visit to the United States by Bayer personnel to study developments in plastics, solvents, and other important products of the petrochemical industry captured that sense well:

We have to catch up in several areas, but the impression we got [in America] is encouraging, too, since we can look with satisfaction on the fact that we are, in several new areas, on the best possible way toward again establishing a starting point for technical development.[23]

Was there any basis for such optimism? If the pressing interest in American developments in petrochemical technology expressed by German firms had been the only factor at work in the early 1950s, the answer would be "hardly." However, many American firms were at least as interested as the Germans in gaining access to technology and know-how from and cooperative agreements with their counterparts. Thus, there certainly were grounds for German optimism.

Technology transfer and cooperative agreements between West German and American firms in the first half of the 1950s

Given the wartime developments in petrochemical technology and the technical intelligence collected from German industry in the aftermath of the war, it may seem surprising that German expertise would hold any attraction for Anglo-Saxon firms; however, that it did is indisputable. For one thing, there were limits to the usefulness of written intelligence reports on German technology, because effective applications often required hands-on experience, which only the German firms possessed. In addition, American petrochemical producers showed considerable interest in German acetylene chemistry. Walter Reppe and other researchers at I.G. Farben's Ludwigshafen plant (BASF) had developed techniques for handling acetylene at high pressures and for using it to manufacture a wide variety of products, including butadiene (needed for synthetic-rubber production) and plastics intermediates. At first, a number of products of Reppe chemistry proved impossible to reproduce via chemistry based on the less ex-

substantially different from the German." H. Miessner, "Interessante Entwicklungen aus der Verfahrenstechnik in USA," *Chemie-Ingenieur-Technik* 23(1951):231. See Peter Spitz, *Petrochemicals: The Rise of an Industry* (New York: Wiley, 1988), esp. chapters 3 and 4 and pp. 135–8, 346–7, for U.S. technical superiority; quotation, p. 346. An interesting mixture of both points of view is found in a study-visit report by BASF's Dr. Rudolf Gäth, "Vortrag am 30.5.52 vor der Werksleitung bzw. der Direktionspostsitzung über meine Amerika-Reise," 10 June 1952, BASF, F9/134/4.

[23] "Bericht über Studienreise der Herren Dr. Hagedorn/Dr. Weinbrenner nach den USA in der Zeit vom 12.9. bis 8.11. 1952," BWA, 700/453.1.

pensive petrochemical feedstocks. Representatives of U.S. chemical companies, hoping to use natural gas rather than coal to produce acetylene, were therefore extremely interested in Reppe chemistry. In addition, U.S. firms had automated chemical production extensively in their large-scale factories and were using centralized laboratories for product analysis. They were interested in the complementary plant-stream analyzers pioneered by the Germans to allow on-the-spot product analysis.[24] And those were only some of the areas that interested American firms.

As a result of such proven technological capabilities, companies such as BASF, beginning in the early 1950s, attracted a steady stream of visitors from the American chemical industry. American interests varied widely, demonstrating the widespread appeal of German technology, despite war and occupation. High-ranking representatives of the chemical engineering firm M. W. Kellogg arrived in Ludwigshafen in March 1951 to negotiate for rights to a BASF process for the cracking of methane in the presence of steam and oxygen in order to produce hydrogen and carbon monoxide. Kellogg was also interested in BASF's process for producing acetylene from methane "without using an electric arc," the Sachsse process.[25] Shortly thereafter, Monsanto negotiated an option on BASF's butynediol-related acetylene processes (part of Reppe chemistry). Sidney Caldwell, from the U.S. Rubber Company, arrived in Ludwigshafen later in 1951 to begin talks on purchasing know-how in the plastics area.[26]

Such expressions of interest in BASF's technical prowess undoubtedly were flattering, but in the short term they brought little financial remuneration. That changed by 1953 when the Pittsburgh-based Koppers Company purchased technical information from BASF for the design of a commercial plant for production of polyethylene. In addition to bringing in badly needed dollars, that agreement constituted recognition of BASF's technological capabilities in a petrochemical process. On the other hand, Koppers was just entering that area of production; an agreement in early 1954 to provide Monsanto, a more firmly es-

[24] M. H. Bigelow (Plaskon Division of Libbey-Owens-Ford Glass Co.), one of the technical investigators, conveyed American excitement in "Reppe's Acetylene Chemistry," *Chemical and Engineering News* 25(1947);1038–42. Some firms later acted on that matter. Monsanto was one; for material on their negotiations with BASF, see BASF, B4/1395 and F9/248. On acetylene chemistry's potential to produce goods that petrochemical technology at first could not, see Walter Reppe, "Die Bedeutung der Acetylenchemie für die Industrie der Kunststoffe im Vergleich mit anderen Grundstoffindustrien," *Chemische Industrie* 3(1951):602; BASF Patentabteilung, "Bericht über den Besuch der Herren Wilson und Menke der Monsanto Chemical Co. vom 15., 16. und 19 März 1951," March 29, 1951, p. 6, BASF, B4/1395. On plant-stream analysis, see B. Sturm, "Betriebskontrolltechnik," p. 19.

[25] On the Sachsse process, see Spitz, *Petrochemicals*, p. 400.

[26] "Besuch der Herren Warren L. Smith, Präsident von The M. W. Kellogg Company, New York, und Z. A. Toula, Vizepräsident von Kellogg, Paris, in Ludwigshafen am 5. März 1951," 5 March 1951, BASF, B4/1815; "*Entwurf* of Monsanto-BASF agreement," 13 April 1951, and letter BASF (Walter Reppe and Hans Freiensehner) to Monsanto (W. K. Menke), "Subject: Reppe Chemistry," 19 April 1951, BASF, B4/1395; BASF Patentabteilung (Kleber) (*Aktennotiz*), "Betr. Besuch von Dr. Sidney Caldwell am 1.8.19511," 2 August 1951, BASF, B4/1813.

tablished chemical producer, with similar information signaled to other companies that BASF was a force to be reckoned with in the petrochemical area.[27]

Bayer A.G., although it was far from being a force in that new area until later in the 1950s, nonetheless had similar experiences with American firms. Especially prominent in the fields of synthetic-rubber technology, synthetic fibers, insecticides, dyes, and pharmaceuticals, Bayer had much to offer foreign companies. There was therefore a steady stream of visitors from the United States to Leverkusen and Uerdingen (and vice versa) in the first half of the 1950s, and even early in the decade the positive results for Bayer were evident. A document prepared to help convince the Allies of the necessity for a visit by Ulrich Haberland to the United States in late 1951 lists some of them. Geary Chemical Company, for instance, had cooperated with Bayer to build a parathion plant in Pittsburgh and was considering building another. Allied Chemical & Dye sought technical assistance from Bayer for its caprolactam and Perlon plants. Pittsburgh Plate Glass was interested in a possible cooperation in the field of silica fillers and polyester resins. U.S. Rubber, Goodrich Chemical, and Goodyear[28] all wanted to acquire Bayer know-how and to secure further cooperation on research and production of vulcollan, "an important new elastic plastic." Interchemical Corporation and Pittsburgh Coke & Chemical sought technical assistance from Bayer in dyestuff manufacturing, and Schenley Laboratories and Parke, Davis & Co. were interested in exchanging technologies and know-how for production of pharmaceuticals.[29] Dow Chemical Company was also interested in acrylonitrile technology.[30]

Common to all of these examples, whether drawn from the BASF or Bayer experience, was that important American firms sought out German help in technological development; in other words, many German firms possessed the technological hard currency with which to trade in information that would secure their long-term competitiveness. One of the most important areas in that regard was that of polyethylene production, and it will be useful to explore the development of that technology in more detail.

The international context of technological development: the case of polyethylene

Generally unknown before World War II, polyethylene was one of the most important plastics of the postwar period. It was a material suitable for a wide variety of applications, from wire insulation and shielding of cables to a host of

---

[27] Agreement (Koppers and BASF), 6 April 1953, BASF, F9/31/1; correspondence from April and May 1954 on exchanges of technical information between Monsanto and BASF, BASF, F9/248.

[28] Otto Bayer to Walter Lee (Goodyear), 6 January 1951, in BWA, O. Bayer Korr.; Cauer, "Bericht über Besprechung mit Goodyear Tire and Rubber Co. über Patent- und Vertragsfrage auf dem Polyurethangebiet am 19. Januar 1951 in Leverkusen," 22 January 1951, BWA, O. Bayer Korr.

[29] (Untitled document in English), 13 November 1951, BWA, Sekretariat Dr. Haberland (hereafter, Haberland), 271/1.1.92.

[30] L. C. Chamberlain, Jr. (Dow Chemical, director of plastics research), to Otto Bayer, 6 August 1951, BWA, O. Bayer Korr.

consumer goods, the most prominent of which was packaging. The first plant, constructed by Imperial Chemical Industries (ICI), began production in Britain on 1 September 1939, with a capacity of 100 tons per year. ICI was producing 1,500 tons per year at the end of the war, and virtually all of the wartime production had gone to applications in the electrical industry, "primarily for airborne radar installations." By 1954, the worldwide demand for polyethylene stood at 200 million pounds, and it grew to 600 million pounds in 1958, and to 1.2 billion pounds in 1960.[31]

As its name suggests, polyethylene is a polymer (a formation, generally in the presence of a catalyst, of small molecules linked in any number of ways into very large molecules) of one of the most basic of chemicals, ethylene, and is made up of units with the chemical composition CH_2. A number of scientists had stumbled onto the material in their research during the first third of this century, often without being able to identify it. In 1932, a team of ICI scientists, including J. C. Swallow, Michael Perrin, E. W. Fawcett, and R. O. Gibson, while working on potential applications for high-pressure chemistry, came up with the first primitive process for making it, quite by accident. Frustrated in their attempts to repeat the experiment, the team stopped work temporarily on polymerization of ethylene. Perrin and two others, however, took up the work again in December 1935. They managed, again partly by accident, to produce more polyethylene than before; they had used slightly less pure ethylene as a feedstock, with the oxygen "contaminant" in the ethylene serving as catalyst for polymerization. Bringing the laboratory process (which had produced only about ten grams of polyethylene) up to industrial scale required a number of other innovations, one of the most important of which was the construction of an autoclave reactor with a stirrer to keep the polyethylene from sticking to its sides while it was being formed. By virtue of a British patent of February 1936 and a United States composition-of-matter patent filed soon after, ICI controlled the worldwide rights to the basic technology for producing high-pressure polyethylene in the immediate postwar period. I.G. Farben had developed its own, slightly different process for making *Lupolen* (its brand name for polyethylene) during the war, but BASF still was indebted to ICI for basic production technology after the war.[32]

ICI's British patent expired in February 1956[33] and in 1952 a district court in New York had ruled, for antitrust reasons, that ICI would have to sell nonexclusive licenses to its technology in the United States to all who wished them.[34] Still, for all of the world through 1952, and for the world outside of the United States until 1956, companies that wished to join in the polyethylene bonanza had little choice: either purchase a license and know-how from ICI or try to develop alternative technologies.

---

[31] Spitz, *Petrochemicals;* pp. 257–64.   [32] Ibid., pp. 258–61.

[33] "Competition in Polythene," *Economist* (13 August 1955), seen in BWA, B700/1214.

[34] "Besprechung in Leverkusen am 15.10.52 [Oskar Loehr with Swallow (Chair, ICI Plastics Division), Williams (Research Director, Plastics Div.), Perrin (Research Adviser, ICI), and de Haas (ICI Frankfurt]," 18 October 1952, in BWA, O. Bayer Korr.; Spitz, *Petrochemicals*, p. 264.

BASF's top managers chose the first route and tried to negotiate an exclusive license for Germany. In practice, that proved impossible, because a small former I.G. facility in Upper Bavaria, Anorgana, in Gendorf, already had feedstocks available and production technology in place and had acquired the first license from ICI, mainly because the British firm feared confrontation with American authorities (in whose zone Anorgana lay), in view of pending antitrust actions against ICI in the United States. Anorgana also had the rights to sell polyethylene produced by ICI in Germany.[35] Still, Anorgana's production level would remain small, and BASF's negotiators hoped to gain the rights to produce the lion's share of polyethylene in Germany. At about the same time, in early 1952, Bayer approached the British chemical giant to purchase nonexclusive licenses for polyethylene production. For that reason, ICI patent attorneys tried to convince BASF's negotiators to accept a licensing program in West Germany that would extend beyond just the Ludwigshafen firm, but they reported to Bayer in mid-February 1952 that "we have good reason to believe our present negotiations [with BASF] will be successfully concluded and that if they are, we should be precluded from any negotiations with your firm."[36] In October 1952, at a meeting with Oskar Loehr in Leverkusen, high-ranking ICI executives (including Swallow and Perrin) notified Bayer that Anorgana and BASF had signed licensing agreements to use ICI technology. Contracts would soon be signed. BASF had not achieved an exclusive contract, but had put enough pressure on ICI so that the British firm was still reluctant to grant an additional nonexclusive license to Bayer.[37]

What accounted for ICI's hesitation? J. C. Swallow, the chairman of the Plastics Division, presented some of the reasons in the meeting with Oskar Loehr in the fall of 1952. Swallow noted that the Alkali Division was responsible for

[35] "Besprechung in Leverkusen am 15.10.52," 18 October 1952, BWA, O. Bayer Korr. Swallow indicated that Anorgana had been given the license "bereits vor längerer Zeit." On the fear of antitrust action, see BASF Patentabteilung (Kleber), (Aktennotiz), "Betr. Polyäthylen/Vertrag mit ICI," 17 December 1951, BASF, o.S. (ohne Signatur, i.e., still not classified numerically), Polyäthylen, ICI Patente 1939–1952. Anorgana GmbH was a company formed under the auspices of I.G. Farben in 1939. It began production in 1941, focusing for the most part on explosives, but also branching into other applications (such as ethylene oxide) for its main feedstock, ethylene. Near the end of the war, technology for one such application, polyethylene, appeared in the form of production equipment from Ludwigshafen, which was moved owing to Allied bombing attacks. [BASF Patentabteilung (Kleber), "Bericht über die Besprechung mit Mr. Clifford von der ICI, London, über Polyäthylen-Lizenz, am 11.7.1951," 21 July 1951, p. 2, in BASF, o.S., Polyäthylen, ICI Patente 1939–1952.] After the war, under U.S. administration, and separated from its former parent company, Anorgana branched out still further into plastics, detergents, emulsifiers, textile auxiliaries, and other organic chemical products, but it remained a relatively small facility. See Peter Hayes, Industry and Ideology; I.G. Farben in the Nazi Era (Cambridge University Press, 1987), p. 333; Anorgana, "Produktion–Anwendungstechnik–Verkauf. Stufen zum Erfolg," Chemische Industrie 4(1952):A573–5.

[36] Dr. Mez (Patentabteilung, Leverkusen), "Polythen," 18 January 1952 (carbon), BWA, B700/1214; Dr. Ball (leader, ICI Patent Department) to Bayer Patent Department, "Polythene," 13 February 1952 (Abschrift), BWA, O. Bayer Korr.

[37] "Besprechung in Leverkusen am 15.10.52," 18 October 1952, BWA, O. Bayer Korr.

granting licenses for polyethylene production technology, but he said that he would endorse Bayer's request for a nonexclusive license. Still, he summarized some of ICI's concerns. Production of polyethylene at an ICI-licensed plant had to be at least 5,000 tons per year for technical and commercial reasons. He went on to say that as the export for polyethylene was not accessible to the Germans (because of licensing agreements and because American firms had access to very inexpensive ethylene feedstocks), he questioned that the West German domestic market was large enough to justify more than just the BASF output (plus Anorgana's small production).[38]

Loehr quickly tried to counter those arguments, pointing out that there was no single source of ethylene in Germany that would be able to provide all of the feedstocks that would eventually be needed for large-scale polyethylene production. Because of the dispersion of ethylene suppliers, he claimed, sooner or later even BASF would have to produce in more than one plant. Loehr contended that ICI should anticipate that inevitable development by giving Bayer a license from the beginning. Loehr concluded that "this argument appeared to be reasonable to Mr. Swallow." Loehr and his colleague Knopf followed up on the conversation on 1 December with a letter to Swallow that summarized and expanded on Loehr's previous arguments.[39]

Bayer's determined efforts to obtain a nonexclusive license were in vain. Swallow answered Loehr on 8 December 1952, indicating that he would send A. Renfrew, the development director of the Plastics Division, to Leverkusen to explain the complexities of the situation to Loehr. I have not been able to locate a record of Renfrew's visit, but the basic message was clear to Bayer already: A handwritten notation on Swallow's letter reads simply "ICI can give no license."[40] ICI's unwillingness to grant the license may have been the most important factor keeping the Leverkusen-based company out of polyethylene production. In any case, some Bayer personnel at least attempted to convey the impression to visitors that Bayer's absence from the polyethylene market was a part of a deliberate strategy, in effect trying to make a virtue of a necessity. Speaking with visitors from Monsanto in March 1956, Otto Bayer concluded his presentation on polyethylene research at the Bayer corporation, saying that "we do not at present have in mind producing polyethylene here in Germany."[41]

The fact that the Bayer corporation had been actively engaged in research on polyethylene during the first half of the 1950s, even though not yet producing it, indicated that Bayer, like other major German and non-German firms and some independent researchers, had been pursuing the second route: development of alternative technologies. That was ongoing even as the firms negotiated with ICI for rights to its technology. One of the first and most promising processes

[38] Ibid.
[39] "Besprechung in Leverkusen am 15.10.52," 18 October 1952, BWA, O. Bayer Korr.; FF Bayer (Loehr, Knopf) to ICI (Swallow), "Polythene," 1 December 1952, BWA, B700/1214.
[40] Swallow to Loehr, 8 December 1952, BWA, B700/1214.
[41] Dr. Schneider, "Aktennotiz Betr. Monsanto Chemical Co./Polyäthylen, Besprechung am 1. März 1956 in Leverkusen," 2 March 1956, BWA, O. Bayer Korr.

came from the laboratory of Karl Ziegler, leader of the Max Planck Coal Research Institute, in Mülheim, on the Ruhr.

Ziegler's major field of expertise was organometallic chemistry, not plastics, but his research proved of major consequence for the plastics industry, both in the production of polyethylene in particular and in the production of polyolefins (e.g., polypropylene) in general. His success in that area had to do, in part, with a historical accident: Ziegler had had access to lithium during the war, and because lithium will react with hydrocarbons, he had begun research on reactions of lithium compounds with olefins. He found that by combining lithium hydride with ethylene, then adding additional ethylene to the resulting mixture, and repeating the addition over and over, he was able to induce "chain growth," producing linear polymers. Ziegler and his fellow researchers also came up with a catalyst system for producing polyethylene: a mixture of titanium and aluminum alkyl. The new process differed from the ICI process in a number of respects: It operated at low pressures, it required no external heat source to start it, and the product, although still called "polyethylene," had properties markedly different from those of the polyethylene produced by the high-pressure process. Low-pressure polyethylene was a linear polymer of relatively high density (thus the designation HDPE, high-density polyethylene) that was "particularly good for applications where hardness, rigidity, and high strength were important." High-pressure polyethylene was a branched polymer of relatively low density (thus the designation LDPE, low-density polyethylene) "used for its flexibility, toughness, and the clarity of its films."[42]

High-pressure producers at first feared competition from low-pressure producers, because low-pressure polyethylene production appeared the less expensive process: Its capital-equipment expenditure would be smaller, because reaction vessels would not have to be as sturdy, and its energy requirements would be lower.[43] In practice, however, the costs did not differ markedly. In a conversation with Dr. Knauff of Bayer on 23 April 1955, for instance, R. J. Wilson of the Monsanto Chemical Company reported that there was no real cost advantage to low-pressure production of polyethylene. Still, the alternative process was interesting because of the different characteristics of the end products in the two cases.[44] Chemical companies like Monsanto, BASF (which purchased rival low-pressure polyethylene technology from Phillips Petroleum), and many others often were interested in the products of both high-pressure and low-pressure processes, seeing them as complementary rather than competing technologies.

Ziegler became quite wealthy by licensing his invention to companies around the world (although some claim that he could have done even better had he not insisted on marketing his ideas on his own). Hoechst, Ruhrchemie, and Hibernia were some of the West German firms that purchased licenses, along with

---

[42] Spitz, *Petrochemicals*, pp. 263–4, 331–8; quotation, p. 264.

[43] Werner Kneip, "Polyäthylen – Die Entwicklung eines Kunststoffes," *Chemische Industrie* 7(1955):299.

[44] Dr. Knauff, "Aktennotiz über eine Besprechung mit Mr. R. J. Wilson, Monsanto Chemical Co., am 23.4.55 in Leverkusen," 25 April 1955, BWA, O. Bayer Korr.

DuPont, Bakelite Co., Dow Chemical, W. R. Grace, Celanese Corporation of America, Monsanto Chemical, Hercules Powder Co., and other American firms. Because Ziegler did not have the resources of an industrial research-and-development laboratory, let alone the experience of actually producing polyethylene on an industrial scale, the companies that purchased licenses for his process had to develop their own production technologies, with the result that a thriving sub-market in Ziegler know-how developed. Hercules Powder, for instance, purchased exclusive American rights to Ziegler know-how from Hoechst, which had started production at the world's first low-pressure poly-ethylene plant in 1955. Celanese sought to purchase know-how for operating the process from other German firms with at least pilot-plant experience in Ziegler production.[45]

Peter Spitz claims that Ziegler's success in selling the rights to his invention to all comers was a function of major changes in the international chemical industry following World War II. The growing number of producers in the field

made it easer for an inventor to find a potential new producer willing to sponsor research work on the basis that success in such research would then allow the sponsoring firm to have suitable technology to enter the field in question. . . . [T]he inventor was now also in a much better position to strike a more favorable bargain with an existing producer.[46]

Ziegler, then, epitomized a new breed of inventor-entrepreneur on the scene in the postwar period.

But if Ziegler represented a new force in the international chemical industry, much important work continued to be done in the laboratories of the major firms. For instance, Phillips Chemical Co., a wholly owned subsidiary of Phillips Petroleum, developed an important process for producing low-pressure polyethylene that competed with the Ziegler process. The Phillips process differed from Ziegler's in a number of ways, including the catalyst systems employed (i.e., the catalyst plus the additional materials used to make a catalyst solution and the processes for purifying the end product).[47]

As the competing processes themselves differed in terms of patents and technologies, Phillips also determined to follow a licensing policy completely different from that of Ziegler. When Hermann Kleber of BASF's Patent Division wrote to Phillips in September 1955 to inquire about acquiring a license, P. M. Arnold, the Phillips research-and-development manager, answered as follows:

I wish to make it plain that Phillips is not interested in doing what Professor Ziegler has done. That is, we do not wish to disclose information about our process to numerous

[45] Dr. Hagedorn, "Bericht über den Besuch mit Celanese Corporation of America am 28.4.1955 in Uerdingen," 3 May 1955 (carbon), BWA, B700/1214; BASF, untitled report on low-pressure polyethylene processes, n.d. (ca. late 1955, early 1956), pp. 12–14, in BASF, K311; a list of German firms acquiring licenses is in the brief note "Verwertung der Zieglerschen Patente für Olefine," *Chemische Industrie* 6(1954):637.

[46] Spitz, *Petrochemicals*, pp. 331–2; on the changes in the industry, see pp. 338–42.

[47] Spitz, *Petrochemicals*, p. 336; BASF, untitled report on low-pressure polyethylene processes, n.d. (ca. late 1955, early 1956), pp. 3–4, in BASF, K311.

organizations in return for only a payment of a few hundred dollars. We wish to restrict detailed knowledge of our process to those organizations which will build plants and utilize our process, returning us a substantial royalty income over an extended period of time. We believe that our process is unique, and that we will have a commanding patent position with respect to it.[48]

The contract conditions that Arnold spelled out were, as Kleber commented in a cover memorandum when distributing the letter to major figures at BASF, "very hard." Kleber also reported that a Hamburg importer with whom he had discussed the subject "had declared this demand completely insane."[49] In order to get an exclusive license, BASF would have to pay $250,000 up front for the license, which would be credited against future royalties. The German firm also would have to obligate itself to build a plant "of sufficient capacity to supply a reasonable proportion of the anticipated German market." For the five years after Phillips started operations at its 25-million-pound-per-year plant, BASF would commit itself to paying royalties based on the capacity of BASF's projected plant *whether or not BASF actually built it*. The royalty would amount to 7 percent of the selling price of polyethylene for the first five years and would drop to 6 percent for the following five years. There were also to be the usual agreements on sharing technical information, at least for the first five years of plant operation.[50]

Despite the tough conditions, BASF did acquire the American technology, with the first payment of $250,000 transferred to a Phillips bank account on 2 May 1956.[51] In its 1957 annual report,[52] BASF announced construction of a large-scale production facility using the process at its Rheinische Olefinwerke (ROW) subsidiary. Despite the "very hard" contract conditions, BASF's Bernhard Timm noted in a 1988 interview that they "seemed better than those for the Ziegler process," in part, at least, because Phillips itself produced using its own system and shared its know-how with its licensees. Regardless of the expense of acquiring the technology, it was money well spent, because BASF experienced few start-up problems using the Phillips process, in contrast to the experiences of those firms using the Ziegler process.[53]

While BASF and Hoechst acquired alternative polyethylene production technology from outside their firms, Bayer concentrated on developing its own processes, especially after unsuccessful negotiations with Ziegler for a license for his process in 1953.[54] In March 1956, Professor Otto Bayer (Figure 4.1) reported to a group of visitors from Monsanto about a Bayer low-pressure process

[48] Arnold to Kleber, 7 October 1955, BASF, K311.

[49] Kleber, "MARLEX 50/Phillips Petroleum Co., Bartlesville," 14 October 1955, BASF, K311.

[50] Arnold to Kleber, 7 October 1955, BASF, K311.

[51] Kleber to Arnold, "Polyolefin Agreement (A-319-56)," 28 May 1956, BASF, K311.

[52] BASF, *Bericht über das Geschäftsjahr 1957*, p. 15. ROW was a 50:50 subsidiary of BASF and Shell. For more on this, see Chapter 5.

[53] Interview with Bernhard Timm, BASF Ludwigshafen, 10 August 1988.

[54] Bayer Patentabteilung (Stroh, Knopf), "Aktennotiz, Besprechung mit Professor Ziegler, Max-Planck-Institut, Mülheim/Ruhr, am 13.5.1953 über die Dimerisation von Olefinen mit Aluminiumtriäthyl," 15 May 1953 (mimeograph), BWA, B700/1214.

Figure 4.1. Otto Bayer, head of the main scientific laboratory and member of the managing board of Bayer A.G. (Courtesy Bayer Firmenarchiv, Leverkusen.)

that used catalysts different from that of Ziegler and did not infringe on Phillips' patents. A pilot plant was in operation, but the quality of the output was not yet satisfactory. He also described a completely new medium-pressure (ca. 300 atm) process and showed the Monsanto representatives polyethylene film produced using that process. Those processes never became very important, in part because, as Professor Bayer noted in the meeting, the Bayer corporation did not intend to produce polyethylene in Germany.[55] Although Bayer was and remains a major force in the plastics area, the decision to eschew polyethylene production may be seen as an example of adherence to the firm's decision after 1945 "to produce no mass[-produced] plastics, but rather products with special technical qualities."[56] That decision, however, must be seen in the context of Bayer's thwarted attempts to acquire ICI and Ziegler technology earlier in the 1950s.

[55] Dr. Schneider, "Aktennotiz Betr. Monsanto Chemical Co./Polyäthylen, Besprechung am 1. März 1956 in Leverkusen," 2 March 1956, BWA, O. Bayer Korr.
[56] Erik Verg, *Meilensteine* (Leverkusen: Bayer, 1988), p. 329.

Still, whether the firm in question was Bayer, BASF, Hoechst, or another German company, this case study of the development of polyethylene production technology in the first half of the 1950s indicates how well the West German chemical industry was integrated into international trade in technology by the middle of the decade. Companies such as BASF – in ways that were not much different from those of their counterparts abroad – were able to choose between competing German and American technologies in low-pressure polyethylene production; American companies lined up to purchase from Germany not only the rights to a new, low-pressure process but also the know-how to implement it.

Concluding remarks

Writing to Bayer's Ulrich Haberland in September 1953, the vice-president of Interchemical Corporation, Bromley Ault, spoke admiringly of the Leverkusen firm's accomplishments since 1945. He mixed his admiration with some regret, however: "So many of the things you predicted in 1950 have come to pass, that I am sorry we were so short-sighted that we did not subscribe to the $30,000,000 you needed for your business."[57] Many other potential investors may have shared that regret, for the accomplishments of the West German chemical industry in the decade after the war were indeed impressive.

Many of them were earned by dint of hard work, vigorous salesmanship, astute investment, and technological expertise. The last factor, in particular, was significant: German firms were able to deal with their foreign counterparts from a position of surprising strength and to move once again into technologies at the forefront of developments in organic chemistry. Still, there were other factors at work beyond the control of West German engineers, scientists, and industrialists. The international political and economic climate had changed substantially in the years following the war, and the German chemical industry was particularly well situated to take advantage of many of those changes. It happened to be in the interest of German bureaucrats to campaign actively on behalf of the industry, although of course the companies themselves undertook most of the negotiations for technology transfer and international cooperation. And, finally, the industrialists were able to take advantage of personal contacts and of a durable reputation for quality – the legacy of the I.G. period – in postwar dealings with foreign firms.

Given all of those advantages, one might ask, Why did the industry not change more quickly than it did? Some answers are provided in the following chapters, and my article "Technology and the West German *Wirtschaftswunder*" outlines some of the arguments more generally.[58] Here, a brief discussion of issues connected with the division between old and new thinking, as outlined in Chapter 3, is in order.

---

[57] Bromley Ault to Ulrich Haberland, 18 September 1953, BWA, Sekretariat Dr. Haberland, 271/1.1.2.

[58] Raymond G. Stokes, "Technology and the West German *Wirtschaftswunder*," *Technology and Culture* 32(1991):1–22.

As pointed out in Chapter 1, German chemical industrialists, from the very beginnings of their industry, engaged in extensive foreign trade, but emphasized domestic self-sufficiency in their domestic-market strategies, raw-materials procurement policies, and manufacturing practices. During the National Socialist period, of course, limitations on foreign trade in chemical products and greater emphasis on the domestic market were added to those other aspects of autarky, or economic self-sufficiency. It is clear that at the beginning of the 1950s there was consensus in West Germany on rejecting the foreign-trade component of autarky, but just the same, at least some of the chemical manufacturers, often supported by the government, clung to old ideas on domestic-market strategies, raw-materials procurement, and manufacturing.

The slowly changing tariff laws regarding petrochemical feedstocks and the products of acetylene chemistry, coupled with the preferences given to products from coal-chemical plants, as described in Chapter 3, indicated the emphasis on the domestic market. In the 1950s as well, West German firms continued to think primarily in terms of domestic manufacturing capacity, although the beginnings of a strategy of manufacturing abroad may be detected in some cases. In terms of raw materials, the Germans continued in the early 1950s, despite the prominence of American petrochemistry, to think primarily in terms of coal. A 1950 article in the trade journal *Chemische Industrie,* for instance, indicated that in the future the role of petroleum in chemical production undoubtedly would be significant, but it would vary from country to country, depending on "for example available sources of raw materials and particular economic and technical – including financial – aspects of the situation."[59] Another article in the same journal pointed more clearly to the need for coal-based chemistry:

Our poverty forces us to the relentless use of all possibilities that the most important raw material, coal, offers. If America, which is rich in raw materials, already today attains pure materials from petroleum and uses them technically, those in Germany must make that much more effort to exploit correspondingly the pure preparations of hard-coal tar. Development work in this special area is being carried out with great intensity at present in Germany. The most recent publications and patent applications in this area provide convincing testimony of this.[60]

A year earlier, another article in *Chemische Industrie* pointed out that it was critical for the West German chemical industry to take advantage of its ability to produce plastics to regain world markets for Germany. Only two countries in the world had been of approximately the same rank in the past, the article went on: the United States and Germany. The author concluded with the expectation "that in the future as well the coverage of the world's requirements of plastics would be satisfied to a reasonable extent by Germany especially since *the necessary raw materials for the most part can be obtained domestically.*"[61]

[59] "Die wirtschaftliche Entwicklung der Erdöllchemie," *Chemische Industrie* 2(1950):213.
[60] Eduard Moehrle, "Möglichkeiten des Steinkohlenteers," *Chemische Industrie* 2(1950):209–10.
[61] Richard Blankenfeld, "Probleme und Aufgaben der deutschen Kunststoffindustrie," *Chemische Industrie* 1(1949):22, my emphasis.

Nevertheless, pressured by competition from abroad, and able, because of the refinery-building program of the early 1950s, to take advantage of less expensive olefins from German refineries, many in the industry were clearly changing their outlook, as indicated by a number of developments in the mid-1950s. They are dealt with on a firm-by-firm basis in the case studies in the following five chapters.

Part III
Alternative paths to plenty:
case studies from the
mid-1950s

5

Fifty-fifty with the petroleum multinationals: BASF, Shell, and Rheinische Olefinwerke

Badische Anilin- und Soda-Fabrik (BASF) has had a long and distinguished history in the international organic chemical industry. The first to produce synthetic indigo dye from coal tar, BASF also pioneered in the area of high-pressure chemistry during the first decades of this century. It was thus no accident that when I.G. Farben was formed in late 1925, the new chemical giant was the legal successor to BASF. BASF's ongoing importance in the new firm extended beyond mere legal formality: The chairman of its managing board, Carl Bosch, became the first chairman of the managing board of the I.G. That meant, among other things, that I.G. Farben would emphasize some of the same high-pressure synthesis technologies that BASF had stressed in its research and production programs.[1]

---

[1] BASF, *Chemie für die Zukunft* (Ludwigshafen: BASF, 1990). For a brief synopsis of some of the most relevant work on the early years of BASF, see Raymond G. Stokes, *Divide and Prosper: The Heirs of I.G. Farben under Allied Authority, 1945–1951* (Berkeley: University of California Press, 1988), pp. 87–90. For BASF's role in the new I.G., see Helmuth Tammen, *Die I.G. Farbenindustrie A.G. (1925–1933)* (Berlin: Verlag H. Tammen, 1978); Peter Hayes, *Industry and Ideology: I.G. Farben in the Nazi Era* (Cambridge University Press, 1987); and Peter Morris, "The Development of Acetylene Chemistry and Synthetic Rubber by I.G. Farbenindustrie Aktiengesellschaft,

Despite its tradition of excellence and leadership in new developments in organic chemical technology, there were some reasons that one might have expected BASF to hesitate about moving into petrochemical technology in the immediate postwar period. For one thing, BASF, alone among the major successors to I.G. Farben, had, by the spring of 1953, achieved clear title to its own coal mine: the Gewerkschaft Auguste Victoria. Assured of its raw-materials supply, BASF might have been expected to be less interested than others in developing technologies that would involve surrendering direct control over its source of raw materials and energy. Furthermore, BASF had at its disposal what appeared to be a promising new set of technologies in Reppe chemistry. Developed by its own Walter Reppe, those technologies employed acetylene made from German coal to manufacture a full range of modern plastic products.[2] Related to that, there was a natural tendency for BASF and other major German organic chemical producers to stick with the feedstock – coal – with which they had already demonstrated success. The Germans thoroughly understood the science behind coal-based technologies, and therefore they hesitated to plunge into the messier petroleum-based processes, the science of which was little understood in the 1940s and 1950s. Unencumbered by any notions of the "elegance" of chemical reactions, chemical engineers in the United States had pioneered in petrochemical production.[3]

West German firms were indeed slow to embrace petrochemical technology. The engineers and scientists working in those firms were more comfortable with coal-based technology; and that accounted, in part, for the lag in petrochemical development in West Germany. But there were numerous counterarguments to set against the other points in the preceding paragraph: Auguste Victoria did not supply coal appropriate for Reppe chemical processes; rather, the mine's output was most suitable for production of nitrogen (which was not an organic chemical), and it could supply up to 70 percent of BASF's requirements for nitrogen production. Acetylene for Reppe chemistry could be obtained from either coal or petroleum, which meant that development in that area would not necessarily restrict BASF to coal chemistry.[4]

Aside from the admittedly quite significant psychological reorientation that would be necessary for BASF chemists and engineers to move away from coal-

---

1926–1945" (dissertation, Oxford University, 1982). On Carl Bosch, see Karl Holdermann, *Im Banne der Chemie. Carl Bosch – Leben und Werk* (Düsseldorf: Econ, 1953).

[2] Morris, "The Development of Acetylene Chemistry"; Morris, "Strategy and System: Reppe and the Development of Organic Chemicals in I.G. Farben" (paper presented at the 1991 meeting of the Society for the History of Technology, Madison, WI, 3 November 1991).

[3] A. Lawrence Waddams, *Chemicals from Petroleum: An Introductory Survey,* 3rd ed. New York: Wiley, 1973), pp. 12–13. Waddams claims that those working for established chemical companies generally found it difficult to make the conceptual switch necessary for the new technology. Petroleum producers, in contrast, were relatively unencumbered by that traditional regard for "elegance." Peter Morris makes a similar point with regard to the choice of feedstocks for synthetic rubber at I.G. Farben in the late 1920s and 1930s in "The Development of Acetylene Chemistry," pp. 197–8.

[4] Morris, "The Development of Acetylene Chemistry," pp. 379–80.

based chemistry, there were few strong impediments to the adoption of petrochemical technology. On the other hand, a number of positive factors pushed BASF's managers into the petrochemical field more rapidly than their counterparts in other West German firms. The company had extensive contacts in the international chemical and petroleum industries. Furthermore, it had a well-developed tradition of internal development of cutting-edge technologies. Some of those have been discussed already. In the current context, however, a brief closer look at BASF's development of polyethylene technology (the products of which the company sold under the trade name Lupolen) will be useful.

The news that Imperial Chemistry Industries (ICI) had developed a process for producing polyethylene in 1936 traveled rapidly to Ludwigshafen. The BASF Patent Section had a copy of the British patent (which had been accepted on 6 September 1937) by 16 October 1937, and I.G. Farben scientists had samples of the product by the summer of 1938.[5] By 1939, a small polyethylene facility was in operation in Ludwigshafen. Up to that time, ICI had not patented its invention in Germany, and the war prevented ICI from doing so until the early 1950s.[6] Ludwigshafen could therefore conduct research on polyethylene and eventually produce it (albeit never in large quantities) without a license, although I.G. Farben's patent attorneys in Ludwigshafen recognized their debt to the British firm from the beginning. Once the war (an inconvenient disruption to normal business operations) was over, I.G. Farben planned to get a license through normal channels. In 1939, in responding to the matter if ICI's Austrian patent for polyethylene granted in 1937, BASF's Dr. Kleber wrote that "we will not speak out against the . . . patent registration, since we are lacking suitable material to support objections. Moreover, we have in mind – following the resumption of normal relations with England – to cooperate with ICI in this area and to come to a contractual understanding."[7]

During the war, production of the new polymer became significant at Ludwigshafen only in 1944, when it amounted to 14 tons per month. That minuscule figure (by contemporary standards) was nonetheless crucial to the German war effort. Just as in the Allied countries, polyethylene figured prominently as insulation in electrical apparatus in Germany. Air attacks on Ludwigshafen late in the war (Figure 5.1) prompted a partial dismantling of the installation and its reassembly at I.G. Farben's subsidiary, Anorgana GmbH, in Gendorf, in Upper Bavaria, although it did not produce there until the 1950s.[8]

---

[5] Patent specification 471,590, "Improvements in or Relating to the Polymerisation of Ethylene," BASF Unternehmensarchiv, Ludwigshafen (hereafter, BASF), o.S. (ohne Signatur, i.e., still not classified numerically), Polyäthylen, ICI Patente 1939–1952; ICI Dyestuffs Group to Dr. Ambros, "Polythene," 27 July 1938, BASF, o.S., Polyäthylen allg. 1938–1946.

[6] BASF (Reppe and Hopff) to Firma Dynamit A.G., Troisdorf (H. R. Dufour), "Polyäthylen," 18 August 1950, BASF, o.S., Polyäthylen–Troisdorf 1939–1950.

[7] I.G. Farben Patentabteilung (Kleber) to Patentabt. Photo- und Kunstseide Wolfen, "Betr. Patentanmeldung A 2974-37/39 – Oesterreich. ICI Ltd., London," 12 December 1939, BASF, o.S., Polyäthylen allg. 1938–1946.

[8] Application from BASF to Inter-Allied Chemical Products Committee to resume production of Lupolen, n.d. (ca. 22 November 1946), BASF, o.S., Polyäthylen allg. 2 1946–1952; BASF

Figure 5.1. Damage to the BASF factory in Ludwigshafen, 1945. (Courtesy BASF Unternehmensarchiv, Ludwigshafen.)

After 1945, the need for insulation materials for electrical apparatus was again critical in Germany, although BASF's production capacity was by that time practically zero. Supported by the French occupation authorities, in 1946 BASF applied to the Allies for permission to reconstruct the plant to a capacity of 60 tons by 1949. By the fall of 1947, the company was producing Lupolen H once again. Just four years later, in November 1951, BASF leaders noted with pride that "at present, three units for the production of 50 tons per month of Lupolen H each are under construction. The quality of our Lupolen H is now good, approximately equal to that of DuPont, and better than that of ICI." Because they had produced polyethylene in the past and because they were not beholden to ICI for know-how, BASF managers were hopeful that the ongoing negotiations with the British firm would proceed smoothly and satisfactorily, which they did by late 1952.[9]

Patentabteilung (Kleber), "Bericht über die Besprechung mit Mr. Clifford von der ICI, London, über Polyäthylen-Lizenz am 11.7.1951," 21 July 1951, p. 2, BASF, o.S., Polyäthylen, ICI Patente 1939–1952.

[9] Application from BASF to Inter-Allied Chemical Products Committee to resume production of Lupolen, n.d. (ca. 22 November 1946), BASF, o.S., Polyäthylen, allg. 2 1946–1952; documents on the resumption of production in 1947 are in the same file; quotation is from BASF Patentabteilung (Kühn), "Bericht über die Besprechung am 26.11.1951 betr. Lizenzvertrag mit der ICI über Polyäthylen," 27 November 1951, BASF, o.S. Polyäthylen, ICI Patente 1939–1952; agreement on polyethylene signed by ICI and BASF, 1953 (1 January), BASF, F9/43.

For BASF, then, the question was not its ability to come up with competitive technologies for producing plastics (especially polyethylene) and other organic chemicals via the petrochemical route; the firm already had significant experience in that area. Rather, the primary concern of the company's leadership was the security of its feedstock supply. To ensure that, it would be necessary to cooperate with a major oil firm, preferably one with some experience in the petrochemical field. That last point was crucial: Because they already possessed much of the technological competence necessary for petrochemical production, BASF's managers had the luxury of being able to choose from among the largest and most well established petroleum producers in the world.

This chapter centers on developments leading to the establishment in 1955 of the Rheinische Olefinwerke GmbH (ROW), the first factory in Germany devoted exclusively to the manufacture of organic chemical products from petroleum. Although the founding of ROW was made possible by broader political and economic developments, such as the re-establishment of the I.G. successors, changes in tax and tariff policies, and so on, and although ROW was founded in the same year that the Federal Republic of Germany gained its sovereignty from the Allies, most of the story of the founding of the firm was centered on politics somewhat more narrowly conceived: It arose from discussions between two very large concerns with international interests.

Rheinische Olefinwerke

In its 1953 corporate report, BASF announced an agreement with Deutsche Shell A.G. to found the first German chemical factory to be devoted wholly to petrochemical production: the ROW. The two companies, each of which would have a 50 percent stake in the new corporation, planned to use the new facility to produce Lupolen and ethylbenzene, an intermediate produced by alkylation of ethylene, primarily for the manufacture of polystyrene. Construction was to be completed by the second half of 1955. Feedstocks for the new factory would come from refinery gases produced in "a neighboring oil refinery," that is, from the Union Rheinische Braunkohlen Kraftstoff A.G. in Wesseling, near Cologne.[10] A former hydrogenation (petroleum products from coal) producer founded by a number of Rhenish brown-coal producers, Union Kraftstoff had ensured retention of its production facilities after 1945 by switching from coal hydrogenation (banned by the Allies) to the refining of crude oil, especially heavy petroleum residues. By virtue of that transition, its connection with Shell had become close. In May 1948, the petroleum-trade newsletter *Erdölinformationdienst* announced that Shell had agreed to supply imported crude to Union for refining. Production was to start on 1 July 1948. Monthly throughput would be 30,000 tons of crude, although the distillation capacity was to increase to 750,000 tons per year shortly thereafter.[11]

[10] BASF, *Bericht über das Geschäftsjahr 1953*, p. 13.
[11] "Uebereinkunft Shell-Wesseling," *Erdölinformationdienst* 1, Nr. 22, 15 May 1948.

Just as in the United States, petroleum refining at Union Kraftstoff had as its primary goal the production of gasoline, kerosene, diesel fuel, and other fuels, but olefins, which could be used as chemical feedstocks, were unavoidable by-products of refining. From mid-1948, Union thus had available surpluses of petrochemical feedstocks that it could sell to chemical producers. Two factors retarded movement in that direction in the late 1940s. First, the quantities of feedstocks produced were quite small initially, although production at Union increased rapidly. More important, technical considerations constrained the choices available to Union and Shell. Large-scale transportation of ethylene feedstocks over long distances was problematic in the late 1940s, although that problem was later overcome. In West Germany in the immediate postwar period, that meant that any potential large-scale purchaser of feedstocks would have to be located close to Wesseling.[12]

Bayer, with its main plant at Leverkusen, about 10 kilometers from Cologne, was the only existing facility in the surrounding area that was a realistic possibility to purchase the feedstock, but its top officials, as will be detailed in the next chapter, were interested in working with Shell's competitors, Standard Oil of New Jersey and British Petroleum. Building a new petrochemical production facility near Wesseling was the only option left, and that would take some time even if a willing partner could be found immediately.

According to Bernhard Timm (Figure 5.2), who eventually carried through the negotiations between BASF and Shell and who in the 1960s served as chairman of BASF's managing board, Shell's representatives were already searching for partners in 1948. Timm claimed that two representatives of Shell, one from the Shell Group in London and one from Deutsche Shell, showed up in Ludwigshafen sometime in 1948 to explore the possibility of supplying BASF with feedstocks for a wax-cracking venture. He immediately seized that opportunity to begin pushing for much more extensive cooperation that would involve large-scale petrochemical production and closer technical collaboration between the two firms. The French, in whose zone that occurred, knew about the negotiations, but looked the other way.[13] Although I have been able to find no documentation of that meeting, a number of its features give it the ring of truth. For one thing, it makes sense that Shell would have been looking for a partner in 1948, when the firm began supplying Union Kraftstoff with crude and petroleum residues; furthermore, its representatives would have been thinking in terms of small supply contracts involving transportable waxes, which were also by-products of refining. Timm's tale of the response of the French occupiers also fits in with their peculiar patterns of behavior during the occupation: Because the French were interested in exploiting BASF in the short term as well as in the long term, their policies often entailed decisions that would benefit the German

---

[12] Interview with Bernhard Timm, BASF Ludwigshafen, 10 August 1988. Timm claimed that he and others at BASF had hoped that the ROW plant could be located at Ludwigshafen or Oppau. Technical problems of transporting the feedstock – which later were overcome – prevented that.

[13] Timm interview.

Figure 5.2. Bernhard Timm, member of the BASF managing board, ca. 1950. (Courtesy BASF Unternehmensarchiv, Ludwigshafen.)

firm's long-term competitive prospects. Finally, given Timm's personality and his enthusiasm for petrochemical technology, his suggestion of closer collaboration than that envisaged by Shell's representatives is plausible.[14]

In any case, full-fledged cooperation between the firms was delayed. It may well have been that one factor involved was BASF's close relationship with Standard Oil of New Jersey (Esso).[15] Timm claimed that BASF eventually decided against working with Esso and turned to Shell because BASF's leaders did not want to compromise the reputations of the American firm's managers, who were under suspicion for having aided BASF and I.G. Farben to the detriment of U.S. national security before the outbreak of the war.[16] Equally likely, Esso officials may have avoided their BASF counterparts for precisely the same reason. A number of other factors undoubtedly influenced the delay, including the shortage of capital in Germany, the decisions still pending on the breakup of I.G. Farben, the problems with moving foreign-exchange earnings out of West Germany, and the careful deliberation that characterized West German firms contemplating the move into petrochemical production. Thus it was no accident that serious negotiations on the issue started at about the time BASF was re-founded as an independent company (officially, that took place on 30 January 1952), nor that the foreign-exchange issue was extremely important in the negotiations. The hard line that BASF took in the negotiations indicated both its surprising

[14] On the French occupation and relations with BASF, see Stokes, *Divide and Prosper,* pp. 86–106.
[15] Hayes outlines some of the details of the relationship between Standard Oil of New Jersey (Esso) and I.G. Farben in *Industry and Ideology,* pp. 37–8, 115, 139–41, 183, 209–10, 335–6, and 355.
[16] Timm interview.

strength in the aftermath of the war and its managers' careful consideration of the path on which they were embarking.

Negotiations began in earnest in mid-January 1952 after Shell managers in London decided that they wanted to cooperate with a well-respected firm in Germany, such as BASF, in the development of petrochemicals.[17] At the beginning, Union Kraftstoff was also to be included as a partner.[18] Representatives of the two larger firms decided that they would discuss the details of the venture in an upcoming meeting. The topics on the agenda included matters related to supply of feedstocks, BASF's potential role as plant operator, a framework for reaching further agreements, and exchange of technical information.[19]

Representatives of all three companies met in Ludwigshafen on 23 and 24 January 1952. Shell sent representatives not only from its London office but also from Shell Hamburg (Deutsche Shell A.G.) and from N.V. De Bataafsche P.M. (BPM, or Shell, the Hague, in the Netherlands). The oil giant's delegation was eight strong, and two additional delegates were present for the first day of the meeting. They included Mr. Mitchell (London) and Mr. Boeder (Hamburg), who had been the first Shell representatives to appear in Ludwigshafen in 1948.[20] Union Kraftstoff's primary representative was Mr. Nowotny, although two others joined him on 23 January. Bernhard Timm led the nine-member BASF delegation, which swelled to eleven on 24 January. The purpose of the discussions was to develop plans for the project as well as means for pushing them forward as rapidly as possible.[21]

BASF's representatives, the acting hosts, started the discussion. They noted that they wanted to find out, first, about the materials that would be available for the plant (what kinds, how much, and when) and, second, what role Farbwerke Hoechst was playing in the plans of Shell and Union Kraftstoff. The representatives of the two petroleum companies pointed out that although they could not commit to precise figures because of the dependence of production figures on the composition of the cracking gas, they would be bringing a cracking and reforming facility on-line at Union's plant in Wesseling in September of 1952. They mentioned some minimum production figures for various products and underscored the fact that the olefins from the plant would not be pure, so that a separation facility would have to be constructed. Shell's delegates asked BASF's representatives if their plant at Ludwigshafen would be able to absorb the transportable fractions of the cracked gases. BASF, its delegates replied, would be able to take small quantities soon, and more eventually. But increasing the

[17] Bernhard Timm, "Notiz über ein Telefongespräch mit Mr. Mitchell, Shell Petroleum London, am 14.1.1952, 11 Uhr" ("streng vertaulich"), 14 January 1952, BASF, F9/165.

[18] Timm interview, confirmed by a document that speaks of "the joint interest of all three partners," from 1952. Timm, "Text des Telegramms v. 14.1.52 an Shell Petroleum, London," BASF, F9/165.

[19] Timm, "Text des Telegramms v. 14.1.52 an Shell Petroleum, London," BASF, F9/165.

[20] This according to Bernhard Timm in Timm interview. Citations for material presented in the remainder of the paragraph follow.

[21] "Bericht über die Besprechung mit der Shell-Gruppe und Wesseling am 23. und 24. January 1952 in Ludwigshafen." 25 January 1952, p. 1, BASF, F9/165.

BASF capacity so that it could accept the full output of the cracking plant would require some time. Delivery of small quantities of propylene to Ludwigshafen, further discussion revealed, would not be economic. Therefore, it would be preferable from the start to design the separation facility to accept Union's entire output of olefins. In any case, the complexity of the discussions, including various technical matters and the question where to build the plant, necessitated breaking up the larger group into smaller ones to deal with individual issues. Most of the detailed negotiations, all agreed, would have to be delegated to a technical group that would meet later.[22]

What Shell's representatives had to say about the Hoechst question was more intriguing. They announced that Farbwerke Hoechst had recently expressed interest in absorbing part of the olefins produced at Union. W. Alexander Menne, "member of the future supervisory board of the Farbwerke Höchst A.G. [Menne was already a member of the Hoechst managing board at the beginning of 1952[23]]," had emphasized that Hoechst could not sit idly by if it did not get part of Union Kraftstoff's olefin production. According to Hoechst, the agreements of the Allied breakup of the I.G. precluded any arrangement between Shell–Union Kraftstoff and another former I.G. plant if such arrangement did not give preference to Hoechst. Union's representatives were willing to skirt that issue; they announced that they had nothing against selling the lion's share of the output of olefins to BASF, while at the same time allowing a certain share to Hoechst.[24]

BASF's delegates complained that Hoechst, although it had had every opportunity to do so in talks between the two I.G. successors, had not mentioned that problem. Hoechst's participation in the project was, for BASF, "not . . . desirable." In particular, it was important that Hoechst not gain valuable technical knowledge from BASF. It would be different if the matter were a mere "over-the-counter transaction" (*Ladentischgeschäft*), BASF's representatives insisted, and Hoechst were simply lining up with BASF to purchase propylene, but that was not the case. Instead, the project would involve close technical cooperation by all of the partners. BASF's personnel were absolutely opposed to any participation on the part of Hoechst.[25]

By May 1952, things had become somewhat more clear. For one thing, Hoechst was no longer in the picture, as the discussions at a June meeting revealed. For another, the two major parties were ready to look at property in Wesseling on which to build the new plant. In addition, Shell, supported by BASF, had decided to block Union from participation in the potentially very lucrative project. According to a note regarding a telephone conversation between Timm and Shell's general director, de Graan (Deutsche Shell A.G., Hamburg), on 26 May de Graan had broached the subject with Dr. Müller von

[22] Ibid., pp. 1–4.
[23] Farbwerke Hoechst A.G., *Geschäftsbericht 1952*, pp. 2–3.
[24] "Bericht über die Besprechung mit der Shell-Gruppe und Wesseling am 23. und 24. January 1952 in Ludwigshafen," 25 January 1952, p. 4, BASF, F9/165.
[25] Ibid., pp. 4–5.

Blumencron at Union, suggesting that it would be in the smaller firm's best interest to build a gas-separation plant, leaving the polyethylene business to Shell and BASF. Dr. Blumencron replied that he did not see any point in participating in the upcoming meetings in the Hague if BASF and Shell were to be the only partners. De Graan told Timm, however, that he had convinced Dr. Blumencron that it was necessary for a representative of Wesseling to be present. One very good reason for that was to convince Union to withdraw from the project voluntarily:

It is, however, the common interest of Shell and BASF in these negotiations to make ethylene chemistry as unattractive as possible in the presentation to Wesseling in order to maneuver Wesseling definitively out of the Lupolen business. Therefore, in the negotiations at the Hague, we should indicate that the maximum proceeds of polyethylene production are just 4.20 RM [sic], in order to lengthen the pay out time. BPM [Shell] will prepare itself internally for this tactical turnabout.

In other words, the two larger firms would, at Shell's suggestion, misrepresent the potential profitability of the plant, making it less attractive to Union. Timm went on to note that BASF personnel would be in Wesseling to look over possible sites for the new plant on 29 May 1952. De Graan recommended strongly that Timm be there as well to help convince Dr. Blumencron to pull out of the ROW project voluntarily.[26]

The meeting at the Hague to which Timm referred in his conversation with de Graan took place on 4 June 1952, although it is not clear that the planned subterfuge was carried out there.[27] In any case, by the next meeting, on 18 June 1952, in Hamburg, Union's Dr. Blumencron had resigned himself to the situation: The smaller firm would not be able to participate in either the gas-separation plant or the chemical plant, because it simply did not have the necessary investment capital at its disposal. It could be, of course, that Union's response to exclusion from the Lupolen business had been to withdraw from the gas-separation plant as well. Still, Dr. Blumencron said that Union would remain at the service of the new joint venture "insofar as this is necessary and possible." Concretely, that help would extend to putting workshops and nitrogen at the disposal of the factory and engaging in cooperative ventures with regard to water supply. Sewerage and steam were two areas in which Union could not help.[28] Clearly, although Dr. Blumencron knew that he was being closed out of the joint venture, it was impossible for him to make a clean break with the other partners. Shell, after all, was the major supplier to his plant.

Blumencron also made it clear that he and his fellow managers would prefer that the facility be located northwest of his factory; a proposed site to the south, although Union had preferred it initially, had housing settlements on two sides of

---

[26] B. Timm, "Notiz über ein Telefongespräch mit Herrn Gen. Dir. de Graan, Deutsche Shell AG, Hamburg, am 26.5.1952, 11 Uhr," 26 May 1952, BASF, F9/165.

[27] Memo from Timm to Dir. Dr. Bülow, "Betr.: Dienstreise nach den Haag," 27 May 1952, BASF, F9/165.

[28] "Bericht über die Besprechung in Hamburg am 18.6.1952," 20 June 1952, BASF, F9/165. Timm claimed in the interview that Wesseling pulled out on its own.

it. A third site to the east was also a possibility. For the two larger firms, one of the most important criteria in site selection was its possibilities for expansion. There would have to be enough room to build a propylene-separation facility and another small production plant, and because the possibility existed that in the near term some 15,000 tons of ethylene feedstocks per year would become available from Union, the polyethylene processing capacity at the joint venture would have to be expanded accordingly. BASF, in particular, noted that the site would have to be chosen with an eye toward new synthesis technologies and improvements of existing ones.[29]

Two other points on the agenda were the role of Hoechst and the security of the raw-materials supply. BASF's representatives informed the others that "Hoechst has now definitely agreed not to disturb the plans for olefin refining in Wesseling. There is no longer any ill feeling at Hoechst either."[30] The reasons for the turnabout are not clear, but may well have resulted from Hoechst's intensification of research, beginning in 1952, into producing feedstocks at its own factory and moving into petrochemicals without the backing of a major oil company.[31]

Regarding raw-materials supply, Shell gave BASF new information, noting that it and Union had signed a ten-year supply/refining contract on 1 January 1952. Shell would be able to extend the contract by five or ten years. The supply of feedstocks would pose no problem, especially because more and more German crude was becoming available, "and already the importation of crude oil for German refineries is going down."[32] The negotiators were referring to the fact that exploration for new petroleum sources in West Germany had been remarkably successful in the late 1940s and early 1950s, a success that would continue into the 1960s: Already in 1951 the Federal Republic was producing crude oil domestically at almost the same rate as had greater Germany in 1940. By 1968, when domestic crude production peaked, the country was producing almost six times as much petroleum as in 1951.[33]

The meeting continued with more detailed discussions of technical, legal, and financial matters, though Dr. Blumencron left at that point, after pointing out that those were matters that concerned only Shell and BASF. After he had gone, those remaining discussed the gas-separation facility and steam generation in the joint venture, the question of the relative participation of each partner in the project (London would decide the Shell participation, which could be anything between 30 : 70 and 50 : 50), and the raising of investment capital. De Graan believed that Deutsche Shell probably would be able, with some difficulty, to

[29] "Bericht über die Besprechung in Hamburg am 18.6.1952," 20 June 1952, BASF, F9/165; Timm interview.

[30] "Bericht über die Besprechung in Hamburg am 18.6.1952," 20 June 1952, BASF, F9/165.

[31] See Chapter 7.

[32] "Bericht über die Besprechung in Hamburg am 18.6.1952," 20 June 1952, p. 3, BASF, F9/165. The downturn in crude imports proved temporary.

[33] Raymond G. Stokes, "German Energy in the U.S. Postwar Economic Order, 1945–1951," *Journal of European Economic History* 17(Winter 1988):627.

free up about DM 8 million from a promissory note that had just been floated. He also thought that the possibilities for raising capital on the open market would be good and that stock in the company would sell well, especially to holders of "blocked" marks, that is, marks on which the West German government had imposed foreign-trade restrictions. BASF, on the other hand, was thinking in terms of financing the project internally. In addition, the two groups discussed the question of getting a rebate on tariffs paid on oil for the production of olefins for chemical feedstocks. BASF did not see that as a realistic possibility at the moment and promised to update Shell on previous efforts in that direction.[34] Finally, "the wish was stressed on both sides that other business relationships between Shell and BASF should become closer." The next meeting was scheduled to take place in London.[35]

Five days after the Hamburg meeting, most of the participants (including, for a time, Dr. Blumencron and another delegate from Union Kraftstoff) met once again in London at Shell's headquarters. The first points on the agenda concerned the areas in which the interests of the joint venture and Union would overlap. Choosing a site was one of those, and BASF's representatives insisted that the southern site was the only real possibility as far as they were concerned. Union's delegates agreed, somewhat reluctantly. For tactical reasons, they also agreed that they would negotiate with the owner of the land to purchase it, although BASF's Herr Thurm would take over as soon as possible.[36] The second area of interest to all three parties was the precise ways in which Union would provide assistance to the new factory. The joint venture would buy its electrical power from the large-scale energy concern Rheinisch-Westfälisches Elektrizitätswerke (RWE), but Shell and BASF asked for and got Union's agreement to an emergency power line in case of blackout. The smaller firm also placed its workshops and small amounts of nitrogen at the new firm's disposal. Other areas in which Union would help would be worked out in the future. Finally, the delegates from the three companies discussed the disposition of the propylene, ethylene, and isobutylene produced by and for Union. Shell would be happy to allow Union Kraftstoff an option on 5,000 tons of propylene per year for use in the production of chemicals, but it needed to know soon if the managers of the former hydrogenation facility would exercise that option. BASF had nothing against such an agreement in principle, because Union would be producing phenol and acetone from its feedstocks. BASF had no intentions of manufacturing those products; in fact, the firm might even be interested in purchasing phenol from Union. But BASF's delegates wanted to know if propylene would be available for use by BASF if it were needed. De Graan – seconded by Mitchell – of Shell answered that BASF need not worry about that. Ethylene, all agreed, was

---

[34] The law revising the tariff structure for petroleum used in petrochemical plants did not take effect until 1953. See Chapter 3 for a discussion of this.

[35] "Bericht über die Besprechung in Hamburg am 18.6.1952," 20 June 1952, pp. 3–4, BASF, F9/165.

[36] "Aktenvermerk, *Betr.:* Krackolefine, Besuch bei Shell, London, am 23.6.1952," 25 June 1952, pp. 1–2, BASF, F9/165.

a subject that did not concern Union. Isobutylene was a subject that BASF and the feedstock producer would have to discuss further. Finally, BASF's representatives asked once again for an official confirmation that supplies of raw materials were secure. Shell's representatives gave their BASF counterparts the same positive answer they had earlier, when they had informed BASF of the agreement between Shell and Union of 1 January 1952.[37]

When Union's negotiators left, BASF and Shell continued their discussions. The two groups were at odds over the proper ratio between polyethylene production and ethylbenzene production in the joint venture. Shell considered the payoff time for ethylbenzene manufacture too long, and Shell thought that German and foreign markets would be able to absorb 10,000 tons of polyethylene per year, instead of the 6,500 tons foreseen by BASF. BASF's representatives were opposed to that plan, because BASF planned to use the ethylbenzene for production of polystyrene. Shell negotiators were angling for a stake in BASF's polystyrene production – they suggested either a high price (DM 1,200–1,250 per ton) for the ethylbenzene produced in the joint venture or a share of the profits from polystyrene production. BASF's delegates considered DM 1,000 per ton more reasonable in terms of domestic and perhaps international markets and simply did not take up the question of profit-sharing. They held that the markets would be able to absorb 6,000 tons of polyethylene without any problem in about 2.5 years, but they thought that domestic and international markets would have to be cultivated substantially to absorb 10,000 tons. BASF's minute-takers noted no retort from Shell.[38] Here, the caution of the German firm's representatives is worth underscoring.

The question remaining before the two groups was the organization and financing of the joint venture. Shell believed that DM 55–65 million would be necessary to launch it. The parties agreed that the best course was to raise the capital internally, rather than going to the banks. How, though, should they raise the money – in the form of basic capital or in the form of loans from parent companies? The Shell group – above all, its representative Guepin – noted that a crucial point in that regard was one that was primarily political: the question of currency convertibility. In France, despite frequent changes in regimes, devaluation of the currency, and general economic difficulties, it was clear that foreign capital was treated well, and Shell and other large companies had no problem investing there. They had no such faith in the West German regime, although they hoped that the current negotiations about foreign debt would clarify the problem. One question, for instance, would be whether or not blocked marks earned by foreign investors could be used to buy such things as pipes for export from Germany, or for payment of shipping fees. The possibility of selling the products of the joint venture (ROW) at cheaper prices to Shell so that Shell could turn a foreign-exchange profit was raised; "however this idea was not pursued any further."[39]

[37] Ibid., pp. 2–4.   [38] Ibid., pp. 5–7.
[39] Ibid., pp. 8–19.

It is worth pausing briefly here in the analysis of that meeting to reflect on Shell's apparent preference, even in 1952, for France rather than Germany as a place to invest. Shell's hesitancy reflected more general problems associated with attracting foreign capital to Germany in the immediate postwar period. A discussion from 1949, found in the files of the British Foreign Office's German Section, was telling in that regard. A personal letter of 28 April from Colonel Vigers, a London businessman, to C. John Macfarlane of the German Section set it off. Vigers reported that the German industrialists with whom he had spoken during a recent visit to the country were clamoring for an end to restrictions on foreign investment and expected money to flow in bountifully once they were lifted. In four pages of handwritten commentary ("Minutes") by five different German Section members, the consensus was that, owing to currency restrictions, those German expectations were unrealistic. One of the most incisive – and withering – critiques of German hopes was that by L. B. Richards of 4 May 1949:

When I was in Germany recently . . . there was ample and disturbing evidence that the German authorities are all subject to this dangerous hallucination that foreign capital is bound to rush joyfully to their rescue as soon as barriers are removed: They for some odd reason even think their housing schemes should be financed in this way. The reasons for this seem to be of a complex order: I suspect they must include (a) memories of the Dawes and Young Loan period; (b) the attitude of mind fostered by GARIOA [a U.S. program for Government Aid and Relief in Occupied Areas], Marshall Aid and other windfalls; and (c) the Germans' profound conviction that they are so important to the world and so very much more deserving than anybody else that (a) and (b) are bound to be repeated.[40]

Despite Shell's hesitancy, however, it was clear that by 1952 the attitudes of foreign investors were beginning to approach West German expectations. At the London meeting, both BASF and Shell favored a 50 : 50 relationship for the joint venture, although Shell wanted to make that dependent on the treatment it got from the West German government. BASF would provide the personnel to run ROW, and they would retain their rights as white-collar employees of the West German chemical firm. Polyethylene would be sold by BASF with the support of its Dyes Section. Patents and know-how for the production in the facilities would come from BASF, with polyethylene produced under a sub-license from ICI through BASF. Both parties would place their product and process improvements at the disposal of the firm and could use any improvements gained in the joint-venture operation, although the contract over that matter would still have to be negotiated. BASF also made it clear that it could not wait forever to get a decision from Shell about the possibility of licensing its polyethylene

---

[40] All materials from Public Record Office, London (Kew), FO 371/76919. GARIOA was the United States "Government Aid and Relief in Occupied Areas" program, through which considerable quantities of food and fuel flowed into western Germany prior to the establishment of the Marshall Plan. For a consideration of some of the dimensions and implications of that program, see Stokes, "German Energy," pp. 624, 627; and Stokes, "German Oil and the American Occupation, 1944–47" (M.A. thesis, Ohio State University, 1981), chapters III and IV.

know-how in the United States. All agreed that the final organization of the firm would have to await detailed negotiations between technical personnel from Deutsche Shell and from BASF, upcoming in about four weeks.[41]

By late summer 1952, Timm felt comfortable enough with the negotiations thus far to go on vacation to the seaside in Schleswig-Holstein. Even while on holiday, however, he insisted on being provided with detailed information on the progress in selecting a site. One of BASF's directors, Mr. Santo, wrote to him on 1 August. Of the two sites seriously investigated to date, Santo considered that only one was at all suited to BASF's needs, and that only with reservations; the other was not at all suitable. The main problem with each of the sites was the limited space available – for expansion (always a crucial consideration in the fast-changing chemical industry) and for allowing, in the event of a war (and making use of the hard-won experience from the last war), "the possibility of a dispersed development on air-protection technical grounds." (That such should have been a consideration at all in 1952 is, of course, astonishing, reflecting either a holdover from the war or renewed concerns in the face of heightened Cold War tensions and impending West German rearmament.) A new site north of Wesseling might well allow the firm much more of the crucial space it wanted, but would, according to estimates by Dr. Mach, require that the firm spend an additional DM 3 million for water and sewer lines. Santo believed the site would be worth the investment if indeed it could more adequately meet the future needs of the factory, and he suggested a detailed study of the site to see if it could meet those and other technical and economic criteria. If the results were negative, the joint venture would have to seek out a new site in the south as close as possible to the Union Kraftstoff plant.[42]

Timm wrote to Dr. Hans Freiensehner of the BASF Patent Section a few days later (4 August), noting that the search for a larger site was a good idea. He continued that "the extra expense does not frighten me, if it can be viewed as a down-payment on closer and more comprehensive cooperation between Shell and us. And I believe, petroleum chemistry offers such chances." Higher stakes would thus necessitate closer ties between the two companies. In addition, he continued (showing once again his attention to diplomatic subtleties), BASF could always threaten to build on a larger site and possibly keep competitors at bay longer. BASF should secure Shell's agreement to that strategy in principle as soon as possible. In the meantime, the final negotiations in London over the organization would have to be postponed until the end of September.[43]

On 20 August 1952, Santo, Freiensehner, and Bülow from BASF, Stok and Krönig from Deutsche Shell, and Manz, Auer, and von Noostwijk from Shell,

[41] "Aktenvermerk, *Betr.:* Krackolefine, Besuch bei Shell, London, am 23.6.1952," 25 June 1952, p. 9–10, BASF, F9/165.

[42] Santo to Timm, 1 August 1952, BASF, F9/165. Santo had been active in assessing sites for I.G. Farben, including that for the firm's Buna-rubber factory near Auschwitz. See Morris, "The Development of Acetylene Chemistry," pp. 331–40. My thanks to Dr. Morris for bringing this to my attention.

[43] Bernhard Timm to Dr. Hans Freiensehner, 4 August 1952, BASF, F9/165.

the Hague, met in Wesseling to look over the site that had been suggested by BASF to the north of the Union Kraftstoff plant between the *Autobahn* and the Cologne–Bonn railway. The discussion focused on infrastructure at the plant, including the number of pipelines to and from Union and the number of rail lines needed, as well as their costs. All agreed that the site was suitable and indeed preferable to all others. Shell London had agreed in principle, although only if the total cost of the project remained in the range of DM 53–60 million. Shell's representatives also wanted to discuss in more detail the investment costs and payout time, but BASF's people said that too many variables were still outstanding; such discussions should therefore be postponed. There was also a discussion of the price of cracked gas from Union. Union wanted to charge a relatively high price for deliveries to the joint company; Shell promised to put pressure on Union not to do that. Finally, all parties agreed that *all* remaining points would be discussed on 8 and 9 September in Ludwigshafen.[44]

The meeting took place as planned. All high-ranking representatives of BASF, Deutsche Shell, and Shell London who had taken part in the negotiations to that point attended. The report of the "organizational-legal group" indicated that all agreed on a 50 : 50 partnership for the new firm. Shell insisted (and a feeling-out of Shell executives by Heintzeler confirmed that they would consider no other course of action) that the company take an organizational form that would avoid putting Shell in the position of only bankrolling the scheme; the representatives of the oil firm considered their relationship with BASF different and closer than that. BASF warned that such a course of action would essentially eliminate the possibility that the new company could participate in BASF's electricity-supply contract, but Shell was determined to stick to its guns. The capital for the firm would come half from shares (*Gesellschaftskapital*) and half from loans (*Gesellschaftsdarlehen*), and each of the two owners would be responsible for raising half of each of those amounts. Shell's portion of the capital would come from Deutsche Shell, while the parent (called "Anglo-Saxon" here) would pay Shell's portion of the loan in blocked marks.[45]

As far as the personnel of the firm, there would be two plant managers. BASF would appoint the de facto plant manager, the man in charge of production in the factory. Shell would appoint someone who, although officially equal in status, would in fact be a more junior, up-and-coming manager. He would be responsible for duties outside production and for sales. The negotiators did not spell the matter out in the meeting, but presumably that meant that Shell's plant manager would be in charge of maintenance, personnel, and other functions subsidiary to the operation of the facility. Shell also wanted to appoint an assistant plant manager of German nationality, a chemist to lead the plant laboratory, and two additional chemists or engineers. An oversight committee modeled on the rela-

[44] BASF Patentabteilung (Freiensehner), "Aktenvermerk, *Betr.*: Aethylenanlage Wesseling," 22 August 1952, BASF, F9/165.

[45] BASF Rechtsabt., Dr. Dribbusch, "Aktennotiz, *Betr.*: Polyäthylenanlage Wesseling, Besprechung in Ludwigshafen am 8. und 9. September 1952, Rechtlich-organisatorisch Fragen," 15 September 1952, pp. 1–2, BASF, F9/165.

tionship between Shell and the French chemical producer St. Gobain would consist of two members from BASF, one from Shell London or the Hague, and one from Deutsche Shell; it would make mid-level decisions and would serve as a nucleus for continuity in partners' meetings. BASF's Bülow estimated total personnel needs at about 10 academics, 40 white-collar workers, and a maximum of 300 workers. All except the highest levels of managers would have rights and responsibilities only in the new company, with upper management committed to five years minimum.[46]

In the course of discussing a "referee clause" (*Schiedsrichterklausel*), it became obvious that the Shell Group was anxious to have the new company legally a cooperative venture between Deutsche Shell and BASF, in a strategy typical of Shell Group contracts. BASF insisted, however, that because the Shell Group would have a reserved seat on the oversight committee and because it would be privy to technical know-how arising from the cooperation, the Shell Group should sign some sort of agreement with BASF to deal with such matters.[47] The remaining decisions involved, for the most part, listing the various agreements and contracts the partners would sign.[48]

Concluding remarks

Although BASF did not announce the agreement publicly until early 1954 (in its 1953 corporate report), which was more than a year after the negotiations had taken place, the basic framework for the cooperation between Shell and the West German chemical firm had been in place by late 1952. Like many such negotiations between large corporations with international interests, the Shell–BASF face-off closely resembled the diplomatic parrying that occurs between sovereign nations. Representatives of Shell and BASF, though clearly having several common objectives, and obviously respecting one another as worthy adversaries, ruthlessly pursued their own selfish interests, with little regard for morality, as when the two larger firms exiled their smaller partner, Union Kraftstoff, cutting it off from the most profitable future initiatives of the joint operation. Each demonstrated firm notions of the value of everything it would bring to bear in founding and operating the firm. The processes of feeling out the other side before advancing proposals and, after long discussions, carefully hammering out compromises were extremely important to the negotiations.

The policy and practice of the West German state had a major impact on the negotiations, as should be apparent from the fact that the possibility of tax rebates on oil used for chemical production figured prominently in the negotiations and the fact that the state had a considerable measure of control over currency policy, including blocked marks, which would have an effect on investment. Shell's surprising view that the attitude of the French government toward foreign investment was far more friendly that than of the federal government in West Germany was one indicator of the importance of that aspect of

[46] Ibid., p. 2.   [47] Ibid., pp. 3–4.
[48] Ibid., pp. 5–6.

government policy. Furthermore, German corporation law also played a role in the negotiations. Still, the primary actors in the drama were drawn not from the state but from the ranks of the two internationally renowned private firms.

It is less remarkable that such "great power" diplomacy between two great corporations could take place than that it took place between Shell, one of the world's foremost petroleum producers, and BASF, a firm only recently re-created out of the ruins of I.G. Farben, whose facilities had been severely damaged during the war, which had ended only seven years earlier. BASF's representatives demonstrated that they were neither intimidated by the giant Shell nor excessively eager in discussing the exact terms of the joint venture with Shell. BASF moved deliberately – as an equal partner – in the negotiations toward embracing what would, in significant ways, be a new technological system (even though BASF would be providing much of the initial production technology) that would differ considerably from the systems in which they had had decades-long experience, primarily because it appeared that the ROW plant would increase its capacity for manufacturing polyethylene and other petrochemical products far more rapidly than originally expected.

Even while the ROW factory was under construction (i.e., through 1955), its capacity to produce Lupolen increased from 6,000 to 10,000 tons per year, primarily because of process improvements. The plant was already producing at full capacity during 1956. Although Lupolen output had originally been meant primarily for the domestic market, even the higher production figures could not satisfy the demand; therefore, given the additional impetus of the expiration of some key ICI patents, Shell and BASF decided in that same year to invest an additional DM 140 million to increase capacity 3.5-fold, partly by introducing new production technologies. The firm also broadened its palette of offerings of traditional high-pressure, low-density polyethylene products so as to meet the needs of a wider variety of customers.[49] In addition, in 1957, ROW acquired, through its parent companies, the right to manufacture high-density polyethylene by means of the Phillips Petroleum low-pressure process. Construction of a new facility began in the same year.[50] By 1959, the co-owners of ROW decided to expand their capacity for polyethylene production once more, and their total production capacity for Lupolen (including both high- and low-pressure polyethylene) reached 125,000 tons per year, placing them in the same league as the

---

[49] BASF, *Bericht über das Geschäftsjahr 1956*, p. 33.

[50] BASF, *Bericht über das Geschäftsjahr 1957*, pp. 15, 28. Interestingly enough, BASF had developed its own low-pressure process before 1945 [reported, for instance, in BASF ZK Labor (Dr. Hopff), "Aethylen-Polymerisation," 11 April 1947, BASF, o.S., Polyäthylen allg. 2 1946–1952]. Because the Ziegler process bore some similarities to the BASF patent, it was possible for BASF to bring suit against Ziegler in the mid-1950s. Eventually, Ziegler decided to settle it by agreeing to a series of licenses for different Ziegler processes (especially for production of polypropylene) on terms advantageous to BASF. BASF Patentabteilung (Kleber) to Patentanwalt Dr. Ing. von Kreisler, "Betr. Polyäthylen-Verfahren," 26 February 1956, BASF, K311; BASF Patentabteilung (Kleber), memorandum, "Betr. Polyäthylen/Ziegler Verfahren," 13 May 1958, BASF, K311.

Figure 5.3. Aerial photograph of the Rheinische Olefinwerke (ROW) in Wesseling, 1963. (Courtesy BASF Unternehmensarchiv, Ludwigshafen.)

world's largest producers.[51] In 1963, continued high demand prompted a further expansion (Figure 5.3) of total high- and low-pressure polyethylene capacity to a total of 190,000 tons per year.[52]

The chemists and engineers seconded by BASF to the Wesseling facility immediately faced the problems inherent in producing on a scale they had never before encountered. That involved many new challenges, not only in the development of new products and new production processes but also in terms of quality control, automation of production, and product testing. Although the BASF personnel met those challenges effectively, steadily increasing their production to try to meet the apparently insatiable demand for petrochemical products, the company did not abandon its investment in its traditional stronghold: coal-chemical production. In fact, coal continued to be a vital feedstock for the company's production program through most of the 1950s.

Its prevailing technological traditions provide part of the explanation for the relatively slow and deliberate progression by which BASF adopted petrochemical technology, but there was another important factor as well: The confusion

---

[51] BASF, *Bericht über das Geschäftsjahr 1959*, p. 33; BASF, *Bericht über das Geschäftsjahr 1961*, p. 28.
[52] BASF, *Bericht über das Geschäftsjahr 1963*, p. 41.

engendered by some unsettling (at least from the perspective of contemporaries) developments regarding energy and feedstock sources played a role in BASF's slow pace in adopting petrochemicals and their associated technologies. Coal prices were increasing significantly in the first half of the 1950s, and the increasing production of chemicals meant that the domestic sources of coal were experiencing strain. In its 1956 corporate report, for instance, BASF reported that "our coal demand could be met only in part from the production of the Auguste Victoria coal mine." Use of heating oil was one way to close the "energy gap," but the Suez crisis made that difficult and, apparently, in the long term, problematic. BASF therefore turned in the short term to imports of coal from the United States, but the resulting increases in energy and feedstock costs forced the firm to seek alternatives. In dealing with the problem in 1956, BASF's managers turned to a traditional solution: They expected an improvement in the situation "from the hastened expansion of a new shaft at our Auguste Victoria mine."[53]

Increases in the price of coal continued during the second half of the 1950s. Still, it is noteworthy that it was not until 1957 that the price factor became decisive in BASF's decision-making on technological change. It started in BASF's traditional stronghold, ammonia:

On account of the rising price of solid fuel, which, as is well known, we can obtain from our subsidiary Auguste Victoria only at fixed list prices, we have begun to switch over to other starting materials [i.e., petroleum or gas] in production of synthesis gas for a substantial portion of our ammonia production.[54]

By 1962, the firm reported that it had gone over to petroleum in a big way:

Our requirements for acetylene cannot be covered in the long run from expensive electro-carbide. We are thus building a large facility with a capacity of 60,000 tons of acetylene per year, for which liquid hydrocarbons will serve as raw material. The process . . . delivers, besides acetylene, carbon monoxide and hydrogen also, and thus contributes to the broader transition of production of synthesis gas to a petroleum basis.[55]

Still, BASF's 1961 corporate report showed that the company had hedged its bet in adopting the new petrochemicals and related technologies. Although the company reported that it was using more petrochemical feedstocks, it also noted that it had adopted a new process for producing synthesis gas that allowed it "within broad limits to use solid and liquid fuels interchangeably, allowing us to adapt the production branch that depended on those fuels elastically to current market relationships." In their opportunistic use of coal or oil, BASF's managers elected to emphasize maximum flexibility in adapting to unstable market conditions.[56]

In other words, even as late as 1961, the first year in which West German chemical producers used petroleum to produce more than 50 percent of organic

[53] BASF, *Bericht über das Geschäftsjahr 1956*, p. 11.
[54] BASF. *Bericht über das Geschäftsjahr 1957*, p. 17.
[55] BASF, *Bericht über das Geschäftsjahr 1962*, pp. 20–1.
[56] BASF, *Bericht über das Geschäftsjahr 1961*, p. 17.

chemicals, the leadership of BASF was not willing to commit itself fully to petrochemical feedstocks and technologies. Instead, the company's managers showed a striking (although completely understandable) ambivalence, choosing instead to focus on technologies that would allow BASF to adopt at will the feedstock that was currently least expensive. By cooperating in a joint venture with one of the world's foremost petroleum producers, BASF made sure that it would be poised to move into the petrochemical field wholeheartedly in the 1960s should that prove the more lucrative and competitive option, although its unwillingness to go it alone was yet another indication of the company's deliberate and relatively slow adoption of the new technology. Much the same can be said of its rival, Bayer, whose cooperation with British Petroleum is the subject of the next chapter.

6

Fifty-fifty with the petroleum multinationals: Bayer, British Petroleum, and Erdölchemie

Farbenfabriken Bayer A.G., like BASF, has had a long and distinguished tradition of technical and commercial excellence within the international chemical industry. Prominent in the dyestuffs industry in the late nineteenth century, the company moved into pharmaceuticals at the end of the nineteenth century and the beginning of the twentieth. Carl Duisberg, one of the firm's leading chemists during that period, also proved to be an organizational innovator and an effective administrator. His plans for Bayer's Leverkusen facility, which remains the company's headquarters and an important manufacturing operation, constituted the first attempt at large-scale coordination of production, transportation, and other services in a single chemical plant that was also designed to accommodate the rapid and often unforeseen changes of the chemical industry. Duisberg's ideas about the need for coordinated financing, purchasing, research, and production in the German chemical industry, in order to meet the intense competition in foreign markets, were also behind the formation of I.G. Farbenindustrie A.G. Thus, it is no surprise that like BASF's Bosch, Duisberg and other Bayer managers played prominent roles in the new chemical giant. Duisberg himself became chairman of the I.G.'s supervisory board.[1]

[1] Eric Verg, *Meilensteine* (Leverkusen: Bayer A.G., 1988); Raymond G. Stokes, *Divide and Prosper: The Heirs of I.G. Farben under Allied Authority, 1945–1951* (Berkeley: University of Cali-

Bayer differed considerably from BASF, however, in terms of the primary source of its reputation and in the focus of its production. BASF's renown derived primarily from its technological expertise, whereas Bayer's reputation was based mostly on its commercial acumen. Both companies started out in the last third of the nineteenth century producing dyestuffs, and dyes remained important components of their production palettes well into the twentieth century. But BASF moved into high-pressure chemistry, producing synthetic nitrogen, methanol, and, later, synthetic gasoline. Bayer concentrated its efforts on pharmaceuticals, pesticides and insecticides, synthetic fibers, and synthetic rubber.

As for the immediate postwar period, it is more readily apparent for Bayer than for BASF why the company did not pursue petrochemicals wholeheartedly after it began its recovery in the late 1940s and early 1950s. Its primary production and its main areas of technological expertise lay in dyes, pharmaceuticals, and pesticides and insecticides, all of which were high-value-added sectors that, in addition, shared the characteristics of industries that had begun in the era before the Industrial Revolution: Although they all depended heavily on scientific research (which, of course, distinguished them from their pre–Industrial Revolution predecessors), they also were produced by small numbers of skilled workers in batch processes. In those kinds of sectors, the use of petroleum rather than coal feedstocks held little attraction, at least at first. The high markups for such products and their production by batch processing (with its attendant high labor and processing costs) meant that the feedstock contributed a relatively small part to the total price charged for a product, thus providing a large cushion for more expensive feedstocks. That was one of the reasons that petrochemicals made their first inroads in continuous-process sectors of the chemical industry, sectors that had the potential for significant savings due to economies of scale.

For Bayer, the potential exceptions to the rule (in terms of scale of production and possible applicability of petrochemical processes) were, first, synthetic fibers, which involved more modern production methods than did many of Bayer's other products, but which shared with them, to a large extent, the characteristic of high value added during manufacture, and, second, synthetic rubber, the manufacture of which was in any case prohibited by Allied decree from 30 June 1948 through most of 1951. Still, despite the disincentives to moving into the petrochemical field, Bayer, like BASF, dabbled in it in the late 1940s and early 1950s. Bayer managers recognized the potential inherent in that new area of organic chemical production. Accordingly, they authorized significant funds for internal research-and-development work in petrochemicals. In addition, they sought to use their expertise in other areas and their limited capital to acquire petrochemical technology from outside sources. In that they were largely unsuccessful. By the mid-1950s, Bayer's managers had decided to cooperate with an established oil company in developing petrochemical capacity, a possibility

fornia Press, 1988), pp. 64–85; Ernst Homburg, "The emergence of research laboratories in the dyestuffs industry, 1870–1900," *British Journal of the History of Science* 25(1992):91–111, esp. pp. 104–6, 110–11.

they had been investigating since the early 1950s. And again like BASF's negotiators, Bayer personnel dealt from a position of surprising strength, keeping
one major oil producer waiting in the wings while they pursued a possible deal
with another. This chapter details Bayer's changing strategies for moving into
the field of petrochemicals, which culminated in 1957 in the formation, together
with British Petroleum (BP), of the Erdölchemie GmbH in Dormagen.

Early strategies

Bayer's leadership recognized fairly early after 1945 the importance of
petrochemicals,[2] but they did not make any significant moves in that direction
until the end of 1952. They then followed a number of different strategies, for
the most part simultaneously. They concentrated first on finding a secure source
of supply for their petrochemical feedstocks, but they also attempted to purchase
turnkey technologies from American chemical engineering firms, engaged in efforts to acquire licenses to produce polyethylene using technology developed by
other firms, established a research team at Bayer to develop technology internally, and, finally, negotiated with large petroleum companies. Some of the materials on how those strategies unfolded, and what their implications were, have
been covered in other chapters,[3] but a brief review of the material will be helpful
in the current context.

Bayer signed a contract at the end of 1952 with the Ruhrbau company in Mülheim, which had "the objective for 'Bayer' of tapping a new source for raw materials on the basis of petroleum, primarily for olefins and aromatics."[4] Ruhrbau
possessed distillation apparatus for cracking 250,000 tons of crude oil each year,
yielding about 25 percent straight-run gasoline of poor quality, 40 percent diesel
fuel, and 35 percent heating oil. One of Bayer's first projects, therefore, was to
expand those facilities and to alter the output of the Ruhrbau plant, changing its
production mix to favor petrochemical feedstocks rather than fuels. To that end
they turned to Hydrocarbon Research, an American engineering firm, for help in
planning and building plants. Five men from Bayer visited the United States at
the end of January 1953 to get further information about a process developed
by Hydrocarbon. They also were assigned the task of "looking around in
petroleum-based chemistry and as far as possible ascertaining the current state
of cracking processes and of petrochemical-chemistry [sic]." Hydrocarbon took
the responsibility for facilitating introductions in the United States.[5]

Hydrocarbon Research's top management included people who were well
known at Bayer because of Bayer's former affiliation with I. G. Farben. Mr.

[2] Bayer A.G., "25 Jahre Gruppe 'Petrochemie' jetzt ZB ZF Petrochemie und Verfahrensentwick-
   lung der Bayer AG, 1953–1978," n.d. (surely 1978 or early 1979), Bayerwerksarchiv, Leverkusen
   (hereafter, BWA), 9/L.
[3] See, for instance, Chapters 3 and 4.
[4] H. Hanisch, "Eindrück und Ergebnisse einer Amerikareise, Vortrag bei der Direktoren-Konferenz
   in Leverkusen am 14. April 1953," p. 1, BWA, 700/1302.
[5] Ibid., pp. 2–3; quotation, p. 2.

Keith, the firm's president, for instance, had previously worked for M. W. Kellogg, a major American chemical engineering firm, and was acquainted with "many of the former members of the managing board of the I.G." Hydrocarbon's chairman for Europe, Dr. Ringer, had actually worked for the I.G. and had carried out negotiations between I.G.'s Sparte I and the Standard Oil companies. The German branch of the firm, Hydramin, had its seat in Düsseldorf, and half of it belonged to "Herr Stinnes."[6]

Still, H. Hanisch, who reported back to Leverkusen on the visit to the United States, complained about the inability of Hydrocarbon to supply Bayer personnel with sufficient information or the contacts they needed. He soon enlisted the aid of Dr. Oskar Loehr and Dr. Heinrich Bütefisch in gaining access to larger engineering firms such as Lummus A.G., Stone & Webster, Kellogg, Koppers, Girdler Corp., and others. Those companies could offer more suitable resources for planning and equipping Bayer's proposed plants than could Hydrocarbon; for instance, Hanisch appended to his report an example of a schematic of "a turnkey facility" that Lummus A.G. could deliver "at anytime." In addition, the Bayer team spent a considerable amount of time in New York "in a large number of conversations in the large offices of the engineering and petroleum companies, such as Standard Oil, etc."[7]

By mid-1954 it became necessary to shut down the Ruhrbau plant; Bayer's management had become better informed about the state of the art in the petrochemicals field, and it was clear that the Ruhrbau option was not viable in the long term.[8] Still, the efforts of company personnel during 1953 to try to build up a domestic feedstock base using, in part, U.S. technology revealed an important characteristic of West German decision-making on technological change. The Leverkusen-based company was able to utilize prewar contacts made through I.G. Farben to gain access to firms that had the technologies required to make the transition from coal to petroleum feedstocks. Because of Bayer's considerable reputation, the American firms that were contacted were interested in coming to some sort of agreement to work with Bayer.

At the same time, Bayer's contacts and reputation did not ensure success in such negotiations, as the company's experience in trying to obtain licenses to produce polyethylene had demonstrated.[9] During 1952, Loehr and others from Bayer had negotiated with ICI in an effort to obtain a nonexclusive license to the British giant's polyethylene production technology, but lost out to BASF and Anorgana when ICI, owing to market projections, decided it wanted to limit production of high-pressure, low-density polyethylene in West Germany. Bayer also tried unsuccessfully in mid-1953 to obtain rights to produce low-pressure, high-density polyethylene by the Ziegler process. It is not entirely clear why those negotiations were unsuccessful, because Ziegler appeared willing to sell to

---

[6] Ibid., p. 3. [7] Ibid., pp. 3–4.
[8] The actual date of the shutdown is unclear, but a memorandum of August 1954 notes that it had been announced earlier. Langheinrich, "Aktennotiz, Betr. Verwertung Ruhrbau – Besprechung mit BP am 13.8.1954 in Leverkusen," 18 August 1954, BWA, 700/1366.
[9] For a more detailed treatment of these negotiations, see Chapter 4.

all comers.[10] One clue came out in a conversation between Dr. Kluge from Hoechst A. G. and Karl Ziegler at the end of July 1953. Kluge noted that

until now he [Ziegler] has only signed an option contract with the F[arb]W[erke] Hoe[chst]. For some time, though, interest in this matter has become loud from the Farbenfabriken Bayer, which is especially interested in the manufacture of butadiene from ethylene via butylene. The negotiations have remained unsuccessful so far, since Le-[verkusen] is only offering a "gratuity" [*ein "Trinkgeld"*].[11]

In the meantime, even before the decision to close down the Ruhrbau plant, and probably as a result of rebuffs by ICI and Ziegler, Bayer began intensive research of its own into petrochemical processes. At the end of 1953, Hermann Holzrichter (Figure 6.1) organized Bayer's petrochemical development group, which eventually provided a number of upper-level managers for the Erdölchemie GmbH.[12] Born in 1911, Holzrichter earned his doctorate in chemistry in 1937 and joined I.G. Farben at Leverkusen. He remained in the Bayer Group throughout his career. "The major areas in which he worked were large-scale technical development of new, continuous polymerization . . . processes for synthetic rubber and later the construction of high-pressure hydrogenation facilities that manufacture starting materials for plastics." A major figure in the creation of Erdölchemie, he became a member of the Bayer managing board in 1957 as his company and BP completed negotiations to build the new factory. In that capacity he was responsible for the areas of organic chemicals, rubber, and polyurethane.[13]

Beginning work early in January 1954, Holzrichter's group started out rather small. It had employed just four chemists by the end of the year: Walter Kroenig, Walter Bayer, Gerhard Scharfe, and Arno Meckelburg. Kroenig, born in 1900, was by far the oldest (all of the rest were under age thirty), and Holzrichter appointed him to lead the group. He came to Bayer with considerable experience, having previously worked for BASF, the I.G., Lurgi, and Deutsche Shell. In addition to the chemists, there was a single secretary for the group and twenty-two white- and blue-collar workers who ran the laboratory, operated the group's experimental plant, and performed other technical duties. The number of chemists associated with the group grew only gradually, to five in 1955 and to six in 1957; indeed, because of the founding of the Erdölchemie in 1958, the number had dropped to four until 1960, when it rose to seven chemists. The number increased gradually throughout the 1960s and 1970s to nineteen in 1977. In the meantime, however, the number of technicians and workers associated with the group's operations nearly doubled from 1954 to 1955 (from twenty-two to thirty-seven in all) and continued to grow rapidly through the early 1960s. By 1962,

---

[10] For more on the Ziegler process and its licensing, see Chapter 4.

[11] Hoechst ZW Labor (Dr. Kluge) (Aktennotiz), "Besprechung mit Herrn Prof. Zielger im MPI für Kohlenforschung . . . am 28.7.1953 betr. Olefinpolymerisation," 1 August 1953, Hoechst Firmenarchiv, Hoechst.

[12] Bayer A.G., "25 Jahre Gruppe 'Petrochemie'," pp. 1–2.

[13] Bayer A.G., Presse-Information, "Dr. Hermann Holzrichter gestorben (21 April 1978)," BWA, Personalia Hermann Holzrichter (hereafter, Holzrichter).

Figure 6.1. Hermann Holzrichter, organizer of the Bayer petrochemical development group and participant in the founding of Erdölchemie GmbH. (Courtesy Bayer Firmenarchiv, Leverkusen.)

such personnel totaled seventy-nine. Staff cuts in the following year dropped the total to just forty-one, although the number of technicians and workers rebounded during the rest of the decade, reaching a total of ninety-six in 1970 before cutbacks in the 1970s dropped the number to seventy in 1977. The total establishment in 1977, by then including three secretaries, was 153 personnel.[14]

Bayer did some research – with mixed results – into the possibility of developing new processes for production of polyethylene that would allow the company to produce that thermoplastic without infringing on any of the Ziegler, Phillips, or ICI processes.[15] Nevertheless, initially the petrochemical production group's main task was to work out a thermal cracking process for producing ethylene and propylene from crude oil. The group's objective was to come up with a process that, unlike those employed in the petroleum industry, would result in

[14] Bayer A.G., "25 Jahre Gruppe 'Petrochemie'," pp. 38, 39, 45.
[15] See Chapter 4.

a nearly complete transformation of crude oil into gaseous olefins.[16] In other words, Bayer researchers wished to devise an entirely new way to produce petrochemical feedstocks, one that would avoid, insofar as possible, "by-products" such as gasoline and diesel fuel. If they could do that, it would liberate the Leverkusen-based company from the usual pattern for chemical companies: their dependence on oil companies not just for crude oil, but also for actual olefin feedstocks.

The technical problems involved in the process, however, were daunting. The desired cracking temperatures of 750–800° stood 250–300°C higher than those used in catalytic crackers in petroleum production. Besides designing equipment to withstand such extreme temperatures, Bayer researchers would have to devise means for maintaining those levels of heat in the reaction vessels. To solve those and other technical problems, Bayer negotiated cooperative agreements with other German firms. The management chose Lurgi Gesellschaft für Wärmetechnik, a major designer of reaction vessels for the petroleum and chemical industries, and Ruhrgas, which had extensive experience in producing and handling gases.[17]

By the summer of 1955, the group had already made considerable progress. They had designed, in conjunction with Lurgi and Ruhrgas, an experimental plant with a capacity of one ton of crude-oil input per hour. The problem of maintaining the high reaction temperatures was solved in part by using heated fine-grain sand as a circulating heat source. Still a number of problems remained. Holzrichter was forced to write to the federal Ministry of Economics to seek relief from taxes and tariffs imposed on petroleum used in experimental processes in the chemical industry, even though a 1953 change in tariff law had absolved new chemical processes *used in full-scale industrial production* from the tariffs and taxes. On the technical side, it was still necessary for the gases to be stored for some time to determine their exact compositions and quality, instead of being used immediately, and the researchers were still having difficulty in attaining the temperature levels they desired for the reactions.[18]

Within the next several months, researchers in the Bayer petrochemicals development group had decided to solve that last problem by switching raw materials: Instead of crude oil, they began using naphtha, or raw gasoline, as the primary input. That had the virtue of allowing lower reaction temperatures, while at the same time increasing the yields of gaseous olefins. On the other hand, it had the potential drawback of making Bayer more dependent on an oil company.

[16] Bayer A.G., "25 Jahre Gruppe 'Petrochemie'," p. 1.
[17] F.F. Bayer (Holzrichter and Casper) to Bundeswirtschaftsministerium (BMW) (Dr. Lenz), "Betr.: Entwicklung der Erdölchemie bei Farbenfabriken Bayer A.G.," 22 July 1955, in Bundesarchiv, Koblenz (hereafter, BAK), B102/36054; Bayer A.G., "25 Jahre Gruppe 'Petrochemie'," p. 1.
[18] F.F. Bayer (Holzrichter and Casper) to BWM (Dr. Lenz), "Betr.: Entwicklung der Erdölchemie." For the role of this process in the discussions about relief for the chemical industry from petroleum tariffs, see Chapter 3.

Yet even as Bayer pursued other options (cooperation with other German firms, purchasing technology, or generating its own processes through internal research and development), its managers were negotiating with major petroleum producers to come up with some sort of cooperative arrangement so that the German firm could enter the field of petrochemical production. In early 1953, a Bayer team visiting the United States began discussions with Standard Oil of New Jersey and other oil companies based in New York.[19] Consultations developed into negotiations as the Leverkusen-based company's other options came to nought or did not appear to be proceeding quickly enough: It was forced to shut down the plant at Mülheim; negotiations with ICI and Ziegler for polyethylene technology fell through; and the company's own research was moving too slowly. By 1957, Bayer's management negotiated a favorable deal with an oil company, British Petroleum (BP), which would guarantee supply, rapidly give Bayer significant experience in petrochemical production, and allow it to use its thermal cracking process more quickly than it could on its own in a new petrochemicals plant near the Bayer factory at Dormagen. We now turn to the story of the founding of the Erdölchemie GmbH.

Erdölchemie GmbH, Dormagen

Through the fall of 1956, Standard Oil of New Jersey (Esso) and its German affiliate, Esso Germany (Esso A.G.), appeared to be the leading candidates for a cooperative arrangement with Bayer as it edged into the petrochemical industry. Still, throughout the entire period, Esso was not the only potential partner. From mid-1954, when the shutdown of the Ruhrbau plant was announced, Deutsche BP "had . . . tried to come into conversation with the Farbenfabriken Bayer and at least to step in as a supplier of raw materials, and perhaps also to come to a closer cooperation in the petroleum-chemical area."[20]

BP's first move was to start talks with Bayer on the possibility of taking over Ruhrbau directly. Bayer's Dr. Kimmerle (who worked in Mülheim) informed BP's sales director in Cologne, Dr. Bauer, that another firm was interested in Ruhrbau. BP, Kimmerle indicated, had better demonstrate its interest quickly. Consequently, the technical member of the BP managing board, Dr. Bockelmann, was sent to Leverkusen on 13 August 1954 to negotiate with Drs. Loehr, Langheinrich, and Kimmerle. The talks did not pan out; Bockelmann apparently had no clear sense of how Mr. Müller-Jahn, the chairman of the managing board of Deutsche BP in Hamburg, planned to proceed with the eventual cooperation. There were more substantive and technical problems as well. Clearly, Mülheim was an excellent location for such a plant. But the Ruhrbau facility, in the course of processing 200,000–250,000 tons of crude per year, yielded 40,000–50,000 tons of low-octane gasoline. That, according to Bockelmann, presented an "in-

---

[19] Hanisch, "Eindrück und Ergebnisse einer Amerikareise," pp. 3–4.
[20] Aktennotiz (Langheinrich), "Betr.: Verwertung Ruhrbau; Besprechung mit BP am 13.8.1954 in Leverkusen," 18 August 1954, BWA, 700/1366.

superable obstacle," not just because the amount of low-grade gasoline produced was too large, but also because crude with a lower gasoline content was
not available, at least not to Bockelmann's company: All of BP's crude, coming
exclusively from the Middle East and Persia, was too uniform in composition to
allow a solution to the problem through a change in supply. Although Bockelmann was pessimistic, he noted that the final decision whether or not to purchase the Ruhrbau plant would have to come from the BP business managers in
London.[21]

Bockelmann notified Bayer of BP's decision not to become involved in the
Ruhrbau in a letter to Loehr dated 1 September 1954. He noted that "in its current condition" Ruhrbau's production would involve yields of low-octane gasoline that would be too large, especially in view of the glut of gasoline on
European markets. Even its favorable location could not convince BP, especially
because the company had already signed a number of "refining contracts with
West German petroleum firms." At the same time, he noted, BP would be
pleased to cooperate with Bayer more closely in the area of petrochemicals,
"whether as supplier of crude oil or as supplier of preliminary products that you
want to use for further processing."[22]

BP apparently was quite serious about that offer, as indicated in a letter dated
10 November 1954 from Bayer's Dr. Langheinrich to his superior, Ulrich
Haberland (Figure 6.2). Langheinrich wished to inform his chief, who had just
returned from a two-month trip to the United States, that Müller-Jahn, the
head of Deutsche BP, had written and Bockelmann had telephoned to try to
set up a meeting between Bayer and BP to discuss general cooperation in the
petrochemical area. Bockelmann, at the beginning of November, had suggested
a meeting with Mr. Ornstein, the representative of Anglo-Iranian Oil Co.
(British Petroleum's official name at that time) in Germany. Ruhrbau was
unlikely to be the theme of the discussion; rather, BP probably wanted "a large-
scale cooperation in the petrochemical area." Langheinrich suggested that it
was also possible "that BP [Germany] was thinking of a financial participation.
It is well known that its mother company, Anglo-Iranian, will be very liquid
for the next few years through the payments it receives under the terms of
the Abadan Agreement from the Persian government and American petroleum
companies."[23]

Bayer appears to have pursued those negotiations with BP in only desultory
fashion. Still, the company continued its program of research in petrochemicals,
while seeking out (and being sought out by) other potential partners in the petrochemical area. For instance, during Haberland's visit to the United States in
the fall of 1954, he visited the chairman of the board (R. G. Hollis) of Standard
Oil Company of California in San Francisco and discussed California's activities

[21] Ibid.
[22] BP (Bockelmann) to Bayer (Dr. Löhr), 1 September 1954 (photocopy from Langheinrich's files),
BWA, 700/1366.
[23] Langheinrich to Haberland, "Betr.: Zusammenarbeit mit BP, Hamburg," 10 November 1954,
BWA, 700/1366.

Figure 6.2. Ulrich Haberland, chairman of the managing board, Bayer A.G. (ca. 1960). (Courtesy Bayer Firmenarchiv, Leverkusen.)

in chemical manufacturing.[24] Haberland also planned a visit to the Enjay petrochemicals plant in Baton Rouge (owned by Standard Oil of New Jersey).[25]

A few months later, in June 1955, Stevinson, Hardy & Co. Ltd. of the United Kingdom wrote a surprisingly condescending letter to Bayer with an offer of a cooperative venture with "friends of ours overseas" who wished to build a petrochemical plant that would use "as raw materials products from a refinery." The "friends" would be willing to "provide half of the required capital outlay." F. V. Boschan, of the Oil Department of Stevinson, noted that "we feel that this proposition may be of interest to you, provided you have the technical knowledge of petro-chemical equipment and have achieved success in this field of activity."[26] Bayer's reply indicated that its managers were not pleased about the

[24] Haberland to Follis, 12 November 1954, BWA, 271/1.1.92.
[25] (Preliminary plan of) "Reise Prof. Dr. Haberland/Canada–U.S.A.–Mexico," (planned for 17 September to 4 November 1954), 23 August 1954, BWA, 271/1.1.92.
[26] F. V. Boschan (Stevinson, Hardy & Co.) to F.F. Bayer, 7 June 1955, BWA, 700/1302.

tone or the substance of the offer. Holzrichter and Knauff of Bayer replied that "though we have done considerable research work in this direction we have not yet any of the basic processes such as cracking and fractionation of gases in commercial plant operation. We therefore doubt whether we would be a suitable partner for your friends." The two suggested that Stevinson make contact with Friedrich Uhde GmbH, "an engineering firm, which is a subsidiary of Farbwerke Hoechst A.G., another successor unit of the former I.G. Farbenindustrie Aktiengesellschaft."[27] In a follow-up letter, Boschan noted that he was taking their advice in writing to Uhde, but he also pointed out, rather peevishly, that "as a matter of fact we were under the impression that you have been manufacturing for some time perlon, and possibly also some other chemicals from petroleum."[28]

Occasional contacts with other potential partners notwithstanding, the major lead that Bayer pursued until the fall of 1956 was a possible cooperative agreement with Esso Germany (and with its powerful parent in the United States). Only when the possibility of cooperating with Esso fell through did Bayer turn – very quickly – to BP in earnest to negotiate an agreement in the area of petrochemicals.

After years of only general discussions, serious negotiations with Esso began at the start of 1956. Hermann Holzrichter of Bayer A.G. visited Esso in Hamburg on 25 January to discuss an upcoming visit by Ulrich Haberland to the United States in the fall. He spoke with Dr. Theel and Messrs. Kratzmüller, Harneit, and Scheibitz. The Hamburg office would arrange for Haberland to meet with top executives of Esso in New York, but its representatives insisted he should keep in mind that the actual agreement and its details would be worked out independently between Esso Hamburg and Bayer; although the main company would have to give final approval to the agreement, a large degree of independence was typical in the company. The men from Esso also noted that

on the American side a clear aversion to a close form of incorporation of the joint company type is ascertainable. Lately, the gentlemen of Esso, on account of their earlier cooperation with the I.G., and in view of the strong antitrust movement in the USA, are having inhibitions about establishing firm ties again with the I.G. successor factories. In Hamburg's estimation, this does not close off the possibility that close ties between Esso-Hamburg and FFB [Bayer] could be brought about, but only on the basis of agreements and not on the basis of independent new corporations.

They asked that Haberland keep that "psychological attitude" in mind during his visit to New York. At the same time, when the discussion turned to technical matters, the Esso Hamburg people agreed in principle with Holzrichter's suggestion that the two companies jointly produce olefins. They asked, however,

[27] Holzrichter and Knauf (Bayer) to Stevinson, Hardy & Co., 13 June 1955, BWA, 700/1302.
[28] Boschan (Stevinson, Hardy & Co.) to Bayer, "Subject: Chemicals from Petroleum," 17 June 1955, BWA, 700/1302.

that no final decision be reached at that time, because "the strongest insecurities still existed precisely in this area of manufacture of olefins." Esso USA was, however, definitely interested in expansion of butyl rubber production in Germany.[29]

All in all, it seemed clear that Esso was quite interested in cooperating with Bayer in the area of petrochemicals; only the details of the extent of cooperation would have to be worked out. A follow-up letter from Esso Hamburg noted that Dr. Theel had contacted Esso USA to arrange meetings with Haberland and enclosed a letter of introduction to Mr. John Wright, the expert for petrochemical questions in the office of refining coordination in New York, who would be responsible for taking Haberland to see the right people.[30]

In the meantime, Esso's German subsidiary and Bayer met several times to do preliminary work for the New York meetings. In a March meeting, for instance, the two sides agreed that cooperation was desirable in three major areas: production of butadiene for making Buna S, production of isobutylene for production of butyl rubber, and production of olefins, specifically ethylene and propylene. Esso's German representatives said that they were ready "immediately" to work on those problems together, "but now, as before, still [shy] away from every new [joint] company." They thus requested that Bayer's managers not think in terms of a joint venture at that time. Instead, they should allow the relationship to develop organically; they should leave it to "the [general] course of development" "whether or not one or another cooperation automatically would lead to closer ties." Regardless of the optimism of the Esso personnel, however, the meeting revealed deeper rifts than anticipated, especially in the area of cooperation in producing olefins. Esso representatives explained that to make their refineries as productive as possible, they would need to produce ethylene, and they suggested that Bayer itself purchase raw ethylene from Esso refineries.[31] Bayer, however, was planning to enter the field of petroleum cracking on its own, as we shall see shortly.

A summary of the results from a meeting between representatives of the two companies at the end of May 1956 noted, however, that "Esso had come to terms with the fact that Bayer itself wants to step into cracking chemistry." In addition, the oil firm "hopes to be considered as a possible supplier of raw materials." The meeting indicated no major issues separating the two firms; indeed, cooperative agreements seemed probable in all of the areas under consideration.[32]

---

[29] Holzrichter (Bayer), "Aktennotiz über eine Besprechung mit der ESSO am 25.1.1956 in Hamburg," 26 January 1956, BWA, 700/1358.

[30] Theel (Esso Hamburg) to Haberland, 25 January 1956; Theel to H. G. Burks, Jr., Attn. Mr. John Wright (Refining Coordination, Standard Oil [NJ]), 25 January 1956, BWA, 700/1358.

[31] Holzrichter to Haberland, 10 March 1956, BWA, Holzrichter, "Duplikate" 1.1.1955–31.12.1960.

[32] Bayer (Holzrichter) (Aktennotiz), "Betr.: Zusammenarbeit Esso–Farbenfabriken Bayer," 2 June 1956, BWA, Holzrichter, "Duplikate," 1.1.1955–21.12.1960.

As preparations continued for Haberland's visit to New York (planned for late October 1956[33]), Holzrichter supervised the in-depth planning of Bayer's move into "petrochemistry." He presented his findings in a confidential memorandum (which was actually written by Walter Kroenig, the head of the petrochemical development group) dated 3 July 1956. Bayer's plans for expansion of the Dormagen works would proceed, according to that recommendation, in two major steps. The first would involve production of basic chemical feedstocks (olefins) and their processing into products such as ethylene oxide, ethylene glycol, ethylene diglycol, and isopropyl alcohol. In the second stage, Bayer would build a factory with a yearly capacity of 45,000 tons of cold rubber. The entire project would take four to five years and would involve a yearly investment of DM 35–40 million.[34]

Holzrichter's planning, and especially his detailing of the second expansion stage, presumed close cooperation with the American firm. He wrote that he was recommending that stage "on account of the cooperation we planned with Esso." By virtue of the establishment of 45,000 tons of capacity yearly for cold rubber, he claimed, "we would therefore accommodate Esso's idea of entering as many areas as possible as a raw materials supplier for the chemical industry and would at full capacity guarantee the acceptance of large amounts of n-butane."[35]

Even before Haberland's visit to the United States, however, it became clear that the projected cooperative venture between Bayer and Esso was in difficulty. Meeting with Esso Hamburg's G. Geyer (the head of the Hamburg operation), Harneit, and Dr. Weber in late September 1956, Haberland and Langheinrich tried to force the oil company's hand. It was necessary, the two claimed, to decide by the end of 1956 on the possibility and the extent of cooperation between the firms. They also presented some technical demands; for instance, Bayer would be able to use n-butane with smaller amounts of n-butylene as a preproduct in rubber production, but would not take any "specially produced butadiene." Haberland and Langheinrich kept their strongest ammunition until last, that is, their ongoing discussions with BP. They informed Esso's representatives that BP was thinking about building a refinery right next to Bayer's Dormagen factory and "had taken up negotiations on the subject of a cooperation with Bayer in the petrochemicals area. Mr. Ornstein [of Anglo-Iranian] will come to Leverkusen on 26 September 1956."[36]

According to those who attended the meeting for Bayer, "Esso was visibly shaken by this news" and did not appear to have any prior knowledge of the possible BP-Bayer deal. The immediate response of the Esso representatives indicated that their firm had not seriously considered the possibility of cooperating

[33] Planning document, "U.S.A. (ab 22. Oktober 1956)," n.d., BWA, 271/1.1.92.
[34] F.F. Bayer (gez. Holzrichter, written by WK [Walter Kroenig]), "Betr. Erdölchemie" (Vertraulich!), 3 July 1956, pp. 1, 14, BWA, 700/306.
[35] Ibid., p. 12.
[36] F.F. Bayer (Langheinrich) (Aktennotiz), "Betr.: Erdölchemie – Zusammenarbeit mit Esso," 21 September 1956, BWA, 271/1.1.92.

with Bayer in a joint subsidiary. At the same time, Esso wanted to sell olefins to Bayer, but only under the condition that the price paid to the oil giant would have to include a part of the profits from Bayer's processing. "Should this not be the case, Esso would have to step into chemical processing more strongly than previously planned." Nonetheless, the two firms did not break off their negotiations just yet. Geyer noted that he would be in New York beginning in the middle of October and would be pleased to accompany Haberland when he talked with American Esso.[37]

The climax of the negotiations came on 30 October 1956 in Rockefeller Center at an early afternoon meeting between Bayer representatives, led by Haberland, and several top Esso officials. The Esso group included the following: S. P. Coleman, P. T. Lamont, and M. W. Boyer, all members of the board; O. V. Tracy, the president of Enjay, Esso's chemical subsidiary; W. C. Asbury, of Esso Research; G. Geyer and F. K. Scheibitz from Esso Hamburg; W. A. Greven, the deputy coordinator for marketing; R. M. Jackson, Esso's coordinator for chemical research, and his deputy, N. F. Myers. Esso believed that its new refinery close to Dormagen would be able to provide Bayer with the necessary feedstocks for its petrochemical operations at the lowest costs. At the same time, it became clear once again that Esso wished to produce butadiene, "which did not correspond to Bayer's interests." Haberland informed Esso of Bayer's intention to move into that area in petrochemical production.[38]

Even as it became clear that the interests of the two firms were significantly at odds, officially there was no break in relations between them. In the report on that meeting, in fact, Bayer's E. M. Pflueger went so far as to note that it was clear that the Esso managers "lay great value on coming to a long-term agreement with Bayer in the area of petro-chemistry." The two firms even agreed to make plans for Haberland and Geyer to meet again in Germany to continue the discussions.[39]

Bayer's strategy in the aftermath of the apparent end of negotiations with Esso is apparent from a memorandum describing a meeting on 16 November 1956 involving Haberland, Dr. Bayer (director of research), Holzrichter, and Langheinrich (who had been involved in negotiations with both Esso and BP). That small group decided on some guidelines for future negotiations with oil companies. Ties to Esso would not be severed entirely, even though the outlook for some sort of an agreement had grown bleak indeed. Langheinrich, in his minutes, noted that "at present there [is] no apparent practical way to cooperate with Esso. The negotiations should thus continue to be pursued dilatorily." BP's offer of a 50 : 50 partnership, on the other hand, "appears interesting. The negotiations with BP should thus be continued." What is more, the group added further to the list of possibilities. Because Bayer's need for olefins (in part owing

---

[37] F. F. Bayer (Langheinrich) (Aktennotiz), "Betr.: Erdölchemie – Zusammenarbeit mit Esso."

[38] Bayer (E. M. Pflueger), Memorandum für Herrn Prof. Dr. Haberland, "Notiz über den Besuch von Herrn Prof. Dr. Haberland bei der Standard Oil Company of New Jersey am 30. Oktober 1956," 1 November 1956, BWA, 271/1.1.92.

[39] Ibid.

to its own cracking facility) was "modest" in relation to the ability of BP to supply that need, Holzrichter suggested trying to interest other large users of olefins, specifically Hoechst and Hüls, "in a cooperation in the petrochemical area."[40]

Within three months, however, Bayer had begun cooperating extensively with BP, which had been waiting for just such an opportunity for some time, unaccompanied by fellow olefin users. That cooperation would eventually lead, later in 1957, to the founding of Erdölchemie. Holzrichter, however, with some trepidation, finally informed Esso of the final suspension of their negotiations on 13 June. He was happy to report to the Bayer directors, however, that, "through indiscretions within the petroleum firms," Esso had already heard of the partnership. "The conversation could thus be conducted in the most friendly tone," and the two sides promptly turned to proposals for Esso's new refinery near Dormagen to supply the Bayer factory with C_4 products.[41]

Before taking up the details of the emerging cooperation between Bayer and BP, it will be useful to explore why it took Bayer's managers so long to come around to that idea. After all, it was clear early on that Esso did not intend to enter into as close a cooperation as Bayer wished, whereas BP clearly was anxious from at least 1954 to come to just such an agreement. Furthermore, the importance of petrochemical production was becoming increasingly evident, and yet Bayer continued discussions with Esso through late 1956 and even then did not make a clean break with the American petroleum giant. The answers to those puzzles are not clear. Nonetheless, existing organizational and personal long-term relationships between Bayer (through I.G. Farben) and Esso undoubtedly played a role. The Leverkusen firm's reluctance to enter into an agreement prematurely and its exploration of a range of possibilities, other than cooperation with a petroleum firm, for entering the petrochemicals business were also significant factors in accounting for the postponement of cooperation with BP.

Nevertheless, when negotiations with Esso broke down, Bayer informed BP of that, and BP immediately made it clear that it was interested in forming a "joint company" with Bayer. It would focus on production of olefins "as well as their refining through further processing steps." Both parties moved swiftly to transform that idea into reality. British BP invited a party from Bayer (including Holzrichter, Langheinrich, Graulich, and Kroenig) to visit its petrochemical production facilities in Grangemouth, 25–27 February 1957. At the same time, the prospective partners were to compare the performance of the Lurgi-Ruhrgas cracking process, which Bayer had developed further, with that of the BP "tube cracker" process. They also hoped to harmonize their calculations regarding the economic basis for the new company. BP's delegation to the

[40] Langheinrich (Aktennotiz), "Betr: Petrochemie. – Zusammenarbeit Bayer/Ölgesellschaften" 26 November 1956, BWA, Holzrichter, EC Betrachtungen über Ausbaumöglichkeiten (Anlage).
[41] Holzrichter (Aktennotiz), "Betr: Besprechung bei der Esso am 13.6.1957 in Hamburg," 14 June 1957, BWA, Holzrichter, "Duplikate" 1.1.1955–21.12.1960.

talks, which included many members of the board, stressed from the beginning "the great interest of BP in a cooperation with the Farbenfabriken Bayer."[42]

One thing that the visit to Grangemouth (a facility owned by British Hydrocarbon, a 50:50 company of BP and The Distillers Co.) made clear to Bayer was the importance of economies of scale in petrochemical production. Bayer's managing board had agreed to finance expansion of their petrochemical facilities to the tune of DM 69.3 million. The largest facility would be a Lurgi-Ruhrgas cracker (which would be combined with a Linde apparatus for breaking down gases) to produce 15,000 tons of ethylene per year. BP stressed to the Bayer delegation that it was necessary to think in larger terms. All sorts of companies were expected to enter the petrochemical field in the coming years, and that would entail rapid expansion. For that reason, "there was no way a joint facility could be any smaller than the facilities of the competition." Capacity, BP argued, was crucial, and its representatives produced figures to show that whereas ethylene produced in a 15,000-ton facility would cost DM 0.583 per kilogram, that produced in a 30,000-ton facility would cost DM 0.36 per kilogram. That very low price was accurate even though the Suez Crisis had pushed up the price of full-range gasoline (the anticipated raw material) from its previous price of DM 120 per ton to DM 141.10 per ton.[43] In contrast to the case of BASF in its negotiations with Shell, BP, the foreign firm, was pushing for larger-scale cooperation, anticipating potential future competition.

Bayer's own production palette would help ensure profitability. As Bayer's Dr. Graulich noted,

it became obvious in the course of the entire discussion, which was at times downright difficult and which went into quite a bit of detail, that the profitability of the ethylene unit will stand or will fall on the economic utilization of the C_3 and C_4 fractions. The Farbenfabriken Bayer finds itself in this area in an excellent position, since, because of the new dehydrogenation process for butylene that the A-Factory [A-Fabrik] has come up with, it will be possible to produce cheaply the entire amount of butadiene needed by the new rubber factory (45,000 tons) from the C_4-fractions of Esso, Shell, and the joint company.[44]

In closing, the memorandum noted several items for the Bayer managing board to consider. First, the company had already decided to spend DM 70 million on expanding Dormagen's facilities for production of petrochemicals. If a new firm were created with BP, Bayer would have to share the profits resulting from that investment, "so that the question of the sense of such a new establishment is to be posed." A second consideration was that because many oil firms were moving into the production of petrochemicals, a small factory unit

---

[42] F.F. Bayer (signed Holzrichter and Graulich) (Aktennotiz), "Betrachungen über Ausbaumöglichkeiten auf dem Gebiet der Petrochemie im Rahmen der Farbenfabriken Bayer," 14 March 1957, pp. 2–3, BWA, 9/L.
[43] Ibid., pp. 1, 3.   [44] Ibid., p. 4.

would not be optimal in terms of profitability. At the same time, it was necessary to keep in mind the potential of petrochemistry for the future: Using only 1 percent of crude-oil production, the U.S. Chemical industry was at that time able to produce goods accounting for 25 percent of total chemical-industry turnover.[45]

All in all, there were considerable advantages to a cooperation with BP: Bayer could get feedstocks at a good price, would have the opportunity to sell by-products in the fuel sector, if necessary, and would be able to build a larger, more competitive plant. The last consideration was quite important, because the profitability for a larger, commonly owned plant would be much greater than that for a smaller one owned exclusively by Bayer. On the other hand, Bayer would have to come up with an additional DM 60 million to get in on the project.[46]

The report ended on an optimistic note, stressing the advantages of a timely, bold stroke, couched in terms reminiscent of those Bernhard Timm had used in arguing for more, rather than less, cooperation between BASF and Shell:

Since the preconditions for a rapid and successful start may be characterized as very favorable, it would be possible through cooperation with BP to become – apart from the Rhein[ische] Olefin Works – the first large-scale producer of olefins on the Rhine. It may be assumed that through this the plans for expansion of the others interested [in this area], such as Shell and Esso, would be affected negatively.[47]

The two firms agreed to found Erdölchemie GmbH in September 1957, although they still had to work out a number of details on the relationship between the two partners. Among many outstanding questions was whether Bayer would make a cooperative agreement with BP Hamburg or with BP London. Part of the problem concerned taxes: BP London owned BP Hamburg outright; so if it became a partner together with Bayer and BP Hamburg in Erdölchemie, there was a danger that "either Erdölchemie or BP Hamburg as places of business of BP London could be dealt with in the sense of German tax law and of the German-English double-taxation agreement." There were also the questions of prestige (Bayer did not want to sign the contract with the subsidiary) and of making sure that profits and losses were shared by the two parties. Finally, assurances of feedstock supply, of exchanges of know-how, and of adequate capital resources to cover the losses expected in the first three years of operation were necessary.[48]

Besides those sorts of issues, Bayer managers discussed the changing economics of the rapidly growing petrochemical industry. Whether or not to establish a major presence in polypropylene, in the face of enormous competition and

---

[45] Ibid., pp. 5–6; quotation, p. 5.   [46] Ibid., p. 6.

[47] Ibid.

[48] August Fürnrohr and Werner Friedrich (Rechtsanwälte, Fachanwälte für Steuerrecht) to BP Benzin und Petroleum Gesellschaft, "Betr.: Steuerliche Auswirkungen der Vereinbarungen über Erdölchemie," 12 December 1957 (Abschrift), Bayer A.G., Rechtsabteilung, 1.21/44/9, Fiche 10.

potential patent disputes, was the basis for one such discussion in January 1958.[49]

Finally, however, on 20 March 1958, BP London and Bayer A.G. signed a more detailed basic agreement to cooperate in the petrochemical field. Geographically, the agreement was limited to the Federal Republic of Germany and West Berlin, although in the event of reunification it would apply to all of Germany. The basic agreement did little more than that, however: It noted that the two companies "have now decided to co-operate in the manufacture of petroleum chemicals"; it established that Bayer would carry out its side of the co-operation directly, but that BP Hamburg would represent the interests of BP London; and it called for BP Hamburg and Bayer therefore to "enter into a contract laying down the details of co-operation."[50]

In September 1958, the first input of raw gasoline to Erdölchemie's first cracker took place, and the factory's production expanded rapidly after that[51] (Figures 6.3 and 6.4). In subsequent years, Erdölchemie produced ethylene, propylene, butadiene, benzene, and toluene by thermal cracking of raw gasoline. BP supplied the raw gasoline, and Bayer absorbed Erdölchemie's butadiene, benzene, and toluene production directly. Bayer also further processed its production of ethylene oxide, ethylene glycol, ethanol, and propylene oxide into a full range of chemical products. Cracking gasoline, a by-product of the production process, was hydrogenated and then sent back to BP, where it was used as an additive to BP gasoline.[52]

Under the agreement between the two firms, research-and-development work in the area of petrochemicals remained with the principals. The petrochemicals development group at Leverkusen, which had been founded in 1953, therefore continued to be of some importance in that area. In addition, Leverkusen's development group provided many high-ranking production managers for Erdölchemie.[53]

Concluding remarks

In a memorandum on "The Development of Erdölchemie GmbH through 1962," a Bayer manager (Holzrichter, or a member of his staff) asked the question, "Was our path into petrochemistry the right one?" Not surprisingly, he concluded that it had indeed been correct, but some of his comments in making his argument are worth noting. He pointed out that "already for a number of years the growth rates of aliphatic chemistry [have superseded] those of aro-

[49] F.F. Bayer, Verkauf Chemikalien, Abt. LK, Besprechungsnotiz: "Konkurrenzprodukt Polypropylen," 18 January 1958 (Vertraulich) (carbon copy), BWA, 700/1214; Otto Bayer to Ulrich Haberland and others, "Polyäthylen–Polypropylen," 12 March 1958 (mimeograph), BWA, 700/1214.

[50] "Basic Agreement . . . between The British Petroleum Company Limited, London, . . . and Farbenfabriken Bayer Aktiengesellschaft, Leverkusen, . . . regarding co-operation in the field of petroleum chemicals," 20 March 1958, Bayer A.G., Rechtsabteilung 1.21/44/3.

[51] Erdölchemie GmbH, *Zehn Jahre EC. 1957–1967* (brochure, n.d.), p. 6, BWA, 9/L.

[52] Bayer A.G., "25 Jahre Gruppe 'Petrochemie,' 1953–1978," p. 2, BWA, 9/L.

[53] Ibid.

Figure 6.3. Butadiene extraction plant, Erdölchemie GmbH, Dormagen (ca. 1963). (Courtesy Bayer Firmenarchiv, Leverkusen.)

matic chemistry." The United States was the first to move along that path, but the Europeans quickly followed. The Germans, handicapped at first by the residual effects of the war, followed more slowly, but by the early 1960s more than half (in terms of value) of all organic chemicals produced in West Germany were being produced from crude oil. Therefore,

the correctness, yes the necessity of the activity in petrochemicals is demonstrated for Europe and Germany. It is clear that we [Bayer], as the largest chemical firm in the Federal Republic, could not escape this development. We believe it would have been impossible for us to hold our rank in the chemical industry in the long term without petrochemistry.[54]

Having said that, the author turned to the additional question whether or not the particular form of Bayer's entry into the field (i.e., the cooperative venture with BP) had been the best route available. He claimed that Bayer had recog-

[54] "Die Erdölchemie GmbH in ihrer Entwicklung bis zum Jahre 1962" (manuscript, n.d., probably spring 1962), BWA, 9/L.

Figure 6.4. Aerial photo of Erdölchemie GmbH, Dormagen. (Courtesy Bayer Firmen-archiv, Leverkusen.)

nized "already in the middle of the previous decade" (i.e., the 1950s) the in-creasing tendency of oil producers to enter the petrochemical field and thus undermine chemical companies. To neutralize that threat, to assure feedstock supplies, and to have an outlet for the oil by-products of petrochemical produc-tion, Bayer decided to cooperate "with one of the large international oil cor-porations." The cooperation provided other advantages as well, because Bayer's capital resources were not so strained as they might otherwise have been. The availability of additional funds from the partner meant a rapid translation of plans into action. The new firm could also optimize its profits through econo-mies of scale. Finally, cooperation with a major oil firm allowed rapid adjust-ments to changes in markets. For all of those reasons, the question whether or not Bayer's course had been a wise choice was "to be answered with a clear 'Yes'." Interestingly, however, the author did not argue that there were any spe-cific advantages to cooperation with BP.[55]

Even in that rather crude, probably self-serving analysis from 1962, we get an impression of the extent to which Bayer's path into petrochemicals was a matter of choice rather than necessity. Although the company probably would not have been able to maintain its position in the West German chemical industry without a major presence in petrochemicals, Bayer would have continued to thrive even if it had decided not to enter that field. Even given its decision to do so, Bayer

[55] Ibid., pp. 7–8.

could have chosen not to cooperate with BP; it could have chosen from among a number of BP's competitors. Furthermore, in evaluating the inevitability of that technological/economic change, we have to keep in mind that the eventual scale of the enormous growth in petrochemical markets was far from clear in the early 1950s, when many of the key decisions were made.

In any case, the issue whether to go it alone, to cooperate with BP, or to work with another company clearly was an open question through 1956, at least. When, exactly, the decision was made was relatively unimportant. What was significant was that from the time of its re-founding in late 1951 and early 1952, Bayer, like BASF before it, could choose from among a range of options. Oil companies, foreign chemical firms, and engineering contractors all courted Bayer from the beginning. However, Bayer's management moved slowly and deliberately to pursue the options it believed to be most compatible with its interests.

Although internal development of petrochemical technology might have been the ideal option for the company (from its perspective), Bayer managers came to the conclusion that they would have to work with an established petroleum producer. They would have preferred to work with Standard Oil of New Jersey (Esso) toward that end; however, Haberland and his associates at Leverkusen were not so eager to work with Esso that they would do so regardless of the costs. Like the negotiations between BASF and Shell over the Rheinische Olefinwerke, the discussions between Bayer and Esso were far from one-sided. Rather, the West German firm acted like Esso's equal and was treated as such, demanding concessions from the oil firm, but also offering to compromise when it seemed appropriate. When Esso, unlike Shell, proved unwilling or unable to meet Bayer's terms, Bayer quickly turned to another powerful and capable partner that had been waiting in the wings: BP. Although the package of technological knowledge, production experience, and capital that BP was able to offer was not equal to what Esso could have offered, it was at least comparable. In addition, the company's representatives, both in Hamburg and in London, were clearly excited about cooperating with Bayer.

Cooperation with BP therefore seemed to Bayer personnel to be a safer way to move into the tempestuous and unfamiliar petrochemical industry than did internal research or any other potential path. As the author of the piece "Was our path into petrochemistry the right one?" stated,

petrochemistry is to a very great extent subject to changes which often make necessary substantial alterations in the production program. If one sits here in the same boat with one of the large petroleum corporations, the implementation of this change in direction is incomparably simpler than if one is bound through delivery and purchase contracts for the long term to outside [fremde] petroleum corporations.[56]

In other words, even as Bayer (and BASF) was moving deliberately into petrochemical technology by slowly evaluating its options, it chose an option that was itself a way of hedging the bet. Risking only half the requisite capital, and re-

[56] Ibid.

lying on its partnership with an established producer to make its way into petrochemicals, Bayer also would realize only half the profits from an industrial sector that would expand far more rapidly than anyone had dreamed possible. Hoechst A.G., the subject of the next chapter, chose differently, with different results.

7
Going it alone: Hoechst

When it was founded at the end of 1951, Farbwerke Hoechst A.G. was the smallest of the "Big Three" I.G. Farben successor corporations. Like BASF and Bayer, Hoechst had originally been founded in the 1860s; it had begun as a small dye producer and then had expanded its product line into pharmaceuticals and other organic chemicals in the late nineteenth and twentieth centuries. Like BASF and Bayer, Hoechst has had a long and distinguished tradition of research, product development, and marketing. Finally, like the two other members of the Big Three, Hoechst initially intended to continue its reliance on coal-based feedstocks; only slowly and deliberately did the firm's management choose to move into petrochemical production. However, the Hoechst group, unlike the other two large I.G. successors, had fallen on hard times, especially during the interwar period. Major Hoechst managers had been underrepresented among the top members of the managing board of I.G. Farben, and the investment plans of the chemical giant during the period from 1925 through 1945 neglected Hoechst plants, as compared with their treatment of the BASF and Bayer groups.[1]

---

[1] Raymond G. Stokes, *Divide and Prosper: The Heirs of I.G. Farben under Allied Authority, 1945–1951* (Berkeley: University of California Press, 1988), pp. 49–52.

Partly as a consequence of the relative neglect of investment in the plants of the Hoechst group, they ended the war in a contradictory situation: The Allies had not bombed them as heavily as they had other plants, especially those of BASF, because the Hoechst plants simply had not been as important to the German war effort. Therefore, after minor repairs, they were ready to produce again immediately after the war was over; on the other hand, the plants of the Hoechst group had only relatively outdated technologies and equipment.

Unquestionably, the legacy of underinvestment in plant, underrepresentation in the upper levels of I.G. Farben management, and relative technological backwardness played a role in the postwar history of the Hoechst group, especially when the management of the group decided to move into petrochemical technology beginning in the early 1950s. Unlike BASF and Bayer managers, Hoechst's leadership had difficulty in coming to cooperative agreements with any of the major oil producers at the time Hoechst was seeking to move into petrochemical production. After some failed attempts to do so, they instead decided to rely primarily on a strategy of internal development of petrochemical technology (including, unlike BASF and Bayer, *both* crude-oil cracking and chemical-intermediates production technologies) and cooperation with domestic firms rather than foreign oil producers.

That strategy was quite successful, for a number of reasons. The massive growth in demand for plastics throughout the 1950s favored all producers – to some extent regardless of raw-materials and feedstock costs. Moreover, it is important to keep in mind that although Hoechst was relatively backward vis-à-vis the other I.G. successors, it shared the I.G. traditions of technological excellence with those other firms, its laboratory facilities were quite good, and even its production technologies were adequate in the early 1950s. A talented new management team led by Karl Winnacker built on that tradition to ensure the firm's competitiveness, not just in international markets, but also at home. Hoechst's newfound parity with the other large I.G. successors was symbolized in 1961 when it, too, abandoned the crude-oil cracking business and opted instead for supply agreements with foreign-owned producers. This chapter explores the ways in which Hoechst differed from the other major successor companies as it moved gradually away from coal-based chemistry and into petrochemical technology in the postwar period.

Competing technologies in the immediate postwar period

Chapter 3 described in detail the negotiations between the Allied occupation forces and the Hoechst group seeking to retain the A.G. für Stickstoffdünger in Knapsack, near Cologne. Knapsack, by far the most important carbide producer in what was to become West Germany, was critical to the Hoechst production program, which featured a broad range of products based on acetylene, which in turn came from the carbide produced at Knapsack. Hoechst entered the postwar period at a disadvantage compared with the other two major successors of the I.G., and therefore gaining control of Knapsack was high on the agenda of the

Hoechst leadership and, eventually, of the American occupiers as well. One of the major problems hindering that disposition was the fact that Knapsack was located in the British zone of occupation. Only after long and complicated negotiations did Hoechst finally gain control of Knapsack as a wholly owned subsidiary, in conjunction with the official re-founding of Farbwerke Hoechst A.G. vormals Meister Lucius & Brüning in December 1951.

The Hoechst group's management gave serious attention to the matter of moving systematically away from coal-based chemical production and into petroleum-based organic chemical manufacturing only after the resolution of the Knapsack question and other issues surrounding the breakup of I.G. Farben. One reason for that delay was that Hoechst managers, like those in other firms, continued to believe in the economic viability of acetylene derived from coal as the primary basis for organic chemical production. That was clearly illustrated when high-ranking Hoechst officials met on 7 July 1950 with members of the I.G. Farben Dispersal Panel (FARDIP), a German committee charged with recommending to the Allies how to proceed with the breakup of I.G. Farben. When the discussion turned to Knapsack, Hoechst's Kurt Möller, who was a member of the firm's managing board from its re-founding in 1952 through the end of March 1954, demonstrated in his presentation

that acetylene chemistry on the basis of carbide is indeed experiencing a certain reduction because of ethylene chemistry on the basis of petroleum, but that it [acetylene chemistry] will still retain a broad field of application since its price will be in order, and it will maintain its justification by virtue of the dependency of the petroleum basis on imports. German crude oil is, according to von Möller, not competitive in terms of price vis-à-vis carbide for the next ten years.[2]

Other Hoechst officials attending that meeting supported Möller's observations on the competitiveness of German crude.

Möller's remarks are of central interest for at least two reasons. For one thing, they demonstrate clearly once again that German industrialists foresaw a world in which coal-based acetylene chemistry and petroleum-based ethylene chemistry would co-exist. Ethylene feedstocks might be more flexible and safer than acetylene, but acetylene chemistry would remain viable because of the breadth of its production palette and because petroleum would, for German companies, involve dependence on imported oil. Second, Möller's comments reveal certain fundamental assumptions about the security of raw materials. German coal, of course, was and would continue to be the fundament for the German organic chemical industry, but even when considering petroleum as a source of chemical feedstocks, Möller chose to emphasize *German* crude oil as coal's primary competitor, not foreign sources of crude. The argument that reliance on petroleum produced abroad would result in an unacceptable dependence on imports apparently was convincing to everyone involved in the discussion.

[2] Dr. Engelbertz, "Aktennotiz über Besprechung bei FARDIP, Ffm., am 7.7.1950," 12 July 1950, p. 2, reprinted in *Dokumente aus Hoechst-Archiven*, vol. 49, part 1: "Der Hoechst-Konzern entsteht" (Frankfurt-Hoechst: Hoechst A.G., 1978), p. 73.

Still, changes were already under way. In a 1952 letter to Vice-Chancellor Blücher that outlined his firm's future investment needs, Karl Winnacker, the chairman of the Hoechst managing board, emphasized the need to invest in new technologies: "The relationships in supply of our solvents and plastics section are more difficult, since the section, in parallel with American developments, in part must move from the acetylene basis to petroleum hydrocarbons, for which considerable means are necessary."[3] By 1954, the need to move into petrochemicals had become more pressing. As Hoechst's public-relations officer, Ernst Bäumler, reported in his official history of the firm, it was clear by then that the twofold problem associated with coal-chemical production (high costs and insufficient capacity) required some sort of alternative technology:

Even the strings of barges on the Main [River] laden with coal from the Ruhr and carbide from Knapsack – which despite new ovens had to be bought in greater and greater quantities at higher and higher prices – no longer sufficed, to cover demand, which was growing gigantically. There was only one way: . . . The hour of petrochemistry was at hand.[4]

Bäumler's account of the rapidity and finality with which Hoechst decided to move into petrochemicals[5] is overly dramatic and assumes a single possible trajectory of events. Still, he is correct to point out that the company began serious work in petrochemical technology in 1952. The extent of its commitment to the new means of producing organic chemicals increased over the course of the following decade.

The move into petrochemicals

Hoechst's managing board announced in the firm's corporate reports for 1952 and 1953 that research into "petroleum-chemical work" had become a central focus of the Hoechst research program,[6] and, as will soon become clear, that research quickly paid off with an internally developed cracking process. Still, Hoechst, like the other major I.G. successors, pursued a number of alternative strategies as it cast about for the most effective means for competing in world markets in the 1950s.

Hoechst's corporate report for 1954, for example, noted that one of the key problems it faced was the need to expand its raw-materials base. The directors reported two quite different but complementary ways of dealing with that problem. One way was to explore new technologies for increasing the output of the German organic chemical industry's most important feedstock: coal-based acetylene. Thus, Hoechst reported that it was proceeding with the construction of "a carbide oven constructed according to the latest technical views," which was soon supposed to begin production. The idea was to enhance the compet-

---

[3] Winnacker to Vice-Chancellor Blücher, 5 April 1952, p. 3, in *Dokumente*, 50, Teil 2, p. 198.
[4] Ernst Bäumler, *Ein Jahrhundert Chemie* (Düsseldorf: Econ, 1963), pp. 139–40.
[5] Bäumler, *Ein Jahrhundert*, pp. 139–64.
[6] Farbwerke Hoechst A.G., *Geschäftsbericht 1952*, p. 7; Farbwerke Hoechst A.G., *Geschäftsbericht 1953*, p. 7.

itiveness of traditional acetylene chemistry in world markets through technological improvements. The second way of expanding the company's base in raw
materials was to explore alternative sources. As the directors noted,

the expansion of our own raw materials basis was also one of the grounds for our activity
in the new area of petrochemistry, which is becoming of supreme importance in the production of plastics and solvents. A petroleum cracking process of our own which was
developed at Hoechst has demonstrated its complete usefulness at the pilot plant level.
The first large-scale plant is currently under construction and will supply even this year
olefins for further chemical processing into plastics, solvents, and raw materials for completely synthetic fibers.[7]

The new cracking process reported by the directors was, of course, a result of
the firm's research efforts in 1952 and 1953, and it will be useful in the next
section of this chapter to take a closer look at the process and the way it was
deployed at Hoechst. Before doing that, it will be necessary to explore further
the technological alternatives that Hoechst pursued in the first half of the 1950s.

In addition to examining two complementary techniques for expanding the company's raw-materials base through the firm's internal research into acetylene and
petrochemical production processes, Hoechst's managers engaged in cooperative ventures with other German firms and purchased technology from outside
the firm. Hoechst's relationship with Deutsche Erdöl-Aktiengesellschaft (DEA)
was its most important cooperative arrangement in the 1950s. DEA, a German
oil company that had begun its existence in 1899 as a drilling contractor, moved
into the area of crude-oil production and refining after 1905. During World
War II, DEA had been one of the most important petroleum firms in Germany,
and its importance in the industry expanded after the war when it discovered
significant new petroleum deposits around Kiel and Speyer, as well as natural
gas near Pfungstadt.[8]

Hoechst and DEA had agreed by early 1954 to build a pipeline from the gas
field at Pfungstadt to Hoechst's main factory, and the chemical company used
the methane to produce various chemicals, pharmaceuticals, and plastics. Still,
the amounts of gas involved were fairly small, and it was not entirely clear even
late in 1954 that the field would be able to meet the needs of Hoechst over the
long term.[9] More important, DEA was involved in supplying Hoechst's
continuous-coking facility (discussed later) with crude oil, although again the

[7] Farbwerke Hoechst A.G., *Geschäftsbericht 1954*, p. 8.
[8] A. E. Gunther, *The War Structure of the German Crude Oil Industry, 1934–1945: Private Industry*
[London: British Intelligence Objectives Sub-Committee, n.d. (ca. 1949)], BIOS Final Report No.
1017, p. 5; "Oel aus deutscher Erde," *Hamburger Anzeiger, Sonderbeilage* (26 March 1955);
"Erdöl-Chemie bleibt optimistisch," *Deutsche Zeitung und Wirtschafts-Zeitung* (9 July 1955).
[9] "Erdgasleitung durch den Main," *Frankfurter Neue Presse* (29 March 1954); Thies, "Aktennotiz
über eine Besprechung mit Herrn Bergassesor Schlicht, DEA, am 14.9.1954 in Essen," 19 September 1954, Hoechst Firmenarchiv, Frankfurt-Hoechst (hereafter, HFA).

relationship was not exclusive: Hoechst kept a certain distance from any single petroleum supplier in the 1950s, considering offers from Standard Oil of New York (Socony) and British Petroleum as well.[10]

DEA and Hoechst, together with Mannesmann, also cooperated more closely through their joint venture Kohle-Oel-Chemie GmbH, which was founded in 1955 to produce polyethylene and polyvinyl chloride for pipes. The joint-venture company drew its feedstocks in part from olefins in the off-gases from coking operations at mines owned by DEA and Mannesmann, and in part from DEA's petroleum, which was added to the off-gases to increase the yield of olefins in the coking operation. The joint venture was to produce 12,000 tons of polyethylene per year beginning in 1957, which would double to 24,000 tons shortly thereafter. Again, though, that was a relatively small operation, and Hoechst kept its distance in that case as well. The chemical company insisted on developing its plastics production technologies independently of, and with no obligations to, the joint venture.[11] The pattern of the relationship between Hoechst and DEA, then, remained consistent during the 1950s: There was cooperation, but often it was halfhearted, and in terms of Hoechst's total production picture it was not of great significance.

Purchase of outside technology was much more important for the company's development in the 1950s. In their 1954 report to stockholders, Hoechst managers noted that they had obtained the rights to manufacture low-pressure, high-density polyethylene from Karl Ziegler. Work on applying that process proceeded swiftly, so that the firm could begin producing a new line of polyethylene beginning in early 1955. From the outset, the trade name for the product, Hostalen, met "with unusually great interest in the processing industry."[12]

The personal relationship between Ziegler and Otto Horn, who headed Hoechst's solvents and plastics research laboratory, clearly was a factor in the cooperation between Ziegler and Hoechst. Horn had come to the company from the Kaiser Wilhelm Institut für Kohlenforschung in Mülheim, in the Ruhr district, where he had served as assistant to the leader of the institute, Franz Fischer (of the Fischer-Tropsch process). Ziegler, an independent researcher based in Halle, whom Horn already knew, had come to the Ruhr institute during the last part of the war. He had succeeded Fischer as head of the institute shortly before the war ended, and he and Horn had become friends. Their friendship, Horn later claimed, combined with the offer to Ziegler of an honorarium of fertilizer, rather than money, in the period before the currency reform, convinced Ziegler to give a lecture at Hoechst, thus ending a bitter prewar dispute over patent rights to the production of phenyl sodium. Horn also took advantage of his friendship with Ziegler and his earlier contacts with the institute to negotiate Hoechst's acquisition of a share of the Studien- und Verwertungsgesellschaft

---

[10] Thies, "Aktennotiz," 16 September 1954; Krekeler and Kamptner to Thies, "Betr.: Rohölversorgung des Kokers," 15 January 1955, HFA.

[11] Thies, "Aktennotiz," 16 September 1954; "Erdöl-Chemie bleibt optimistisch."

[12] Farbwerke Hoechst A.G., *Geschäftsbericht 1954*, p. 9.

mbH, the institute's patent-exploitation company, thus obtaining "the right to take licenses on processes from the institute from now on."[13]

Horn was responsible for encouraging a formal relationship between Ziegler and Hoechst beginning in 1952. In a visit to Horn's apartment in mid-February, Ziegler told Horn about his recently patented work in the area of ethylene polymerization. Asked if he would be interested in cooperating with Hoechst in that area, and whether or not he had agreements with other firms regarding his new technology, Ziegler replied that he would be interested in cooperation. He had no obligations to other firms yet. Using aluminum-based catalysts, he was able to produce polyethylene in small quantities. According to Ziegler, the process was "independent of ICI [Imperial Chemical Industries], but could surely not reach with his methods the high rate of polymerization [of the ICI process]. It seemed to him much more interesting that he could dimerize, for example, propylene and butylene and thus attain octane, which, through aromatization, supplied p-xylene [for polyester]." Horn, in his memorandum of the meeting, suggested that his firm take up formal contact with Ziegler.[14]

What was so interesting about Ziegler's process? It is clear that Hoechst's management did not have much hope for the commercial possibilities of Ziegler-based polyethylene production until late 1953. For most of 1952 and 1953, Hoechst was particularly intrigued by the potential that Ziegler offered for producing p-xylene.[15] Just as the initial formal feelers between Horn and Ziegler were going out, Hoechst was involved in negotiations for a license from ICI to produce the British chemical firm's polyester fiber: Terylene. To manufacture approximately 50,000 tons of the synthetic fiber per year in Germany, the amount that both Hoechst and ICI had in mind, there were insufficient quantities of p-xylene available in Germany. Ziegler's process appeared to offer a means for overcoming that shortfall.[16]

In early April 1952, Ziegler visited Hoechst to give a talk about his process, so that members of the firm's patent department could judge whether or not it was in Hoechst's interest to purchase an option. After evaluating his remarks in light of the ongoing negotiations with ICI, the patent department wrote to Ziegler to say that Hoechst was very interested in the process and wished to conclude a contract with Ziegler. The contract, which gave Hoechst the right to begin research on applications and to examine the commercial possibilities of Ziegler's "processes for polymerization, including dimerization and mixed po-

---

[13] Otto Horn, "Entwicklung des Polyäthylens nach Ziegler aus der Sicht von Hoechst," 2 October 1973, HFA.

[14] O. Horn, Aktennotiz "Besuch von Herrn Prof. Ziegler . . . am 15.2.1952 in Höchst," 15 February 1952, HFA.

[15] In a meeting with Ziegler to negotiate an options agreement in July 1952, the head of the plastics department, Dr. Möller, identified production of p-xylene as the primary interest of the firm in Ziegler process. Hoechst was also interested in the possibility of producing polyethylene ("wenn möglich das hochmolekulare Produkt") using a similar process. Hoechst AG, Laboratorium für Lösungsmittel und Kunststoffe (Dr. Krekeler), "Bericht über einen Besuch am Kohlenforschungsinstitut . . . am 2.7.1952," 8 July 1952, HFA.

[16] Horn, "Entwicklung des Polyäthylens," pp. 2–3.

lymerization, including mixed dimerization of olefins or mixtures of olefins in the presence of organometallic compounds," took effect in the fall of 1952. The firm had the option to make a further agreement on commercial exploitation of the process during the contract period (one year, with the possibility of extensions). Hoechst paid Ziegler DM 50,000 for those rights.[17]

During 1952 and 1953, Hoechst's laboratory for solvents and plastics conducted research on possible applications for the Ziegler process of producing *p*-xylene, and the firm went so far as to invest in an experimental production plant. By July 1953, however, it was clear that they had reached a dead end: "It can already be said today, that this process for the production of *p*-xylene is no longer of interest, since *p*-xylene can today be produced very cheaply via the petrochemical process." In West Germany, Standard Oil of California was selling *p*-xylene using the petrochemical process at prices far lower than Hoechst could match.[18]

Still, Hoechst decided in July to negotiate with Ziegler to extend its contract option; during the first half of 1953, the firm had become more interested in the process's potential for producing polyethylene. In the opinion of its management, Hoechst probably had no possibility of gaining a license from ICI for manufacturing the polymer using its process, and so it would be necessary to try to find an alternative process, and Ziegler's seemed a possible candidate. In addition, other chemical firms had been working with the Ziegler process in that same direction, and Montecatini had even begun production on a small scale.[19]

As negotiations continued throughout the summer and fall of 1953, Hoechst representatives repeatedly emphasized their strong interest in polyethylene production using Ziegler's process. In November, for instance, Horn and Dr. Scherer of the Hoechst central laboratory "told Prof. Ziegler that Hoechst was very interested in polyethylene and at the conclusion of the first option contract had thought primarily, in addition to now-outdated *p*-xylene, in terms of polyethylene."[20] In mid-January 1954, Ziegler and Hoechst agreed to extend their contract "to its full extent . . . without raising the option amount."[21]

For its second try, Hoechst's priorities for exploiting the process were more clear. By February, a working group under Dr. Sieglitz began development, at laboratory scale, of Ziegler-based production of polyethylene. The group's Dr. Grams, speaking in mid-June at a meeting of Hoechst scientists and technicians working on "applications technology for solvents, plastics, and raw materials

---

[17] Dr. Bergmann, Hoechst Patentabteilung, Aktennotiz "Besprechung mit Herrn Prof. Dr. Ziegler . . . am 1.4.52," 2 April 1952, HFA; Hoechst (Möller and Eishold) to Karl Ziegler, 28 April 1952, HFA; Horn, "Entwicklung des Polyäthylens," p. 3.

[18] Hoechst Patentabteilung, Aktennotiz "Besprechung am 2. Juli 1953 . . . über Verlängerung des Optionsvertrages mit Professor Ziegler," 6 July 1953, HFA; Horn, "Entwicklung des Polyäthylens," p. 4. Quotation from former.

[19] Hoechst Patentabteilung, Aktennotiz, "Besprechung am 2. Juli 1953."

[20] Hoechst (Horn and Scherer), Aktennotiz "Besuch bei Herrn Prof. Dr. Ziegler . . . am 20.11.1953," 25 November 1953, HFA.

[21] Hoechst (Dr. Scherer), "Notiz über den Besuch bei Herrn Prof. Dr. Ziegler . . . am 27. und 28. Januar 1954," 29 January 1954, HFA.

for fibers," reported that so far the group had tried 300 different runs in the apparatus, of about 200 grams each. The product was not the usual polyethylene, however:

The Ziegler polyethylene product is differentiated from the well-known polyethylene types (ICI, BASF, DuPont, Bakelite) generally by its softening range, which is higher; by its greater hardness and stiffness; as well as by a greater firmness. The differences may have their origins in:
1. its higher molecular weight;
2. less branching;
3. the greater tendency to crystallization (conditioned by 1 and 2).
The first products manufactured demonstrated the characteristics mentioned to a particularly high degree. Possibilities for processing do not appear to be available outside of pressing. It was attempted to steer the development toward softer products which would approach more closely those usually available in trade.

Those attempts were successful, although there remained considerable variations in the characteristics of the Ziegler polyethylene, as compared with "normal" polyethylene. Still, the product type that resulted from those experiments was chosen as the working basis for further development work.[22]

In other words, as late as mid-1954, just a year and a half before the firm took up industrial-scale production of low-pressure, high-density polyethylene, Hoechst scientists were still trying to alter or fine-tune the Ziegler process so that they could produce a substance that would mimic more closely the characteristics of "normal" (low-density) polyethylene. Just as had been the case earlier when Hoechst researchers and managers had favored concentrating on producing p-xylene rather than polyethylene using the Ziegler process, they did not anticipate the full commercial possibilities of the new polyethylene type. Thus, Hoechst's management clearly was excited about the possibilities of the new technology, and they directed the firm's research teams to explore those possibilities as thoroughly as possible, but it was not until 1955 that they realized that Ziegler polyethylene could establish itself in a market niche entirely separate from that of low-density polyethylene.

That market niche, lucrative as it was, paid added dividends to Hoechst, which, by virtue of its development work on the Ziegler process, already possessed considerable practical experience. Ziegler sold his licenses nonexclusively around the world, and they were for a largely untested production process, because Ziegler had neither the resources nor the desire to do the development work. Hoechst's experience with the process was therefore an important commodity, especially in establishing the firm as a major player in the international arena.

Hoechst's management used their Ziegler experience to aid them in another facet of their strategy to restore the firm's status as a major force in the international chemical market, that is, to move into the U.S. market. They acquired

[22] Dr. Grams, "Referat Nr. 3, Stand der Polyäthylen-Arbeiten (Produkt K 24), in Dr. Heuck (ATA-Kunststoffe), "Sitzung der Unterkommission 3 c, 'Anwendungstechnik für Lösungsmittel, Kunststoffe und Faserrohstoffe' am 18.6.1954," 14 June 1954 [sic], HFA.

the majority of Metro Dyestuff Corporation, "a small, productive dyes factory," during 1954. In the same year, they also cooperated with W. R. Grace in building a chemical factory that used "electrolysis of chlorine alkalies" to produce pesticides, solvents, and textile auxiliaries. In addition, they tried to reacquire trademarks and to rebuild their foreign-sales offices.[23]

Hoechst's Ziegler know-how appeared to offer a way to further the concern's interests in expanding its presence in the United States, in particular through strengthening its ties to W. R. Grace. In November 1954, Hoechst officials began negotiations with Ziegler to obtain a license for a prospective cooperative production venture between Hoechst and Grace in the United States. Ziegler made it clear that it would be difficult to give preference to the Hoechst-Grace venture, especially because he had already sold three licenses in the united States (to Gulf Oil – Goodrich, Koppers, and Hercules Powder). In addition, negotiations were under way to sell an additional three licenses (to Dow, Monsanto, and Union Carbide and Carbon), and DuPont and "about 10 additional corporations" had shown interest in licenses. Ziegler told the Hoechst officials that he feared that Dow, Monsanto, and Union Carbide would lose interest if Grace were given preference at that point. Because each license cost $400,000 at that time, up from the original price of $300,000 each (plus royalties from production), failure to sell those licenses would represent a considerable loss in revenue for Ziegler. There was, of course, a way around that, but "he [Ziegler] hardly believed, that Grace was ready to pay $1.2 million as a substitute for the negotiations in process." Ziegler suggested, instead, that Grace and Hoechst build a joint polyethylene production facility in Brazil, instead of in the United States, or that the firms look into another sort of factory in the United States for their joint venture. Hoechst's representatives "indicated that Grace had very much decided to go into chemistry and was in addition very potent, and that we had promised our support. A clear statement from Prof. Ziegler was not to be had."[24]

Hoechst's Drs. Engelbertz and Horn visited Ziegler in his office in Mülheim in February 1955 to try to get him to clarify his position. Ziegler reported that all three companies with which he had negotiated at his last meeting had signed (or would sign within the next two days) licensing agreements with him, and an additional three companies (DuPont, Standard Oil of New Jersey, and National Distillers) were on the verge of signing. The last three would pay the new base price of $700,000 per license. Ziegler believed "that it indeed would be simplest if Hoechst would implement these plans [for a cooperative venture in the United States] with one of the firms that had purchased a license from him to this point." Still, he was prepared to grant a license to Hoechst and Grace, provided that a number of conditions were met. Among them were the following: that the license would be exclusively for polyethylene production; that Ziegler would

---

[23] Farbwerke Hoechst A.G., *Geschäftsbericht 1954*, p. 7.

[24] Hoechst (Dr. Horn, Dr. Kneip), "Aktennotiz über Besprechung mit Herrn Prof. Dr. Karl Ziegler . . . am 11.11.1954, Bert.: Polyäthylen-Lizenz/Grace Hoechst," 12 November 1954, HFA.

receive a payment of $700,000 on the day the contract was signed; and that Hoechst and Grace would give Ziegler a firm commitment to his terms within two days. The reasons for that last condition were that Ziegler was about to go on a four-week vacation and that he had delayed accepting the licensing agreements suggested by Standard of New Jersey and National Distillers because of Hoechst's interest. He was not, however, prepared to lose those firm offers while awaiting Hoechst's decision. Drs. Horn and Engelbertz replied that it was unlikely that a decision could be reached so rapidly, but they promised to let him know the outcome within two days.[25] In fact, deciding so quickly proved impossible, and Horn phoned Ziegler on 9 February to ask for a two-week extension. Ziegler agreed to an eight-day extension, but also raised the price: "on tax grounds" he insisted on a direct transfer of $800,000 from the United States. Horn agreed to let Ziegler's attorney know Hoechst and Grace's decision within eight days.[26]

In the end, swiftly changing alliances in the international chemical industry changed everything. Grace did, in fact, acquire a license late in 1955, although without the cooperation of Hoechst; by 1957 its plant had a capacity of 50 million tons per year. In the meantime, Hoechst signed an agreement with Hercules Powder to provide the U.S. firm with exclusive American rights to Hoechst's Ziegler know-how.[27] Grace and Hoechst decided, in the end, to take Ziegler's advice, establishing a cooperative venture in 1955 in Brazil, due to come on line in 1957.[28]

Hoechst's experience with the Ziegler process thus proved a boon for the firm's prospects and performance during the 1950s. Production of polyethylene proved a lucrative business, and later in the decade it was possible to move from there into newer areas of plastics production, including, for instance, polypropylene, using another version of the Ziegler process as modified by the Italian chemist Giulio Natta.[29] Thus, Hoechst was able to make its way into petrochemical production of thermoplastics using largely German technology, while preserving, for the most of the 1950s, its commitment to traditional acetylene-based chemistry, based partly on coal. At the same time, during the 1950s, the firm's management was most proud of its achievements in the area of petroleum cracking, which had resulted from research done within the firm.

[25] Dr. Horn, "Aktennotiz über die Besprechung mit Herrn Professor Dr. Ziegler . . . am Nachmittag des 7.2.1955, Bert. Polyäthylen-Lizenz/USA," 8 February 1955, HFA.

[26] Dr. Horn, "Aktennotiz über ein Telefongespräch mit Prof. Dr. Ziegler . . . am Nachmittag des 9. Februar 1955, Betr. Polyäthylen-Lizenz/ USA," 9 February 1955, HFA.

[27] Peter Spitz, *Petrochemicals: The Rise of an Industry* (New York: Wiley, 1988), p. 338; Dr. Hagedorn, "Bericht über den Besuch mit Celanese Corporation of America am 28.4.1955 in Uerdingen," 3 May 1955 [carbon], Bayerwerksarchiv, Leverkusen (hereafter, BWA), 700/1214; BASF, untitled report on low-pressure polyethylene processes, n.d. (ca. late 1955, early 1956), pp. 12–14, in BASF Unternehmensarchiv, Ludwigshafen (hereafter, BASF), K311; a list of German firms acquiring licenses is in the brief note "Verwertung der Zieglerschen Patente für Olefine," *Chemische Industrie* 6(1954):637.

[28] Farbwerke Hoechst A.G., *Geschäftsbericht 1955*, pp. 11–13.

[29] Bäumler, *Ein Jahrhundert Chemie*, pp. 183–4; Spitz, *Petrochemicals*, pp. 333–8.

The Hoechst "coker" and high-temperature pyrolysis

After the collapse of the negotiations for supply of olefins from Union Kraftstoff in the second half of 1952 (see Chapter 5), Hoechst's managers decided to develop their own technologies for manufacturing petrochemical feedstocks. They were immediately faced with a decision about what to use as a starting material for the process: raw gasoline, which was used most often, or crude oil. Price considerations and the location of the firm's main factory convinced them that the latter would be the better choice: Crude oil was "not only really cheap, but less subject to price fluctuations than the products obtained from it by distillation," and Hoechst's location away from the main centers of the West German petroleum industry – and especially its refining sector – made it necessary to think in terms of "producing olefins independently of industries having other objectives."[30]

Researchers at Hoechst began work on a new process for cracking crude oil in 1953, with the objective of maximizing production of olefins (gaseous feedstocks for the chemical industry) and minimizing output of fuels. By 1954 they were able to construct the first pilot plant using the Hoechst "indirect-coking" or "continuous-coking" process (Figure 7.1). Using coke pellets 5–12 mm in diameter (called "pebbles") that were by-products of manufacturing electrodes in the Hoechst factory at Griesheim, the initial stage of the process involved heating coke indirectly in tube bundles to high temperatures (the process proceeded at 700–800° C). Indirect heating of the coke, which served to transmit the heat used in the cracking process, eliminated the side reactions that occurred when coke was heated directly to such high temperatures; hence the term "indirect coking."[31]

The reaction began when preheated crude oil was introduced into the reaction vessel, which already contained the heated coke. Any additional coke needed for the reaction was produced as a by-product of the cracking process; hence the term "continuous coking." When the crude oil injected into the vessel came into contact with the coke, part of it became gaseous, and both the gas and liquid portions of the crude were split, or "cracked," into simpler hydrocarbons, including gases, liquids, and coke. In the cracking process, the coke used initially was cooled somewhat and was reheated in a regenerator to the desired temperature of reaction, using heating gas or a part of the coke formed in the reaction for fuel.[32]

Hoechst's process was not the only continuous-coking process available in 1954. The Lummus continuous-contact coking process and the Standard Oil

---

[30] Dr. Krekeler, "The Hoechst Continuous Coking Process," 21 September 1954, pp. 1–2 (draft of presentation before World Petroleum Congress, 1955), HFA; "Petrochemie Hoechst 1957, Zusammenfassung," HFA.

[31] H. Kamptner, "Aktennotiz Betr. Höchster Coker," 10 March 1959, HFA; Krekeler, "The Hoechst Continuous Coking Process."

[32] Kamptner, "Aktennotiz Betr. Höchster Coker"; Krekeler, "The Hoechst Continuous Coking Process."

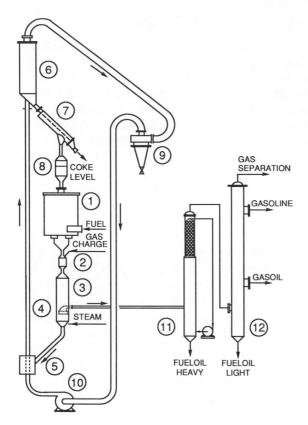

Figure 7.1. The Hoechst coking process. (Courtesy Dr. Krekeler, "The Hoechst Continuous Coking Process," 21 September 1954, Hoechst Firmenarchiv, Frankfurt-Hoechst.)

fluid-coking process were two examples of technologies already in use. The major differences between those two processes and that developed at Hoechst were as follows (Table 7.1): The reaction temperatures in the Hoechst process were higher; the Hoechst process occurred at normal atmospheric pressure, rather than under higher pressure; and, most important, the Hoechst process yielded a far higher output of olefinic gases that could be used as petrochemical feedstocks. In fact, gases accounted for about 60 percent of the yield, by weight, from the Hoechst continuous-coking process, compared with 14.5 percent in the Lummus process and 8 percent in the Standard Oil process. It should be noted that both of the latter processes were designed to maximize yields of gas oils, rich in hydrogen, which could be further processed in catalytic cracking plants.[33]

---

[33] Kamptner, "Aktennotiz Betr. Höchster Coker"; Krekeler, "The Hoechst Continuous Coking Process."

Table 7.1. *Comparison of the Lummus, Standard Oil, and Hoechst coking processes, 1954*

Characteristic	Lummus "CCC process"	Standard Oil "FC process"	Hoechst "IC process"
Average coke size	12 mm	0.5 mm	2–15 mm
Coke temperature entering reactor	555°C	540°C	650°C
Coke temperature leaving reactor	490°C	450°C	565°C
Type of reheating for coke	Direct	Direct	Indirect
Movement of coke	Mass lift	Fluidized-bed transport by means of agitation and pressure difference between reactor and regenerator	Gas lift using cracking gases as transport medium
Operational overpressure in reactor	2.5 atm	0.5 atm	No pressure
Production yield in % by weight			
C_3 & lighter	1.45	8.0	Gas 60% of weight
C_4-gasoline	22.0	18.4 (1.7 C_4)	Liquid 20% of weight
Gas oil	51.0	57.5	Coke 20% of weight
Coke	12.5	16.1	
Main product	Gas oil & coke	Gas oil & coke	Gases
Average reactor temperature	512°C	495°C	607°C

Source: H. Kamptner, "Aktennotiz Betr.: Hoechster Coker," 10 March 1954, Hoechst Firmenarchiv, Frankfurt-Hoechst.

Soon after the pilot plant started processing about 5 tons of crude per day in 1954, Hoechst's management gave the green light for construction of an industrial-scale "coker." Dr. Krekeler, one of the primary researchers leading the project, reported on the process at the World Petroleum Congress in 1955, and the coker began production on 1 February 1956.[34]

Even as the firm began cracking crude oil to supply its needs for petrochemical feedstocks (primarily ethylene), it had already begun to explore ways of expanding such production. Hoechst's need to increase its supply of acetylene beyond what the coal-based carbide ovens of Knapsack could produce was one major factor in the company's search for a petroleum-based alternative. Despite

[34] Krekeler, "The Hoechst Continuous Coking Process;" Bäumler, *Ein Jahrhundert Chemie*, pp. 146–51.

new technologies for improving the yield of acetylene produced from coal at Knapsack, Hoechst's needs – mainly to supply demand in the booming plastics market – outstripped production. Finding an alternative source was crucial, because even as late as 1957 (and, in its planning in that year, through 1961) Hoechst relied heavily on acetylene chemistry to manufacture polyvinyl chloride, vinyl acetate, and a host of other key products. Therefore, research on a petroleum-based process that would yield a mixture of ethylene and acetylene, research that ultimately led to the firm's high-temperature pyrolysis (HTP) process, began in April 1954.[35]

As the economics of the petroleum industry began to change in the mid-1950s, the wisdom of Hoechst's decision appeared to be confirmed. Cracking of crude in traditional refineries yielded a variety of products of differing specific gravities (fractions), including heating oil, gasoline, and various heavy residues. It was possible, by using different crude oils from various sources and by altering the reaction conditions and other factors, to optimize the output of one fraction over another, but the undesired fractions were bound to be present in the final output, even if in small amounts. Producers in the United States in the second half of 1949 and the first half of 1950, for instance, had to dump heating oil on the high seas "in order to avoid the overfilling of storage tanks and thus a complete standstill." The beginning of the Korean War and the consequent increase in demand for heating oil put an end to that environmentally (and economically) dubious practice.[36]

In West Germany, a tremendous expansion in refinery capacity in the 1950s required adjustments of output to fit the market, which quickly began to favor heating oil over gasoline to fire industrial and domestic boilers (the vast increase in the number of automobiles in West Germany did not occur until the 1960s). However, light fractions, including gasoline, were unavoidable by-products of the production of heating oil, and the consequence was an oversupply on the West German market in the mid-1950s. It was only a matter of time before the prices of those products, which were less expensive and easier to use for production of petrochemical feedstocks than was unrefined petroleum, would approach that of crude oil. Hoechst therefore moved into middle-temperature pyrolysis (MTP) in 1957. Employing raw gasoline to produce olefins, MTP involved technology similar to that used in ethane and propane cracking.[37] Again, though, the primary product was ethylene, and in the search for petroleum-based acetylene production, it was necessary to develop a new technology. Hoechst researchers and engineers came up with high-temperature pyrolysis (HTP).

HTP was a process distinguished chiefly by the extreme temperatures of the reaction and by the unusual and, for Hoechst, highly desirable mixture of its end products (Figure 7.2). It took place in a two-chamber vessel. In the first chamber, combustible off-gases from the cracking facility were burned together with oxygen to produce temperatures higher than 2,000° F (with flame temperatures

[35] "Petrochemie Hoechst 1957," p. 2; Bäumler, *Ein Jahrhundert Chemie*, pp. 139–40.

[36] Kamptner, "Aktennotiz Betr. Höchster Coker," p. 1, HFA.

[37] Bäumler, *Ein Jahrhundert Chemie*, p. 155.

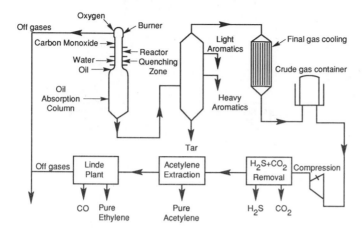

Figure 7.2. High-temperature pyrolysis at Hoechst, 1957. [Courtesy Karl Winnacker, "Petrochemie und Kunststoff-Industrie," *Kunststoffe* 47(1957):402.]

as high as 4,000° F). Introduced into the second chamber together with pre-heated hydrocarbons, the resulting combustion gases were then cracked into a gas mixture containing ethylene and acetylene, with the richness and composition of the mixture depending on the hydrocarbon employed. After a series of steps to purify the main products, the result was very pure petrochemical feedstocks, at the ratio of about 30 parts acetylene to 70 parts ethylene.[38]

Once the industrial-scale apparatus for HTP was in place, beginning in 1959, it was clear that the firm was in possession of a series of complementary cracking processes that would allow it maximum flexibility in its choice of a starting product from which to manufacture petrochemical feedstocks (Figure 7.3).

Investment in petrochemical processes constituted the lion's share of Hoechst's investments in works facilities in the years 1957–9, and HTP development was no small part of that. HTP had entailed investments of about DM 260 million by the time it came on-line, and it was capable of supplying the firm with 12,000 tons of acetylene and 36,000 tons of ethylene per year.[39] Hoechst's managers were naturally delighted with the success of their investment, but the reason for their joy was, from a current-day perspective, surprising: They were happy that they had finally secured their source of acetylene. As explained in a 1957 lecture anticipating that the HTP facility would come on-line in 1959, "Hoechst has at its disposal, after the completion of these projects, a viable basis for the production of petrochemical products on the basis of crude oil. *The*

---

[38] Karl Winnacker, "Petrochemie und Kunststoff-Industrie," *Kunststoffe* 47(1957):402; Spitz, *Petrochemicals*, pp. 440–3; Bäumler, *Ein Jahrhundert Chemie*, p. 158.

[39] Farbwerke Hoechst A.G., *Geschäftsbericht 1957*, p. 14–15; Farbwerke Hoechst A.G., *Geschäftsbericht 1958*, pp. 12–14; Farbwerke Hoechst A.G., *Geschäftsbericht 1959*, pp. 16–17; figures on investment and production capacity drawn from Hermann Holzrichter, "Aktennotiz Besuch bei Professor Dr. Winnacker, Hoechst, am 21.8.1958," 28 August 1958, BWA, 9/L: Erdölchemie GmbH: Sek. Dr. Haberland, 1958–1961.

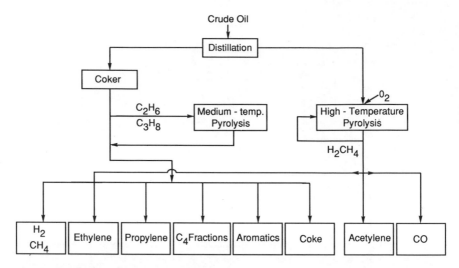

Figure 7.3. Crude-oil cracking operation at Hoechst, 1957. [Courtesy Karl Winnacker, "Petrochemie und Kunststoff-Industrie. *Kunststoffe* 47(1957):402.]

difficulty in supply of acetylene, which had inhibited the development of acetylene chemistry at Hoechst for decades, is finally set aside."[40] Furthermore, despite the lower price and easier processing of raw gasoline, the firm still remained committed to crude oil. As the lecturer noted, "the decisive advantage of the coker lies in its raw material, crude oil, which is universally available, whereas in contrast pyrolysis of raw gasoline, which today supplies cheaper ethylene, has the insecurity of the price-formation of its raw material. For a chemical factory which is not bound to a refinery, crude oil is always preferable as a raw material for cracking reactions."[41]

In choosing HTP, the actions of Hoechst's management had, by and large, positive consequences for the firm, as was the case for many of their other decisions about the development of petrochemical technologies in the mid-1950s. The company, at a significant disadvantage at the beginning of its existence, as compared with the other major I.G. successors, began the 1960s in a vastly improved position. In the late 1950s and early 1960s, the firm invested steadily increasing sums of money in new and improved technologies, in part through retained earnings and in part by expanding its basic capital. In addition, because of the firm's performance, the managing board found itself in a position to recommend that yearly dividends of 18 percent be paid to shareholders.[42] Unquestionably, the astuteness of the firm's managers and engineers, the abilities of its salesmen, and the skill of its workers were all factors in that success, but those factors do not explain fully what happened to the firm in the 1950s, as should be

[40] Petrochemie Hoechst, 1957," p. 9; my emphasis.   [41] Petrochemie Hoechst, 1957," p. 5.
[42] Farbwerke Hoechst A.G., *Geschäftsbericht 1960*, pp. 8, 11–12, 34; Farbwerke Hoechst A.G., *Geschäftsbericht 1961*, pp. 17–19, 21, 40; Farbwerke Hoechst A.G., *Geschäftsbericht 1962*, pp. 16, 27, 40; Farbwerke Hoechst A.G. *Geschäftsbericht 1963*, p. 11.

clear from the preceding discussion. Many of Hoechst's successes in choosing particular technologies had as much to do with accident as with deliberate choice. To put it another way, the deliberate choices of the firm's managers were, in retrospect, good ones, but their intentions at the time they made those decisions failed to anticipate the actual outcomes.

Not long after the HTP process came on-line, at the end of 1960, Hoechst's management made yet another decision that they had never anticipated in the late 1950s. They decided to shut down all of their facilities for cracking or distilling crude oil, although Bäumler's official history of the firm's first 100 years, published in 1963, noted that the facilities were retained because of continuing uncertainty about the future: "The coker and the refinery owned by the works serve today as a sort of strategic reserve. None can forecast with certainty whether they will not one day have to be reactivated, since the petroleum business is rich with surprises and sudden changes."[43] Bäumler also contended that the firm's activities in the petroleum production area had been of considerable value to the firm:

When the time required it and the new olefin plastics were mature, one had at his disposal the raw products which in other places at this point in time were not at hand. The most important thing, though was: a valuable treasure of experience came into being, gained by a large number of first-class experts, who now will master every new task in this working area, which is so important and interesting for Hoechst.

Hoechst's "nonconformism" in petrochemistry preserved [the firm's] freedom of maneuver and created the breathing space until some petroleum corporation would decide after all to establish itself in the Frankfurt region, which was industrially of ever increasing significance.[44]

The long-awaited refinery was completed in 1963. In 1961, in anticipation of its construction, Hoechst had signed a long-term contract with Caltex, which built a refinery in Kelsterbach near Hoechst's main plant. At about the same time, Union Kraftstoff signed an agreement to supply Knapsack with olefins. Combined, those contracts guaranteed the firm's supply of ethylene feedstocks for the foreseeable future and, in effect, made Hoechst's MTP and HTP cracking processes redundant.[45]

Concluding remarks

Of the three major successors to I.G. Farbenindustrie A.G. established in the early 1950s, Farbwerke Hoechst had the least resources in terms of capital, personnel, experience, know-how, and technology. Thus, unlike its better-equipped counterparts, Hoechst was not often sought out and pursued by the petroleum multinationals and chemical firms eager to exchange information on the newest developments in chemical technology, especially in the area of petrochemicals. Disadvantaged as it was, though, the firm shared the experience of the other

---

[43] Bäumler, *Ein Jahrhundert Chemie*, p. 161.   [44] Ibid.
[45] Bäumler, *Ein Jahrhundert Chemie*, p. 162; Spitz, *Petrochemicals*, p. 442.

members of the West German Big Three insofar as its managers explored a number of different alternatives for technological change during the 1950s. Even as it continued its investments in research and development to improve coal-based acetylene production technologies, Hoechst moved into petrochemical technology, in part through purchase of technology, in part through cooperation with outside firms (although that was not highly significant), and most importantly through internal development of technology.

Hoechst's management decided on that course for a variety of reasons. Since the late 1940s it had been clear that petrochemicals would become a major production area for internationally competitive organic chemical producers, even though, from a contemporary perspective, it seemed equally clear that the industry would not be based entirely on petroleum feedstocks, let alone primarily on ethylene.[46] Hoechst, with aspirations of continuing to be a player in the organic chemicals industry, needed to establish a presence in the new petrochemical production area. Obviously, Hoechst's inability to find a worthy partner from the international petrochemical industry was one factor in determining the course that Hoechst ultimately followed, but there were others as well. Because of its relatively disadvantaged geographic position, it had, arguably, more to gain from going it alone. As Karl Winnacker, Hoechst's chairman of the managing board, put it in 1957, petrochemical technology held the promise of releasing the firm from the geographic shackles imposed by its earlier reliance on coal and gas:

These remarks [in Winnacker's article] have shown, that the chemist is in the position to produce all of the products which the plastics industry needs for starting materials on the basis of coal, oil, or natural gas. The possibilities, thus to start with crude oil and so to become independent of industries that are bound to particular areas – insofar as they are based on coal and gas – make it possible for the German chemical industry as well to attain everything that the plastics industry calls for.[47]

Despite that compelling dream, the evidence demonstrates time and again that Hoechst managers did not gamble on a specific technology or feedstock. In fact, they chose to develop the continuous-coking process (which could employ many different hydrocarbon sources) and high-temperature pyrolysis (which complemented the coking process) precisely to avoid exclusive reliance on either crude or light gasoline. As late as 1963, Bäumler wrote of the coker and HTP as constituting a "strategic reserve" for the firm in case of fluctuations in the oil industry. Hoechst was also unwilling to abandon acetylene chemistry even into the 1960s, although it did switch to acetylene produced from petroleum, for the most part, rather than from coal. Eventually, Hoechst, like the other major I.G. successors, combined forces with foreign and domestic oil firms for supply of olefins, and for many of the same reasons as the others. In 1957, Hoechst announced internally its intention to seek an outside partner in a venture to secure

[46] This continued to be the perception for much of the 1950s. See, for instance, Winnacker, "Petrochemie und Kunststoff-Industrie," pp. 400–1.
[47] Winnacker, "Petrochemie und Kunststoff-Industrie," p. 403.

its supply of petrochemical feedstocks to meet future needs, as well as to share the risk of the venture.[48] Winnacker indicated the same desire in a conversation with Hermann Holzrichter of Bayer on 21 August 1958. The coker and HTP were important in providing his firm with feedstocks. But, Winnacker continued,

the coverage of Hoechst's requirements of ethylene and of acetylene in Knapsack is with this still not secured in the long term. Hoechst is thus forced in the next 3–5 years to implement an additional petrochemical expansion, which must be secured either by Hoechst or a subsidiary alone, through a joint company of the ROW and EC type, or through a long-term supply contract with Esso or other interested parties.[49]

But was the move into petrochemicals, and indeed into ethylene-based chemistry, preordained? Peter Spitz thinks it was. He points out that the "superior economics of ethylene – versus acetylene-based processes – for making vinyl chloride spelled the end of hydrocarbon cracking processes [such as HTP] designed to produce mixtures of the two reactive hydrocarbons [ethylene or acetylene].[50]

Given the evidence presented in this chapter, however, one must ask why, if the economics of ethylene (or petrochemicals in general) were so obvious, conventional steam cracking or today's petrochemical processes were not preferred from the start. It might be argued that Hoechst was either unable or unwilling to see the handwriting on the wall. Perhaps those responsible for running the company were unable. But that is not a likely explanation, because there were contacts with outside petrochemical producers from the early 1950s, and the evidence indicates that Hoechst was *able* to make such a deal, but was unwilling to do so if the price was too high. Perhaps, then, the company's managers simply were unwilling to take the plunge into petrochemicals and a cooperation with an outside producer. Their obstinacy may certainly have been a factor, or another explanation may have been that they were not smart enough to embark on that course.

Neither explanation seems satisfactory, however. Their pursuit of a number of different options simultaneously and their consistent choice of lucrative technologies and production areas argue against both explanations. What remains? The most likely explanation is that the "superior economics" of which Spitz writes were not at all obvious – and indeed may not, at that time, have existed – from the perspective of those operating in the late 1950s.

Something lurks behind Spitz's contention, which (like those of many other commentators) tends to see technological change as economically preordained. His explanation is based on the assumption that our present-day context also governed decision-making in the past. In fact, if one thinks oneself into the 1950s, one can conceive of alternative scenarios that would have changed the "superior economics" of ethylene-based petrochemicals. The economic-determinist argu-

---

[48] "Petrochemie Hoechst 1957," p. 10.
[49] Holzrichter, "Aktennotiz Besuch bei Professor Dr. Winnacker."
[50] Spitz, *Petrochemicals*, p. 443.

ment presumes, for instance, easy access to petroleum supplies, an assumption that the Suez Crisis of 1956 made somewhat questionable. It presumes that the economic order dominated by the United States was fated to continue its hegemony, a matter that was unclear at the height of the Cold War, especially as the second Berlin crisis intensified beginning in 1958 and continued into the construction of the Berlin Wall in 1961. The ultimate outcomes of such developments were not at all obvious in the middle or even in the late 1950s.

One of the most important areas that the argument for economic determinism of technological change overlooks is that of politics, which also helped shape technological choices in the West German chemical industry. That is the subject of the next chapter, which explores the experience of the Hüls firm in the area of cold rubber in the 1950s.

8
State's interest and technological change: Hüls and cold-rubber technology

Situated in Marl, near Reckinghausen, in the Ruhr district, the Hüls chemical factory had its origins, in part, in the National Socialist policy of autarky, or self-sufficiency; it was built under pressure from the state to supply the Nazi war economy with Buna synthetic rubber. But more conventional business interests were also instrumental in shaping the plant: Chemical industrialists used criteria such as proximity to related plants, raw materials, coal, and transportation – in other words, factors that would ensure its long-term commercial viability – to decide on a site, though the National Socialist Government saw the site as vulnerable to air attack. Hüls was founded in 1938 and began operations in August 1940 as Germany's second major Buna producer, accounting for about 45 percent of Germany's total wartime synthetic-rubber output. I.G. Farbenindustrie A.G. owned 74 percent of the new company, and Hibernia, a mining company owned by the Prussian government, controlled the remaining 26 percent.[1]

[1] For additional material on Hüls, see Paul Kränzlein, *Chemie im Revier. Hüls* (Düsseldorf: Econ, 1980); Peter Morris, "The Development of Acetylene Chemistry and Synthetic Rubber by I.G. Farbenindustrie Aktiengesellschaft, 1926–1945" (dissertation, Oxford University, 1982); and Morris, "Transatlantic Transfers in Synthetic Rubber Technology, 1930–1960" (unpublished manuscript). For materials on the relationship between the National Socialist regime and I.G.

Because the I.G. was Hüls's principal owner and because of its heavy involvement in Buna production, the decision whether or not Hüls would continue to exist after 1945 proved complicated and difficult. Following the dictates of Allied trust-busting policy, the I.G. was disbanded, and Hüls became an independent corporation just after the war. Independence, of course, had its advantages, but they were more than offset by the disadvantages: Hüls was cut off from its research facilities, because the I.G.'s central rubber laboratory was located at Leverkusen; it lost access to the purchasing and sales organizations of the I.G.; and its primary source of investment capital, again the I.G., was cut off. To make matters worse, Allied demilitarization policies in the immediate postwar period specifically identified synthetic-rubber production as a war-related industry. Initially, the Allies waived the prohibition in view of the needs of the German and European economies in the immediate aftermath of war. By 30 June 1948, however, they had banned Buna production altogether. Cut off suddenly and completely from their primary area of production, Hüls managers were forced to expand or to develop other product lines in organic chemistry.[2]

Hüls's position in the immediate postwar period, then, did not compare at all favorably with the positions of the three major successors to I.G. Farben. Its former heavy dependence on the facilities of the large firm for a range of vital services made its prognosis for success under the new regime seem doubtful. Its tight focus on synthetic-rubber manufacture through 1945 (Buna production accounted for about 60 percent of total sales by the end of the war), in light of Allied intentions to ban rubber production, did not augur well for the company's chances. On the other hand, Chemische Werke Hüls possessed the hardware necessary to compete in the postwar organic chemical industry, and its hardware was of relatively recent vintage. In addition, top prewar and wartime managers continued in their positions after the war. They were led by Paul Baumann, who had headed the Hüls Production Group from the firm's founding and whom the Allies named plant manager on 26 June 1945. Their experience, including that in the banned synthetic-rubber area, was invaluable. Eventually Hüls was allowed to resume the business of synthetic-rubber manufacture owing to changes in the Allied policies, although the experience of the production ban and the development of new, lucrative product lines, especially in the area of plastics, had fundamentally changed the nature of the company.

This chapter focuses on the decision-making process whereby Hüls was allowed to resume production of synthetic rubber. It reveals the important role of the state and political considerations in key technological decision-making, as well as details about the process of technology transfer from the United States to Germany.

Farben and on the discussions surrounding the location and construction of Hüls, see Peter Hayes, *Industry and Ideology: I.G. Farben in the Nazi Era* (Cambridge University Press, 1987), passim, esp. pp. 188–93; and Morris, "The Development of Acetylene Chemistry," passim, esp. pp. 297–304, 308. My thanks to Dr. G. Franz of the Hüls Unternehmensarchiv for his comments on this chapter.

[2] Kränzlein, *Chemie im Revier*, pp. 46–53; H. Gröne, "Kautschuk: Der Weg zu Hüls;" *Der Lichtbogen* 37 (September 1988):16.

Reorienting the firm: Hüls and the Allies in the initial occupation period

Although the British occupation authorities permitted production of Buna in the Marl facility in the immediate postwar period, owing to severe shortages in Germany and the rest of Europe, Hüls managers recognized from the start that such good fortune would not last: Allied occupation planning before 1945 had specifically identified synthetic-rubber production as a war-related industry and called for its banning, a policy written into the Potsdam protocols of August 1945. Baumann and his top managers had anticipated that probable development even before war's end, when they had created a Section for the Realization of Technologies (*Verwertungstechnische Abteilung*) on 27 April 1945. Its charge was to research and develop alternative products based on the existing machinery and reaction vessels, which were heavily, although not exclusively, oriented to Buna productions. Scientists and engineers working in that section were expressly directed to limit the capital costs of their suggestions.[3]

Thus, when the anticipated ban on Buna production went into effect on 30 June 1948, Hüls's management was prepared. Their most effective short-term device was simply to utilize much of the acetylene that normally would have been used as a feedstock in synthetic-rubber production to manufacture solvents instead. In addition, a facility for producing polyvinyl chloride (PVC) was already under construction when the ban took effect; Hüls hoped to take advantage of the fact that most German PVC capacity lay in the Soviet zone of occupation and thus was largely inaccessible in the West. Hüls's first vinyl chloride reactor began operating on 12 October 1948. Hüls personnel also discovered that if the proportions of the ingredients in their recipe for producing Buna (i.e., 70 parts butadiene and 30 parts styrene) were reversed (i.e., 30 butadiene to 70 styrene), they could manufacture a new product that did not violate the Allied ban, and that product, "upside-down Buna," found a market in the German linoleum industry.[4]

In the early 1950s, through such improvised measures, and because of its systematic and deliberate embrace of new production technologies (such as PVC), Hüls became a much more broadly based chemical producer. The factory produced, among other things, plastics, solvents, chlorohydrocarbons, textile auxiliaries, and technical gases. Still, it did not have the same freedom of movement as the Big Three. That was in part owing to the fact that Hüls was beholden to them – in particular to BASF and Bayer – for many licenses and patents. In May 1952, Paul Baumann reported to H. von Rospatt, an official of the federal Ministry of Economics who played an important role in the breakup of I.G. Farben, that negotiations with BASF to gain certain necessary licenses were proceeding satisfactorily; on the other hand, in June he also wrote that the price for such cooperation was that Hüls would avoid direct competition with the I.G. successors in a number of key areas.[5] In addition, Hüls was at a disadvantage

---

[3] Kränzlein, *Chemie im Revier*, pp. 48–9.   [4] Ibid., pp. 67ff.

[5] Paul Baumann to H. von Rospatt, 6 May 1952, Bundesarchiv, Koblenz (hereafter, BAK), B102/411; Paul Baumann, "Produktionsprogramm der Chemischen Werke Hüls," 13 June 1952, BAK, B102/442, Heft 1. For more on this, see Chapter 3.

with regard to its research, sales, purchasing, and other auxiliary organizations. Thus, Allied experts who reported their recommendations on the breakup of the I.G. and the future composition of the successors in the summer of 1950 warned that Hüls's future prospects would be shaky if it were not permitted to resume synthetic-rubber production. Buna, after all, was a known quantity for the firm's production teams, but many other types of polymer chemistry were new to them.[6]

Negotiators from the West German government had been able to achieve some success in regard to lifting the ban on Buna production by 3 April 1951, when the three Western Allies relaxed many of their restrictions on the German economy. After the Allied High Commission approved a specific production plan, Hüls was able to resume Buna production on 29 November 1951.[7]

As the company prepared during 1952 and most of 1953 for its "re-founding" as an independent joint-stock company under reorganized ownership on 16 December 1953, however, its leadership faced two major problems. First, it would be necessary to expand capacity. The Allied policy change in 1951 allowed only limited manufacture of synthetic rubber – in fact, just 500 tons per month, or 6,000 tons per year. By way of comparison, Hüls had produced 40,000 tons of Buna in 1944, and Baumann believed that the smallest economical capacity in the early 1950s would be 30,000 tons per year.[8] The second problem that the Hüls leadership faced was somewhat of a contradiction to the first: Having laboriously broadened their firm's production palette through 1951, they understandably were unwilling to return to the very heavy commitment to rubber production that had existed through 1945. Hüls managers saw the erosion of their diversification inherent in renewed emphasis on Buna as too risky in light of the frequent and often substantial price fluctuations. Thus, although they sought to expand their capacity and to become a major presence in the arena of synthetic-rubber production, Hüls managers refused to take that risk alone. Instead, they sought to found a joint company in cooperation with other chemical firms and rubber processors, and they sought state assistance in financing the joint company.[9] The complexities involved in negotiating those arrangements were substantial. Nonetheless, unraveling them will allow us to examine important issues related to technology transfer, interactions between technology and foreign policy, and the role of the state in technological change.

---

[6] "Report of the Tripartite Investigation Team Appointed to Consider Dispersal Problems Relating to I.G. Farbenindustrie A.G.," August 1950 (signed October 1950 by the principal authors, Amick, Brearley, and Denivelle), pp. 24–5, Public Record Office, London (Kew) (hereafter, PRO), FO371/85684.

[7] Kränzlein, *Chemie im Revier*, pp. 89–92.

[8] Ibid., pp. 89–91, 38; Bundeswirtschaftsministerium (BWM), IV B 1, "Vermerk, Betr. Ausbau der deutschen Buna-Produktion, Besprechung vom 17.3.1953 . . . beim Herrn Minister Prof. Dr. Erhard," 18 March 1953, BAK, B102/9576, Heft 2.

[9] BWM, IV B 1 (Lenz), "Vermerk über eine Besprechung bei Herrn Dr. Prentzel am 20.2.1953 betr. Ausbau der deutschen Buna-Produktion," 23 February 1953, BAK, B102/9576, Heft 2.

The politics of technological change: Hüls and synthetic rubber

Although Hüls's managers recognized that in the long run they would have to make some changes in their synthetic-rubber production technology in order to remain competitive, they began Buna manufacture again in November 1951 using their four-stage process based on acetylene produced from coke-oven gas, from the off-gases of hydrogenation plants, or from natural gas. The operation was a high-cost endeavor, partly because of hardware heavily used during the war and an outmoded process and partly because of the production limit the Allies imposed on the plant (500 tons per month). A short-term solution to the problem of high production costs had to be found while a higher production limit was negotiated. The solution, which came from the rubber processors' trade association (Wirtschaftsverband der deutschen Kautschukindustrie, or WDK), drew on Germany's past experience in maximizing economic self-sufficiency and minimizing its outlay of foreign exchange.[10]

At the request of the WDK, and with the cooperation of Hüls, the federal minister of economics, Ludwig Erhard, issued a regulation on 17 May 1952 creating a "Rubber Price Equalization Fund." It required rubber processors to pay a fixed amount into the fund (originally DM 0.12, and later DM 0.20) for each kilogram of imported and processed rubber. Hüls could then draw on that fund to reduce the selling price of its Buna from DM 4.55 per kilogram to DM 3.00. Buna produced at Hüls could thus compete effectively with imported rubber, whether natural or synthetic, without the German government having to take the politically risky step of imposing a tariff on imports.[11] The solution was a creative way of easing the pain of West Germany's entry into international markets in the 1950s.

Later in 1952, Hüls's management began to orchestrate an effort to change both Allied policy and the basis of their Buna technology. Baumann sent a letter in November to the Economics Ministry analyzing the synthetic-rubber problem: Owing to Allied limitations, Hüls's Buna capacity was "much too limited to be interesting from an economic or business perspective." Baumann's firm was also interested in changing its feedstock for the process, probably to petroleum. Given the potential savings in foreign exchange and the "significance for the political economy" of large-scale rubber synthesis, Baumann called for a meeting with Economics Minister Erhard by January 1953. Hüls would not be the only company to send representatives; Baumann suggested that West Germany's other Buna producer (Bayer) and a representative of the WDK also attend the meeting.[12]

The projected meeting with Erhard would take place somewhat later than originally suggested, but in February 1953 there was a preliminary meeting to prepare for it. Chaired by Felix Prentzel, head of the Economics Ministry's Chemicals Section, it was attended by Otto Friedrich of the Phoenix Gummi-

---

[10] Kränzlein, *Chemie im Revier,* pp. 114–15.   [11] Ibid.
[12] Chemische Werke Hüls [Baumann and (Beckmann?)] to the Federal Ministry of Economics, "Betr.: Neuregelung des Mineralölabgabesystems," 8 November 1952, BAK, B102/9576, Heft 2.

Werke; Dr. Otto Ambros of the supervisory board of the Hibernia mining company;[13] Dr. Conrad of Bayer; Dr. Friedrich Zobel of Chemische Werke Hüls; Dr. Hermann Richter of Düsseldorf (who later became the first chairman of the Hüls supervisory board); and two other members of the Chemicals Section, Drs. Lenz and Blankenfeld.[14]

Friedrich started the discussion by pointing out that, for political reasons, rubber from the Far East might be in short supply, with the result that West German producers would have to depend on synthetic substitutes. Because of difficulties in getting a clear overview of the situation, and because of the political risks involved, chemical and rubber producers needed some insurance before dealing with the situation. Ambros expanded briefly on Friedrich's remarks, noting that he was already involved in negotiations with French and Italian rubber producers; it seemed possible that the three countries could cooperate to solve the supply problem. Hüls's representative, Dr. Zobel, then stated that his firm was willing, in principle, to expand its production of rubber to 30,000 tons per year, up from the current 6,000; a precondition, however, was access to other European countries for sales of finished product.[15]

Prentzel and the others then turned to a detailed discussion of the financial conditions under which Hüls would undertake such a project. It would cost DM 50–60 million to expand current capacity to 30,000 tons per year. Because of that high cost, and because Hüls was not willing to place synthetic rubber at the center of its production program again, Zobel argued for creation of a joint company owned by a number of chemical and rubber companies. Still, the project would be too large and too expensive even for such a coalition from private industry. Federal funding would be a prerequisite, possibly including direct aid, tax concessions, or loan guarantees.[16]

About three weeks later, on 17 March, the meeting with Erhard himself finally took place. It was larger than the earlier meeting with Prentzel, and the representatives of the various firms were higher-ranking than those who had met earlier. Friedrich was joined on the rubber side by H. A. Fritz of the WDK and by Herr Grupe of Continental Gummi-Werke. Baumann represented Hüls, and

[13] Ambros is a key figure here. He had been head of the Buna program at I.G. Farben. For that reason, he had been deeply involved in the decision to locate one of the plants near the Auschwitz death camp and in the construction of the facility (it never produced synthetic rubber during the war). His implication in that matter led directly after the war to Ambros being found guilty of slavery and aiding in mass murder, for which he received a sentence of eight years imprisonment. Released early, Ambros did not participate actively as a member of the successor companies, but remained active in the West German chemical industry. See Hayes, *Industry and Ideology,* pp. 206–7, 347–68; Siegfried Balke, "Der I.G.-Farben-Prozess in Nürnberg," *Chemie-Ingenieur-Technik* 21(1949):34; Raymond G. Stokes, *Divide and Prosper: The Heirs of I.G. Farben under Allied Authority, 1945–1951* (Berkeley: University of California Press, 1988), pp. 151–6.

[14] BWM, IV B 1 (Lenz), "Verkmerk über eine Besprechung bei Herrn Dr. Prentzel am 20.2.1953 betr. Ausbau der deutschen Buna-Produktion."

[15] Ibid., pp. 1–2. Ambros had had experience in dealing with Italian synthetic-rubber producers during the 1940s. See Morris, "The Development of Acetylene Chemistry," pp. 345–7.

[16] BWM, IV B 1 (Lenz), "Verkmerk über eine Besprechung bei Herrn Dr. Prentzel am 20.2.1953 betr. Ausbau der deutschen Buna-Produktion," p. 3.

Ulrich Haberland took part in the discussions as Bayer's representative. Ambros and Richter also attended, and the contingent of lower-ranking officers from the Economics Ministry had increased to nine.[17]

Prentzel opened with a summary of the main points of the discussion from the previous meeting: They needed to get the Allied High Commission to alter Law 24 so as to allow Hüls to expand its capacity. Because the company planned to make the transition from coal-based feedstocks to either butane (from petroleum) or ethyl alcohol, it would also be necessary to purchase new technology and/or know-how from the United States. In undertaking that task, Hüls would need partners, not just in private industry, but also in the federal government. Erhard's first question was obvious: Why could private industry not undertake the project by itself, without state aid? Ambros countered that if one looked at the countries currently involved in or considering synthetic-rubber production, they all featured "considerable" state participation. They included the United States, the Soviet Union, Great Britain, France, Italy, and the "Eastern Zone" (East Germany).[18]

Baumann then took the floor to outline the details of the Hüls project. The smallest possible economical capacity for the plant would be 30,000 tons per year. To build it at the current Hüls facility would cost DM 60–66 million – expensive perhaps, but a bargain compared with the DM 120–132 million it would cost to build it "from green fields." The planning costs for the project would also be higher than normal, about DM 1 million, mainly owing to outlays to U.S. firms for licenses prior to beginning productions; those licenses, he noted, would also require the approval of the U.S. State Department. All in all, Baumann continued, the risks involved in the project were very high, especially because "at present significant [technological] developments . . . are in motion." For all of those reasons, it would be necessary to found a company separate from Hüls, the capital for which would come from a number of sources, and the investments in which would be eligible for rapid write-offs.[19] It is worth noting that although the discussions focused on ways for German industry to catch up with the United States technologically, the cost of entry into the more modern and sophisticated end of synthetic-rubber production would be less expensive than starting from scratch: The new plan could make good use of its interdependence with other production and subsidiary facilities already in existence at Hüls.

Erhard was convinced, declaring that he was "all for the project." He asked for some idea of how much the state would have to contribute to the project. Haberland and Friedrich made it clear that Bayer and the rubber industry were both strapped for cash and had other projects with higher priorities, although Friedrich indicated that the rubber industry might be more forthcoming if there were tax incentives. One of the representatives of the Economics Ministry, Dr. Kramer, indicated that such incentives might be possible.[20] The upshot of the

[17] BWM, IV B 1, "Vermerk, Betr. Ausbau der deutschen Buna-Produktion, Besprechung vom 17.3.1953 . . . beim Herrn Minister Prof. Dr. Erhard."
[18] BWM, IV B 1, "Vermerk, Betr. Ausbau der deutschen Buna-Produktion, Besprechung vom 17.3.1953 . . . beim Herrn Minister Prof. Dr. Erhard," pp. 1–2.
[19] Ibid.   [20] Ibid., p. 3.

meeting was that the state would have a major and vital role to play in the realization of the project.

Erhard moved quickly to translate his enthusiasm into action. On 26 March 1953, he sent a letter drafted by the Chemicals Section to Konrad Adenauer to ask the chancellor to take up the cause in his upcoming trip to Washington, D.C. Germany, he wrote, was the birthplace of synthetic rubber, but companies in the United States had taken the technology much further. In addition, their use of only petroleum feedstocks had made it possible to produce at less expense, with the result that Germany and the rest of Europe had become dependent on the United States for supplies of synthetic rubber. "The German rubber industry view this situation with grave concern," he reported. Referring to his meeting with executives from the rubber and chemical industries, Erhard also communicated the fears of those executives that Southeast Asia, for political reasons, would no longer be able to deliver natural rubber to Germany and that the United States, for reasons not specified, could also "be lost [as a rubber supplier]."[21]

Again referring to the 17 March meeting, Erhard noted that it would be possible for German industry to expand its capacity only by using the latest American know-how. Hüls had already begun negotiations with an American firms, which had indicated that it was quite willing to come to an agreement. Transferring that know-how to foreign firms would require U.S. State Department approval. Erhard therefore asked Adenauer to take up the issue during his trip to Washington. He provided one set of arguments that obviously were meant to help the chancellor present the request in internationalist terms, indicating that the know-how would be used to supply not only the Federal Republic but also the rest of Europe with synthetic rubber. Erhard's subsequent remarks, however, showed that he and his ministry were thinking in purely nationalist terms. Italy and France, Erhard reported, were also planning to purchase the latest U.S. technology and know-how to produce synthetic rubber; it was not acceptable that the Federal Republic would be cut out of that extremely important area.[22]

The good news was not long in coming. By late April 1953, Freiherr von Maltzan of the Trade Policy Section of the West German Foreign Office wrote to Erhard that the U.S. State Department was entirely in sympathy with allowing Hüls to purchase the know-how for the latest process for producing butadiene. Maltzan went on to report that it was likely that the Allied High Commission would be sympathetic to a request for expansion of capacity as well.[23]

Given the green light, Hüls began preparations, but the matter soon took an unexpected turn. In a letter to Dr. Lenz dated 13 July 1953, Baumann introduced

---

[21] Erhard to Adenauer, "Betr.: Projekt eines Ausbaus der Bunafabrikation bei den Chemischen Werken Hüls," 26 March 1953 (copy signed by Erhard), BAK, B102/9576, Heft 2.

[22] Ibid.

[23] Auswärtiges Amt, Abt. IV (HaPol) (von Maltzan) to Erhard, "Betr. Ausbau der Buna-Fabrikation bei den Chemischen Werken Hüls – Genehmigung des Department of State zur Abgabe von Lizenzen," 28 April 1953 (original), BAK, B102/9576, Heft 2.

a new factor into the equation. He reminded Lenz that the two crucial starting products for synthetic rubber at Hüls were styrene and butadiene. Styrene was already available at Hüls, although some expansion of existing facilities would be necessary. Butadiene would be available from two different, competing sources. The first used *n*-butane, a by-product of fuel production, and the technology could be provided (for a fee) by either Houdry Process Corporation or Standard Oil Development Company. The second process used ethyl alcohol to produce butadiene. The French government had offered to supply the necessary ethyl alcohol at a final cost to Hüls of FF 25 per liter. From independent sources, the company knew that the alcohol – the result of French overproduction of red wine – cost the French government FF 85 per liter, which obviously meant the French government was providing an enormous subsidy. By mentioning both possibilities for the production of butadiene, Baumann implied that both were very real contenders in the minds of the Hüls leadership. Because of the enormous subsidy, however, he noted "that a decision about using subsidized alcohol from France had to be made in the first instance from the political and not from the technical perspective."[24]

Baumann soon came back to the topic of feedstock selection for the new plant. In the meantime, he had decided, without government guidance, between the competing options in the area of cold-rubber production technology.[25] He reported that his firm had been holding negotiations with Goodrich Chemical Company. Otto Friedrich had, however, arranged a meeting between Hüls and Firestone Tire and Rubber Company on 13 July. Baumann went on: "We will be able to decide after this conversation with which firm we will come to an agreement on the issue of making available technical processes."[26] Thus, although Hüls was smaller, weaker, and more dependent on outside help than were the three major successors to the I.G., it, too, was in a position to command respect abroad and to make its choice from among established American firms and their technologies. Indeed, the smaller firm had something to offer: In August 1954, Hüls decided to acquire cold-rubber technology from the Firestone Company, in part because the American firm was interested in Hüls's styrene process (for a plant in India) and its know-how in polyamides and PVC.[27]

---

[24] Hüls (Baumann) to BWM Abt. Chemie (Lenz), "Betr. Vorarbeiten für das Projekt 'Synthetischer Kautschuk Hüls'," 13 July 1953, BAK, B102/9576, Heft 2. Interestingly enough, I.G. Farben had introduced alcohol-based synthetic-rubber processes to the French during the German occupation. See Morris, "The Development of Acetylene Chemistry," pp. 347–9.

[25] "Cold-rubber technology" referred to processes that employed temperatures for polymerization that were relatively low compared with those used in previous synthetic-rubber processes. Chemists at I.G. Farben worked on the process before 1945, but U.S. firms developed it to industrial scale. On the development of cold-rubber technology in the United States and its transfer to West Germany, see Peter Morris, "Transatlantic Transfer in Synthetic Rubber Technology;" pp. 46–53, 53–60.

[26] Hüls (Baumann) to BWM Abt. Chemie (Lenz), "Betr. Vorarbeiten für das Projekt 'Synthetischer Kautschuk Hüls'."

[27] Morris, "Transatlantic Transfers in Synthetic Rubber Technology," p. 58; Kränzlein, *Chemie im Revier*, p. 125.

Baumann returned to the matter of feedstock selection in a lengthy memorandum to the Economics Ministry dated 6 October 1953. He reported with a prospective French partner, the Societé des Etudes du Caoutchouc Synthetique à Base d'Alcool (SECASAL), that might lead to a joint venture to use French red wine to produce ethanol. Ethanol would, in turn, be used to produce butadiene. The red wine, whose delivery could be assured through a long-term contract, would be subsidized by the French government and would cost Hüls FF 25 per liter. SECASAL would provide technical assistance and also would come up with 40–50 percent of the capital needed for constructing the plant. In the end, the plant would cost considerably less to build than would those using competing feedstocks.[28] Although he asked for guidance from the Economics Ministry in deciding among the competing feedstocks, Baumann's letter clearly implied that he thought that ethanol produced from French red wine would be the best choice.

Baumann's request for guidance received intensive scrutiny within the Economics Ministry in Bonn. On 17 October, Mr. Schneider of the Economics Ministry's Petroleum Section discussed the viability of competing feedstocks and technologies. He stressed the limited ability of either the country's petroleum industry or its liquid-gas industry to satisfy Hüls needs. Both industries, he contended, were already selling virtually all of their current production; neither was in a position to expand significantly. In addition, Hüls's location was unfavorable in terms of shipping petroleum by-products or liquid gas from their production sites in West Germany to Marl. For the same reason, Schneider went on, ethanol from liquid gas was not a satisfactory option.[29]

Only in the penultimate paragraph of his memorandum did Schneider turn to the question whether or not imported hydrocarbons – as opposed to those produced within Germany itself – could be used. He stressed from the outset that an import was an import, whether it was petroleum, liquid gas, or alcohol; imports of either of the first two products would be no more "secure than delivery of ethyl alcohol from France." He conceded that there was an economical source of n-butane from petroleum in Pernis, Holland, if it could be shipped by barge, or of liquid gas from Brüx in Czechoslovakia. Supplies from both sources would be uncertain, however, especially "since the intentions of these factories [in Pernis and Brüx] in the petrochemical or other areas are not known." Having thus dismissed all other options, Schneider came to his recommendation in his final paragraph:

Thus it appears, especially when one considers the financial participation offered [by France] and the securities given for long-term supplies of French alcohol, and not least

[28] Chemische Werke Hüls to BWM, IV, "Betr. Erzeugung von synthetischem Kautschuk," 6 October 1953, BAK, B102/9576, Heft 2. SECASAL was a society set up by French industry and sponsored by the French government to promote use of alcohol in producing synthetic rubber, both within France and abroad. "Protokoll," 22 July 1953, Anlage I to the foregoing.

[29] BWM, IV B 3 (Schneider), "Stellungnahme zu dem Projekt der Chemischen Werke Hüls; Erzeugung von 30 000 t/Jahr synth. Kautschuk (Tieftemperatur-Polymerisat)," 17 October 1953, BAK, B102/9576, Heft 2.

also the more limited capital requirements, that the plan of the C W H [Chemische Werke Hüls] to use French alcohol as a raw material for the production of butadiene is the most economical.[30]

Although other Economics Ministry officials disagreed with Schneider's assessment, he was not alone in advocating alcohol rather than coal as Hüls's primary feedstock for synthetic rubber. In early November 1953, Otto Friedrich, chairman of the managing board of Phoenix Rubber Works A.G., notified the Chemicals Section of the ministry that he was in favor of exploring the project further. Although he could not speak for all rubber processors, and although there were some drawbacks, Friedrich believed that the project had much to recommend it: "Although it is not very pleasant to construct long-range plans on a politically based state subsidy in France for the price of alcohol, it appears to me that, based on the results of the negotiations of the chemische Werke Hüls with the French, the project is capable of realization."[31]

Before Friedrich wrote his comments, however, Dr. Blankenfeld of the Economics Ministry's Chemicals Section had already delivered a response to Schneider's memorandum, on 30 October. Outlining Schneider's views, Blankenfeld pointed out that the main argument was that "petrochemistry will be able to develop only to a limited extent in the Federal Republic," because fuel production would completely occupy the refineries. Blankenfeld thought it possible – indeed necessary – to take a less extreme position: "In my view, not everything can revolve around motor fuels. In the final analysis, no automobile can run without tires." He countered Schneider's views with an analysis that took into consideration the relationship between increasing use of automobiles and the subsidiary industries associated with that increase. As an example relevant to the current discussion, he pointed out that if "motorization" proceeded at the current rate; the rubber industry would require supplies of 2.5 million tons of raw rubber per year by the mid-1950s, and 3 million tons by 1960. Current supplies from rubber plantations and from synthesis facilities would be able to meet the projected need only through 1955; undersupply in 1956 would amount to about 22,000 tons, and that would rise to about 150,000 tons by 1958. He went on: "It is by no means clear that a removal of this potential bottleneck will be successful." Already the Americans were expanding their synthetic-rubber capacity to meet the projected shortfalls, as were the French, the Italians, and the British.[32]

Of course, Schneider had not been arguing against synthetic-rubber production per se, but rather for manufacturing it using ethyl alcohol as the primary feedstock. Blankenfeld finally came around to discussing that in his final three paragraphs. The suggestion of using the inexpensive French alcohol as a feed-

[30] Ibid.

[31] Otto Friedrich to Economics Ministry, "Betr: Ausbau der deutschen Buna-Produktion," 5 November 1953, BAK, B102/9576, Heft 2.

[32] BWM, IV B 1 (Blankenfeld), "Vermerk Betr. Stellungnahme des Referates IV B 3 vom 17.10.1953 zum Projekt der Chemischen Werke Hüls GmbH . . . ; Erzeugung von 30.000 t/Jahr synth. Kautschuk (Tieftemperatur-Polymerisat)," 30 October 1953, BAK, B102/9576, Heft 2.

stock, he conceded, "has . . . much going for it." His primary objection was that exclusive reliance on French alcohol, and in particular on the French government's price and supply guarantees, was dangerous. Turning Schneider's argument – which stressed the security concern regarding the domestic supply as a primary criterion for rejecting petroleum and liquid gas – against him, Blankenfeld argued "that the dependence for supply of raw materials on imported alcohol, despite whatever assurances given by the foreign supplier, will always remain a risk, and especially in times of crisis can lead to severe disturbances. In contrast, one can always fall back on domestic production in the case of hydrocarbons." A similar level of security in the domestic supply of alcohol would be possible only if the Bundestag were to revise and update the Alcohol Monopoly Law to guarantee supplies to the chemical industry.[33]

As a parting shot, Blankenfeld noted that synthetic-rubber production facilities based on alcohol in the United States had been shut down because the alcohol process was too expensive. Given that and other considerations, he suggested renewed attention to the problem of supplies of hydrocarbons, "because . . . a better constancy of production seems possible through extensive use of domestic supplies of raw materials."[34]

While those internal discussions were taking place in the Ministry of Economics, its representatives asked their counterparts in the Finance Ministry for input on the question of exempting alcohol meant for Buna production from tariffs and from sales taxes, in addition to allowing it the same special legal and financial perquisites accorded the existing alcohol monopoly (Branntwein-Monopol). The Finance Ministry reported that the current legal basis for dealing with those issues was insufficient; to achieve those objectives, it would be necessary to make three major changes to existing laws.[35] Obviously, those in the Ministry of Economics would have to be strongly committed to the Hüls project to go to such trouble.

Not long after the Economics Ministry received that finding from the Finance Ministry, the stage was set to decide, "finally," how to proceed with the Hüls request. A meeting was held on 5 March 1954; Prentzel met with a number of bureaucrats from the Economics Ministry and Finance Ministry, representatives from the Alcohol Monopoly Administration, and officials from the Economics Ministry of North Rhine-Westphalia.[36] Prentzel and the other participants began by reviewing the state of negotiations to that point. Referring to the Hüls memorandum of 6 October 1953, Dr. Lenz, who wrote the minutes, outlined in some detail the reasons that the use of French alcohol was so attractive. Not only was it available in sufficient quantity at a reasonable price, but also it would have the advantage "that the investment needed is less than when one uses the hydro-

[33] Ibid.   [34] Ibid.

[35] Bundesminister der Finanzen (Dr. Kunz) to Bundesminster für Wirtschaft (Section V), "Betr.: Errichtung einer neuen Buna-Produktionsanlage der Chemischen Werke Hüls G.m.b.H.," 2 December 1953, BAK, B102/9576, Heft 2.

[36] BWM, IV B 1, "Notiz für Herrn Dr. Prentzel, Betr. Besprechung über Buna-Projekt Chemische Werke Hüls A.G. am 5. März 1954," 1 March 1954, BAK, B102/9576, Heft 2; BWM, IV B 1 (Lenz), "Vermerk Betr. Erzeugung von synthetischem Kautschuk in der Bundesrepublik," 8 March 1954, BAK, B102/9577.

carbons *n*-butane or *n*-butylene." In addition, the French supplier, SECASAL, offered a number of other advantages: The time period of the contract was flexible (seven, twelve, or seventeen years); SECASAL would provide about 40 percent of the capital for the project; and the French desired an option to purchase each year 12,000–15,000 tons of the Buna produced by Hüls.[37]

The major drawback was that despite the use of subsidized alcohol, world prices for natural rubber were so low that the factory would have to be subsidized by the West German government as well. The French would subsidize the alcohol at a rate of DM 15.35 million per year; in addition, the Germans would have to chip in DM 12.59 million per year, either in the form of write-offs and tax concessions or in the form of a running subvention directly from the Finance Ministry. Lenz made it clear in his minutes that even Hüls had second thoughts about that idea, especially because it was currently engaged in negotiations with a potential American supplier of *n*-butane. It had therefore been possible to delay a decision on the French plan. Lenz made his complete opposition to the red-wine plan clear in an acid commentary: "Thus it was possible to postpone a decision on the economically unusual measure of constructing a DM 100 million project on the basis of a raw material subsidized in another country." Press reports from February 1954, however, indicated that the French side was pressing for a final decision on their offer, which Hüls in turn requested from the Ministry of Economics in a letter of 17 February.[38]

In effect, the decision not to go with the French had already been made, but there were complications. Participants at the meeting noted that in addition to the various technological and economic advantages offered by the alcohol route to butadiene, there were political advantages as well:

Even in initial deliberations, the assumption was that the factory at Hüls should be a European one and that, from there, other European markets should be supplied [in addition to the German market]. The factory could therefore have served as a model for a European integration. This idea was supported through the offer of the French side to participate in terms of capital investment and to take an option on a part of the production.

In relaying to Hüls the decision not to support the French solution, therefore, it would be necessary to note "that the concept of European integration is not being discriminated against and that administrative difficulties alone make it impossible to give further consideration to the project of production of Buna on the basis of French alcohol."[39] That was communicated to Hüls in a letter dated 13 March, sent by Krautwig and drafted by the Chemicals Section of the Economics Ministry. It recommended that Hüls inform the French of the "unimplementability" of the project and asked the German firm to submit a new proposal.[40]

[37] BWM, IV B 1 (Lenz), "Vermerk Betr. Erzeugung von synthetischem Kautschuk in der Bundesrepublik."

[38] Ibid.   [39] Ibid.

[40] Der Bundesminister für Wirtschaft, IV B 1 (signed Krautwig) to Chemische Werke Hüls, "Betr. Erzeugung von synthetischem Kautschuk in der Bundesrepublik," 13 March 1954, BAK, B102/9576, Heft 2.

Lenz's final remarks on the project, from 8 March, bear some examination, however. Dr. Blankenfeld of the Chemicals Section of the Economics Ministry had reported to the meeting that alcohol-based facilities in the United States had proved uneconomical and that even Hüls was beginning to come around to the idea of basing its production on petroleum. The prerequisite for that would be a secure and inexpensive source of n-butane. If Hüls went that route, the proposed French subsidy for the Buna project, amounting to DM 15.35 million in the case of the red-wine route, would, of course, cease to be a consideration. On the other hand,

the federal government's subsidy amount of DM 12.59 million . . . would continue to be necessary. A so-called "Lex-Buna" or "Lex-Hüls" would thus also in this case be required if it is not possible to attain a satisfactory regulation through the "Law on the Takeover of Loan Guarantees for the Promotion of the German Economy."[41]

In other words, "administrative difficulties" and the proposed high subsidies per se had had nothing to do with the decision against alcohol. Instead, the primary reason had been uncertainty over the security of the supply and the fact that West Germany could not have substituted effectively for the imported alcohol feedstocks with any domestic resources in the event of interruption of the supply from France.

During 1954 and 1955, Hüls did work out a new proposal for its project. Before going on to discuss that, we should try to sum up the major issues raised in those discussions of feedstocks and related technologies. Few historians have paid any attention whatsoever to that episode. Those who have, including Paul Kränzlein, in his official history of Hüls, and Peter Morris, in a paper on technology transfer and the synthetic-rubber industry, have downplayed its significance, mentioning it primarily as a curiosity.[42] Kränzlein, in particular, used most of the space he devoted to the episode to recount the humor with which contemporaries viewed the matter. Wine connoisseurs, claimed one wit, would be able to identify the vintage of a given tire, and he went on to suggest that tires he named after wine-producing regions, such as Beaujolais or Burgundy. Another suggested that regardless of the decision on the technology, a red-wine pipeline should be laid immediately between the south of France and Hüls.[43]

From today's perspective – and, indeed, given what Kränzlein reported, for contemporaries as well – the idea of using red wine to produce rubber does seem odd, even funny. But that does not necessarily imply that it was trivial. Indeed, the willingness of the French government to subsidize the business and even to allow a French company to invest heavily in it, the apparent enthusiasm for the project by the leadership of Hüls and by some bureaucrats in the Economics Ministry, and the length of time (about six months in all) devoted

[41] BWM, IV B 1 (Lenz), "Vermerk Betr. Erzeugung von synthetischem Kautschuk in der Bundesrepublik."

[42] Kränzlein, *Chemie im Revier,* pp. 120–2; Morris, "Transatlantic Transfers in Synthetic Rubber Technology," p. 57.

[43] Kränzlein, *Chemie im Revier,* p. 121.

to intensive scrutiny of the project within the ministry all indicate that the historical actors took it quite seriously, and therefore perhaps the historian should as well.

The red-wine episode demonstrates just how unclear it was in the early 1950s, even to experts in private industry and government, whether or not petroleum-based chemistry would be the wave of the future. It shows the extent to which political considerations – such as rapprochement with the French – influenced the discussions about which feedstock or technology to adopt. It illustrates the West German willingness to use extensive tariff and non-tariff measures to protect domestic industry and to foster technological development, and hence the country's slow and deliberate re-entry into the economy of the Western world. And it underscores the extent to which the West German government served to coordinate the public interest and diverse private interests (or at least the interests of certain sectors of large-scale industry).[44]

Certainly the decision by the West German government not to support the plan to produce Buna from French wine is understandable: On the face of it, the arguments against the project – that it would require both a large subsidy (in whatever form) and extensive legislative action – were compelling. But to admit that is not to admit the economic or technological supremacy of petroleum as a chemical feedstock, at least not in the early 1950s. One must keep in mind that *all* of the alternatives for producing butadiene for synthetic rubber at that time would have required both subsidies and legal and/or administrative changes. Thus, the basis for the decision was not which process would be most profitable, which feedstock would be least expensive, or even which would be ''best'' technologically; rather, the decision involved a host of considerations, including the transportability of the feedstock, foreign-policy objectives, the security of supply, and the related issue of the possible necessity of substituting domestically produced raw materials for imported ones. At the end of the day, the last two factors constituted the most compelling case against French alcohol.

Could the outcome of the lengthy deliberations in late 1953 and early 1954 over the Hüls plan have been otherwise? An answer requires some speculation, which in turn requires some caution, but such might well have been possible. The length and intensity of the discussions within the Economics Ministry provide one indication of how close Hüls came to choosing alcohol over oil. A closer (and especially public) identification of the project with European integration, a more positive position on the issue by the alcohol monopoly, or a powerful advocate within the Ministry of Economics (Schneider, the early advocate, did not participate in any of the ensuing discussions), whereas Lenz, the early opponent, did, and he often wrote the minutes of the key meetings) – any

[44] See, for instance, Werner Abelshauser, ''The First Post-Liberal Nation: Stages in the Development of Modern Corporatism in Germany,'' *European History Quarterly* 14 (1984):285–318; Abelshauser, ''Korea, die Ruhr und Erhards Marktwirtschaft: Die Energiekrise von 1950–1951,'' *Rheinische Vierteljahrsblätter* 45(1981):287–316; Diethelm Prowe, ''Economic Democracy in Post-World War II Germany: Corporatist Crisis Response, 1945–1948,'' *Journal of Modern History* 57(1985):451–82.

one or any combination of those factors might have caused the decision within the ministry to go the other way.

But so what if it had? Would it have made any difference to the subsequent development of the West German chemical industry? Exploring alternative scenarios for a historical episode is even more dangerous than speculation, and the past is not an experiment that can be run a second time with a single variable altered. On the other hand, given that some possibilities appear to have been more likely than others, it is worth pursuing this line of thought further, at least briefly.

Given the extensive growth in the uses of synthetic rubber in the 1950s and 1960s, an alcohol-based plant of the size initially planned by Hüls could have met only a fraction of the demand in West Germany, let alone in Europe or the world. On the other hand, Hüls's choice of an alcohol-based process might have set a precedent for the rest of Europe, and certainly using the process on the industrial scale would have led to higher efficiencies. Also, expansion of the plant might have been possible, just as was the case with the petroleum-based plant that was actually constructed.

One might raise objections: Although the world's oil resources are not without limits, certainly oil is available in far greater quantities than are supplies of grapes for alcohol; oil supplies are more amenable to being marshaled to meet fluctuations in demand; the supplies of petroleum are not subject to the natural disasters that can befall the supplies of agricultural products. Many would contend that these assumptions are themselves problematic, but let us entertain them for the moment. It is possible to imagine a situation in which alcohol- and petroleum-based processes might have co-existed. Indeed, given the astonishing increases in European agricultural productivity since the 1950s, it is possible to imagine that alcohol from wine or other agricultural products could have provided a substantial part of the butadiene needed by the synthetic-rubber industry. The European Community's ocean of wine overproduction might have found an outlet; and the world might have been provided a key example of the use of renewable resources rather than nonrenewable resources in chemical production.

What actually occurred was substantially different. Baumann met with Prentzel to present his firm's revised proposal of the Buna plant on 24 March 1955. Ethanol clearly was no longer in the running as a feedstock; instead, n-butane was preferred. Baumann presented two proposals for plants of different sizes, one with a capacity of 30,000 tons per year, the other 45,000 tons per year. The smaller plant naturally would cost less (DM 119 million vs. DM 142 million), but its output would also be higher-priced (DM 2.82 per kilogram vs. DM 2.60). The latter price, in particular, compared favorably with (but was still higher than) the price of imported synthetic rubber in Hamburg, which was DM 2.55 per kilogram. Baumann proposed that the plant be operated by a new firm, for which Hüls would supply half the capital. The Big Three successors to I.G. Farben would together subscribe the other half of the capital, with the costs of building and operating the plant borne by the chemical industry and by a loan guaranteed by the federal government. Such state aid would be necessary given the project's continuing risks, despite its improved competitiveness. Those risks included the possibility of a downturn in motorization, resulting in decreased demand for Buna, and a possible collapse in the price of natural rubber. Baumann, supported by the Chemicals Section of the Economics Ministry, requested that Erhard make a firm commitment to support, in principle, the federal government's willingness to provide "protection against certain risks." The Chemicals Section, significantly, explicitly rejected calling that a subsidy, preferring instead to use the term "backing" (*Rückendeckung*).[45]

In Prentzel's judgment, the new version of the project would be internationally competitive. Accordingly, he arranged a meeting with Erhard, Baumann, Krautwig, Menne (head of the chemical-industry trade association), and Lenz on 25 March. Erhard apparently agreed to support the effort to gain federal loan guarantees for the project.[46]

It soon became evident that the precise nature and extent of Erhard's commitment were matters of dispute. Husung and Kuhfuss from Hüls called on Lenz and another ministry bureaucrat (Weniger) on 27 October 1955 to report on the recent meeting of the supervisory board of the new company formed to produce synthetic rubber: the Buna-Werke Hüls GmbH (BWH). BWH had been formed as expected during 1955 by Hüls and the three I.G. Farben successors. The main purpose of the visit was to inform the ministry of the supervisory board's "disappointment" that the agreement by Erhard in March 1953 and March 1955 to seek federal participation in the Buna project had thus far come to nought; it might not be possible for the new firm to proceed unless a final, favorable decision was reached by the ministry. Specifically, the two representatives of Hüls wanted a loan guarantee of DM 40 million, half guaranteed by the federal government and half by the province of North Rhine-Westphalia. Under what circumstances would such a loan guarantee be possible?[47]

Bureaucrats from the Economics Ministry denied that there had been a fundamental change in policy. Erhard's agreement had been to the proposition that the Buna project was of "economic significance," and that remained his belief. But circumstances had changed, limiting the options of the federal government. They recommended once again that the financing of the project be reviewed, so as to avoid reliance on loan guarantees, and they suggested as well that the new firm take up negotiations with the finance ministries of the individual provinces for special write-offs.[48] Although Lenz apparently did not enumerate the reasons for the reluctance of the Economics Ministry to provide state

[45] BWM, IV (Krautwig) to Erhard via the State Secretary, "Betr.: Ausbau der deutschen Bunaproduktion," 25 March 1955, BAK, B102/9576, Heft 2.

[46] BWM, IV B 1 (Lenz), "Buna-Projekt der Chemischen Werke Hüls AG," 10 September 1955, BAK, B102/9576, Heft 2.

[47] BWM, IV B 1 (Lenz), "Vermerk Betr: Buna-Projekt Chemische Werke Hüls A.G.," 28 October 1955, BAK, B102/9576, Heft 1.

[48] Ibid.

aid to BWH, the ministry's state secretary, Dr. Westrick, did so in an internal memorandum dated 22 December 1955. In a conversation with Menne, Westrick noted his belief that "the stockholders of this firm were in a position on the basis of their general situation to obtain the necessary credits – this especially since the rubber-consuming industry guarantees losses of up to DM 50 million."[49]

In the course of the next two years, the new firm, BWH, began construction of a synthetic-rubber facility using technologies from the United States, without any aid from the federal government in Bonn. That did not stop the BWH representatives from continuing to push for state aid, in particular because some savings that had been achieved through research and development and efficiency measures were being eroded by increasing labor costs and other costs, with the result that the cost per kilogram of finished product remained about DM 0.20 higher than the cost of rubber imported from the United States.[50]

Baumann, for instance, wrote to Erhard in mid-August 1957 to thank him for recently visiting the construction site of the new Buna works, but the main purpose of the letter was to remind the economics minister of the firm's "concerns." Capital costs had increased substantially since Erhard had originally recognized the project's "economic significance," from DM 70–90 million in 1953 to a projected DM 180 million. In part as a result of that, the cost of rubber would be DM 2.65 per kilogram, as compared with DM 2.45 for imported American synthetic rubber. Baumann noted other factors as well, including the price of butadiene for BWH (about 2.5 times as much as in the United States), the smaller capacity of the Hüls facility vis-à-vis those in the United States, and the higher start-up costs of the West German plant. Baumann stressed that start-up costs for the U.S. plants had been borne by the state. He also complained that attempts to get capital participation or loan guarantees from the federal or state governments had been unsuccessful, that the capital for the new plant (which had been raised privately) was subject to a capital tax of 3 percent, and that the finished product would be subject to a "turnover equalization tax" to which imported Buna was not subject.[51]

Certainly, if Baumann could complain about the treatment his firm received at the hands of the Economics Ministry in general, no such accusation could be made against the ministry's Chemicals Section. Hans Beckmann of Hüls wanted to send a quick follow-up letter to the minister in late August to ask that Erhard support a guarantee, through the Rubber Price Equalization Fund, against losses of up to DM 10 million per year for the first five years of the facility's operation. He sent a draft of the letter to the Chemicals Section, and Lenz provided a detailed commentary on it within two days, although the actual letter, as further amended according to suggestions from the WDK, did not go

[49] Der Staatsekretär (Westrick), Abt. L4, "Notiz Betr. Buna-Projekt in Hüls/Bundesbürgschaft," 22 December 1955, (Abschrift), BAK, B102/9576, Heft 1.

[50] Beckmann to Lenz, "Betr. Buna-Projekt," 29 August 1957, and attachment, BAK, B102/9577.

[51] Baumann to Erhard, 14 August 1957, BAK, B102/9577.

to Erhard until 25 October.[52] The Chemicals Section also supported the application of BWH in 1958 for relief from the turnover tax.[53]

The synthetic-rubber plant at Hüls went into operation on 15 September 1958 without having received any news regarding its application for tax relief. The request was denied seven months later, despite the efforts of the Chemicals Section, for two reasons: First, if such a preference were extended to Hüls, other companies in other industries would demand the same treatment, the result being an unacceptable loss of revenue to the federal government. The second reason concerned the impact of tax relief on the competitiveness of West German Buna production. In a January 1959 memorandum, "Misgivings about the Buna application," an official of the Economics Ministry noted that "the application of the Buna Works is justified by and large on the basis of the deficient international competitiveness of Buna manufacture in the Federal Republic. Freeing [the firm] from the turnover tax is not seen as a suitable means to improve the competitiveness of a branch of the economy."[54] Both considerations figured prominently – indeed, using virtually the same wording – in subsequent letters from Westrick to the federal minister of finance (recommending denial of the Hüls request) and from Erhard to Baumann (informing Hüls of the bad news).[55]

Concluding remarks

Usually it is a dreary task to examine in detail the negotiations between private industry and the state. The tangled and often obscure discussions within the federal Ministry of Economics on whether or not to allow tax relief to BWH were no exception. Nonetheless, the examination is useful because of the light it sheds on the role of the West German state in the technological and ideological changes that occurred during the postwar period. The Hüls case admittedly was somewhat extreme in terms of the degree of state involvement in the decision-making process, mainly because synthetic-rubber technology, more than most others, was tied up with foreign-policy considerations (i.e., limitation of German war potential, German reconstruction, international transfer of technology) and because Hüls requested heavy subsidies from the government. Still, the role of the Chemicals Section of the Economics Ministry as advocate for the chemical industry, and the frequent consultations between state bureaucrats and

---

[52] Beckmann to Lenz, "Betr. Buna-Projekt," 29 August 1957, and attachment; Lenz to Beckmann, "Betr. Buna-Projekt," 31 August 1957; Bunawerke Hüls (Baumann and Holzrichter) to Erhard, "Betr. Preisausgleichskasse Kautschuk," 25 October 1957; all in BAK, B102/9575.

[53] Correspondence in BAK, B102/9577, especially meeting of 3 July 1958 chaired by Ministerialrat Schulze-Brachmann, BWM I B 6, "Vermerk über den Antrag der Buna-Werke Hüls auf Erweiterung [UStdB:] . . . zur Freistellung von der Umsatzsteuer am 3.7.1958," 14 July 1958.

[54] Dr. Bodsch to Abteilungsleiter I, "Betr. Antrag der Buna-Werke Hüls auf Umsatzsteuerfreiheit," (9?) January 1959, BAK, B102/9577.

[55] Westrick to Bundesminister der Finanzen, "Betr.: Umsatzsteuer; hier Befreiung der Lieferungen synthetisches Kautschuks von der Umsatzsteuer," 6 March 1959 (Abschrift); Erhard to Baumann, "Betr.: Antrag auf Erlaß der Umsatzsteuer für Bunalieferungen," 28 April 1959; both in BAK, B102/9577.

industrialists on technological and commercial problems, can be seen as typical of West German business-government relations in the postwar period and to some extent belied Ludwig Erhard's rhetoric about the "market economy" aspect of his "social market economy." The West German government thus continued well into the 1950s to follow the activist tradition of intervention in the economy dating from the Nazi period and the immediate postwar period, although the ultimate outcome of the negotiations on possible subsidies and tax breaks for the synthetic-rubber plant at Hüls indicated a growing tendency for the state to force (or, depending on one's perspective, to allow) business to compete in a more open market. That occurred only gradually during the course of the 1950s, however.

Similarly, there was a gradual change away from traditional thinking about autarky, or economic self-sufficiency, during the 1950s, which the Hüls case highlights. The anticipated wartime necessity for self-sufficiency in synthetic rubber was the reason that the Hüls plant came into existence in the first place. But even after the war, the desire to avoid German reliance on foreign sources of synthetic rubber was a key consideration prompting the government and industry to press for removal of Allied restrictions. That desire to attain some measure of self-sufficiency in such an important production area also constituted much of the spirit behind the establishment of the Rubber Price Equalization Fund. The security of domestic supply – of feedstocks and of finished product – was also central to the arguments of the Economics Ministry bureaucracy in discussions about competing feedstocks for Hüls in the early 1950s. Again, emphasis on full integration into the economy of the Western world (at the cost having to rely on foreign sources of raw materials and markets abroad) came only gradually, and it was tempered throughout the 1950s by the tendency to hedge bets, to choose technologies that would allow a retreat to German domestic sources of raw materials should that become necessary.

Still, however qualified, the importance of American cold-rubber technology to BWH and the plant's eventual reliance on petrochemical feedstocks represented a break with the past, both ideologically and technologically. Other companies and other technological sectors had more difficulty in breaking such ties, as we shall see in the coming chapter on coal-based Fischer-Tropsch technology.

9
End-game strategies: the German coal industry and the Fischer-Tropsch process

Speaking before the annual meeting of the German Society for Petroleum Research and Coal Chemistry on 25 September 1953, Dr. Bernhard Löpmann outlined some of the ongoing research-and-development efforts at his plant, a Fischer-Tropsch facility in Bergkamen, in the Ruhr district. Löpmann concluded enthusiastically that "in my view, we stand at present in Bergkamen at the very beginning of a new development of hydrocarbon synthesis from the raw material coal, which is so valuable."[1] By the late 1950s, however, it was clear that Bergkamen, which was owned by Ruhr coal interests, was in deep trouble. In early 1962, the factory shut down its Fischer-Tropsch plant. It had, in the meantime, been acquired by the Berlin-based Schering chemical concern and had begun to produce pharmaceuticals, industrial chemicals, and chemical catalysts. Other Fischer-Tropsch facilities in West Germany had stopped production even earlier, by the mid-1950s, the victims of escalating coal prices and competition from petrochemicals.[2]

---

[1] Bernhard Löpmann, "Betrachtungen zur Fischer-Tropsch-Synthese unter besonderer Berücksichtigung der Arbeitsweise der Chemischen Werke Bergkamen," *Erdöl und Kohle* 7(October 1954):622–6.

[2] Heinz Nedelmann, "The German Coal-Chemical Industry" (paper presented to the American Coke and Coal Chemicals Institute, Rye, NY, 17 May 1954), p. 20, from collection of Dr. Nedel-

What happened? How could Dr. Löpmann have been so wrong? Was his talk simply an example of whistling in the dark while catastrophe loomed? In this chapter I shall argue that in the early 1950s, Löpmann and others like him had grounds for optimism regarding the prospects for Fischer-Tropsch production based on coal. Even when coal prices rose dramatically during 1953 and Fischer-Tropsch plants began to lose some of their markets to petroleum-based products, there was reason to believe that Bergkamen and plants like it could continue, by working at lowering their costs of production through technological improvements and finding lucrative niches for their products. This story, then, is one of a gradual closing off of options for Fischer-Tropsch plants. Because that closure process occurred so slowly, at least from the point of view of the contemporary actors, its effects often were imperceptible and its long-term implications therefore unpredictable. The final blow came in 1961, when the West German government rescinded the tax preferences that the products of Fischer-Tropsch plants had previously enjoyed, thus ending a decade that had begun with the triumphant return to production in those Fischer-Tropsch facilities that had survived the war and the postwar dismantling.

The primary focus is on the experience of the Fischer-Tropsch plant at Bergkamen. Bergkamen, according to cost information exchanged with another Fischer-Tropsch plant, and according to postwar evaluation by experts, had been the most efficient of the Fischer-Tropsch facilities during the National Socialist period.[3] Partly for that reason, it was able to survive the 1950s, despite massive economic changes that undermined its competitiveness. Bergkamen is also of interest because its managers were able to make the transition away from the Fischer-Tropsch process in the early 1960s. Finally, the Bergkamen case is significant because its history mirrors important political, economic, and technological trends in twentieth-century Germany: Owned and developed by Ruhr coal firms, the Fischer-Tropsch technology used at Bergkamen and other such facilities had represented the coal industry's challenge to the increasing power and prestige of the chemical industry on its own turf during the 1930s; the decline of the technology during the 1950s was part and parcel of the political and economic decline of the Ruhr coal industry during the same period.

The hopeful years: 1951–3

In the immediate aftermath of World War II, of course, all synthetic-fuel facilities in Germany were under notice that the Allies intended to shut them down

mann, copy in possession of author. Of the six Fischer-Tropsch plants in West Germany (all were located in the Ruhr district), two produced through the spring of 1948 (Wanne-Eickel and Castrop-Rauxel); Bergkamen was added to the list after the removal of Allied production prohibitions in 1951.

[3] Hermann Schwenke, "Entwicklung der Chemischen Werke Bergkamen A.G. vom 2. January 1937–April 1959," 1 July 1959, esp. p. 5, unpublished manuscript from collection of Dr. Hubert, Schering A.G., Bergkamen works, in possession of author. Schwenke uses postwar estimates of the average cost of Fischer-Tropsch production calculated by Dr. Heinrich Bütefisch of I.G. Farben in British Intelligence Objectives Subcommittee (BIOS) reports after the war.

as "war-related industries." The factories were also slated to be dismantled. In the short term, however, the two Allies with such plants in their zones – the British and the Soviets – operated them to supply the fuel needs of the occupation forces. The threat of shutdown and dismantling continued throughout the occupation period, although hydrogenation plants in West Germany were soon exempted from that threat because they converted to using petroleum (supplied by British and American oil companies) rather than coal as their starting material. The Fischer-Tropsch plants, which were neither as large nor as amenable to retrofitting as were their counterparts that employed high-pressure hydrogenation technology, could work out no such deal and consequently remained in danger. In April 1948, the Western Allies followed through on their original plans by banning all Fischer-Tropsch production and scheduling the plants for immediate dismantling.[4]

The motives for the Allies' action at that late date – and just as negotiations to form the Federal Republic of Germany were about to begin in earnest – are not clear. Perhaps the Allies realized that that would be their last chance to implement policies that would inhibit Germany's ability to make war in the future. In any case, their decision provoked a strong German reaction, as industry, labor, and government united to oppose the dismantling order, and in November 1949 that united effort succeeded. The Petersberg agreement between the Federal Republic and the Western Allies removed all of the Fischer-Tropsch plants (along with other plants from other industries) from the dismantling lists, although production prohibitions remained in place. It took another year and a half, until April 1951, to convince the Allies to loosen their restrictions and remove the prohibitions, and shortly after that those Fischer-Tropsch plants that remained in reasonably good repair resumed production. At first, that included only the works at Bergkamen and the Krupp factory at Wanne-Eickel. The Gewerkschaft Victor at Castrop-Rauxel followed later, although the Krupp and Gewerkschaft Victor plants had halted production by 1954.[5]

One major argument that the Germans, led by Heinz Nedelmann of the Coal Chemical Trade Association (Fachverband Kohlechemie, FVK), had used in trying to convince the Allies to rescind their prohibition of Fischer-Tropsch production was that the plants were not war-related at all. In fact, they argued, the National Socialist policy of autarky, with its emphasis on maximizing production of motor fuels from domestic German coal, had led to inefficient and improper use of Fischer-Tropsch technology. The synthesis process was not well suited to the production of motor fuels after all; its output of gasoline, in particular, was of poor quality. Instead, the process was best suited for production of chemical feedstocks for other industries, including alcohols and starting materials for detergents and plastics production, especially because Fischer-Tropsch feedstocks were of uniform aliphatic structure and free of sulfurous

---

[4] See Chapter 2.

[5] Heinz Nedelmann, "Die Chemie im Ruhrgebiet," 20 May 1952, p. 19; Nedelmann, "The German Coal-Chemical Industry," p. 20; both from collection of Dr. Nedelmann, copies in possession of author.

contaminants. In other words, as Nedelmann put it in one memorandum, optimal production using the Fischer-Tropsch process would manufacture "*basic chemical products* for a *pure peacetime economy*," including fatty acids, paraffin, soap, detergent intermediates, softeners and solvents for the plastics and paint industries, and so on.[6]

The idea of "pure peacetime production" is as nonsensical as that of industries geared exclusively to war production. Most industrial production, in fact, has multiple uses, and countries at war need many of the same things (though usually in different quantities) as those at peace. Nevertheless, after the resumption of operations in the Fischer-Tropsch plants in 1951, production tended, for political and economic reasons, to gravitate away from concentration on motor fuels and toward the manufacture of the kinds of producer goods for which the Fischer-Tropsch process was more suited; at the same time, motor-fuel production continued to be both an unavoidable by-product of the synthesis process and a key factor in determining a Fischer-Tropsch plant's commercial viability.

From its beginnings in the 1920s, Fischer-Tropsch synthesis had been intended to allow the German coal industry to turn some of its excess production of coke into products that were in demand. When most of the plants were built, in the 1930s, the demand appeared to be primarily for gasoline, in accordance with National Socialist policies stressing autarky. At the Bergkamen works, which began production in the spring and summer of 1939, the original intention of the designers was to produce as much gasoline as possible. Furthermore, they meant to crack or polymerize most of the by-products of the synthesis process (gases and solids as well as those liquids with boiling points higher than that of gasoline) into motor fuel as well. As it turned out, given the many needs of the economy during the National Socialist period, and especially during the war, those by-products were, in practice, used to manufacture other items. Gaseous products were processed into "gaseous motor fuel and motor butane." Liquids with somewhat higher boiling points than that of gasoline served, for instance, as additives for improving diesel fuel or as raw materials for the production of detergents. Solid crude paraffin was sold as an animal-fat substitute after processing into fatty acids, and other paraffin fractions with higher boiling points (above 450°C) were used in the production of lubricants. Thus, although in 1942–3 (the year of peak production at the Bergkamen plant) the combined outputs of gasoline and diesel fuel made up the lion's share of the plant's production, those other products were of considerable importance in Bergkamen's production palette during the period 1939–45.[7]

When the plant resumed production in April 1951, the changes in economic relationships that had occurred since the end of the war required it to alter its existing technology, although such alterations did not amount to a major change in technological direction for the plant. One new market was for propyl alcohol, which, in part because it was tax-free, was attractive to the cosmetics industry

---

[6] (No author noted, but clearly Nedelmann), Fischer-Tropsch-Industrie, 7 April 1948, Bayerwerks-archiv, Leverkusen (BWA), 186/K1.15.

[7] Schwenke, "Entwicklung der Chemischen Werke Bergkamen A.G.," pp. 2, 5, 7.

and was used as a solvent in the paint industry. Plant engineers developed a process to run the ethylene resulting from the production process "over the cobalt catalysts at a temperature of 160–200 degrees [C]" in order to optimize the output of propyl alcohol. At about the same time, one of the old markets collapsed completely: As animal fats became available once again in the early 1950s, the plant found little interest in its fatty acids from crude paraffin. Bergkamen's engineers therefore erected a thermal cracking facility for it. The gases resulting from the cracking process contained ethylene, which was used to enrich coke gases, thus increasing the yields of alcohol; the liquid products of thermal cracking were sold as gasoline or diesel fuel.[8] In that area, at least part of the original conception of the plant's designers (i.e., to maximize the output of motor fuels) was realized.

Two other products, kogasin I and II, emerged in the early 1950s as the major money-makers for Bergkamen. Kogasin I (boiling point 180–230°C) was "very much sought after" during the first half of the 1950s as a raw material for fine detergents. Kogasin II, the "product which developed into the determinant of the economic viability of the process," likewise was used as a raw material for detergent production, but it also served as a key intermediate in the production of solvents and emulsifiers. Production of kogasin was so important to the commercial viability of the Bergkamen plant that maximizing its yield became one of the driving forces for the engineering staff. To maximize the yields of kogasin II, they redesigned the process so that it took place in one step and could be operated at fairly low temperatures.[9]

As part of the trust-busting of German heavy industry that followed the war, the ownership of Bergkamen was transferred in 1952 from the Essener Steinkohlenbergwerke A.G. to Harpener Bergbau A.G.[10] The new owners were not greatly interested in the Fischer-Tropsch plant and refused to allocate new resources to it. Thus, the money for making the changes just outlined came in part from the plant's profits, but primarily from the West German federal government and from the state government of North Rhine-Westphalia. In all, state loans for reconstructing, updating, and improving the Bergkamen facilities amounted to DM 7.7 million between 1951 and 1957.[11]

More fundamental research-and-development work on the Fischer-Tropsch process occurred during the early 1950s outside the Bergkamen plant – in Germany, in the United States, and in other countries. Melvin Astle, a professor of

[8] Ibid., pp. 13–14.
[9] Ibid., Bundeswirtschaftsministerium (BWM), IV B 1 (Lenz), "Vermerk: Betr. Besprechung mit Herrn Dir. Dr. Werning und Herrn Dr. Limmer über die Chemische Werke Bergkamen A.G. am 13.1.1959," 15 January 1959, Bundesarchiv Koblenz (hereafter, BAK), B102/9432, Heft 1.
[10] Schwenke, "Entwicklung der Chemischen Werke Bergkamen A.G.," pp. 1–3, 13; generally, on the trust-busting of German heavy industry after the war, see John Gillingham, *Coal, Steel, and the Rebirth of Europe; 1945–1955: The Germans and French from Ruhr Conflict to Economic Community* (Cambridge University Press, 1991), esp. pp. 205–17, 266–83, 301–12.
[11] BWM, II A 2, "Betr.: Stillegungen und Betriebseinschränkungen; *hier* Chemische Werke Bergkamen AG; Vorg.: Weisung des Herrn Bundesministers vom 26.10.1957," 14 November 1957 (Abschrift), BAK, B102/9432, Heft 1.

chemistry at the Case Institute of Technology, wrote extensively about the process in his 1956 textbook on *The Chemistry of Petrochemicals*. Major changes to the process after the end of World War II included controlled oxidation of natural gas (instead of using coal) to produce synthesis gas and improvements in heat transfer. The German process used water external to the reaction vessels for heat transfer; postwar practice, especially in the United States, involved introducing "a fluidized catalyst which served as its own heat transfer medium and permitted much larger throughputs of materials at higher temperatures and pressures" than those allowed in the traditional Fischer-Tropsch process. Astle went on to point out that "at the present time the process is thought by some to be competitive with petroleum for the production of fuels and, in addition, to be an excellent source of chemicals."[12] He was, of course, writing about prevailing opinion in the United States, where newer petrochemical technologies were already far advanced compared with those in West Germany. As a result of the research-and-development efforts Astle described, by 1958 there were four different commercial versions of the Fischer-Tropsch process, and three others had reached the pilot-plant stage in the United States and Great Britain.[13]

Despite changes in the production process because of the altered political and economic relationships after the war, and despite ongoing research-and-development efforts, gasoline continued to be the largest single product of the Fischer-Tropsch process, just as it had been through 1945; after 1951, it still amounted to about 50 percent of total production by weight. Gasoline production was also the largest single source of revenue for the Bergkamen factory, contributing about one-fourth to one-third of the plant's total income. Despite the fact that Bergkamen lost some money selling the gasoline it made, proceeds from gasoline sales were vital to the financial health of the plant: It was not possible to operate the Fischer-Tropsch process without making gasoline, and sales of gasoline as a motor fuel continued to be the most lucrative outlet for such production. Thus, in spite of losing money on the transaction, gasoline sales brought in enough revenue so that, together with the plant's other lines (in particular, kogasin II), Bergkamen could turn a profit through the fiscal year 1954–5 (1 October 1954 to 30 September 1955).[14]

The gap between the sales price and the cost of producing gasoline at Bergkamen would have been greater (and the plant would have been in jeopardy even earlier) had it not been for the holdover effects of the earlier German policies favoring autarky. During the late Weimar Republic and the Third Reich, processes utilizing domestic coal to produce motor fuels had been given tax relief

[12] Melvin J. Astle, *The Chemistry of Petrochemicals* (New York: Reinhold, 1956), pp. 5ff.; quotations, p. 10 and p. 5.

[13] *New Technologies for Old Fuels. Hearings before the Subcommittee on Fossil and Nuclear Energy Research, Development, and Demonstration of the Committee on Science and Technology*, 95th Congress, 1st session, 1 November 1977 (Washington, DC: U.S. Government Printing Office, 1977), p. 86.

[14] Schwenke, "Entwicklung der Chemischen Werke Bergkamen A.G.," pp. 15, 17–18; BWM, IV B 1 (Lenz), "Vermerk Betr. Besprechung mit Herrn Dr. Werning, Chemische Werke Bergkamen am 15.10.1957," 21 October 1957, BAK, B102/9432, Heft 1.

vis-à-vis those producing from petroleum. For instance, on 1 December 1939 the German government raised the pump price of diesel fuel from RM 26.40 per 100 kg to RM 31.90. All producers – except those that used hydrogenation or Fischer-Tropsch synthesis – were then required to pay, out of their sales proceeds, an "equalization payment" of RM 5.50, which, for oil-based manufacturers, canceled out the positive effects of the price rise. The payments went into a fund for subsidies. In addition, the Central Petroleum Office (Zentralbüro für Mineralöl), the monopoly organization that had distributed all oil products in the Third Reich, paid different amounts for diesel fuel, depending on the process used: Those that produced diesel from German crude oil received RM 16.50 per 100 kg, whereas those employing hydrogenation or the Fischer-Tropsch process received RM 20.40. The synthetic-fuels producers received an additional subsidy of RM 4.60 per 100 kg. Finally, Fischer-Tropsch works did not have to pay any taxes on the diesel fuel they produced, while others had to pay RM 3.90 per 100 kg.[15]

The West German state (and its predecessors in the early occupation period) continued the practice of subsidizing the products of the plants, although of course that was not necessary during the period of prohibition, from April 1948 through April 1951. As part of the changes in the Oil Tax law passed in 1953,[16] direct subsidies were eliminated. In their place came the "coal preference," which imposed differential rates of taxation of motor fuels, depending upon source, and the differences in tax rates were substantial. Whereas gasoline from crude oil was taxed at a rate of DM 28.65 per 100 kg, that produced via the hydrogenation process was taxed at DM 14.65 per 100 kg. Gasoline manufactured by Fischer-Tropsch plants (at least if they used hard coal, which most did), on the other hand, was taxed at the nominal rate of DM 1.00 per 100 kg![17]

For Bergkamen, that rate represented an extremely important cost advantage. Synthesizing 100 kg of gasoline cost the plant just under DM 58, and the total revenue from it amounted to just under DM 54, a relatively small loss.[18] If the gasoline had been taxed at the same rate as that produced from crude, Bergkamen would have had to increase its prices by DM 27.65 per 100 kg, in other words, by nearly 50 percent. Thus, removal of the concealed subsidy probably would have spelled disaster for the Fischer-Tropsch plants. But until the late 1950s, no serious consideration was given to ending the coal preference. From the perspective of the early 1950s, it appeared that one of the mainstays of those factories' revenues would remain intact for the foreseeable future.

In 1953, then, when Löpmann made the speech cited at the beginning of this chapter, the outlook for the Fischer-Tropsch process did look rosy. Hopes for its

[15] Heinz Nedelmann (Fachverband Kohlechemie), "Preise, Zölle und Steuern in der Mineralölwirtschaft," 6 November 1948, p. 3 and Anlage 3, BWA, 186/K1.8. (Note that the tax break detailed here also applied to hydrogenation plants during the war.)
[16] See Chapter 3.
[17] Schwenke, "Entwicklung der Chemischen Werke Bergkamen A.G.," p. 14.
[18] Ibid., pp. 14–15. The revenues listed in the table on p. 14 indicated an "Abschlagzahlung" of DM 48.90 and a "geschätzte Nachverrechn." of DM 5.00.

future competitiveness rested, indeed, on a concealed subsidy, the coal preference, but the industry was active in seeking technological improvements that
would make it more competitive. Ultimately, however, its long-term competitiveness would depend on coal not becoming substantially more expensive. During 1953, and even more so in the later years of that decade, that began to prove
a vain hope. At the same time, some of the other bases for the competitiveness
of such plants fell apart as well.

The mid-1950s: buffeted by adversity

The first blow to the hopes of the Fischer-Tropsch producers came on 1 April
1953, when coke prices, which had remained at RM 19 per ton during the period
1939–45, and had risen only slightly in the aftermath of the war, rose suddenly
to DM 71.15 per ton, a 3.5-fold increase in the cost of coke, the single most
important raw material in Fischer-Tropsch synthesis (and a large component in
synthesis gas, which accounted for one-third of the cost of production). At the
same time, sales income increased by only 1.7-fold over the same period.[19]
Even a very profitable operation would have had trouble in absorbing such new
costs, and given the marginal profitability of many of the Fischer-Tropsch products, that was a serious blow indeed.

Even as Bergkamen and other Fischer-Tropsch plants struggled to deal with
that increase in the cost of their primary raw material, they faced serious challenges from the relatively new petrochemical industry. As discussed in earlier
chapters, petroleum-based chemistry remained a fairly small operation in the
early 1950s, but by the mid-1950s, especially as the first factory dedicated exclusively to petrochemical production, the Rheinische Olefinwerke GmbH,
came on-line in September 1955, it began to make serious inroads into the markets of traditional coal-based chemistry. Fischer-Tropsch plants were not im-
mune to that incursion, with one of the most serious challenges coming in 1954–
5, when petrochemical substitutes for kogasin I "through tetramer hydrocarbons
stemming from petrochemistry" were found. The new petrochemical products
placed severe downward pressure on prices, so that one of the Fischer-Tropsch
plants' most lucrative products became only marginally profitable.[20] The combined impacts of increased prices for coke and competition from petrochemicals
left Bergkamen as the only active Fischer-Tropsch plant by 1954.

For Bergkamen, still more trouble was on the horizon, for lower-cost substitutes were not the only threats from petroleum-based chemistry in the mid-
1950s. Petrochemical products not only tended to be cheaper but also were often
of better quality than those of coal-based chemistry. In 1959, for instance, a review of the profitability problems for the products manufactured at the Bergkamen plant came to the following telling conclusion: "The unsatisfactory results

---

[19] Schwenke, "Entwicklung der Chemischen Werke Bergkamen A.G.," p. 13; for more on the price
   increases for coal during the 1950s, see Chapter 3.
[20] Schwenke, "Entwicklung der Chemischen Werke Bergkamen A.G.," p. 14.

are, apart from rising coke prices, attributable to the similarly constantly rising demand with regard to the quality of the product, which is caused primarily by progress in petrochemicals."[21]

Large-scale refining of crude oil in West Germany, combined with new developments in refining techniques, allowed production of higher-quality gasoline, which also had an adverse impact on the sales picture for the Fischer-Tropsch plants. At the beginning of the 1950s, BV-Aral, the central sales-and-distribution organization in West Germany for "petroleum" products (whether made from crude oil or coal), required gasoline with an octane number of 72 or higher. Fischer-Tropsch gasoline's octane number was slightly below that (the number stood at 65–66 at Bergkamen, for instance), but through enrichment techniques it was fairly easy to reach the level of quality required by BV-Aral. However, those requirements increased steadily during the 1950s. By April 1959, the organization demanded a minimum octane number of 88.[22] Gasoline from the Bergkamen plant would have to be processed still further to be useful, which would increase its cost, or it would have to be sold at a discount.

The combined effects of the spiraling raw-materials costs and the price and quality pressures from the growing and increasingly aggressive petrochemical industry were devastating to the hopes of those running even the most efficient of the Fischer-Tropsch plants. Bergkamen began to lose money in fiscal year 1955–6, its losses amounting to DM 360,000. In the following fiscal year, its losses exceeded DM 1 million, and they would have been higher still had it not been for the Suez Crisis and a severe winter that caused gasoline prices to rise. Early in fiscal year 1957–8 it was already clear that Bergkamen would face bankruptcy unless swift and drastic action were taken.[23]

To make matters worse, there was a move afoot by late 1957 to reform the Oil Tax Law; one consideration was to remove the coal preference.[24] Removal of that remnant of autarkic policy clearly would mean catastrophe for Fischer-Tropsch technology. In short, then, all signs indicated that the question was not whether or not Fischer-Tropsch technology would survive at Bergkamen and become competitive, but rather when the sole remaining Fischer-Tropsch producer would collapse. The biggest single concern of management, therefore, became the search for a way – any way – out of that end game.

Getting out of the end game: 1957–61

By the fall of 1957, the leadership at the Bergkamen factory recognized the seriousness of their situation and began to look for ways to deal with it. West Germany, despite Ludwig Erhard's free-market rhetoric, operated on a corporatist

[21] Ibid., p. 16.
[22] Ibid., p. 14; BWM, IV B 1 (Lenz), "Vermerk Betr. Besprechung mit Herrn Dr. Werning."
[23] BWM, IV B 1 (Lenz), "Vermerk Betr. Besprechung mit Herrn Dr. Werning."
[24] BWM, IV B 1 (von Buddenbrook), "Vermerk Betr. Besprechung mit Herrn Dr. Werning, Chemische Werke Bergkamen, und Herrn Dr. Limmer am 11.2.1958," 12 February 1958, BAK, B102/9432, Heft 1.

model that featured extensive government-business cooperation, and therefore consultation with personnel in the federal Ministry of Economics seemed appropriate. On 15 October 1957, Dr. Werning, of Bergkamen's managing board, told Dr. Lenz of the ministry's Chemicals Section that the board had already decided "to pursue other paths and, instead of producing gasoline and various primary products (kogasin), to manufacture other chemical products. It is foreseen to allow the production of gasoline to cease on 31 March 1958 and from this point forward to move to reducing the work force considerably." Werning hoped that the new production program could begin within the next few months. In the meantime, the work force would be reduced. Bergkamen's leadership would, as an additional measure, contact chemical firms such as Hüls, Bayer, Hoechst, and BASF, as well as Otto Ambros, who sat on the supervisory boards of Scholven and a number of smaller chemical firms, to explore possible cooperative arrangements.[25]

Much of what Werning told Lenz was vague and preliminary. Still, the threats of job losses, looming bankruptcy, and likely massive changes in property and technological relationships prompted the bureaucracy to probe further. By direct order of Economics Minister Ludwig Erhard, a ministry official visited Bergkamen in early November to investigate the Bergkamen works and to interview members of the managing board. He reported that "the general impression of the equipment in the works was favorable. All of the technical installations have been automated for the most part." Nevertheless, over the preceding two years "it has become evident, that the factory . . . is no longer competitive. . . . The more expensive coal basis is so strongly inferior to petrochemistry, that it is necessary already now to draw the consequences from this, especially since the petroleum industry will extend its competitive superiority still further in the next few years with the expansion of refinery installations."[26]

The managing board drew two conclusions from that evaluation of their situation: On the one hand, they determined that they would move to dissociate the firm from its current owners, who had never displayed any real interest in the plant, and instead attach it to "a large-scale chemical company. Negotiations in this regard are in progress." In addition, the board decided "to change the basis of the work to petroleum," abandoning the coal-based Fischer-Tropsch process entirely. They planned to use "by-products of petroleum" to produce olefins and ethylene oxide at first, with production later expanding into other areas. The investment necessary for that project would amount to about DM 2 million. In an obvious bid to gain the help of the Economics Ministry, members of the managing board dramatically noted that if the supervisory board did not approve that investment strategy (and if no partner firm were found), "the chemical works will have to be designated a 'scrap heap'." They soon made their intentions even clearer, requesting direct subsidies or loan guarantees from the federal government during the transition period. A ministry official discouraged that thinking, refusing to be taken in by the implied threat that the board would scrap the

[25] BWM, IV B 1 (Lenz), "Vermerk Betr. Besprechung mit Herrn Dr. Werning."
[26] BWM, II A 2, "Betr.: Stillegungen und Betriebseinschränkungen."

plant – and its jobs – if such subsidies or guarantees were not forthcoming. Instead, he insisted that it would be necessary for management to work out a viable plan for the transition in cooperation with labor; alternatively, the managing board could allow the plant to become a scrap heap. It was up to them.[27]

The stance of that Economics Ministry official was indicative of the new official attitude in the late 1950s and was similar to that taken by the ministry in its dealings with Hüls at about the same time (see Chapter 8). Whereas earlier there had been little questioning of subsidies, tax breaks, and loan guarantees (in fact, from 1951 to 1957 Bergkamen alone had received DM 7.7 million in state loans to reconstruct and modernize the plant[28]), officials were becoming much more reluctant to undertake such measures, preferring instead to trust the free market. Thus, although consultation and advice from the ministry was readily forthcoming, money was not. That same change in thinking characterized the discussions under way at the same time within the Economics Ministry and Finance Ministry about eliminating the coal preference as part of the reform of the Oil Tax Law.[29]

In the end, the plant did not end up on the scrap heap after all, despite the fact that it continued Fischer-Tropsch production (including gasoline) into 1962. There were three reasons for that. Unquestionably the most important one had to do with the ability of a single product of the plant, kogasin II, to defy the devastating onslaught of the petrochemical industry. Bayer A.G., the main customer for the chemical, was unable to find a suitable and inexpensive petrochemical substitute for it.[30] Because kogasin II was necessary for the production of detergents, some solvents, and emulsifiers at Bayer, the company was prepared "temporarily to pay a very much increased price for kogasin II," which permitted the endangered coal-chemical plant to remain in existence. In the contract formalizing that commitment at the end of 1958, Bergkamen agreed to continue Fischer-Tropsch synthesis until as late as 30 September 1961, provided that the coal preference for by-product gasoline remained in place; if it did not, Bergkamen could opt out of the contract. Either Bayer or Bergkamen could nullify the contract if a suitable and inexpensive petrochemical substitute were found, a research project that both firms undertook. It was already possible to produce kogasin II from petrochemical feedstocks; the major problem outstanding was to

---

[27] Ibid.   [28] Ibid.

[29] Werner Abelshauser, *Der Ruhrkohlenbergbau seit 1945. Wiederaufbau, Krise, Anpassung* (Munich: Beck, 1984), made this point about the change in thinking of government officials in the late 1950s; see, for instance, pp. 80f. For that and other reasons, Abelshauser also saw a rapid "Wende am Energiemarkt" (i.e., a shift from coal to oil) in West Germany starting in 1958; see esp. p. 87 and the graph on p. 93.

[30] In a brief document analyzing the raw-materials situation for Bayer, Hermann Holzrichter, head of the Leverkusen-based firm's petrochemical effort, noted that it would be necessary to think in terms of covering losses at Bergkamen of "max. DM 280.000, . . . Trotzdem glaube ich, ist es richtig, den Weg . . . weiterzuverfolgen, da nur diese Firma auf längere Sicht die Gewähr bietet, preisgünstige Rohstoffe für unsere Fabrikationen an Hand zu geben." Dr. Holzrichter to Director Wehling, "Betr.: Kogasin II-Bergkamen,"14 May 1958, BWA, Holzrichter Papers, "Duplikate 1.1.55–31.12.60."

cleanse the petrochemical product "for the most part from aromatic components," which until the early 1960s was "still too expensive."[31]

The second reason for the relatively smooth transition away from Fischer-Tropsch production at Bergkamen was the continuation of the coal preference until 1961. As an Economics Ministry representative informed members of the managing board at Bergkamen in February 1958, the preference was bound to last for some time, because the government bureaucracy would be quite slow in writing up its new Oil Tax Law. Any reforms would not take effect before the end of 1958. Even if they were to take effect that early, however, the government was preparing to propose interim aid (*Betriebsbeihilfe*), at about the same level as the tax preferences, that would last until 1964.[32]

Armed with those assurances, certain of income from the contract with Bayer during the transitional period, and having developed a detailed plan for moving into petrochemical production, Bergkamen continued its search during early 1959 for "a 'chemical mother' who is strong in terms of capital."[33] That it quickly found one was the third reason for Bergkamen's success in making the transition away from Fischer-Tropsch synthesis. Schering A.G., a Berlin-based chemical firm interested in acquiring facilities in West Germany during the second Berlin crisis (1958–61), purchased the Bergkamen plant from Harpener Bergbau A.G. in 1959. Bergkamen became Schering's main production facility for industrial chemicals, pharmaceuticals, and chemical catalysts, and by 1967 it had become Schering's second headquarters.[34] Fischer-Tropsch synthesis continued through 1961, and briefly during 1962, but then it was closed down owing to the removal of tax preferences and the discovery of an inexpensive petrochemical process for producing an equivalent to kogasin II.[35]

Concluding remarks

There certainly were numerous differences between this case and the others presented earlier. Not only were Bergkamen and the other Fischer-Tropsch facilities *much* smaller than the firms discussed in earlier chapters, but also they were of necessity more strongly committed to coal-based chemistry than were those larger firms. That stemmed, for the most part, from the fact that the Fischer-

---

[31] BWM, IV B 1 (von Buddenbrook), "Vermerk Betr. Besprechung mit Herrn Dr. Werning, Chemische Werke Bergkamen, und Herrn Dr. Limmer am 11.2.1958"; BWM, IV B 1 (Lenz), "Vermerk: Betr. Besprechung mit Herrn Dir. Dr. Werning und Herrn Dr. Limmer über die Chemische Werke Bergkamen A.G. am 13.1.1959"; quotations from first source.

[32] BWM, IV B 1 (von Buddenbrook), "Vermerk Betr. Besprechung mit Herrn Dr. Werning, Chemische Werke Bergkamen, und Herrn Dr. Limmer am 11.2.1958."

[33] BWM, IV B 1 (Lenz), "Vermerk: Betr. Besprechung mit Herrn Dir. Dr. Werning und Herrn Dr. Limmer über die Chemische Werke Bergkamen A.G. am 13.1.1959." Two German chemical firms and two firms form the United States were interested in the plant. Its provisional plan for a five-year transitional period to full-scale petrochemical production focused at first on methylpentene production, followed by production of isoprene.

[34] Schering A.G., *Schering A.G. West Germany: From a chemist's shop to a multinational enterprise* (Berlin: Schering, 1986), pp. 30–2.

[35] Interview with Dr. H. J. Hubert, Schering A.G., Bergkamen-Werk, 3 April 1989.

Tropsch factories were not independent companies. Bergkamen, like other Fischer-Tropsch plants, was a subsidiary of a larger firm that was involved in heavy industry (i.e., the coal and steel industries, Germany's largest and most conservative at that time). During the 1930s and 1940s, Fischer-Tropsch production had represented a challenge on the part of heavy industry to the increasing power and prestige of the German chemical industry, led by I.G. Farben.[36] They were meant to produce high-value-added synthetic fuels and chemical feedstocks, the sales of which would increase the profits of the coal companies. They succeeded under the autarkic policies of the Third Reich, but to a much lesser degree than did the chemical firms and other synthetic-fuel facilities. In the early 1950s, the Fischer-Tropsch plants repeated their challenge, facing off against petrochemicals and the petroleum giant Shell, and having much less success on that second try.[37]

Regardless of their ultimate demise, however, the case of the Fischer-Tropsch plants, and of Bergkamen in particular, is important for understanding the transition of West Germany from coal-based chemistry to petroleum-based chemistry during the 1950s. For one thing exploring the history of those plants in detail demonstrates clearly that through early 1953 there were genuine grounds for hope that Fischer-Tropsch technology would in the long term be competitive with others. Bergkamen and the other producers had turned a profit, and they were relying on internal improvements in technology and cost-cutting measures to maintain their competitiveness.

The truth is that under certain conditions, the products of coal-based Fischer-Tropsch technology were competitive. Extreme examples of such conditions include those existing in National Socialist Germany and, more recently, in South Africa. Nazi policies of autarky and aggression naturally favored processes that utilized domestic coal to produce gasoline. South Africa's adherence to a policy of apartheid alienated it from the international community and forced it into an autarkic posture, but the country's domestic coal reserves permitted it to overcome its ostracism to some degree.[38]

Those are extreme examples. One might also mention the less extreme examples of West (and East) Germany in the early 1950s. The postwar Germanies had rejected most of the ideology associated with Nazism, each in its own way. Still, those in power – whether politically or economically – had come of age in a period in which the prevailing mode of thinking was in terms of maximizing domestic self-sufficiency. It was only natural that such thinking would continue for some time after the war, as the evidence presented in the case studies in this book indicates. In addition, the existing economic and political conditions through the

---

[36] I.G. Farben was challenging the coal industry on its turf at the same time by purchasing coal mines. See Gottfried Plumpe, *Die I.G. Farbenindustrie* (Berlin: Duncker & Humblot, 1990), pp. 165–8.

[37] For an account of that challenge to petrochemicals and to Shell, see Chapter 2.

[38] Hubert interview. Because any coal can be gasified, regardless of its ash content, Fischer-Tropsch technology, as modified in the years following World War II, proved the best available to meet South African conditions.

middle of the 1950s for West Germany (and through 1989, in some ways, for the East Germany) favored a continuation of such habits of thought. It is important to remember in this regard that despite the rhetoric or Erhard and many others, West Germany, even while working its *Wirtschaftswunder,* its economic miracle, continued to face foreign-exchange restrictions at home and considerable difficulties in international markets through the mid-1950s.

Conditions had changed markedly by the middle of the 1950s, and Fischer-Tropsch plants, like other coal-chemical producers, faced the hard reality that petrochemicals were by then both better and less expensive than their own products. That led to the closing of all the Fischer-Tropsch facilities except Bergkamen. As we have seen in this case, niche competition was still possible for coal-based chemicals even in the late 1950s and early 1960s. Bayer, a private firm, was even willing to subsidize Bergkamen's production of kogasin II until a petrochemical substitute of suitable quality and price could be found. Admittedly, that private subsidy had to be matched by a public one; Bergkamen's Fischer-Tropsch production could not have survived until 1962 without the extension of the coal preference. The fact that West German bureaucrats, although loath to subsidize German producers directly, were willing to work out indirect means (such as the indirect-subsidy plan that would have substituted for the coal preference during a transitional period until 1964) demonstrated the tendency among Germans since the last third of the nineteenth century to think in terms of excellence in technology, while at the same time being slow and deliberate about its implementation.

In the end, subsidies from Bayer and the German state enabled Bergkamen to make the transition from a coal-based chemical producer to a full-fledged participant in the new, petroleum-based chemical economy. This chapter has demonstrated, however, that the transition from coal-based chemistry to petroleum-based chemistry was neither inevitable nor as rapid as one might have thought, despite the eventual triumph of petrochemicals.

Part IV
Consolidating the new regime, 1957–1961

10
Petrochemicals triumphant, 1957–1961

The increasing economic disparity between the two German states that were created in the aftermath of World War II precipitated a severe political crisis in the late 1950s and early 1960s. One result of the widening gulf between them was a population hemorrhage from East to West, especially through Berlin, where the border remained open through the early 1960s. Those defections constituted a staggering blow to the German Democratic Republic (East Germany), which lost 2.5 million citizens, permanently, to the Federal Republic between 1949 and 1961. Nearly half of the émigrés were twenty-five years of age or younger.[1] Important segments of the refugee flood had been well educated – many of them professionals. East Gemany was losing many of its most productive and creative people.

Naturally the East German government tried to stem the flow. In December 1957, a new law made "flight from the Republic" (*Republikflucht*) a criminal offense. In November of the following year, the Soviets agreed to help their Warsaw Pact ally resolve the crisis by issuing an ultimatum to the Western Allies

---

[1] Dietrich Orlow, *A History of Modern Germany, 1870 to Present* (Engelwood Cliffs, NJ: Prentice-Hall, 1987), p. 319.

that the status of West Berlin had to be clarified within six months. The climax of the growing tension came on 13 August 1961, shortly after midnight, when the East Germans began construction of the Berlin Wall. The fluid, unstable, and potentially extremely dangerous political-economic situation that had existed in the German Democratic Republic stabilized to a substantial degree following the erection of the Wall, at least until the regime's collapse in 1989–90.

During those same years, 1957 through 1961, the German chemical industry experienced a critical period during which a fluid, unstable technological-economic situation resolved itself. The changes occurring in chemical technology and feedstocks, of course, involved none of the danger and little of the spectacle of the second Berlin crisis. Nevertheless, it was no mere coincidence that the political crisis and the critical period of the chemical industry occurred practically simultaneously: The technological and economic developments in the chemical industry both mirrored and reinforced the unstable political situation at the end of the 1950s, its resolution in 1961, and the consolidation of the newly reinforced fact of the division of Germany (literally set in concrete) in the years that followed.

By the end of 1961, West Germany's chemical industry had committed fully to petrochemical technology, which also meant commitment to the Western world's economic order, dominated by the United States. For the first time, the industry was dependent on overseas countries, not only for markets but also for raw materials. By the end of 1961, East Germany's chemical industry had just as clearly committed itself to integration into the Soviet sphere. Although its leaders were acutely aware of its need to move more fully into petrochemical production, they also continued to think in terms of domestic self-sufficiency in raw materials, to a much greater degree than in the West. As a result of that and other factors, the changeover to petrochemical technology occurred much less rapidly than in the West, and the distance between the two increased over time. This chapter outlines some of the dimensions of the transformation of the West German chemical industry in the late 1950s and early 1960s.

The triumph of petrochemicals

Despite the significant developments in petrochemical technology achieved by major German chemical firms during the mid-1950s, as outlined in the preceding chapters, coal remained the premier – and even preferred – raw material for producing chemical feedstocks into the early 1960s. In 1957 the West German chemical industry still was producing less than one-fourth of its organic chemicals from petroleum or natural gas (Table 10.1). In other words, in that regard West Germany in 1957 was about where the United States had been in the early 1950s. West German firms still used coal to produce about half their ethylene feedstocks, and in two other areas of aliphatic chemistry, production of carbon monoxide and acetylene, they used coal for making about two-thirds of feed-

Table 10.1. *Feedstocks used in producing organic chemicals in West Germany, 1957–63*

Year	Total input (1,000 tons carbon)	Percentage from petroleum or natural gas	Percentage from coal
1957	666	24	76
1958	820	29	71
1959	1,034	40	60
1960	1,300	44	56
1961	1,425	50	50
1962	1,640	57	43
1963	1,803	63	37

Source: Verband der Chemischen Industrie, *Chemiewirtschaft in Zahlen*, 6th ed. (Düsseldorf: Econ, 1964), p. 83.

stocks. Aromatic production (i.e., manufacture of chemicals that include benzene rings) through the early 1960s came almost exclusively from coal-based raw materials.[2]

During the next few years, however, that situation changed dramatically. The percentage of organic chemicals produced from petroleum or natural gas rose to 40 percent in 1959, to 50 percent in 1961, and to 63 percent in 1963. The feedstock and technological transformations in the industry continued during the 1960s and 1970s. By 1980, about 95 percent of all organic chemicals in Western Europe as a whole were produced from petroleum or natural gas, with the percentage in the Federal Republic of Germany approximately on a par with that for Europe as a whole. If one

takes into consideration in addition, that more than 80 percent of the production of chemical products (measured by turnover) come from the organic chemical sector, it works out that at least three-fourths of the raw materials used in production of chemicals comes from petroleum; refinery and liquid gas are, in terms of quantities, hardly of any importance, and natural gas is used primarily in manufacture of ammonia.[3]

The performances of individual firms, of course, varied during that period of rapid transition, and it will be useful to survey briefly the developments at each of the major companies discussed in earlier chapters.

[2] Verband der Chemischen Industrie (VCI), *Chemiewirtshaft in Zahlen*, 6th ed. (Düsseldorf: Econ, 1964), p. 83; VCI, "Petrochemie," n.d. (late 1960), p.3 (one of a series of monographs prepared by the VCI and sent to the CEFIC (European Center of Federations of Industrial Chemistry, in a letter dated 31 January 1961), Bayerwerksarchiv, Leverkusen, 271/1.1.52.15.

[3] VCI, *Chemiewirtschaft in Zahlen*, p. 83; Wolf Rüdiger Streck, *Chemische Industrie, Strukturwandlungen und Entwicklungsperspektiven* (Berlin: Duncker & Humblot, 1984), p. 115; quotation from Streck.

BASF

BASF illustrated most clearly the tendency of West German chemical firms in the early 1950s to hedge their bets in their approach to the new petrochemical technology. Thus, in 1953, just as the firm announced in its annual corporate report the founding of the country's first plant dedicated exclusively to using petrochemical feedstocks, the Rheinische Olefinwerke GmbH (ROW), it reported in a separate official publication on the development of an improved technology for making acetylene from coal. The new "oxygen-thermal" (Sachsse) process, BASF proclaimed, would demonstrate "considerable progress" over earlier processes because it would rely on coke burned in the presence of oxygen to produce the heat needed for the reaction, rather than relying on much more expensive electricity. The new process would have the added advantage of producing carbon monoxide as a by-product, which BASF could also use.[4] In keeping with the fact that the company was still excited about the prospects for coal-based acetylene technology, even as it entered the petrochemical age, BASF displayed caution in founding ROW, preferring to enter into a cooperative agreement with Deutsche Shell A.G. to build the new plant, rather than taking the additional risk of going it alone.

As the 1950s went on, it became obvious that there were good reasons to cease reliance on domestic coal. Coal and coke prices rose steadily throughout the decade (especially in 1953, 1956, and 1957[5]), and even though BASF owned its own coal mines at the Gewerkschaft Auguste Victoria in the Ruhr district, the company was forced to pay the same official price for coal and coke that others paid. The only advantage to owning Auguste Victoria, then, was relative security of supply. Petroleum and natural gas became, in contrast, more attractive relative to coal.

An additional reason for making the move away from coal was the inability of Auguste Victoria to meet all of BASF's growing needs for organic raw materials, as noted in its 1956 annual report. BASF substituted heating oil to take up the slack until the Suez Crisis, when heating-oil shortages and price increases made it necessary to turn instead to U.S. coal. The report went on to note that the company hoped to improve that situation by hastening the sinking of a new pit at Auguste Victoria.[6]

At the same time that coal was becoming increasingly problematic as a raw material for the organic chemical industry, BASF experienced completely unexpected growth in the area of petroleum-based chemistry. ROW's original capacity for Lupolen (BASF's trade name for polyethylene) production was 7,500 tons per year. By 1956, because of process improvements during the construction pe-

---

[4] BASF announced the founding of ROW in *Bericht über das Geschäftsjahr 1953*, p. 13; BASF, *Bericht über die Neugründung 1953–1953*, p. 33, reported on the new technology for producing acetylene.

[5] BASF, *Bericht über das Geschäftsjahr 1953*, p. 9; BASF, *Bericht über das Geschäftsjahr 1956*, p. 11; BASF, *Bericht über das Geschäftsjahr 1957*, p. 17.

[6] BASF, *Bericht über das Geschäftsjahr 1956, p. 11.*

riod, its capacity had increased to 10,000 tons. Still, even though ROW restricted itself to the West German domestic market, the demand continued to outstrip its production capacity. Therefore, BASF and Shell decided in 1956 to expand ROW's capacity to 35,000 tons per year.[7] In 1957, BASF reported that production of polymerization products (including those produced at the parent company and at ROW) was up 31 percent over the previous year,[8] and in 1959 the company reported developing a series of new processes to produce the feedstocks necessary to manufacture those polymerization products for crude oil.[9] By 1961, the year that West Germany passed the halfway mark in its transition toward petroleum-based chemistry, the corporation proudly proclaimed that

ROW, with a total capacity of more than 125,000 tons of Lupolen per year, has secured its position in the ranks of the greatest producers of polyethylene in the world.

A third installation for the production of ethylene was built and brought into use in 1961 for supply of the Lupolen factor. It has a capacity of about 80,000 tons of ethylene per year and is thus the largest facility of this type in the Federal Republic. Total capacity for production of ethylene was brought to nearly 150,000 tons per year through this development.[10]

All of that new production was based on petroleum.

Nonetheless, even as BASF proceeded to develop its petroleum-based chemistry, the company remained active in more traditional areas, demonstrating once again how gradual was the technological transition of the German chemical industry. Acetylene-based "Reppe" chemistry, for instance, continued to play an important role in the company's production program through the mid-1960s. In that, the Germans were not alone: When BASF and Dow decided in 1958 to create the Dow Badische Chemical Company in Freeport, Texas, the new company – which began producing in 1959 using acetylene produced from natural gas – manufactured "acrylic acids and their derivatives" using the Reppe process. As the BASF annual report for 1959 indicated, even the market in the United States was still interested in at least that area of acetylene chemistry: "These products, which have been used for decades by BASF among others for its plastics dispersions, are also gaining in significance on the U.S. market."[11]

Of course, even though BASF used acetylene chemistry to good effect, even in the United States, the preferred feedstock had changed from coal to natural gas. Still, even as late as 1961, the company chose technologies that would allow the maximum flexibility in the choice of raw materials. As its report noted; "our synthesis gas production, which in the course of the past several years was rebuilt from the ground up, allows us within broad limits to utilize solid or liquid fuels interchangeably and to adapt the production branches which depend on that synthesis gas elastically to current market relationships."[12]

[7] Ibid., p. 33.   [8] BASF, *Bericht über das Geschäftsjahr 1957*, p. 15.
[9] BASF, *Bericht über das Geschäftsjahr 1959*, p. 17.
[10] BASF, *Bericht über das Geschäftsjahr 1961*, p. 28.
[11] BASF, *Bericht über das Geschäftsjahr 1959*, p. 35.
[12] BASF, *Bericht über das Geschäftsjahr 1961*, p. 17.

Just two years later, in 1963, the choices had narrowed, and BASF ceased referring to "solid hydrocarbons" at all in regard to the production of synthesis gas and other chemical starting materials. Instead, the company informed its shareholders about "synthesis gas produced on a petrochemical basis for the manufacture of ammonia and methanol," along with ethylene and acetylene produced from petroleum. Still, even at that late date the company touted the virtues of *flexibility* – and thus *independence* – in the technologies it developed:

> To obtain these basic petrochemical materials [synthesis gas, ethylene, and acetylene], we have developed especially economical processes which, on the one hand proceed from refinery products, on the other hand proceed from crude oil itself or from natural gas; thus we can adapt ourselves flexibly to changes in the raw materials situation. Our processes found great attention at the Sixth World Oil Congress in 1963 in Frankfurt am Main.[13]

Bayer

Lacking BASF's long tradition in producing organic chemical raw materials and plastics, Farbenfabriken Bayer A.G. was even slower than BASF to move into petrochemical production. Bayer's managers had already considered such a move in the early 1950s, when they had begun research-and-development work in petrochemicals and, at the same time, had opened negotiations with Esso to cooperate in the field, though ultimately those negotiations were inconclusive. But their first public mention of petrochemicals was in Bayer's corporate report for 1956, when the company noted with pleasure "the successful conclusion of our experiments on further development of the Lurgi-Ruhrgas petroleum cracking process to the level of technical-scale maturity."[14] Bayer also moved later than did BASF in finding and coming to terms with a partner; its deal with BP to establish Erdölchemie GmbH was announced publicly only in 1957 (serious negotiations had begun in 1956).[15]

There were other differences between the two cases as well. Unlike BASF, Bayer did not go in for manufacturing polyethylene, preferring instead to develop more specialized plastics lines. Lacking a Walter Reppe, acetylene chemistry was far less important for Bayer than for its counterpart to the south. Pharmaceuticals, synthetic rubber, pesticides, and herbicides – distributed by a justifiably well regarded sales force with a distinguished tradition – continued to be vital to Bayer's corporate culture, whereas BASF's success rested on heavy chemicals and its world-renowned research-and-development initiatives.

Still, there were extensive and important similarities between the two firms. Like BASF, Bayer decided to use a cooperative agreement with a major oil company as a point of departure into the petrochemical industry, rather than going alone, thus minimizing its risk, but also undoubtedly limiting its prof-

---

[13] BASF, *Bericht über das Geschäftsjahr 1963*, p. 20.
[14] Bayer A.G., *Geschäftsbericht für das Jahr 1956*, pp.12–13.
[15] Bayer, *Geschäftsbericht für das Jahr 1957*, p. 15; see also Chapter 6.

its. Moreover, it is remarkable that Bayer, in announcing its "further development of the Lurgi-Ruhrgas petroleum cracking process" in 1956, described it in much the same terms as did BASF. The corporate report stated with pride that "this especially *flexible* process . . . produces gaseous olefins and diolefins from crude oil or one's choice of heavy or light petroleum fractions."[16] Petroleum-based chemistry clearly was going to be the basis for the process, but Bayer, like BASF, was not going to be captive to a single type of feedstock to operate it.

The late 1950s were characterized at Bayer, just as at BASF, by everincreasing allegiance to petroleum-based processes. In 1958, for example, the company announced extensive improvements and capacity expansion in it isocyanate area:

For foams, new developments of "Desmophen" types on the basis of polyethers stood at the forefront. . . .

These new "Desmophen" types, which are manufactured from cracked olefins from Erdölchemie GmbH, are especially well suited for the manufacture of "Moltopren" soft foams and are about to be introduced into the market. Hard "Vulkollan" types that are resistant to saponification and cold and which are manufactured on a new and economically promising basis, are hard and at the same time highly elastic materials which open promising vistas in the dampening of vibrations, in applications as bearings, etc. New light-true glues and "Desmodur" applications were discovered, which in connection with new saponification-resistant "Desmophen" lines allow us to expect a big business in the paint and coatings sector.[17]

In expanding and improving that and other areas of its production palette, Bayer relied heavily on Erdölchemie, which contributed "the overwhelming proportion of its production . . . to us for further processing. . . . It [Erdölchemie] thus places our supply of raw materials and intermediates for our steadily growing production of organic products on a secure footing."[18] Increasing use of petrochemical feedstocks at Bayer led to substantial expansion in Erdölchemie's capacity in the early 1960s. At the subsidiary early in 1960, "a second cracking facility – a tube cracking facility – was brought on line, so that now 265,000 tons per year of raw gasoline could be processed into olefins." In addition, new refinery capacity in the form of a BP refinery in Dinlaken, which began production in the middle of 1960, meant that Erdölchemie could be supplied with petroleum products domestically, which "had . . . with this wiped out previous imports for the most part."[19]

By the following year, 1961, the Bayer/BP subsidiary undertook "a generous expansion of existing production lines and a construction of new ones, which taken together may be summarized as Expansion Phase II. . . . After these installations are finished, Erdölchemie will be able to crack up to 700,000 tons of

---

[16] Bayer, *Geschäftsbericht für das Jahr 1956*, pp. 12–13, my emphasis.
[17] Bayer, *Geschäftsbericht für das Jahr 1958*, p. 17.
[18] Bayer, *Geschäftsbericht für das Jahr 1959*, p. 22.
[19] Bayer, *Geschäftsbericht für das Jahr 1960*, p. 23.

raw gasoline per year and to further process the resulting olefins."[20] In other words, their plans were to expand feedstock production capacity by more than 2.5-fold. That would involve, among other things, expansion of the propylene oxide and ethanol production facilities and the erection of a third "raw-gasoline cracking facility, which among other things, should produce 70,000 tons each of ethylene and propylene per year." Bayer's own process would be the basis for construction of a new acrylonitrile facility.[21]

Most of those plans for improvements and expansion of capacity had been carried out by 1963, although the explosive growth in demand for petrochemicals still meant that "all installations were for the most part used to capacity." An acrylonitrile facility was expected to start production at the beginning of 1965. In addition, in another blow to coal-based chemistry, Erdölchemie completed a plant for producing aromatics (benzene and toluene) at the end of 1963 and began producing there at the beginning of 1964.[22]

Hoechst

Like BASF's managers, the leaders of the Hoechst corporation recognized soon after the war the importance of petroleum-based chemistry and made research and development in that area one of the company's priorities. They also chose, along with their counterparts to the south in Ludwigshafen, and in contrast to their colleagues to the north in Leverkusen, to move into polyethylene production in the early 1950s.[23] Unlike either of the other two members of the West German Big Three, however, Hoechst decided to go it alone, developing its own crude-oil cracking process and, by the beginning of the 1960s, its high-temperature pyrolysis (HTP) process for producing ethylene and acetylene feedstocks.

Nonetheless, the common thread in the stories of the Big Three in their transitions from coal-based chemistry to petroleum-based chemistry in the 1950s was their gradual and piecemeal adoption of new processes (and giving up old ones). For instance, whereas Hoechst emphasized in its corporate reports for 1954 and 1955 the need to diversify its raw-materials base owing to the increasing cost of coal and the inability of coal-based processes to supply the firm's growing needs,[24] its 1956 report noted the installation of new carbide ovens at Hoechst's Knapsack facility to produce acetylene from coal.[25]

Hoechst's development of the HTP process (construction of the plant began in 1958; and it was completed in 1960) may be seen as an interim step in the move

[20] Bayer, *Geschäftsbericht für das Jahr 1961*, p. 27.

[21] Bayer, *Geschäftsbericht für das Jahr 1962*, pp. 44–45.

[22] Bayer, *Geschäftsbericht für das Jahr 1963*, p. 36.

[23] Farbwerke Hoechst A.G., *Geschäftsbericht 1952*, p. 7; Farbwerke Hoechst A.G., *Geschäftsbericht 1953*, p. 7.

[24] Farbwerke Hoechst A.G., *Geschäftsbericht 1954*, p. 8; Farbwerke Hoechst A.G., *Geschäftsbericht 1955*, p. 12.

[25] Farbwerke Hoechst A.G., *Geschäftsbericht 1956*, p. 9.

away from traditional German organic chemistry. The process yielded both ethylene and acetylene from crude oil.[26] Thus the firm could retain, as did BASF, its attachment to acetylene-based chemical processes while at the same time choosing a new, less expensive raw material for producing the required acetylene. Peter Spitz points out, however, that Hoechst's long-standing allegiance to acetylene chemistry, and thus to the HTP process, could not withstand the challenge posed by ethylene-based petrochemicals:

In any event, the economics of the Hoechst HTP process and of other ethylene and ethylene/acetylene production techniques were never as good as those achieved in conventional steam crackers, except in special situations, such as at Hoechst, which required large amounts of acetylene. . . . [T]he superior economics of ethylene – versus acetylene-based processes – for making vinyl chloride spelled the end of hydrocarbon cracking processes designed to produce mixtures of the two reactive hydrocarbons. Eventually, even Hoechst decided to discontinue manufacture of both building blocks and switched to ethylene as a feedstock, investing in the petrochemical refinery of Union Rheinische Kraftstoff AG, which henceforth supplied ethylene to Hoechst's downstream operation.[27]

However, it was well into the 1960s before Hoechst – and BASF – fully realized the "superior economics" of ethylene-based processes and made the switch away from traditional acetylene chemistry. That was not because the leaders of Hoechst were slow-witted. Instead, the best explanation for their behavior probably is that the idea of "superior economics" is based on an anachronism: Because the economics of ethylene-based processes became "superior" only when the processes were applied on a very large scale, it is implicitly assumed that decision-makers in the chemical and petroleum industries knew in advance that there would be enormous growth in the demand for comsumption of modern thermoplastics. In fact, few had any notion of how massive the expansion in that part of the industry would be during the 1950s and 1960s.

In any case, by the early 1960s the increased scale of Hoechst's own petrochemical production necessitated a change in strategy. Instead of producing its own feedstocks through the HTP and other processes, the firm turned to the outside for the first time. Spitz mentions the agreement with Union Kraftstoff, which was signed in 1961. In addition, in the same year, Hoechst signed a supply agreement with Caltex Oil (Germany) GmbH. Caltex agreed to build a refinery for producing petrochemical feedstocks at Kelsterbach, very close to the Hoechst plant, which would begin operations in 1963.[28] As the firm announced in its 1963 corporate report, "with these two supply sources, the future supply of olefins at economic prices is placed on a secure footing in the long term."[29]

[26] Farbwerke Hoechst A.G., *Geschäftsbericht 1958*, p. 12; Farbwerke Hoechst A.G., *Geschäftsbericht 1959*, p. 16; Farbwerke Hoechst A.G., *Geschäftsbericht 1960*, p. 13.

[27] Peter Spitz, *Petrochemicals: The Rise of an Industry* (New York: Wiley, 1988), p. 443.

[28] Farbwerke Hoechst A.G., *Geschäftsbericht 1961*, pp. 18–19; Farbwerke Hoechst A.G., *Geschäftsbericht 1962*, p. 20.

[29] Farbwerke Hoechst A.G., *Geschäftsbericht 1963*, p. 21.

Hüls

With polymers as its main product line, Chemische Werke Hüls had to monitor changes in raw materials and technology in the organic chemical industry during the 1950s much more closely than did firms with more diverse product lines. For Hüls, as for other major chemical factories, coal-based feedstocks remained key starting materials past the middle of the decade, although the company began to use liquid gas and gaseous hydrocarbons from refineries in 1954 and 1955.[30]

Like BASF and Hoechst, Hüls remained active in acetylene chemistry well into the 1960s, but as early as 1956 the firm's research-and-development efforts were concentrating on the problem of "whether and if the intermediate products of the factory, which until now have been manufactured on the basis of acetylene, could be produced on an olefin basis (petrochemistry)."[31]

Petroleum-based feedstocks were not the only ones the firm considered, however. As the Hüls annual report for 1956 noted,

work on the manufacture of acetylene and ethylene from hydrocarbons – including also crude oil – under application of thermal as well as electrical process was pursued further at the laboratory scale. At the technical scale, work on the manufacture of acetylene and ethylene by thermal cracking of gas liquids in hot incineration gases was taken up.[32]

Once again, an emphasis on flexibility in raw-materials supply characterized the management's thinking.

Already in 1957 the company had curtailed acetylene-based production of butadiene, although that had less to do with payoffs from Hüls's research program than with technological developments abroad. Petrochemical facilities in Great Britain and Italy were producing butadiene in sufficient quantities and at prices low enough that Hüls's management decided to import much of what it needed. In the process, some of the firm's acetylene capacity was freed up, and that was used as a feedstock for production of solvents.[33]

By the early 1960s, Hüls, like most other major organic chemical firms in West Germany, was using petroleum-based feedstocks for the bulk of its production. The firm continued to stress flexibility in its supply of raw materials, although the range had narrowed. At the end of 1962, when oil refineries in West Germany had to cut back production owing to difficulties in water transport, Hüls reported a change in its basic raw materials for feedstock production, but coal was not a factor. Instead, "the fallback position [from crude oil] was thus to use natural gas and raw gasoline to a greater extent."[34]

Concluding remarks

All in all, then, the large organic chemical producers in West Germany had made a major commitment to petrochemicals by the early 1960s. And although

---

[30] Chemische Werke Hüls A.G., *Bericht über das Geschäftsjahr 1954*, p. 17; Chemische Werke Hüls A.G., *Bericht über das Geschäfsjahr 1955*, p. 10.

[31] Chemische Werke Hüls A.G., *Bericht über das Geschäftsjahr 1956*, p. 18.

[32] Ibid.   [33] Chemische Werke Hüls A.G., *Bericht über das Geschäftsjahr 1957*, p. 12.

[34] Chemische Werke Hüls A.G., *Geschäftsbericht 1962*, p. 10.

the major West German firms embraced the new feedstocks and their associated technologies only gradually and in quite different ways, in the last years of the 1950s and during the early 1960s, petrochemicals clearly were displacing traditional coal chemistry. The technological changes mirrored and reinforced the new political and economic positions of the Germanies. Each German successor state had settled firmly into the orbit of a dominant superpower. For West Germans, that entailed full acceptance of petroleum as their primary source of energy and, in the case of organic chemicals, of raw materials. That also meant learning to accept their dependence on overseas sources for a substance vital to the survival of the country, and that required major shifts in traditional practices, not just in politics and business, but also in ingrained cultural attitudes. For the East Germans, their existence in the Soviet sphere involved reinforcement – and, to some extend, realignment – of the traditional ideology and practice of self-sufficiency, which necessitated increased allegiance to traditional coal-based organic chemistry. On the other hand, their needs for foreign exchange, for maximum output of plastics, and for Western recognition of the country's technological accomplishments combined to push the East German chemical industry toward petrochemicals.[35] In each of the German successor states, then, the pace of technological change was determined not by some ineluctable logic internal to the process of "technological development," but rather by a host of interwoven technological, ecomonic, political, social, and cultural factors.

[35] I explored the East German case in "A Peculiar Synthesis: Organic Chemicals and State Policy in East Germany," (presented at a meeting of the German Studies Association, Minneapolis, MN, 3 October 1992).

11
Conclusion

Between 1945 and 1961, West German chemical producers dramatically increased their reliance on oil. At the beginning of that period, coal was the basis for almost all organic chemical production. By 1961, over half of it came from petroleum-based feedstocks. That trend continued during the following decade, until by the early 1980s virtually all organic chemical products were made from petroleum or natural gas. Full participation by West German firms in the technological transformation of the international chemical industry was a key factor in West Germany's remarkable economic success from the 1950s to the present.

One might imagine that the change from coal-based to petroleum-based chemical production was inevitable. Petroleum and its derivatives were, after all, far less expensive than coal and its products; petrochemicals also allowed economies of scale in the production of chemicals far beyond those offered by coal-based chemistry. On the basis of those facts, one might argue that it was inevitable that in the long run the less expensive feedstock and the superior technology would prevail in West Germany just as they had in the organic chemical industry around the world.

But to accept that intuitively plausible explanation would be unfortunate, for at least two reasons. First, that explanation would convey a false impression of the course of technological change in the West German chemical industry during the postwar period. More important, it would obscure an understanding of the gradual transition in cultural attitudes among West German businessmen, bureaucrats, and politicians that took place between 1945 and 1961.

In what manner did all those technological changes occur in the West German chemical industry between 1945 and 1961? On the basis of the evidence presented in this study, one would have to answer gradually, not along any predictable path, and without much uniformity. Individual companies moved slowly into the new petrochemical technologies only after carefully considering their own particular interests.

From the point of view of the principals in the industry in the early and middle 1950s, the ultimate triumph of petrochemicals was far from evident, nor was it at all clear that a single feedstock, whether coal, alcohol, natural gas, or petroleum, would displace all the others entirely (or almost entirely). During that early phase, alternative technologies at times co-existed and at times competed with one another. Over time, the cumulative effects of large numbers of decisions both within and outside the industry combined to tip the scales in favor of petrochemicals. Those effects included, among other things, a relatively free flow of startlingly inexpensive petroleum around the world, which the United States, in particular, had gone to great lengths to ensure,[1] increasing motorization of the German economy; the spiraling costs of coal and coke in the 1950s; unprecedented breakthroughs in petrochemical research that allowed, for instance, the manufacture of petroleum-based aromatics. Over time, more and more companies adopted petrochemical processes for increasing numbers of their products. By the late 1950s, that amounted to a bandwagon effect, a self-reinforcing cycle in which petrochemical feedstocks and technology dominated not because they were necessarily "better" technologically or otherwise but rather because more and more companies pursued research in the field, built plants, and thus affected both the technological effectiveness and the relative costs of petrochemicals.[2]

Not only was technological change in the industry gradual and unpredictable, but also it varied enormously from one company to another. Some companies, especially smaller ones like Bergkamen, relied on traditional coal-based technology far longer than did others (especially compared with the cooperative companies set up by BASF/Shell and Bayer/BP). Even the major companies went about the process of changing technologies and of deciding on the proper mix of new and old feedstocks and technologies in widely differing ways. BASF, for instance, started earlier than the others; Hoechst differed from the other

---

[1] See, for instance, Daniel Yergin, *The Prize: the Epic Quest for Oil, Money, and Power* (New York: Simon & Schuster, 1991).

[2] On the self-reinforcing cycles that tend to separate competing technologies from one another, see W. Brian Arthur, "Positive Feedbacks in the Economy," *Scientific American* (February 1990):92–9; and Arthur, "Competing technologies, increasing returns, and lock-in by historical events," *The Economic Journal* 99(1989):116–31. This idea is closely related to that of "technological momentum," a concept pioneered by Thomas Hughes. See, for example, Hughes, *Networks of Power* (Baltimore: Johns Hopkins University Press, 1983), pp. 140–74.

members of the Big Three by going it alone; Hüls relied, to a much greater extent than the others, on advice and assistance from the West German state. Even when companies embraced petrochemical feedstocks, often there was a lag in adopting "modern" petrochemical technologies. BASF and Hoechst, among others, hedged their bets with acetylene technology, which could use either coal, petroleum, or natural gas, well into the 1960s. Even in the early 1960s, when petrochemical production was increasingly the order of the day for all major West German chemical firms, they chose technologies that would allow maximum flexibility (and thus independence) in the choice of starting materials. The move during the 1950s from coal-based to petroleum-based chemical technology in West Germany was both slower and less wholehearted than one might have expected.

Technology is more than just machines and the means of deploying them; it is also both an expression of and a means of implementing cultural values. This examination of developments in the German organic chemical industry in the 1950s and 1960s thus allows insight not only into how technological change occurred but also into how and when shifts in cultural attitudes occurred among business leaders and politicians in West Germany.

In his book *The Americanisation of West German Industry,* Volker Berghahn identifies the elements of a German model of capitalist organization, including an authoritarian approach to the labor movement, cartelization of domestic industry, and thinking in terms of relatively isolated economic blocs in international economic relations. Berghahn contrasts the German model with the American model of capitalist organization, which emphasizes more egalitarian industrial relations, trust-busting, and thinking in terms of free trade. During the postwar period in West Germany, Berghahn argues, the American model slowly displaced the German one. The transition occurred slowly because of the gradual nature of generational change: Industrial and political leaders in the immediate postwar period were, by and large, firm adherents to the German model, having come of age professionally in the 1920s and, more significantly, in the 1930s; as that generation retired from positions of power in the 1960s and early 1970s, a new generation took over, one that was schooled in and committed to the American model of capitalist organization.[3]

Berghahn's book focuses, for the most part, on the experiences of the heavy industries. The evidence presented in this study of the chemical industry for the period from 1945 through 1961 suggests some refinements to Berghahn's conceptions by contending that even at the end of the period covered (that is, as the generational change was taking place), West Germany was never completely "Americanised," because postwar German approaches to technological change shared key characteristics with those of the period before 1945.[4]

---

[3] Volker Berghahn, *The Americanisation of West German Industry, 1945–1973* (Cambridge University Press, 1986), esp. pp. 3–39.

[4] For more on this argument, see Chapter 4 and Raymond G. Stokes, "Technology and the West German *Wirtschaftswunder,*" *Technology and Culture* 32(1991):1–22.

The chemical industrialists had been some of the most liberal – in economic terms as well as political terms – industrialists in pre-1945 Germany.[5] Always heavily dependent on export markets for their commercial viability, representatives of major German chemical firms had championed free trade to a much greater degree than had their counterparts in other industries. Although they, like leaders in the other industrial sectors, saw the virtues of cartelization, they were unusual among pre-1945 German industrialists in their views on labor relations; even in the 1920s they were much less paternalistic and much more "Americanised" than were leaders in other industries.

Yet even in the organic chemical industry, which quite early had clearly identified itself with many aspects of what Berghahn calls the "American model" of capitalist organization, and which continued to stress the value of foreign trade even in the National Socialist period, the tendency to think in terms of autarky remained pronounced well after 1945. As outlined in Chapter 1, embracing a particular foreign-trade policy (i.e., only such foreign trade as is absolutely necessary) is but one component of autarky. The other components are raw-materials policy and manufacturing policy. In both of those areas, the German organic chemical industry from its beginnings emphasized the importance of the security of a domestic supply of raw materials and tended to favor manufacturing at home to the maximum extent possible. Of course, the "security of a domestic supply of raw materials" meant guaranteed coal supplies, and it is vital to note that during the 1920s and 1930s, chemical firms (and especially I.G. Farben) sought to remain independent of the industrialists who controlled heavy industry by purchasing their own coal mines.

After World War II, and well into the 1950s, the argument that the best sources of raw materials were at home continued to hold sway in West Germany. Because the most important raw material in Germany was coal, the perseverance of that argument affected technological decision-making during the 1950s to a considerable degree, as mainifested not only in the continuing policy of fostering coal-based production technologies but also in the tendency to choose technologies that would permit maximum *flexibility* in feedstock input, so as to preserve at least a semblance of domestic security of supply: If foreign sources of oil dried up, it would be possible to substitute German coal as a starting material for at least some of the production.

In retrospect, then, at least through the mid-1950s, the firms in the German chemical industry did not see petrochemical technology or olefin-based chemistry as fundamentally new. Instead, in those early years, petrochemistry was, for them, a slightly different version of the more familiar acetylene chemistry and coal-based technologies. In a way, they completely missed the point in those early days, for petrochemicals represented a radical departure from coal-based chemistry in at least three ways. First there was a difference in the scale at which production would be optimal, with petrochemical plants being much larger than coal-based plants. Second, the massive scale of the petrochemical facilites re-

---

[5] Peter Hayes, "Carl Bosch and Carl Krauch: Chemistry and the Political Economy of Germany, 1925–1945, "*Journal of Economic History* 47(1987):353–63.

quired new methods of handling materials and a new approach to design, so as to ensure smooth flows of materials through the lengthy production process. Finally, and again to optimize the benefits of the new technology, German designers – who had been trained primarily as chemists – had to abandon their traditional regard for "elegance," that is, for indirect processes with high yields that could be well described theoretically, and instead learn to concentrate on the most direct path to the final product, regardless of how messy, theoretically obscure, or low in yield, relying on recycling part of the reactant to increase yields.[6]

Acetylene-based chemical technologies and companies' emphasis on flexibility in "petrochemical" technologies, however, seemed to represent reasonable compromises for the Germans, because they could use their past experience to try to anticipate a very uncertain future. By the late 1950s and early 1960s, all that had changed. In the cases of BASF and Bayer, their partners in the oil industry provided part of the impetus to begin thinking in terms of heavy reliance on foreign sources of supply, large-scale plants, and abandonment of the traditional notions of elegance. More important, those firms and others in the industry turned increasingly to large-scale petrochemical production facilities in the face of unprecedented and unrelenting demand for new products, rising coal and coke prices, and the inability of coal and coke producers to meet the growing needs of the organic chemical industry.

In sum, the development of West Germany's petrochemical industry in the 1950s and early 1960s reflected a more general German technological tradition that emphasized technological excellence, while at the same time stressing cautious and gradual implementation of new technologies. Far from delaying West German economic success, continuity in that tradition helped bring about and maintain the country's *Wirtschaftswunder,* its economic miracle.[7] What was crucial in the postwar development of the West German petrochemical industry was not the pace at which it adopted the new technology, but rather its willingness to re-evaluate choices repeatedly and critically in the face of a dynamic situation – and then, of course, to act decisively on the basis of those re-evaluations.

The gradual shift in West Germany after 1945 from its overwhelming reliance on coal to a primary reliance on petroleum products to manufacture organic chemicals – and, more broadly, the shift from the "bloc mentality" that stressed eco-

---

[6] A. Lawrence Waddams, *Chemicals from Petroleum: An Introductory Survey,* 3rd ed. (New York: Wiley, 1973), pp. 7–13. Waddams contends that this last problem of insisting on "elegant" reactions was not restricted to German chemical firms; that is one reason why oil companies and practices derived from the oil industry have done so well in petrochemicals.

[7] For more on this, see Stokes, "Technology and the West German *Wirtschaftwunder.*" This continuity in approach to technological change may be part of the reason that Rolf Dumke, in a recent econometric study, found that "reconstruction growth" accounted almost entirely for West Germany's postwar "economic miracle." See Dumke, "Reassessing the *Wirtschaftswunder:* Reconstruction and Postwar Growth in West Germany in an International Context," *Oxford Bulletin of Economics and Statistics* 52(1990):451–91.

nomic self-sufficiency to a mentality of embracing international trade and accepting the inevitable dependence on foreign sources of supply that that entailed – was both an effect and a cause of a power shift within German industry. German heavy industry had emerged from the war with severe problems;[8] but it remained by far the most powerful industrial sector, both economically and politically. Its power derived from three major sources. First, besides contributing heavily to the economy, it had been vital to Germany's military might. Second, it employed massive numbers of workers. Finally, and most important, it controlled Germany's most precious raw material: coal.

Soon after the end of the war in 1945, the basis for the great power of Germany's heavy industries had begun to be called into question in certain quarters. By the end of the 1950s, primarily as a result of the changed international context for German industry, the heavy industries, and especially coal, were on the decline. Their involvement in military-related production obviously had become of less importance, despite West German rearmament. The numbers of workers employed in heavy industry declined as new laborsaving techniques were introduced, as petroleum became West Germany's preferred energy source, and as plastics and other materials were substituted for steel in many applications. Although coal and steel remained vital to the West German economy, the power of the Ruhr industrialists had diminished considerably by the early 1960s.

Much of the dynamism of West German industry was instead to be found among industrialists outside the traditional Ruhr elite. One such group focused on manufacturing consumer goods to meet the demands in the rapidly growing West German economy.[9] Some chemical firms were included in that group, but most of them belonged to another, a group oriented heavily toward export. As this study documents, during most of the 1950s, West German chemical industrialists shared with their counterparts in the Ruhr the assumption that German coal would continue to be their primary raw material and energy source. Yet they eventually abandoned that view, for the most part, primarily because they were willing to accept the risks of becoming dependent on overseas sources of raw materials.

What accounted for that willingness? There were, of course, many reasons. That willingness did not derive from a desire among chemical industrialists to free themselves of the dominance of the heavy-industry elites, because, as mentioned earlier, the chemical industry often controlled its own coal supplies. Instead, the price of petroleum undoubtedly was a factor, as was – in the long term – the demonstrated commitment of the United States to maintaining both price and supply. Moves by competitors abroad to adopt petroleum feedstocks also influenced their decision-making. Still, one of the most important reasons that West German chemical industrialists eventually abandoned domestically

[8] See, for instance, Berghahn, *The Americanisation of West German Industry;* John Gillingham, *Coal, Steel, and the Rebirth of Europe, 1945–1955* (Cambridge University Press, 1991); Mark Roseman, *Recasting the Ruhr, 1945–1958* (New York: Berg, 1992).

[9] Alfred D. Chandler, Jr., *Scale and Scope: The Dynamics of Industrial Capitalism* (Cambridge, MA: Belknap Press of Harvard University Press, 1990), p. 609.

produced coal was that they could substitute other domestic resources that they controlled (at least in part) and still remain competitive internationally: Instead of relying on domestic sources of energy and raw materials, they relied primarily on the sophistication of their work force and of their research-and-development programs to compete in world markets.

Other research-intensive, export-oriented industries in West Germany (such as optics, machine tools, and electronics) did the same. Did industrialists in those industries, for which coal was much less directly vital than for chemicals, also continue to assume that secure domestic supplies of raw materials and domestic manufacturing were crucial criteria in making decisions on technological change? If so, how were they able to remain competitive in world markets? The extent to which such industries shared these and other aspects of the postwar experience of the West German chemical industry has yet to be studied fully. In addition, thorough studies of other countries will be important in assessing the similarities and differences between the West German experience and the experiences of others. Comparisons with developments in East Germany would be particularly useful.[10] Companies in East Germany, after all, often were descended from the same parent firms as those in West Germany, and they therefore shared a common corporate culture in the late 1940s. Yet West German firms were, by and large, far more successful than their East German counterparts. What accounted for that discrepancy? When and how did similar companies in the two countries begin to diverge? Did the rate of divergence depend on the peculiarities of the industry or on other factors? These questions deserve sustained scholarly attention. Moreover, the extent to which changes in technology and business culture in both East and West Germany affected and were affected by broader changes in society at large requires detailed examination.[11] Finally, the effect of Germany's explosive industrial development on the environment is a topic worthy of consideration. Some of the reasons for the importance of and the difficulties in such an undertaking are sketched out next.

In one of the more memorable episodes in crime fiction, in ''The adventure of Silver Blaze,'' Sherlock Holmes, having highlighted one clue in the case, was asked by Inspector Gregory if there were any additional points ''to which you would wish to draw my attention?'' Holmes replied: ''To the curious incident of

[10] For an astute analysis of the East German research-and-development system that contains some historical background, see Raymond Bentley, *Research and Technology in the Former German Democratic Republic* (Boulder, CO: Westview Press, 1992); I have explored the case of the East German chemical industry in ''A Peculiar Synthesis: Organic Chemicals and State Policy in East Germany'' (presented at a meeting of the German Studies Association, Minneapolis, MN, 3 October 1992). Unfortunately, access to the East German material came too late for inclusion in this study.

[11] A recent collection of essays sketches out some of the major themes in this regard. See Hartmut Kaelble, ed., *Der Boom 1945–1973. Gesellschaftliche und wirtschaftliche Folgen in der Bundesrepublik und in Europa* (Opladen: Westdeutscher Verlag, 1992) esp. pp. 6–32. In his introduction, the editor identifies the study of changes in production processes as important not only for their economic effects but also for their societal effects; see p. 15.

the dog in the night-time." "The dog did nothing in the night-time," Gregory countered. 'That was the curious incident,' remarked Sherlock Holmes."[12]

The curious incident in the case of the German organic chemical industry in the 1950s was the remarkable silence of politicians, industrialists, the public, and the press on the issue of the impact of the industry on the environment. Not only did the issue of renewable versus non-renewable resources never enter the debate between, say, alcohol and petroleum-based feedstocks at the Chemische Werke Hüls; but also any discussion of the effects of the massive increases in production of organic chemicals (which was made possible in large part by petroleum-based feedstocks) on German air and water supplies was muted, at best, and cropped up only relatively late in the time period under consideration.[13]

Upon starting intensive research on this subject in 1987, I expected that one of the important themes of this monograph would be gradually dawning environmental awareness. The limited evidence of any such awareness, compiled by searching corporate reports, industry trade publications, and a number of public and private archives, did not permit sustained exploration of environmental issues. After some consideration, I chose, with some minor exceptions in some chapters, to reflect rather than highlight that silence and to comment briefly on the problem in this conclusion. It is, however, clearly a topic worth pursuing, although just as clearly the sources used to research it will have to be different from those used in this study.

The relative silence on that problem during the 1950s, though, is not surprising. No industrial country involved itself too deeply in such concerns until the late 1960s and 1970s; West Germans, in the throes of reconstruction and of working their economic miracle, gave the problem correspondingly little attention in the 1950s and early 1960s. The first public glimmerings, in the late 1950s, of an awareness of the need for action to minimize or offset the environmental impacts of organic chemical production – however faint they were at first – reflected the end of one era and the beginning of another. Obviously there was increasing evidence of environmental damage owing to unbridled industrialization. Just as important, with the economy largely reconstructed, unemploy-

[12] Arthur Conan Doyle, "The Adventure of Silver Blaze," in *The Complete Memoirs and Adventures of Sherlock Holmes* (New York: Bramhall House, 1975), pp. 183–4.
[13] An analysis of the corporate reports of the major West German chemical firms from 1953 through 1963 is telling in this regard. Of the four covered in detail in this study (BASF, Bayer, Hoechst, and Hüls), in the 1950s only Hüls mentioned concern with the environmental impacts of its processes and the need to counteract them. Hüls reported experiments to clean up their plant's wastewater in 1957 and 1958. See Chemische Werke Hüls A.G., *Bericht über das Geschäftsjahr 1957*, p. 23; and *Bericht über das Geschäftsjahr 1958*, p. 19. BASF first publicly mentioned concerns about air pollution in its annual report of 1962. See BASF, *Bericht über das Geschäftsjahr 1962*, pp. 20–1. There was no mention of environmental concerns at Hoechst until 1963, when the firm's annual report noted that the scientific and technical means devoted to keeping the air and water clean had been increased and claimed the "vor einigen Jahren" a special section had been created for "Reinhaltung von Wasser und Luft." Farbwerke Hoechst A.G., *Geschäftsbericht 1963*, p. 18. Bayer did not mention the problem at all in its reports through 1963. The relative inattention to such problems is an indication of a lack of concern not only on the part of the industrialists but also on the part of their shareholders and the general public.

ment down, and the competitive ability of the country's industry being demonstrated more clearly each day, finally there was time and money to contemplate doing something about the deleterious environmental effects of chemical production.[14] Clearly, the initial action in that regard was feeble; much more needs to be known about the problem, not only for the West German chemical industry but also for other industries and for those in other countries, both in western Europe and in eastern Europe.[15] The increasing availability of documentary evidence in public and private archives should make this possible in the coming years.

It would be ironic if at the end of a monograph that has stressed time and again the need to view political, economic, and technological decision-making in context (that is, on the basis of the information that was available to the actors) I were to condemn those actors for not having had the same awareness of environmental issues that many share today. And that is not the purpose here. Rather, my purpose is to underline once again a major theme of the study, that is, the availability of alternatives for the historical actors and the need to view history not as a linear progression but rather as a dynamic, multifaceted process. In this context, it is worth considering that the "uneconomical" paths not taken in the past (e.g., renewable, alcohol-based feedstocks for organic chemistry; relatively small production units; hybrid technologies) might serve as an inspiration for the future. Thinking in terms of the technological alternatives that were available in the past, in turn, allows us to think in terms of using such inspiration to direct technological change along channels that we, as citizens in an industrial society, choose.[16]

[14] The growing awareness of environnental issues in Japan in the postwar period followed a similar course, although a few years later, in the late 1960s and early 1970s. See Chalmers Johnson, *MITI and the Japanese Miracle* (Stanford University Press, 1982), pp. 283–4.

[15] I have surveyed the available literature and summed up some of the key themes that still need to be studied in "The Ecological Burden of the Past: Environmental Aspects of German Unification" (unpublished paper presented at the Michigan Technological University Symposium on German Unification, Houghton, MI, 12 April 1991).

[16] For more on this notion, see, for instance, Langdon Winner, *The Whale and the Reactor* (University of Chicago Press, 1986).

Index

Abs, Hermann J., 58–9
acetone, 35–6, 99, 144
acetylene chemistry (*see also* Reppe chemistry), 5, 25, 44, 49–50, 99, 112–3, 134, 152, 246; at Hoechst, 36, 80–4, 177–80, 189–93, 194–5; at Hüls, 199–201; compared to petroleum-based ethylene chemistry, 247–8; in the late 1950s and early 1960s, 234–7, 240–1, 242; interest of U.S. firms in, 118–9; initial development of, 35–8
acrylonitrile, 117, 120, 240
Adenauer, Konrad, 62, 69, 72, 79–80, 94, 204
Agfa, 18, 29, 73–5, 80, 89
aliphatic chemistry (*see also* ethylene, chemical processes based on; olefins, chemical processes based on; propylene, chemical processes based on), 171–2, 234–5
Allied Control Council (ACC), 52, 91, 93
Allied High Commission (AHC), 48; and breakup of I. G. Farben, 73, 79; and synthetic rubber at Hüls, 200, 203, 204; policy on dismantling and restric-

tion of German industry, 61, 62; and synthetic rubber at Hüls, 200, 203, 204
Ambros, Otto, 202, 226
Amick, Erwin H., 72, 73, 75, 82–3, 200
Anorgana (Gendorf), 122, 123, 157
antitrust, 121, 221
arc process, 24, 85
aromatics, 103, 156, 171–2, 228, 235, 240, 245 (*see also* benzene)
Auguste Victoria, 73, 74, 84, 89; allocation to BASF by Allies, 75–80; supply of coal to BASF, 134, 152, 236
Auschwitz, 38, 147n
autarky, 8, 14, 23, 31–2, 35–6, 39, 70, 81; changes in meaning of, 33, 107–8, 216, 243, 247–9; continuity in thinking into post–World War II period, 107, 129–30, 178, 234; departure from, 48, 216, 243, 245, 246–50; Fischer-Tropsch process and, 219, 220, 222–3, 229–30; security of supply at Hüls and, 84, 197, 206–10, 211
automation, 117, 119, 151

253